THE ESSENTIAL
COMMUNITARIAN READER

THE ESSENTIAL COMMUNITARIAN READER

Edited by Amitai Etzioni

ROWMAN & LITTLEFIELD PUBLISHERS, INC.
Lanham • Boulder • New York • Oxford

ROWMAN & LITTLEFIELD PUBLISHERS, INC.

Published in the United States of America
by Rowman & Littlefield Publishers, Inc.
4720 Boston Way, Lanham, Maryland 20706

12 Hid's Copse Road
Cummor Hill, Oxford OX2 9JJ, England

Copyright © 1998 by Rowman & Littlefield Publishers, Inc.

All chapters were previously published in *The Responsive Community:* chap. 1 in vol. 4(4), Fall 1994; chap. 2, 6(1), Winter 1995–96; chap. 3, 2(1) and 2(2), Winter 1991–92 and Spring 1992; chap. 4, 1(4), Fall 1991; chap. 5, 3(4), Fall 1993; chap. 6, 2(3), Summer 1992; chap. 7, 6(4), Fall 1996; chap. 8, 5(3), Summer 1995; chap. 9, 1(1), Winter 1990–91; chap. 10, 1(4), Fall 1991; chap. 11, 1(3), Summer 1991; chap. 12, 3(4), Fall 1993; chap. 13, 6(1), Winter 1995–96; chap. 14, 6(1), Winter 1995–96; chap. 15, 1(1), Winter 1990–91; chap. 16, 7(3), Summer 1997; chap. 17, 5(4), Fall 1995; chap. 18, 6(1), Winter 1995–96; chap. 19, 5(3), Summer 1995; chap. 20, 4(3), Summer 1994; chap. 21, 3(4), Fall 1993; chap. 22, 3(2), Spring 1993; chap. 23, 3(1), Winter 1992–93; chap. 24, 3(1), Winter 1992–93; chap. 25, 1(2), Spring 1991; chap. 26, 6(3), Summer 1996; chap. 27, 4(2), Spring 1994; chap. 28, 1(2), Spring 1991; chap. 29, 4(3), Summer 1994; chap. 30, 6(2), Spring 1996.
      Chap. 19 is reprinted with permission from the Trust for Public Land; to obtain a copy of *Land and People*, please call 415-495-4014. Chap. 13 is reprinted from the *American Journal of Public Health*, June 1994, © American Public Health Association.

British Library Cataloguing in Publication Information Available

Library of Congress Cataloging-in-Publication Data
The essential communitarian reader / edited by Amitai Etzioni.
      p.   cm.
   Includes bibliographical references and index.
   ISBN 0-8476-8826-7 (cloth : alk. paper).—ISBN 0-8476-8827-5 (pbk. : alk. paper)
   1. Social ethics.   2. Communitarianism.   3. Liberalism.
I. Etzioni, Amitai.
HM216.E755   1998
303.3′72—dc21   97-42335
                                                                           CIP

ISBN 0-8476-8826-7 (cloth : alk. paper)
ISBN 0-8476-8827-5 (pbk. : alk. paper)

Printed in the United States of America

♾ ™ The paper used in this publication meets the minimum requirements of American National Standard for Information Sciences—Permanence of Paper for Printed Library Materials, ANSI Z39.48–1984.

Contents

Introduction   ix
    Amitai Etzioni

The Responsive Communitarian Platform:
Rights and Responsibilities   xxv

Part I: Communitarian Theory

1. Foundations of Communitarian Liberalism   3
    Philip Selznick

2. Community Properly Understood: A Defense of
    "Democratic Communitarianism"   15
    Robert N. Bellah

3. The Limits of Libertarianism   21
    Thomas A. Spragens, Jr.

4. A Moral Reawakening Without Puritanism   41
    Amitai Etzioni

5. The Dangers of Soft Despotism   47
    Charles Taylor

6. Beyond Teledemocracy: "America on the Line"   55
    James S. Fishkin

7. Social Justice: A Communitarian Perspective   61
    Philip Selznick

8. A Precarious Balance: Economic Opportunity, Civil
    Society, and Political Liberty   73
    Ralf Dahrendorf

Part II: Rights and Responsibilities

9. Rights and Responsibilities   97
    Dallin H. Oaks

10. "Absolute" Rights: Property and Privacy   107
    Mary Ann Glendon

11. Permissible Paternalism: In Defense of the Nanny State 115
    Robert E. Goodin

12. Finding a Place for Community in the First Amendment   125
    Roger L. Conner

13. AIDS Prevention vs. Cultural Sensitivity   131
    Ronald Bayer

14. A Gangsta's Rights   139
    Roger L. Conner

Part III: Communitarian Policy

15. A Liberal-Democratic Case for the Two-Parent Family   145
    William Galston

16. How Therapists Threaten Marriages   157
    William J. Doherty

17. Residential Community Associations: Community or
    Disunity?   167
    Daniel A. Bell

18. When Redistribution and Economic Growth Fail   177
    Senator Dan Coats

19. What Makes a Good Urban Park?   183
    Peter Katz

20. The Loss of Public Space   187
    Fred Siegel

21. Rebuilding Urban Communities   199
    Senator Bill Bradley

22. The Libertarian Conundrum: Why the Market Does Not
    Safeguard Civil Rights   207
    Alan Wolfe

23. Drug Abuse Control Policy: Libertarian, Authoritarian,
    Liberal, and Communitarian Perspectives   217
    Mark Kleiman

24. Inner-City Crime: What the Federal Government Should Do 227
    John J. DiIulio, Jr.

25. A Mandate For Liberty: Requiring Education-Based
    Community Service   237
    Benjamin R. Barber

26. Social Science Finds: "Marriage Matters"   247
    Linda J. Waite

Part IV: The Community of Communities

27. Democracy and the Politics of Difference   259
    Jean Bethke Elshtain

28. Pluralism vs. Particularism in American Education   269
    Diane Ravitch

29. Immigration and Political Community in the United States   283
    Daniel J. Tichenor

30. Who Killed Modern Manners?   295
    Judith Martin

Index   303

About the Contributors   321

Introduction

A Matter of Balance, Rights and Responsibilities

Amitai Etzioni

The Responsive Community, the source of the articles assembled here, was created in 1990 with the intention of providing a forum where new communitarian thought could be fashioned. The editors recognized that communitarian ideas can be found throughout history, although the term itself was coined only in 1841 by Barmby, who founded the Universal Communitarian Association. In this and other nineteenth-century usage, communitarian means "a member of a community formed to put into practice communistic or socialist theories." The more common and contemporary usage—"of, pertaining to, or characteristic of a community"—first appeared in *Webster's* in 1909.[1] Communitarian thoughts are found in the writings of the ancient Greeks (for instance in Aristotle's comparisons of life in the small city and the large metropolis),[2] in the Old and the New Testament, in Catholic social thought,[3] and among early sociologists such as Ferdinand Tönnies, Emile Durkheim, Robert Nisbet, Robert E. Park, Talcott Parsons, and William Kornhauser, among others.[4] I myself began my training in sociology and social philosophy under the tutelage of Martin Buber in Jerusalem, who wrote a fine communitarian book, *Paths to Utopia.*[5] Throughout history there have been hundreds of attempts to create new communities; from the Shakers to communal settlements in Palestine. Many of these endeavors were accompanied by considerable communitarian reflections and writings.

In the 1980s a group of political philosophers—Charles Taylor,[6] Michael J. Sandel,[7] and Michael Walzer[8]—challenged individualist liberal opposition to the concept of a common good, although all have been uncomfortable with the label "communitarian."[9] Particularly important works that advanced a communitarian thesis were written by contempo-

rary sociologists, especially Robert Bellah and his associates, and by
Philip Selznick[10] and the political scientist Daniel A. Bell.[11] Furthermore,
communitarian elements are found in the works of other scholars who
usually are not called communitarians. These include, on the liberal side,
Robert D. Putnam,[12] Hans Joas,[13] and John Gray[14]; and on the conservative side, David Willetts[15] and Meinhard Miegel.[16]

The new, post-1990 initiative that launched *The Responsive Community* and formulated the communitarian platform often has been credited
with taking communitarian ideas from the campus to the larger society;
sharing them with public and community leaders and the citizenship at
large, both in the United States and abroad.[17] Indeed, the number of articles about communitarian thinking in the popular press has increased
from a handful in 1990 to many hundred in the years that followed.[18] As
a result, there have been marked changes in the public vocabulary and
dialogue; the term communitarian and communitarian concepts have been
added to that of both liberals and conservatives as a recognized third way
of thinking. To provide but two examples of the many that could be given,
a *Time* Magazine cover story by Robert Wright compared liberal individualists and social conservatives with a distinct communitarian alternative.[19] Also, with the election of Tony Blair as the Prime Minister of the
UK in 1997 came an intensive debate in the British media as to whether
his course would be a gentle Tory one, a return to Old Labour, or a new
communitarian path.[20] Blair, it was pointed out, was influenced by the
American new communitarian group.[21]

The new communitarians have achieved much more than merely the
wide dissemination and publicity of pre-existing ideas, as some detractors
have implied.[22] The main new ideas and conceptions are flagged in the
following pages, and are elaborated upon much more extensively in several books.[23] While the old communitarians tended to stress the significance of social forces, of community, of social bonds, (and in the case of
Asian communitarians—that of social harmony), elements neglected in
the individualistic ideologies they criticized, the new communitarians
have been concerned from the onset with the balance between social
forces and the person, between community and autonomy, between the
common good and liberty, between individual rights and social responsibilities. Thus, for instance, Ferdinand Tönnies' writings as an early and
"old" communitarian, predominantly were concerned with the fragmentation of society under the rise of modern, industrial, urbanizing forces,
and compared unfavorably the rising associational society *(geshelfschaft)*
to the loosing communal society *(gemeischaft)*.[24] Similarly, Robert Nisbet's main subtext is a concern with the loss of community, and with it,
of authority.[25] Michael Sandel's often cited communitarian track[26] focused
on the tendency of liberals to treat individuals as free agents while actually

they are, to a significant extent, social creations reflecting the communities in which they are embedded. None of these authors explored the opposite danger: that a community may be oppressive, authoritarian, and may unduly penetrate the individual. These pre-1990 communitarians did not focus on the issues raised by George Orwell in his negative utopian *1984*. They let others deal with left and right totalitarianism, and religious fundamentalism was not in their sights.

The new communitarians made the question of balance between individual rights and social responsibilities, between autonomy and the common good, a major concern. We assumed from the beginning that the theory of a good society will need to deal simultaneously with both dangers; with a society whose communal foundations are crumbling and with one in which they have risen to the point that they block out individual freedoms. The term "responsive" was coined to indicate that the new communitarians are concerned with a society that is well founded, but also attentive to its members and profoundly democratic.[27] The term has been used both in the Platform, the only manifesto of the new communitarians (included in this volume), and of course, in the name of the journal created to develop new communitarian thinking, *The Responsive Community*. To further stress that new communitarians are not concerned merely with social obligations or responsibility, the subtitle of the journal is *Rights and Responsibilities*. A steady stream of articles in *The Responsive Community* and of books written by new communitarians explore the conditions under which the common good or individual rights need to be shored up, rather than assuming—as has been charged by critics who do not see differences among old and new communitarians—that the community is and should reign supreme.[28] For instance, new communitarians advance the argument that mandatory drug testing is justified only when those tested directly hold the lives of others in their hands (such as train engineers, pilots, police, etc.), rejecting both the liberal ACLU notions that privacy rights preclude testing anybody, and the conservative quest to test one and all indiscriminately.

As in all other intellectual, social philosophical, and even social science bodies of thought, there are significant differences among new communitarians (as illustrated in the following pages). Yet all share the quest for the moral, legal, and intellectual criteria that allow one to characterize a society that carefully balances concerns for the common good and for autonomy, differentiating these societies from those that are leaning toward social anarchy or conformism. This core position was specified further in two ways that cannot be explored here. The first concerns the issues that arise out of the observation that up to a point social order and liberty are mutually sustaining and reinforcing, but that if either is enhanced beyond that point, they become antagonistic and adversarial.[29]

The second concerns the specific criteria that indicate when a society is tilting in the direction of social anarchy or excessive order.[30] A fair number of the articles published in *The Responsive Community* (a select number of which are included here), concern themselves with these issues.

THE GOOD SOCIETY, BEYOND STATE OR MARKET

Another major theme of new communitarians has been to stress that the old opposition between those who favor the market (or private sector) and those who champion the state (or the public sector) is lacking; contrasting individual liberties with command-and-control systems leaves out of consideration a major—if not *the* major—realm: that of society, and the importance of social bonds and the moral voice. Communitarians have pointed out that ideological, political and intellectual debates have been dominated, as everyone is all too familiar, by a confrontation between those who argue that the economy would perform best if markets were as free as possible and those who argue for a greater role for the state, including the pursuits of various social goals from eliminating poverty to protecting the environment. Moreover, when it came to concern for social conduct, from the use of narcotics to abortion, from smoking to the speed of driving, the same arguments were repeated ad nauseam between those who strongly favored that individuals be left alone to make their own choices and those who believed that state control is required to promote virtuous behavior.

Communitarians have highlighted, especially on the pages of *The Responsive Community,* that much of social conduct is, and that more ought to be, sustained and guided by an informal web of social bonds and by moral voices of the community. Thus, communitarians have pointed out that if one simply arrests drug dealers, others will step in and take over their "jobs," and that the government—which has been unable to stop drug dealing even in prisons—is surely unable to stop the problem in free society without itself becoming a police state. At the same time, communitarians also have rejected the notion that people should be left to follow their own conceptions of the good in most matters of social conduct. They have pointed to the fact that when communities appreciate certain forms of behavior (from avoiding drug abuse to not speeding) and censure others (from alcoholism to spousal abuse), these anti-social behaviors are curbed much more effectively, in a more humane way, and at much lower costs to the public than when these matters are left either to the state or to market-driven efforts. A comparison of religious communities, including those of Black Muslims, Hasidic Jews, Amish, Mormons, secular communities in small town America, and ethnic groups that have strong communal bonds, to urban areas in which such bonds are lacking highlight his point. Anti-social behavior is rare in the first and common in the second.

New communitarians hence have tended, as shown here and elsewhere, to favor relying first and foremost on attempts to persuade, rather than coerce, people when seeking to promote pro-social behavior. Following is one of many examples supporting this position. Communitarians have joined the debate about the family. They have agreed, as the Platform indicates and as articles published in *The Responsive Community* show, that a two-parent family is preferable to a single-parent unit; but they have supported peer marriages, ones in which both fathers and mothers have the same rights and responsibilities, rather than delegating child rearing to mothers and gainful employment to fathers (as favored by at least some conservatives). When questioned about how these kinds of families may be fostered, new communitarians opposed suggestions that the states ban divorce or make it more difficult to obtain by a return to fault divorce. Instead communitarians have sought ways to convince the members of society to once again place a higher value on parenting; for communities to appreciate more those who attend well to their children (even at some costs to their career); and to advance non-coercive means to strengthen the family. Communitarians thus have favored measures such as premarital counseling, counseling during marriage, teaching of conflict resolution and communication skills in schools, and the availability of supervows (or covenant marriages),[31] among other measures. They have not excluded economic measures (such as tax credits for new parents and a longer paid leave of absence) and state-based measures (such as extending the waiting period before a divorce is granted). But, as several of the following articles show, they have rejected making them the mainstay of the good, communitarian society.

WHAT CONSTITUTES A COMMUNITY?

From the beginning critics have complained that the new communitarians, like their earlier counterparts, portray community in a fuzzy manner. As I see it, and as expressed on the pages of *The Responsive Community*, communities are webs of social relations that encompass shared meanings and above all shared values.[32] Families may qualify as mini-communities. Villages often are, although not necessarily. Some neighborhoods in cities (such as Little Havana in Miami, Chinatown in New York City) constitute communities. Well-integrated national societies may be said to have communitarian elements. Communities need not be geographically concentrated. One may speak of, say, a Jewish community in a city even if its members are dispersed among the population but maintain their social-normative web around core institutions such as a synagogue, private schools and so on.

Communities are not automatically or necessarily places of virtue. Many traditional communities that were homogenous, if not monolithic, were authoritarian and oppressive. And a community may lock into a set of values that one may find abhorrent, say an Afrikaaner village that legitimates an ideology of lynching. Communitarians who automatically sanctify any and all forms of community leave communitarianism open to the kind of criticism levelled by Steven Holmes, who argues, "Members of the Ku Klux Klan, too, have a 'commonality of shared self-understanding' " (the reference is to Michael Sandell).[33]

However, contemporary communities tend to be new communities that are part of a pluralistic web of communities.[34] People are, at one and the same time, members of several communities, such as professional, residential and others. They can, and do, use these multi-memberships (as well as a limited, but not trivial, ability to choose one's work and residential communities) to protect themselves from excessive pressure by any one community.

What is the scope of communities? It is best to think about communities as nested, each within a more encompassing one. Thus, neighborhoods are parts of more encompassing suburbs or cities or regional communities. These, in turn, often intersect or are part of larger ethnic, racial, or professional communities. And most communities are contextualized by the national society. Ultimately, some aspire to a world community that would encapsulate all people. Other communitarians object to such globalism and suggest that strong bonds and the moral voice, the essence of communities, mainly are found in relatively small communities in which people know one another, at least to some extent, as in many stable neighborhoods.[35]

Communities As Embedded in Societies

Communitarians occasionally are charged with being majoritarian. The argument is that by giving more weight to the needs of the community in determining the course of public policies, individual and minority rights are neglected.[36] For instance, Ira Glasser, executive director of the ACLU, claims, "Communitarians really means majoritarians. The tendency is to make the constitutional rights responsible for the failure to solve social problems."[37] Elsewhere, Charles Derber writes, " 'Consensual' values are, in reality, the voice of one part of the community—usually the majority or an elite minority—against the others."[38] Others fear that the community may engage in such untoward actions as banning books the majority dislikes from public and school libraries. Note that the concern here is not that a local or national tyrant would take over, but that ordinary citizens would instruct their duly-elected city council or school board officials to institute policies that violate basic rights.

A communitarian response is that American society maintains both constitutional and moral safeguards against majoritarianism. These safeguards basically work by *differentiation,* by defining some areas in which the majority does not have (and ought not to have) a say, and those in which it does and should. We are not a simple democracy, but a constitutional one. That is, some choices, defined by the Constitution, are declared out of bounds for the majority.

Clearest among these is the Bill of Rights, which singles out matters that are exempt from majority rule, from typical democratic rule-making, and in which minority and individual rights take precedence. The First Amendment, which protects the right of individuals to speak freely whether or not the majority approves of what they have to say, is a prime example of an area explicitly exempt from majority rule or consensus building. (A person's expressions as a rule are not subject to community rulings.) Similarly, the majority may not deny any opposition group the right to vote; even Communists were not banned in the U.S. during the period when they were most hated and feared. All citizens are entitled to a trial by a jury of their peers, whether they are members of the majority or the minority. And so on.

The Constitution and our legal traditions and institutions clearly indicate, however, that other matters are subject to majority rule. Thus, all Americans must pay their taxes, drive with a license, and refrain from abusing children. It is inconceivable, and there is no moral and legal support for the notion, that everybody would be allowed to decide for himself whether or not he wished to obtain a license, how much taxes he would choose to pay, et cetera.

This constitutional differentiation between the realms of minority and individual rights and majority rule, is not merely a matter of legal provisions. This differentiation is backed up by a set of convictions held by many Americans. That is, differentiation is not affirmed merely in courts of law, but, most times, is also underwritten by community consensus. Thus, when in the early 1990s about 130 universities moved to ban racial slurs and thereby limit free speech, very few of the challenges to this approach found their way into the courts. The primary voices of opposition to any such codes were raised by editorial writers, public intellectuals,[39] columnists (from George Will to Nat Hentoff), and many others who together comprise America's opinion leaders. They evoked a moral claim: we must continue to allow free expression of ideas, words, and sentiments even if these hurt the feelings of minorities and women. The majority ought not to decide what can be said; it is the right of each individual to speak freely. These opinion makers carried the day most of all in the court of public opinion. The so-called hate codes did not spread to most universities; several were canceled, and those that are in place rarely are enforced.

All this is not to suggest that there is no tension between the particular values, mores, and laws of communities and individual rights. However, there are well-ensconced guidelines and safeguards that help determine where the proper "borders" of communities are, and that show that there is no inherent contradiction between a respect for rights and for community ethos. Much more needs to be said on this important complex of issues. Some of this commentary is found in the following pages; some of it waits to be written in future issues of *The Responsive Community* and volumes such as this one.

NEW BEGINNING:
HOW AND WHY OF THE RESPONSIVE COMMUNITY

A brief telling of the way *The Responsive Community* was conceived will help explain the content of what follows. Several writers who specialize in drawing profiles of those individuals somewhat visible in the public eye suggested that the psychosocial roots of my concern with communitarian issues reflect the fact that I grew up in a cooperative village in Israel.[40] More immediately, as I see it, the apple that hit my forehead was a finding that I came upon when teaching ethics at the Harvard School of Business in 1989. This finding reported that the majority of young Americans feel strongly, as they ought to, that they have a right to demand a trial before a jury of their peers if charged with a crime; but that many indicated that they would rather not serve on a jury.[41] It seemed, first of all, that such a position was untenable; if peers will not serve, a jury of one's peers will not be possible. And such a position violates a profound moral precept: that it is unfair to take and not to give, to draw on the commonwealth, but to refuse to contribute. It soon became evident that the attitude towards juries, far from being an isolated phenomenon, was indicative of a general malaise—of people demanding that the government, and above all taxes, be curtailed, while still seeking more government services from education to public health, from housing to protection from crime.[42] More generally, there was an explosion of new rights, some of which were very important and compelling, others that were rather contrived (not paralleled by a recognition that the corollary of rights are responsibilities). It seemed a subject worth exploring.

On returning to Washington, D.C., in mid 1989, I came across the writings of William A. Galston, whom I knew before as an Issue Director of Fritz Mondale's election campaign in 1984. Soon we were having lunch at the George Washington University faculty club, enjoying one of those conversations in which one need not complete a sentence or a thought because the other is already anticipating the next step. We were discussing the polarization of social philosophy: the pull of radical individualists from one side, and the tug of authoritarians from the other. The middle ground, we realized, did not have a platform from which its voice could be raised. We examined a series of issues: what would be a middle ground on public safety (for those who are concerned with the rights of victims *and* of criminals)? Would such a position favor national service, and should such service be mandatory or voluntary? Would it be pro-family (while seeking to ensure equal rights for women and men)? We sensed the outline of a new position.

We invited fifteen colleagues, from across the country and the ideological spectrum (leaving out the extremists of both sides), to a workshop. There was a surprising amount of consensus on the need for a new position and on its main outlines. But where could it be explored and expressed? A new journal seemed the obvious answer. Most members of the original groups, and a few others, agreed to serve as the editorial board; James Fishkin (from The University of Texas at Austin) and Mary Ann Glendon (from Harvard Law School) consented to serve as co-editors with Bill Galston. I was left with the responsibility of editing the new publication.

Most everyone I know writes or wants to write, and wishes to share their ideas with the world at large. I was sure authors would line up on the street next to our office. But for quite a while, all I could see from my narrow window was the hot dog vendor. In preparing for the first issue, we appealed to a long list of established talent, most of whom reported that they were committed to other projects for the next few years and already were behind. Three sent in articles that clearly were prepared for another occasion and had languished in their drawers after prior rejections. Above all, it was difficult to find people to write articles that would fall somewhere within the new territory we were trying to chart. We set no narrow requirements, but we sought authors who would share our approach that tries to reconcile individual rights and community needs. Writers seemed to prefer championing either the libertarian or the social conservative, if not authoritarian, side.

The first author who responded to our invitation wrote about whether free speech on the campus was to be curbed to prevent racial slurs. He gave it the standard libertarian treatment: the First Amendment is sacrosanct; no other values should be taken into account. I called him. "Sure," I tried, "we all are in favor of free speech, and prohibiting racial speech by force of law may indeed not be the solution. But would you agree that if you were on a campus and hounded for the color of your skin, that it would be desirable to have some *non*-legal remedies? For instance, to combat a rash of racial incidents, a college should have a teach-in on racial tolerance, and so on." He seemed to agree, but when the revised manuscript came back it closed with the statement that racial slurs have been with us forever and not much can be done about them. It seemed to slight the pain of those who suffer from racial attacks. When we declined to publish the article, members of the editorial board, various friends, and editors of other publications received a bitter letter from the author and I got my first taste of an editor's life.

I did not have to wait long for the second serving. A colleague sent in an article that was pro-family in nature. The article covered much ground; in effect, it had a page or paragraph dealing with most of the matters that have ever been raised in this area. It touched on divorce; it discussed abortion; it had something to say about equality for women and men; and it mentioned the problems that arise from recognizing gay marriages. We asked the author to expand on any one of the communitarian topics he brought up and leave out some of the others. His overview, it seemed to us, did not focus on issues such as peer marriage, *pre*marital counseling, or covenant marriages.[43] The next thing we heard from him was a claim that we rejected his article because it was pro-heterosexual.

In effect, while we received a good number of rather flattering letters from readers, good press, frequent citations by others and our articles were reprinted (for instance, in *Current*) and assigned as teaching materials, few of the authors we dealt with seemed to be pleased, even when we published their texts. They tended to feel that editorial queries and rewrites diminished their copy. Most insisted on having their piece published in the very next issue. And if we did, many still smarted: "You published someone else's essay in the front of the book—is mine not as sexy?"

KEEPING THE DEBATE CLEAN

Nothing is more challenging than keeping our voice clearly heard so that it adds to the intellectual give and take and avoids mislabeling and framing by irresponsible critics. The norms of debate and mores of criticism seem to have frayed, as have so many others. People and groups with whom we respectfully disagree seem to be ready to characterize our "third," balancing position as an extreme expression of whatever they oppose most. Thus, while we deliberately put rights *and* responsibilities in our title and stressed our commitment to both in every editorial statement, because some of us hold that at this stage in history, and in some areas, responsibilities must be enhanced, we are depicted as authoritarians who wish to impose our moral code on all others.

Tibor Machan, for instance, has written about us:

> . . . the mirage of a unified, organic community with its own needs and its own rights is a myth. Let us not be deceived by it and yield even more of our rights to the renewed but essentially worn-out call for subjugation of the individual. In my view communitarianism is really socialism in a new disguise, with some people wishing to call the shots for the rest of us in line with their own valued objectives.[44]

Wrong address. Our position is deeply democratic. We seek what Benjamin Barber calls a "strong democracy," one that extends beyond occasional voting and finds ways to make the community responsive to all its members.[45] While we search for a moral consensus, the ideas underpinning a moral consensus are mutual dialogue and persuasion, not imposition. And while we all are not completely convinced that animals and trees have rights (although we may well owe them some respect) and are concerned about the proliferation of rights and the decline of a sense of civic duty, minority and individual rights are as dear to us as they are to all supporters of constitutional democracies.

Timothy Sinnot compared our views to those advanced by Mussolini and Hitler, on the basis of a story he read about us in *Business Week*.[46] We have tried to counter this labeling by emphasizing our agreement with those who see the Constitution as a living body that adapts to changing circumstances while striving to maintain the balance between the general welfare and individual rights. In short, we are about as fascist as the founding fathers and the Supreme Court.

While a new quarterly is a place one can easily lose all the money one has and more in a hurry, and is a sure way to lose friends en masse and make new enemies, establishing the journal has been exhilarating because we seemed to have reached out and touched numerous people. We hear from a surprisingly large number of people, from all walks of life and parts of the country and from overseas, that our course is right; that fashioning a communitarian position is of service; that we help them to think about where the balance between rights and responsibilities lies, what constitutes "reasonable" versus "unreasonable" search, how moral education may take place in schools without indoctrination, how the family may be preserved without returning women to an inferior status, and so on. Some readers even explore setting up local discussion groups around *The Responsive Community*'s themes and issues. Several well known political and public leaders endorsed our platform or have explicitly associated themselves with us, ranging from Rudolf Sharoing, the former head of the German Social Democrats,[47] to Senator and Mrs. Charles Robb, former Secretary of State James Baker III, President Emeritus of the Brookings Institution Bruce MacLaury, and CEO of Circuit City Alan Wurtzel, who most recently endorsed our platform, while others are said to have embraced communitarian ideas, or have been influenced by our work—Tony Blair for instance.[48]

The next step is to cultivate our roots. New communitarians started as a group of academicians, drawing on sociological and social philosophical texts. Our following grew rapidly in the community at large (a poll shows the majority of Americans agree with our key positions)[49] and among public leaders, in the USA and overseas. However, as our popularity grew, our academic critics grew louder and harsher. Our next step ought to be to respond to these criticisms, and to highlight our scholarly (and not merely public) contributions without losing our public role.

For more information about *The Responsive Community,* please contact us electronically at comnet@gwis2.circ.gwu.edu or call either (202) 994-4355 or (800) 245-7450. You may also visit our website at http://www.gwu.edu/~ccps.

Washington, DC July 1997

THE RESPONSIVE COMMUNITY
Editorial Board

Charles Taylor, McGill University
Daniel Yankelovich, DYG, Inc.

Editor
Amitai Etzioni, The George Washington University

Co editors
Bruce Douglas, Georgetown University
William A. Galston, University of Maryland
Thomas Spragens, Jr., Duke University

Managing Editor
Daniel Doherty

NOTES

1. Amitai Etzioni, *The New Golden Rule: Community and Morality in a Democratic Society.* (New York: Basic Books, 1997), 39–40.
2. Ronald Beiner, *What's the Matter with Liberalism?* (Berkeley, Cal.: University of California Press, 1992), 4–5; Italo Calvino, *Invisible Critics,* trans. William Weaver (New York: Harcourt Brace Jovanovich, 1978).
3. Alan Jacob, "Auden's Local Culture," *Hudson Review* 47, no. 4 (Winter 1995): 543.
4. Ferdinand Tönnies, *Community and Society,* trans. Charles P. Loomis (East Lansing, Mich.: Michigan State University Press, 1957); Ferdinand Tonnies, *Community and Association,* trans. Charles P. Loomis (London: Routledge & Paul, 1955); Emile Durkheim, *The Elementary Forms of Religious Life,* (1915; reprint, New York: Oxford University Press, 1962; formerly *The Quest for Community: A Study in the Ethics of Order and Freedom* [New York: Oxford University Press, 1953]); Robert Nisbet, *The Social Philosophers: Community and Conflict in Western Thought* (New York: Crowell, 1973); Robert Nisbet, "The Concept of Community: A Reexamination," *Sociological Review* 38, no. 4 (August 1973): 397–416; Robert E. Park and Ernest Burgess, *Introduction to the Science of Sociology* (Chicago: University of Chicago Press, 1924); Talcott Parsons, *The Social System* (Glencoe, Ill.: Free Press, 1951); Talcott Parsons and Edward A. Shils, *Toward a General Theory of Action: Theoretical Foundations for the Social Sciences* (Cambridge, Mass.: Harvard University Press, 1951).
5. Martin Buber, *Paths to Utopia* (Boston: Beacon Press, 1958).
6. Charles Taylor, *Sources of the Self: The Making of the Modern Identity* (Cambridge, Mass.: Harvard University Press, 1989).
7. Michael J. Sandel, *Liberalism and the Limits of Justice* (Cambridge, Mass.: Cambridge University Press, 1982).
8. Michael Walzer, *Spheres of Justice: A Defense of Pluralism and Equality* (New York, Basic Books, 1983).
9. "First a word of caution. Those typically put forward as communitarian critics of liberal political theory—Alasdair MacIntyre, Michael Sandel, Charles Taylor and Michael Walzer—have yet to identify themselves with the 'communi-

tarian movement,'" Daniel A. Bell, *Communitarianism and Its Critics* (Oxford: Clarendon Press, 1993), 4. MacIntyre explicitly repudiated the label in "The Spectre of Communitarianism," *Radical Philosophy* 70 (March/April 1995): 35. Walzer places his work within a context of the "periodic communitarian correction" required by liberalism but considers his basic position liberal. Michael Walzer, "Communitarian Critique of Liberalism," *Political Theory* 18, no. 1 (February 1990): 6–23. The term "communitarian" does not even appear in the index of Sandel's most recent book, *Democracy's Discontent*.

10. Philip Selznick, *The Moral Commonwealth: Social Theory and the Promise of Community* (Berkeley, Cal.: University of California Press, 1992); see also Philip Selznick, "The Demands of Community," *Center Magazine* 20, no. 1 (January/February 1987): 33–54; Philip Selznick, "Dworkin's Unfinished Task," *California Law Review* 77, no. 3 (May 1989): 505–13.

11. Daniel A. Bell, *Communitarianism and Its Critics* (Oxford: Clarendon Press, 1993).

12. Robert D. Putnam, *Making Democracy Work: Civic Traditions in Modern Italy* (Princeton, N.J.: Princeton University Press, 1993).

13. Hans Joas, *Pragmatism and Social Theory* (Chicago: University of Chicago Press, 1993).

14. John Gray, *Post-liberalism: Studies in Political Thought* (New York: Routledge, 1993).

15. David Willetts, *Modern Conservatism* (London: Penguin, 1992).

16. Meinhard Miegel and Stephanie Wahl, *Das Ende des Individualismus: Die Multur des Westens zerstoert sich selbst* (Munich: Verlag Bonn Aktuell, 1993).

17. See Karen J. Winkler, "Communitarians Move Their Ideas Outside Academic Arena," *The Chronicle of Higher Education*, 21 April 1993; Jacob Weisberg, "All Together Now," *New York*, 24 July 1995; Michael Elliot, "What's Left?," *Newsweek International*, 10 October 1994, 13; Murray Cambell, "Movement seeks redefinition of values," *Toronto Globe and Mail*, 17 January 1994.

18. Richard M. Coughlin reports that in 1990 there were 42 citations of communitarianism in nonacademic periodicals; by 1993 the number was well over 400. See Richard M. Coughlin, "Frameworks and Findings: Assessing Etzioni's Contributions to Sociology," in David Sciulli, ed., *Macro Socio-Economics: From Theory to Activism* (Armonk, New York: M.E. Sharpe, 1996), 29.

19. Robert Wright, "The False Politics of Values," *Time*, 9 September 1996: 42–45.

20. British Broadcasting Corporation, "'Analysis' The Next Steps," transcript of a recorded documentary, 29 May 1997, 1–31. See also "Labour's ladder of opportunity," *The Economist*, 8 October, 1994: 57–58; Ray Pahl, "Friendly Society," *New Statesman & Society*, 10 March 1995: 20–22.

21. Melanie Phillips, "The Father of Tony Blair's Big Idea," *Observer*, 24 July 1994; Peter Riddell, "I'm a guru; are you one too?" *The Times*, 7 August 1996.

22. Fareed Zakaria, "The ABCs of Communitarianism, A Devil's Dictionary," www.Slate.com, July 1996.

23. See, for instance, the essays collected in Amitai Etzioni, ed. *New Communitarian Thinking: Persons, Virtues, Institutions, and Communities.* (Charlottesville,

VA: University of Virginia Press, 1995); Amitai Etzioni, *The New Golden Rule: Community and Morality in a Democratic Society* (New York: Basic Books, 1997); Amitai Etzioni, *The Spirit of Community: The Reinvention of American Society* (New York: Simon & Schuster, 1993); Mary Ann Glendon, *Rights Talk* (New York: Free Press, 1991); and Philip Selnick, *The Moral Commonwealth: Social Theory and The Promise of Community* (Los Angeles, CA: University of California Press, 1992); Robert Bellah, et al., *The Good Society* (New York: Alfred A. Knopf, 1991).

24. Ferdinand Tönnies, *Community & Society (Gemeinschaft und Gesellschaft)* (New York: Harper & Row, 1957).

25. See Robert Nisbet, *Community and Power* (New York: Oxford University Press, 1962; formerly *The Quest for Community: A Study in the Ethics of Order and Freedom* [New York: Oxford University Press, 1953]); Robert Nisbet, *The Social Philosophers: Community and Conflict in Western Thought* (New York: Crowell, 1973).

26. Michael J. Sandel, *Liberalism and the Limits of Justice* (Cambridge: Cambridge University Press, 1982).

27. For additional discussion of the term see Amitai Etzioni, *The Active Society: A Theory of Social and Political Processes* (London: Free Press, 1968), and American Sociological Association Presidential Address, "The Responsive Community: A Communitarian Perspective," published in *American Sociological Review*, (February 1996): 1–11.

28. Tony Mauro, "Competing Rights Collide in the Nation's Cities: 'Quality of Life' Concerns Going Head-to-Head with Panhandlers," *First Amendment News* 3, no. 6 (June 1997).

29. See Amitai Etzioni, *New Golden Rule*, Chapter 2, "Order and Autonomy," pp. 34–57.

30. See *The Spirit of Community*, "Notching Principles," pp. 177–190; *New Golden Rule*, pp. 51–53.

31. The Louisiana state legislature recently passed a law establishing voluntary "covenant" marriage. Couples that enter covenant marriages acknowledge that divorce is permitted only under stringent circumstances. For more detail, see Kevin Sack, "Louisiana Approves Measure to Tighten Marriage Bonds," *Wall Street Journal*, 24 June 1997. Advocated in Amitai Etzioni, "How to Make Marriage Matter," *Time*, 6 September 1993, 76.

32. For further discussion of community see David E. Price, *The 'Quest for Community' and Public Policy.* (Bloomington, Ind.: The Poynter Center, 1977).

33. Stephen Holmes, *The Anatomy of Antiliberalism*, (Cambridge: Harvard University Press, 1993), 178.

34. For more discussion see *The Spirit of Community*, 116–160.

35. For a discussion of community definition and the accordant scope of obligation see David Price, "Community, 'Mediating Structures', and Public Policy," *Soundings* 62, no. 4 (Winter 1979): 369–394.

36. See Tibor Machan, "The Communitarian Manifesto," *The Orange County Register*, 12 May 1991.

37. Glasser cited in Aimed Asian, "What Fascists?" *The Responsive Community* 1 (Winter 1990/1991): 13.

38. Charles Derber, "Communitarianism & Its Limits," *Tikkun*, July/August 1993, 29.

39. Arthur Schlesinger, Jr., *The Disuniting of America: Reflections on a Multicultural Society.* (New York: Whittle Communications, 1991); Dinesh D'Souza, *Illiberal Education* (New York: Free Press, 1991).

40. See for instance, Michael D'Antonio, "Tough Medicine for a Sick America," *Los Angeles Times Magazine,* 22 March 1992, p. 50. For a comment along the same lines see Louis Jacobson, "Anti dissing Communitarians," *City Paper* 7 February 1997, p. 56.

41. Morris Janowitz, *The Reconstruction of Patriotism: Education for Civic Consciousness* (Chicago: The University of Chicago Press, 1983), 8.

42. Lawrence Friedman, *The Republic of Choice* (Cambridge, Mass.: Harvard University Press, 1990).

43. See Amitai Etzioni, "How to Make Marriage Matter," op cit.

44. Tibor Machan, op cit.

45. Benjamin Barber, *Strong Democracy: Participatory Politics for a New Age* (Berkeley: University of California Press, 1984).

46. Timothy J. Sinnott, "The Danger of A One-Voice Community," Letter to the Editor, *Business Week,* 1 October 1990.

47. Rudolf Scharping, "Freedom, Solidarity, Individual Responsibility: Reflections on the Relationship Between Politics, Money, and Morality," *The Responsive Community* 6, no. 4, (Fall 1996): 51–58.

48. Phillips, op cit.

49. David Karp, "Americans as Communitarians: An Empirical Study," *Responsive Community* 7, no. 1 (Winter 1996/97): 42–51.

The Responsive Communitarian Platform: Rights and Responsibilities

PREAMBLE

American men, women, and children are members of many communities—families; neighborhoods; innumerable social, religious, ethnic, work place, and professional associations; and the body politic itself. Neither human existence nor individual liberty can be sustained for long outside the interdependent and overlapping communities to which all of us belong. Nor can any community long survive unless its members dedicate some of their attention, energy, and resources to shared projects. The exclusive pursuit of private interest erodes the network of social environments on which we all depend, and is destructive to our shared experiment in democratic self-government. For these reasons, we hold that the rights of individuals cannot long be preserved without a communitarian perspective.

A communitarian perspective recognizes both individual human dignity and the social dimension of human existence.

A communitarian perspective recognizes that the preservation of individual liberty depends on the active maintenance of the institutions of civil society where citizens learn respect for others as well as self-respect; where we acquire a lively sense of our personal and civic responsibilities, along with an appreciation of our own rights and the rights of others; where we develop the skills of self-government as well as the habit of governing ourselves, and learn to see others—not just self.

A communitarian perspective recognizes that communities and polities, too, have obligations—including the duty to be responsive to their members and to foster participation and deliberation in social and political life.

A communitarian perspective does not dictate particular policies; rather it mandates attention to what is often ignored in contemporary policy debates: the social side of human nature; the responsibilities that must be borne by citizens, individually and collectively, in a regime of rights; the fragile ecology of families and their supporting communities; the ripple effects and long-term consequences of present decisions. The political views of the signers of this statement differ widely. We are united, how-

ever, in our conviction that a communitarian perspective must be brought
to bear on the great moral, legal, and social issues of our time.

MORAL VOICES

America's diverse communities of memory and mutual aid are rich resources of moral voices—voices that ought to be heeded in a society that
increasingly threatens to become normless, self-centered, and driven by
greed, special interests, and an unabashed quest for power.

Moral voices achieve their effect mainly through education and persuasion, rather than through coercion. Originating in communities, and
sometimes embodied in law, they exhort, admonish, and appeal to what
Lincoln called the better angels of our nature. They speak to our capacity
for reasoned judgment and virtuous action. It is precisely because this
important moral realm, which is neither one of random individual choice
nor of government control, has been much neglected that we see an urgent
need for a communitarian social movement to accord these voices their
essential place.

WITHIN HISTORY

The basic communitarian quest for balances between individuals and
groups, rights and responsibilities, and among the institutions of state,
market, and civil society is a constant, ongoing enterprise. Because this
quest takes place within history and within varying social contexts, however, the evaluation of what is a proper moral stance will vary according
to circumstances of time and place. If we were in China today, we would
argue vigorously for more individual rights; in contemporary America,
we emphasize individual and social responsibilities.

NOT MAJORITARIAN BUT STRONGLY DEMOCRATIC

Communitarians are not majoritarians. The success of the democratic experiment in ordered liberty (rather than unlimited license) depends, not
on fiat or force, but on building shared values, habits and practices that
assure respect for one another's rights and regular fulfillment of personal,
civic, and collective responsibilities. Successful policies are accepted because they are recognized to be legitimate, rather than imposed. We say
to those who would impose civic or moral virtues by suppressing dissent
(in the name of religion, patriotism, or any other cause), or censoring
books, that their cure is ineffective, harmful, and morally untenable. At

the same time divergent moral positions need not lead to cacophony. Out of genuine dialogue clear voices can arise, and shared aspirations can be identified and advanced.

Communitarians favor strong democracy. That is, we seek to make government more representative, more participatory, and more responsive to all members of the community. We seek to find ways to accord citizens more information, and more say, more often. We seek to curb the role of private money, special interests, and corruption in government. Similarly, we ask how "private governments," whether corporations, labor unions, or voluntary associations, can become more responsive to their members and to the needs of the community.

Communitarians do not exalt the group as such, nor do they hold that any set of group values is ipso facto good merely because such values originate in a community. Indeed, some communities (say, neo-Nazis) may foster reprehensible values. Moreover, communities that glorify their own members by vilifying those who do not belong are at best imperfect. Communitarians recognize—indeed, insist—that communal values must be judged by external and overriding criteria, based on shared human experience.

A responsive community is one whose moral standards reflect the basic human needs of all its members. To the extent that these needs compete with one another, the community's standards reflect the relative priority accorded by members to some needs over others. Although individuals differ in their needs, human nature is not totally malleable. While individuals are deeply influenced by their communities, they have a capacity for independent judgment. The persistence of humane and democratic culture, as well as individual dissent, in Eastern Europe and the Soviet Union demonstrate the limits of social indoctrination.

For a community to be truly responsive—not only to an elite group, a minority, or even the majority, but to all its members and all their basic human needs—it will have to develop moral values which meet the following criteria: they must be nondiscriminatory and applied equally to all members; they must be generalizable, justified in terms that are accessible and understandable: e.g., instead of claims based upon individual or group desires, citizens would draw on a common definition of justice; and, they must incorporate the full range of legitimate needs and values rather than focusing on any one category, be it individualism, autonomy, interpersonal caring, or social justice.

RESTORING THE MORAL VOICE

History has taught that it is a grave mistake to look to a charismatic leader to define and provide a moral voice for the polity. Nor can political institutions effectively embody moral voices unless they are sustained and criticized by an active citizenry concerned about the moral direction of the community. To rebuild America's moral foundations, to bring our regard for individuals and their rights into a better relationship with our sense of personal and collective responsibility, we must therefore begin with the institutions of civil society.

Start With the Family

The best place to start is where each new generation acquires its moral anchoring: at home, in the family. We must insist once again that bringing children into the world entails a moral responsibility to provide, not only material necessities, but also moral education and character formation.

Moral education is not a task that can be delegated to babysitters, or even professional child-care centers. It requires close bonding of the kind that typically is formed only with parents, if it is formed at all.

Fathers and mothers, consumed by "making it" and consumerism, or preoccupied with personal advancement, who come home too late and too tired to attend to the needs of their children, cannot discharge their most elementary duty to their children and their fellow citizens.

It follows, that *work places should provide* maximum flexible opportunities to parents to preserve an important part of their time and energy, of their life, to attend to their educational-moral duties, for the sake of the next generation, its civic and moral character, and its capacity to contribute economically and socially to the commonweal. Experiments such as those with unpaid and paid parental leave, flextime, shared jobs, opportunities to work at home, and for parents to participate as volunteers and managers in child-care centers, should be extended and encouraged.

Above all, what we need is a *change in orientation* by both parents and work places. Child-raising is important, valuable work, work that must be honored rather than denigrated by both parents and the community.

Families headed by single parents experience particular difficulties. Some single parents bravely struggle and succeed in attending to the moral education of their children; while some married couples shamefully neglect their moral duties toward their offspring. However, the weight of the historical, sociological, and psychological evidence suggests that on average *two-parent families are better able to discharge their child-raising duties* if only because there are more hands—and voices—available for the task. Indeed, couples often do better when they are further backed up by a wider circle of relatives. The issue has been wrongly framed when one asks what portion of parental duties grandparents or other helpers can assume. Their assistance is needed in addition to, not as a substitute for, parental care. Child-raising is by nature labor-intensive. There are no labor-saving technologies, and shortcuts in this area produce woefully deficient human beings, to their detriment and ours.

It follows that *widespread divorce,* when there are children involved, especially when they are in their formative years, is indicative of a serious social problem. Though divorces are necessary in some situations, many are avoidable and are *not in the interest of the children,* the community, and probably not of most adults either. Divorce laws should be modified, not to prevent divorce, but to signal society's concern.

Above all, we should cancel the message that divorce puts an end to responsibilities among members of a child-raising family. And the best way to cancel that message is to reform the economic aspects of divorce laws so that the enormous financial burden of marriage dissolution no longer falls primarily on minor children and those parents who are their principal caretakers. Just as we recognized in the 1960s that it was unjust to apply to consumers laws that were fashioned for the dealings of merchants with one another, we must now acknowledge that it is a mistake to handle divorces involving couples with young children with a set of rules that was tailored mainly to the needs and desires of warring husbands and wives alone. The principle of "children first" should be made fundamental to property settlements and support awards.

Schools—The Second Line of Defense

Unfortunately, millions of American families have weakened to the point where their capacity to provide moral education is gravely impaired. And the fact is that communities have only a limited say over what families do. At best, it will take years before a change in the moral climate restores parenting to its proper status and function for many Americans.

Thus, by default, schools now play a major role, for better or worse, in character formation and moral education. Personal and communal responsibility come together here, for education requires the commitment of all citizens, not merely those who have children in school.

We strongly urge that all educational institutions, [from kindergartens to universities], recognize and take seriously the grave responsibility to provice moral education. Suggestions that schools participate actively in moral education are often opposed. The specter of religious indoctrination is quickly evoked, and the question is posed: "Whose morals are you going to teach?"

Our response is straightforward: *we ought to teach those values Americans share,* for example, that the dignity of all persons ought to be respected, that tolerance is a virtue and discrimination abhorrent, that peaceful resolution of conflicts is superior to violence, that generally truth-telling is morally superior to lying, that democratic government is morally superior to totalitarianism and authoritarianism, that one ought to give a day's work for a day's pay, that saving for one's own and one's country's future is better than squandering one's income and relying on others to attend to one's future needs.

The fear that our children will be "brainwashed" by a few educators is far-fetched. On the contrary, to silence the schools in moral matters simply means that the youngsters are left exposed to all other voices and values but those of their educators. For, one way or another, moral education does take place in schools. The only question is whether schools and teachers will passively stand by, or take an active and responsible role.

Let us note that moral education takes place least in classroom lectures (although these have a place) and is only in a limited measure a matter of developing moral reasoning. To a much greater extent, moral education is fostered through personal example and above all through fostering the proper institutional culture—from corridors and cafeteria to the parking lot and sports. In effect, the whole school should be considered as a set of experiences generating situations in which young people either learn the values of civility, sharing, and responsibility to the common good or of cheating, cut-throat competition, and total self-absorption.

Education must be reorganized to achieve a better integration between work and schooling. Educators need to search for ways to connect schooling with activities that make sense to young people; and the many businesses who employ high school students part-time ought to recognize that they are educators too. These early work experiences will either reinforce responsible habits and attitudes, or will serve as lessons in poor civics and deficient work ethics.

WITHIN COMMUNITIES

A Matter of Orientation

The ancient Greeks understood this well: A person who is completely private is lost to civic life. The exclusive pursuit of one's self-interest is not even a good prescription for conduct in the marketplace; for no social, political, economic, or moral order can survive that way. Some measure of caring, sharing, and *being our brother's and sister's keeper,* is essential if we are not all to fall back on an ever more expansive government, bureaucratized welfare agencies, and swollen regulations, police, courts, and jails.

Generally, no social task should be assigned to an institution that is larger than necessary to do the job. What can be done by families, should not be assigned to an intermediate group—school etc. What can be done at the local level should not be passed on to the state or federal level, and so on. There are, of course, plenty of urgent tasks—environmental ones—that do require national and even international action. But to remove tasks to higher levels than is necessary weakens the constituent communities. This principle holds for duties of attending to the sick, troubled, delinquent, homeless, and new immigrants; and for public safety, public health, and protection of the environment—from a neighborhood crime-watch to CPR to sorting the garbage. The government should step in only to the extent that other social subsystems fail, rather than seek to replace them.

At the same time vulnerable communities should be able to draw on the more endowed communities when they are truly unable to deal, on their own, with social duties thrust upon them.

Many social goals, moreover, require partnership between public and private groups. Though government should not seek to replace local communities, it may need to empower them by strategies of support, including revenue-sharing and technical assistance. There is a great need for study and experimentation with creative use of the structures of civil society, and public-private cooperation, especially where the delivery of health, educational, and social services are concerned.

Last, but not least, we should not hesitate to speak up and express our moral concerns to others when it comes to issues we care about deeply and share with one another. It might be debatable whether or not we should encourage our neighbors to keep their lawns green (which may well be environmentally unsound), but there should be little doubt that we should expect one another to attend to our children, and vulnerable community members. Those who neglect these duties, should be explicitly considered poor members of the community.

National and local service, as well as volunteer work, is desirable to build and express a civil commitment. Such activities, bringing together people from different backgrounds and requiring them to work together, build community, and foster mutual respect and tolerance.

Americans should *foster a spirit of reconciliation.* When conflicts do arise, we should seek the least destructive means of resolving them. Adversarial litigation is often not the optimal way; mediation and arbitration are often superior. We should favor settlements that are fair and conciliatory even if we have to absorb some losses. Going for the last ounce of flesh is incompatible with community spirit. (It is said that marriage works better when each side is willing to give 75 percent and expect 25 percent, rather than each give 50 percent and expect 50 percent. The same holds for other close relations.)

We should *treat one another with respect* and recognize our basic equality, not just before the law, but also as moral agents.

Duties to the Polity

Being informed about public affairs is a prerequisite for keeping the polity from being controlled by demagogues, for taking action when needed in one's own interests and that of others, for achieving justice and the shared future.

Voting is one tool for keeping the polity reflective of its constituent communities. Those who feel that none of the candidates reflect their views ought to seek out other like-minded citizens and seek to field their own candidate rather than retreat from the polity. Still, some persons may discharge their community responsibilities by being involved in non-political activities, say, in volunteer work. Just as the polity is but one facet of interdependent social life, so voting and political activity are not the only ways to be responsible members of society. A good citizen is involved in a community or communities, but not necessarily active in the polity.

Paying one's taxes, encouraging others to pay their fair share, and *serving on juries* are fully obligatory. One of the most telling ills of our time is the expectation of many Americans that they are entitled to ever more public services without paying for them (as reflected in public opinion polls that show demands to slash government and taxes but also to expand practically every conceivable government function). We all take for granted the right to be tried before a jury of our peers, but, all too often, we are unwilling to serve on juries ourselves.

Cleaning Up the Polity

We need to revitalize public life so that the two-thirds of our citizens who now say they feel alienated or that the polity is not theirs, will again be engaged in it.

Campaign contributions to members of Congress and state legislatures, speaking fees, and bribes have become so pervasive that in many areas of public policy and on numerous occasions the public interest is ignored as legislators pay off their debts to special interests. Detailed rationalizations have been spun to justify the system. It is said that giving money to politicians is a form of democratic participation. In fact, the rich can "participate" in this way so much more effectively than the poor, that the democratic principle of one-person one-vote is severely compromised. It is said that money buys only access to the politician's ear; but even if money does not buy commitment, access should not be allotted according to the depth of one's pockets. It is said that every group has its pool of money and hence as they all grease Congress, all Americans are served. But those who cannot grease at all or not as well, lose out and so do long-run public goals that are not underwritten by any particular interest groups.

To establish conditions under which elected officials will be able to respond to the public interest, to the genuine needs of all citizens, and to their own consciences requires that the role of private money in public life be reduced as much as possible. All candidates should receive some public support, as presidential candidates already do, as well as some access to radio and TV.

To achieve this major renewal and revitalization of public life, to reinstitute the prerequisites for attending to the public interest, *requires a major social movement,* akin to the progressive movement of the beginning of the century. For even good causes can become special interests if they are not part of such a movement, keeping their strategies and aims in constant dialogue with larger aims and multiple ends. Citizens who care about the integrity of the polity either on the local, state, or national level, should band with their fellows to form a neo-progressive communitarian movement. They should persevere until elected officials are beholden—not to special interests—but only to the voters and to their own consciences.

Freedom of Speech

The First Amendment is as dear to communitarians as it is to libertarians and many other Americans. Suggestions that it should be curbed to bar verbal expressions of racism, sexism, and other slurs seem to us to endanger the essence of the First Amendment, which is most needed when what some people say is disconcerting to some others. However, one should not ignore the victims of such abuse. Whenever individuals or members of a group are harassed, many *non-legal measures* are appropriate to express disapproval of hateful expressions and to promote tolerance among the members of the polity. For example, a college campus faced with a rash of incidents indicating bigotry, may conduct a teach-in on intergroup understanding. This, and much more, can be done without compromising the First Amendment.

Rights vs. Rightness

The language of rights is morally incomplete. To say that "I have a right to do X" is not to conclude that "X is the right thing for me to do." One may, for example, have a First Amendment right to address others in a morally inappropriate manner. Say one tells a Jew that "Hitler should have finished you all" or a black, "nigger go back to Africa," or worse. Rights give reasons to others not to coercively interfere with the speaker in the performance of protected acts; however, they do not in themselves give a person a sufficient reason to perform these acts. There is a gap between rights and rightness that cannot be closed without a richer moral vocabulary—one that invokes principles of decency, duty, responsibility, and the common good, among others.

Social Justice

At the heart of the communitarian understanding of social justice is the idea of reciprocity: each member of the community owes something to all the rest, and the community owes something to each of its members. Justice requires responsible individuals in a responsive community.

Members of the community have a responsibility, to the greatest extent possible, to provide for themselves and their families: honorable work contributes to the commonwealth and to the community's ability to fulfill its essential tasks. Beyond self-support, individuals have a responsibility for the material and moral well-being of others. This does not mean heroic self-sacrifice; it means the constant self-awareness that no one of us is an island unaffected by the fate of others.

For its part, the community is responsible for protecting each of us against catastrophe, natural or man-made; for ensuring the basic needs of all who genuinely cannot provide for themselves; for appropriately recognizing the distinctive contributions of individuals to the community; and for safeguarding a zone within which individuals may define their own lives through free exchange and choice.

Communitarian social justice is alive both to the equal moral dignity of all individuals and to the ways in which they differentiate themselves from one another through their personal decisions.

Public Safety and Public Health

The American moral and legal tradition has always acknowledged the need to balance individual rights with the need to protect the safety and health of the public. The Fourth Amendment, for example, guards against unreasonable searches but allows for reasonable ones.

Thus, while people with AIDS must be vigilantly protected from invasions of their privacy and from job and housing discrimination, the community must be allowed to take effective measures to curb the spread of the disease. While drug dealers' civil rights must be observed, the community must be provided with constitutional tools that will prevent dealers from dominating streets, parks, indeed, whole neighborhoods. While high school students must be protected against wanton expulsion, places of learning must be able to maintain the social-moral climate that education requires.

We differ with the ACLU and other radical libertarians who oppose sobriety checkpoints, screening gates at airports, drug and alcohol testing for people who directly affect public safety (pilots, train engineers, etc.). Given the minimal intrusion involved (an average sobriety checkpoint lasts ninety seconds), the importance of the interests at stake (we have lost more lives, many due to drunken drivers, on the road each year than in the war in Vietnam), and the fact that such measures in the past have not led us down a slippery slope, these and similar reasonable measures should receive full public support.

There is little sense in gun registration. What we need to significantly enhance public safety is *domestic disarmament* of the kind that exists in practically all democracies. The National Rifle Association suggestion that criminals not guns kill people, ignores the fact that thousands are killed each year, many of them children, from accidental discharge of guns, and that people—whether criminal, insane, or temporarily carried away by impulse—kill and are much more likely to do so when armed than when disarmed. The Second Amendment, behind which the NRA hides, is subject to a variety of interpretations, but the Supreme Court has repeatedly ruled, for over a hundred years, that it does not prevent laws that bar guns. *We join with those who read the Second Amendment the way it was written, as a communitarian clause, calling for community militias, not individual gun slingers.*

When it comes to public health, people who carry sexually transmitted diseases, especially when the illness is nearly always fatal, such as AIDS, should be expected to disclose their illness to previous sexual contacts or help health authorities to inform them, to warn all prospective sexual contacts, and inform all health care personnel with whom they come in contact. It is their contribution to help stem the epidemic. At the same time, the carriers' rights against wanton violation of privacy, discrimination in housing, employment, and insurance should be scrupulously protected.

The Human Community

Our communitarianism is not particularism. We believe that the responsive community is the best form of human organization yet devised for respecting human dignity and safeguarding human decency, and the way of life most open to needed self-revision through shared deliberation. We believe that the human species as a whole would be well-served by the movement, as circumstances permit, of all polities toward strongly democratic communities. We are acutely aware of the ways in which this movement will be (and ought to be) affected by important material, cultural, and political differences among nations and peoples. And we know that enduring responsive communities cannot be created through fiat or coercion, but only through genuine public conviction.

We are heartened by the widespread invocation of democratic principles by the nations and peoples now emerging from generations of repression; we see the institutionalization of these principles as the best possible bulwark against the excesses of ethnic and national particularism that could well produce new forms of repression.

While it may seem utopian, we believe that in the multiplication of strongly democratic communities around the world lies our best hope for the emergence of a global community that can deal concertedly with matters of general concern to our species as a whole: with war and strife, with violations of basic rights, with environmental degradation, and with the extreme material deprivation that stunts the bodies, minds, and spirits of children. *Our communitarian concern may begin with ourselves and our families, but it rises inexorably to the long-imagined community of humankind.*

In Conclusion

A Question of Responsibility

While some of the responsibilities identified in this manifesto are expressed in legal terms, and the law does play a significant role not only in regulating society but also in indicating which values it holds dear, our first and foremost purpose is to *affirm the moral commitments of parents, young persons, neighbors, and citizens,* to affirm the importance of the communities within which such commitments take shape and are transmitted from one generation to the next. This is not primarily a legal matter. On the contrary, when a community reaches the point at which these responsibilities are largely enforced by the powers of the state, it is in deep moral crisis. If communities are to function well, most members most of the time must discharge their responsibilities because they are committed to do so, not because they fear lawsuits, penalties, or jails. Nevertheless, the state and its agencies must take care not to harm the structures of civil society on which we all depend. *Social environments, like natural environments, cannot be taken for granted.*

It has been argued by libertarians that responsibilities are a personal matter, that individuals are to judge which responsibilities they accept as theirs. As we see it, responsibilities are anchored in community. Reflecting the diverse moral voices of their citizens, responsive communities define what is expected of people; they educate their members to accept these values; and they praise them when they do and frown upon them when they do not. While the ultimate foundation of morality may be commitments of individual conscience, it is communities that help introduce and sustain these commitments. Hence the urgent need for communities to articulate the responsibilities they expect their members to discharge, especially in times, such as our own, in which the understanding of these responsibilities has weakened and their reach has grown unclear.

Further Work

This is only a beginning. This platform is but a point in dialogue, part of an ongoing process of deliberation. It should not be viewed as a series of final conclusions but ideas for additional discussion. We do not claim to have the answers to all that troubles America these days. However, we are heartened by the groundswell of support that our initial efforts have brought to the communitarian perspective. If more and more Americans come forward and join together to form active communities that seek to reinvigorate the moral and social order, we will be able to deal better with many of our communities' problems while reducing our reliance on governmental regulation, controls, and force. We will have a greater opportunity to work out shared public policy based on broad consensus and shared moral and legal traditions. And we will have many more ways to make our society a place in which individual rights are vigilantly maintained, while the seedbeds of civic virtue are patiently nurtured.

SIGNATORIES

Signatures signify that we are of one mind on the broad thrust of this platform and the necessity of this intervention into the current dialogue, without necessarily agreeing to every single, specific statement.

Rodolfo Alvarez (University of California, Los Angeles)
John B. Anderson (Presidential Candidate, 1980)
Benjamin R. Barber (Rutgers University; signing with exception to moral education section)
Robert N. Bellah (University of California, Berkeley)
Janice M. Beyer (University of Texas, Austin; signing with exception to family section)
John E. Brand (University of Minnesota, former Minnesota State Senator, Representative)
James Childress (University of Virginia)
Bryce J. Christensen (President, The Family in America, The Rockford Institute)
Henry Cisneros (Former Mayor, San Antonio, Texas)
John C. Coffee (Columbia University Law School)
David Cohen (Co-Director, Advocacy Institute)

Anthony Cook (Georgetown University Law School)
Harvey Cox (Harvard Divinity School; signing with exception to cleaning up the polity section)
Thomas Donaldson (Georgetown University)
Thomas W. Dunfee (Wharton School, University of Pennsylvania)
Stuart E. Eizenstat (Attorney, Washington, D.C.)
Jean Bethke Elshtain (Vanderbilt University)
Amitai Etzioni (George Washington University)
Chester E. Finn, Jr. (Vanderbilt University)
James Fishkin (University of Texas, Austin)
Carol Tucker Foreman (Attorney, Washington, D.C.)
William A. Galston (University of Maryland)
John W. Gardner (Stanford University)
Mary Ann Glendon (Harvard Law School)
Jeffrey R. Henig (George Washington University)
Albert O. Hirschman (Institute for Advanced Study, Princeton)
James Hunger (University of Virginia)
Daniel Kemmis (Mayor, Missoula, Montana; signing with exception to second amendment section)
George C. Lodge (Harvard Business School)
Malcolm Lovell, Jr. (President, National Planning Association)
Jane Mansbridge (Northern University; signing with exception to family section)
Gary Marx (Massachusetts Institute of Technology)
Thomas McCollough (Duke University)
Newton N. Minow (Former F.C.C. Chairman; Attorney, Chicago, Illinois)
Ilene H. Nagel (U.S. Sentencing Commission and Indiana University)
Richard John Neuhaus (President, Religion and Public Life Institute)
William C. Norris (Chairman, William C. Norris Institute, Minneapolis, Minnesota)
Michael Pertschuk (Co-Director, Advocacy Institute)
Terry Pinkard (Georgetown University)
David Popenoe (Rutgers University)
Alice S. Rossi (Former President, American Sociological Association; Amherst, Massachusetts)
Isabel Sawhill (Senior Fellow, The Urban Institute)
William D. Ruckelshaus (Chairman of the Board and Chief Executive Officer, Browning-Ferris Industries, Houston, Texas)
Philip Selznick (University of California, Berkeley)
Albert Shanker (President, American Federation of Teachers)
Fred Siegel (Cooper Union)

Gillian Martin Sorensen (President, National Conference of Christians
   and Jews)
Thomas Spragens, Jr. (Duke University)
Margaret O'Brien Steinfels (Editor, *Commonweal*)
Adlai E. Stevenson (Chicago, Illinois)
William Sullivan (LaSalle University)
Robert Theobald (New Orleans, Louisiana)
Lester C. Thurow (Dean, Sloan School of Management, Massachusetts
   Institute of Technology)
Daniel Thursz (President, The National Council on the Aging)
Kenneth S. Tollett (Howard University)
Barbara Dafoe Whitehead (Amherst, Massachusetts)
Dennis H. Wrong (New York University)
Daniel Yankelovich (President, Public Agenda Foundation)

I

Communitarian Theory

1

Foundations of Communitarian Liberalism

Philip Selznick

The contemporary communitarian movement is sometimes seen as anti-liberal. Indeed, the "communitarian-liberal" debate is a staple of recent political philosophy. The contrast is too stark, however, and can be very misleading. Today's communitarians are not antiliberal if liberalism means a strong commitment to political freedom, social justice, constitutional rights, the rule of law, full citizenship, and special concern for the poor and the oppressed. If communitarians criticize specific liberal doctrines, it does not follow that they reject, or fail to appreciate, the main ideals and institutions of liberalism.

Liberal ideals and institutions have taken different forms over the past two centuries and have been supported by a variety of political theories. Hence, it is best to think of liberalism as an ethos or a loose tradition, rather than as a tight system of ideas. This way of thinking invites us to consider how ideas develop and how they are deployed. We see ideologies as historical realities, bound to be composed of often conflicting strands such as, in liberalism, classical vs. welfare liberalism and popular vs. theoretical liberalism.

We are or should be "communitarian liberals" or, if you prefer, liberal communitarians. Like John Dewey, we should combine a spirit of liberation and a quest for social justice, with responsible participation in effective communities. This is not a wholesale rejection of liberalism. Rather, it is a call for a deep reconstruction of liberal theories and policies.

In this essay I want to focus attention on the ideals of liberalism: equality, liberty, and rationality. These ideals were hallmarks of eighteenth and nineteenth century "classical" liberalism; and they continue to guide today's "welfare" liberals. They are the true starting points for liberal reasoning; and each has made major contributions to social progress and moral well-being.

At the same time, each ideal has suffered degradation within liberal thinking; each has taken forms that are ill-adapted to our times.

Therefore we must criticize and reject some of the ways these ideals are used in drawing policy conclusions. Our main target is intellectual and practical excess. In contemporary liberalism, both popular and theoretical, there is too much reliance on the power of abstractions; too much hope that some single principle will be an unerring guide to social policy; and too little appreciation for implicit boundaries, competing values, and unintended effects. These criticisms are communitarian because they give great weight to the social frameworks within which all ideals find their limits as well as their opportunities.

EQUALITY: MORAL AND OTHERWISE

As used by Jefferson in the Declaration of Independence and by Lincoln in the Gettysburg Address, equality means *moral* equality. This is the postulate that all persons have the same intrinsic worth. They are unequal in talents, in contributions to social life, and in valid claims to rewards and resources. But in principle, as a starting point for moral reasoning, every adult is to be considered a responsible moral actor; and every person, grown-up or not, is equally an object of moral concern. This is not a distinctively liberal or modern idea; it has religious roots. But the secular doctrine of moral equality has been a centerpiece of liberal thought and practice; a powerful weapon against all forms of the caste principle; a great resource for overcoming prejudice, contempt, and moral stigma; and a summons to concern for individual growth and flourishing. By decisively reinforcing this ideal, and by giving it secular legitimacy, liberalism has made a major contribution to the cause of humanity.

There are, however, troubling downsides in the ways equality is perceived and invoked. A major issue is the complex connection between *moral* equality and *social* equality. How much and what kinds of social equality—effective access to health care, for example—are called for by the promise of moral equality? This question has led to significant divisions within the liberal tradition. Classical liberalism, more concerned with form than substance, was ready to accept grave inequalities of condition, as suggested by Anatole France's sardonic comment that "the law, in its majestic equality, forbids rich and poor alike to sleep under bridges, beg in the streets, or steal bread." American liberalism has come a long way from that perspective. A decisive advance was made by Franklin D.

Roosevelt's New Deal, which acknowledged collective responsibility for poverty and unemployment, and when the Supreme Court, taking judicial notice of historic subordination and oppression, gave special protection to African-Americans and other victims of invidious discrimination.

These developments were anchored in history and in genuine problems. The current zest for equality, however, which we find in popular liberalism, lacks such an anchor; indeed it lacks a rudder as well. Popular liberalism has come to suppose that every kind of privilege, authority, coercion, classification, or segregation is an actual or potential affront to the subject's dignity as a person, and therefore to moral equality. Equality becomes a powerful but untamed abstraction, a premise from which we are supposed to draw specific conclusions about social policy. On many issues, such as separate education for boys and girls, or mainstreaming handicapped or unmotivated students, there is an unwarranted leap from a premise of moral equality to a social policy rejecting segregation. Specific circumstances and competing values are given short shrift, if not ignored. Insofar as the Constitution is successfully invoked, the states and local communities are unduly limited in the choices they can make and in the diversity of practices they can countenance. In this way, ideological thinking impoverishes the textured, nuanced, problem-solving experience of community.

More important, these days, is a too easy transition from moral equality to moral *autonomy*. In contemporary liberalism—theoretical as well as popular—moral equality has been given this central meaning: To treat people as equals, invested with inherent dignity and responsibility, is to grant them the right to define the good and pursue the good in their own way. Stated abstractly, and applied to much ordinary experience, this makes eminent good sense. And among liberal theorists like John Rawls, a limiting framework of moral principles is taken for granted. But in popular liberalism, and to some extent in theoretical liberalism as well, moral autonomy has come to have a more fateful significance—it is said to necessarily produce deep-seated differences in peoples' values and outlooks. To respect these differences is to accept profound moral pluralism as a salient feature of the human condition, or at least the condition of modernity. Thus moral equality, which begins as an appeal to shared identity and therefore to what we have in common, becomes a celebration of difference and a source of misunderstanding and distrust. In contemporary popular liberalism, equality as difference threatens to swallow equality as humanity.

There is surely an important connection between moral equality and respect for diversity. But historically the principle of respect was a way of showing how distinctively human characteristics, shared by all peoples, can transcend particularities of kinship, locality, custom, and religion.

Therefore cosmopolitan liberals rejected ethnocentrism and affirmed natural (or human) rights. At the same time, they disparaged localism as the breeding ground of ignorance and bigotry. In rejecting that disparagement, today's apostles of multiculturalism have also rejected the cosmopolitan ideal.

Up to a point this rejection is congenial to communitarian liberalism. In contrast to cosmopolitan liberals, we take seriously the claims of particularity. This is so in part because we think ordinary people are entitled to respect, and the respect they want has much to do with the culture that gives them a sense of authenticity and rootedness. Such a culture very often depends on special local, religious, ethnic, or racial identities. (There are, of course, other good reasons for respecting and nurturing families, localities, churches, and other "mediating" groups.)

Does this mean we should accept, or fail to criticize, the currently fashionable politics of identity? Not so. To acknowledge that moral equality requires respect for diversity does not mean we must yield to parochial passion, or accept distortions of moral principle. When we are told, for example, that cultural assimilation amounts to genocide, or that every difference of origin or disposition is a radical difference, we should strongly object. These are prescriptions for fragmentation. They cannot build that unity of unities we call community.

LIBERTY: FROM LIBERAL TO LIBERTARIAN

For most of its history the liberal tradition has not been libertarian. Today, however, the libertarian element has become stronger and less restrained, with important support in philosophy and in constitutional interpretation. The idea of *ordered* liberty, once central, has lost much of its hold on the liberal imagination. This is what troubles communitarian liberals.

If we now express concern, it is not because we dislike liberty. On the contrary, in many settings we are glad to cry "let freedom ring." Furthermore, we accept and cherish a *culture* of liberty, which is by no means limited to basic protections against potentially oppressive government. Something more than the Bill of Rights is wanted. A culture of liberty provides effective opportunity for personal growth, expression, and the pursuit of individual life plans; for free inquiry and unburdened communication; and for the chance to grow up and be educated in an atmosphere that encourages criticism, reflection, and experimentation. I trust there are few among us who would wish to abandon, or even to dampen, these elements of the liberal spirit.

But contexts are decisive. It is the context that tells us what *kinds* of liberty are appropriate and what *limits* are desirable. We cannot apply what Dewey called "the method of intelligence" without continuing awareness of how contexts make a difference for abstract ideals or for models of motivation and conduct. Contexts point to purposes and functions, which invite attention to important variations in what makes sense for persons, institutions, and practices. Only if we appreciate contexts can we truly act with integrity, that is, in principled ways. As I have written elsewhere:

> Integrity has to do with principles, and therefore with principled conduct. ... A political, administrative, or judicial decision is principled if it is guided by a coherent conception of institutional morality, that is, of appropriate ends and means. A principle is not an idée fixe; not an instrument of ideological thinking; not a prejudice; not a rule to be applied mechanically. It belongs to a larger whole, which includes textured meanings and concrete understandings as well as abstract ideas. Only if that whole is implicated can there be genuinely principled judgment. (*The Moral Commonwealth,* p. 323)

Failures of contextual thinking are especially prominent in current controversies over freedom of speech. Because the value at stake is so important, people are tempted to turn it into an absolute, with the result that variations in kinds of speech, and in the appropriateness of constitutional protection, are ignored or resisted. In this country a watershed of sorts was reached when freedom of speech became freedom of expression, thus widening the category of protected utterance and detaching it from the contexts of deliberative democracy, institutional integrity, or even personal well-being—indeed from context of any kind.

We now have a situation in which almost any utterance can be thought to deserve constitutional protection. This is more true of popular culture than of law, for in fact our constitutional law of free speech does recognize some important distinctions, which have drawn the fire of libertarians. But the rhetoric of free speech, even in judicial opinions, strains toward absolutism. People come to think that all speech is morally equivalent, and that any regulation is oppressive.

This strain toward absolutism in popular liberalism finds sustenance in the writings of some liberal theorists. According to Ronald Dworkin, for example, the constitutional doctrine of free speech cannot be understood or justified if we consider only the "instrumental" worth of speech, that is, its contribution to political democracy or to restraining the abuse of power. Rather, free speech has "intrinsic" worth, derived from the premise that all adults, except any who are incompetent, must be treated as responsible moral agents. Such agents rightly "insist on making up their own minds about what is good or bad in life or in politics, or what is true or false in matters of justice or faith;" their dignity is violated if opinions are withheld from them on the ground that they are not fit to consider them; and they have a compelling desire to express their convictions to others, a desire that must be honored if their integrity as moral agents is to be respected. (See Ronald Dworkin's "The Coming Battles Over Free Speech," *New York Review of Books,* 11 June 1992.)

Here the concept of moral agency carries a great deal of freight, and Dworkin's postulates are by no means self-evident. For example, it is easy to suppose that responsible moral agents, for their own good reasons, may wish to defer to the authority of others, including the authority of a tradition, rather than make up their own minds on every issue. And the desire for self-expression is highly variable, to say the least. More important than these overreachings, however, is the very idea that we can draw specific conclusions about freedom of speech from a general theory of moral responsibility. In fact we cannot know what it means to be responsible apart from knowing what it means to be a good citizen, a good physician, a good journalist, a good teacher, a good student. There is quite a leap from the abstract idea of moral responsibility to the conclusion that *"any* censorship on grounds of content is inconsistent with that commitment."

I agree with Dworkin that freedoms of speech and expression have intrinsic worth. This has two relevant meanings: first, such freedoms have intrinsic worth because they are prized, not only for the social benefits they bring but also for the direct contributions they make to personal well-being; and second, because they have the capacity to sustain and enrich a wide range of values. (It follows that the contrast between "instrumental" and "intrinsic," like many such dichotomies, is not hard and fast. Ultimately, values are tested by their consequences, and in that sense are instrumental; but that does not mean they are narrowly instrumental.) Uncoerced communication, to others and to oneself, is important for intellectual, emotional, and moral growth; and freedom of speech is valuable for many purposes, including science, education, and professional consultation, as well as self-government. Hence I also agree that the protection of free speech should extend beyond "deliberative democracy" to include many other institutions and practices.

But even so broad a commitment to free speech cannot be a substitute for focused inquiry as to how far, in what forms, and with what limits free speech will be governed by appropriate standards, including its relation to other values and purposes. In every context there are boundaries to be set and exclusions to be considered. Free speech in the classroom is surely prized in part for its intrinsic worth, but it is also constrained by the requirements of academic order and purpose. In the larger arena of the public forum we may also ask: Does protected speech extend to the words used by panhandlers, to verbal abuse by frustrated motorists, to indecent exposure as a form of self-expression? These and many other questions cannot be answered by appeal to a premise of moral responsibility.

I do not mean to endorse a strategy that "turns away from general principle to the pragmatic (anti)principle of considering each situation as it emerges," assessing "in every case what is at stake and what are the risks and gains of alternative courses of action," as Stanley Fish put it in his recent book, *There's No Such Thing as Free Speech.* Rather, we give effect to a principle, such as freedom of speech, by establishing a presumption that is to be afforded great weight in familiar contexts. When we define limits by taking account of the setting, including relevant purposes and other values at stake, we make sense of the ideal and give it the force it should have. This is affirmation, not abandonment.

RATIONALITY: THE LIMITS OF SPECULATIVE REASON

A third ideal of liberalism is rationality. It was a prime objective of the Enlightenment to release people from ignorance and superstition so that the light of rational understanding might prevail. Science and technology gained immensely from this celebration of unfettered and rational thought. So did the moral order, which was fortified and civilized by the demand that reasons be given to justify power, policy, and custom. Thus rationality joined with equality and liberty to form a liberal bulwark against arbitrary judgment and power.

The most important contribution of liberal rationality to human well-being is its support of the idea of—and the authority of—critical morality. Critical morality is our best effort to apply intelligence to moral issues. It postulates that every purported moral truth is subject to inquiry and open to correction. As Kant and other Enlightenment figures understood very well, however, the conclusions of critical morality *may either confirm or amend* conventional or received morality. Therefore critical morality should not be understood as wholly different from or counterposed to conventional morality.

The trouble is that the liberal quest for a wholly rational morality often leads to excessive reliance on abstract and speculative reasoning about human nature and social life. As the history of intellectual controversy and policy failure shows, many premises are ill-examined and the reasoning is very often seriously flawed. These exercises fail to recognize that reflection, far from being self-certifying, can lead to stupid and even disastrous policies, and that the tacit knowledge of custom is often wiser than a scheme based on explicit theorizing. This is the truth in Edmund Burke's rejection of "speculative reason."

A great deal can be lost when we fail to appreciate beliefs and practices we cannot fully justify (at least right now) by a clear chain of reasoning or by readily available facts. Consider, for example, John Stuart Mill's famous "harm principle": "The only purpose for which power can be rightfully exercised over any member of a civilized community, against his will, is to prevent harm to others. His own good, either physical or moral, is not sufficient warrant. He cannot rightfully be compelled to do or forbear because, in the opinion of others, to do so would be wise, or even right." This is a noble idea, and a worthy defense of liberty, but only if its implied limits are understood. Mill took for granted a reasonably stable and viable culture, as his reference to a "civilized" community suggests. Moreover, in focusing on harm to *individual* others, Mill's principle slights the significance of a moral environment. The decay of a moral environment may be subtle, and perhaps long-term, yet such decay can be crucial, not only for the community's identity and character (which indeed should be open to criticism and change) but also to the elementary conditions of social order.

We cannot escape the sociological truth that participation in a viable culture is an indispensable source of personal stability and social discipline. The loss of culture—especially as it affects basic expectations of everyday life regarding personal behavior and social interaction—produces widespread anxiety and a weakening of social control. Although *some* anxiety and *some* lack of discipline must be accepted as costs of cultural change or renewal, it is folly to neglect the dangers of cultural destruction. Cultural destruction brings lack of motivation, including the capacity to care for children, hold a job, or resist self-destructive gratifications. It is remarkable that liberal social scientists, who have done so much to deepen our understanding of the significance of culture for human life, have failed to provide guidance for the defense of culture against destruction from within.

It may well be easier, and apparently more rational, to identify direct harms to individuals than to offer reasons for, say, restricting pornography or preserving an atmosphere that upholds civility as well as freedom. But the want of easy answers is not, in itself, a want of rationality. We may find, perhaps too late, that there were good reasons for preserving the core of conventional morality. We simply did not understand them.

A MEAGER COMMON GOOD

Compared to the ideals of equality, liberty, and rationality, the notion of a common good is more gingerly embraced in the ethos of liberalism. For communitarians this is a major concern. Of course many liberal writers

and statesmen have explicitly sought the "public good," "the public interest," or, as in the preamble to the U.S. Constitution, "the general Welfare." And many liberals, especially welfare liberals, have insisted that the
liberal ideal of rationality requires cooperative action for rationally defined collective goals.

Yet much in liberalism has undercut the pursuit of what James Madison
called, in his famous definition of faction, "the permanent and aggregate
interests of the community." A pervasive rhetoric of individualism, and a
preference for individual-centered models of thought and action, has
tended to marginalize conceptions of the common good. For many contemporary liberals, the so-called common good must be, inevitably, a partial and self-serving perspective, a justification for imposing the will of
some people over others. Therefore, as J. Donald Moon observed in *Constructing Community: Moral Pluralism and Tragic Conflicts*, "the whole
point of the liberal project is to discover a way in which people with
different values may live under principles that they regard as just and
legitimate, and the obvious way to do that is to limit the scope of political
authority to unproblematic areas and to provide space within which citizens can pursue their own conceptions of the good."

On this view, the common good will be served by limiting the reach of
collective decision. If we stick to "unproblematic" areas—social utilities,
we might say—then the unity of the political community will be preserved, and unity is surely a common good.

But can politics and government be divorced from fundamental values?
Communitarians say no. Such a divorce too drastically restricts what can
be done through collective action, including representative government
to solve the community's problems and meet its responsibilities. These
problems have to do with the allocation of resources; with taming as well
as liberating the play of interest and power; with the quality and direction
of our institutions; with the substance of education; with how we respond
to discrimination, poverty, and disorder, with the fate of the environment;
with our responsibilities as a nation within a world made new by technology and shadowed by fragmentation; and much, much more that can
hardly be called "unproblematic" or innocent of value choices.

It is sometimes said, by liberals fearful of domination, that there is no
"common good." There are only plural and competing goods. The implication is that we need not bother with an elusive but integral conception
of the good; we need only worry about the choice of specific goods. But
what criteria shall we use in making such choices? How shall we establish
priorities and make tradeoffs? Just because we have competing interests
and many goods, we must make collective decisions about priorities and
tradeoffs; and this requires a collectively established conception of what
will make the community better off or worse off. On a great many issues,

including major value choices, we must pull ourselves together, as a community, and take thought as to what kind of a people we are and how we should deal with our urgent problems.

In the liberal project, as currently defined by liberal theorists, the political community is a bare framework within which autonomous choices can be made. We are not to seek, through politics and government, the kind of community that will best redeem the promise of human fellowship or most closely approximate the potential for human growth, creativity, and responsibility. As John Rawls writes in *Political Liberalism,* the liberal state can no more act to "advance human excellence . . . than it can act to advance Catholicism or Protestantism, or any other religion."

On the contrary, within a liberal community there is much room for secular judgment as to what the community may aspire to as well as what it must guard against. These aspirations, and the way to achieve them, are inevitably contested, sometimes very vigorously. That is where democracy comes in. A constitutional framework limits what democracies can do, especially by indicating what rights must be protected in the course of collective judgment. Beyond, however, lies a realm of democratic opportunity, governed by the morality of deliberation and by a shared commitment to determine and implement the public interest.

It is a parody of democracy to say that democratic institutions are mainly geared to managing diversity; and that the main evil to be considered is moral coercion, that is, the burden of accepting, as legitimate, conclusions that offend one's moral convictions. We should have greater confidence in human resilience and in the possibilities of accommodation. We should be more realistic and focused in what we take to be unacceptable moral coercion. We should not leap to the conclusion on specific issues that differences are deep and opaque, impervious to argument, wholly irreconcilable.

People often ask, who decides what is the common good? The answer is we all decide, not by abandoning our special interests and perspectives but by transcending them as necessary and by discovering ways of binding them to more comprehensive interests and ideals. The objective is to advance social learning, through deliberative institutions, and to encourage knowledge of and sacrifice for the common good. Therefore democracy looks to substance as well as to procedure.

We cannot and should not expect a fully shared conception of the common good; we must always presume plurality and dissension. Nevertheless, democracy is, above all, a way of exercising collective will. That will is tied down, as Jefferson said, "by the chains of the Constitution." But the mission of democracy is to make a virtue out of the necessity of common life, and to do so by solving problems and bringing people together, not mainly by keeping them from one another's throats.

In short, a communitarian morality recognizes the compelling power of liberal ideals while also noting that much liberal rhetoric, philosophy, and policy has been overly individualistic, ahistorical, and insufficiently sensitive to the social sources of selfhood and obligation. These deficiencies have nurtured the abstract, uncontextual modes of thought, and the strains toward absolutism, which I have discussed above. The communitarian response seeks a new blend, one that treasures liberal values and institutions but also takes seriously the promise of community and the perils of ignoring the need for community.

2

Community Properly Understood: A Defense of "Democratic Communitarianism"

Robert N. Bellah

The word "community" leads a double life. It makes most people feel good, associated as it is with warmth, friendship, and acceptance. But among academics the word arouses suspicion. Doesn't community imply the abandonment of ethical universalism and the withdrawal into closed particularistic loyalties? Doesn't it perhaps lead even to ethnic cleansing?

The word community is a good word and worthy of continued use if it is carefully defined. My fellow authors and I attempted such a definition in *Habits of the Heart*, but it was often ignored. The primary problem is that the word is frequently used to mean small-scale, face-to-face groups like the family, the congregation, and the small town—what the Germans call *Gemeinschaft*. There is a long tradition of extolling this kind of community in America. But when that is all that community means, it is basically sentimental and, in the strict sense of the word, nostalgic. And nostalgia, as Christopher Lasch wrote, is merely a psychological placebo that allows one to accept regretfully but uncritically whatever is currently being served up in the name of progress. It inhibits, rather than serves, serious social criticism.

Thus if the term community is to be useful, it must mean something more. Those philosophical liberals who tend to reject the term community altogether see society as based on a social contract establishing procedures of fairness, but otherwise leaving individuals free to serve their own interests. They argue that under modern conditions, if we think of community as based on shared values and shared goals, community can exist only in small groups and is not possible or desirable in large-scale societies or institutions.

15

A deeper analysis, however, reveals that it is possible to see this supposed contrast of contract versus community as a continuum, or even as a necessary complementarity, rather than as an either/or proposition. Surely procedural norms of fairness are necessary in large-scale social institutions; but any group of any size, if it has a significant breadth of involvement and lasts a significant length of time, must have some shared values and goals. Consequently societies and institutions can never be based solely on contract, striving to maximize the opportunities of individuals. They must also, to some extent, be communities with shared values and goals

But this reformulation leads to a further problem. Those who think of community as a form of *Gemeinschaft,* as well as their liberal critics, tend to think consensus about values and goals must be complete or nearly complete. Is such complete consensus realistic, or even desirable, in modern societies?

The answer, of course, is no. Yet this lack of unanimity need not create problems for supporters of community. While community-shared values and goals do imply something more than procedural agreement—they do imply some agreements about substance—they do not require anything like total or unarguable agreement. A good community is one in which there is argument, even conflict, about the meaning of the shared values and goals, and certainly about how they will be actualized in everyday life. Community is not about silent consensus; it is a form of intelligent, reflective life, in which there is indeed consensus, but where the consensus can be challenged and changed—often gradually, sometimes radically—over time.

Thus we are led to the question of what makes any kind of group a community and not just a contractual association. The answer lies in a shared concern with the following question: "What will make this group a *good* group?" Any institution, such as a university, a city, or a society, insofar as it is or seeks to be a community, needs to ask what is a good university, city, society, and so forth. So far as it reaches agreement about the good it is supposed to realize (and that will always be contested and open to further debate), it becomes a community with some common values and some common goals. ("Goals" are particularly important, as the effort to define a good community also entails the goal of trying to create a good one—or, more modestly and realistically, a better one than the current one.)

THE INDIVIDUAL RECONSIDERED

Even given the claim that community does not require complete consensus, some people view with skepticism any effort to reach some common agreement about the good. Such a view is rooted in our culture's adherence to "ontological individualism"—the belief that the truth of our condition is not in our society or in our relation to others, but in our isolated and inviolable selves. It is this belief that tempts us to imagine that it is opportunity that will solve all our problems—if we could just provide individuals the opportunity to realize themselves, then everything else would take care of itself. If we focus on individual opportunity then we don't need to worry about substantive agreement or the common good, much less force any such notion on others. Each individual can concentrate on whatever good he or she chooses to pursue.

In seeking to solve our problems through individual opportunity we have come up with two master strategies. We will provide opportunity through the market or through the state. The great ideological wars of our current politics focus on whether the most effective provider of opportunity is the market or the state. On this issue we imagine a radical polarity between conservative and liberal, Republican and Democrat. What we often do not see is that this is a very tame polarity, because the opponents agree so deeply on most of the terms of the problem. Both solutions are individualistic. Whatever their opponents say, those who support a strong government seldom believe in government as such. They simply see it as the most effective provider of those opportunities that will allow individuals to have a fair chance at making something of themselves. Those who believe in the market think free competition is the best context for individual self-realization. Both positions are essentially technocratic. They do not imply much about substantive values, other than freedom and opportunity. They would solve our problems through economic or political mechanisms, not moral solidarity.

And yet the world of these ideological opponents, composed as it is of autonomous individuals, markets, and states, is not the world that anyone lives in—not even the free enterprise or welfare liberal ideologists. This ideological world is a world without families. It is also a world without neighborhoods, ethnic communities, churches, cities and towns, even nations (as opposed to states). It is, to use the terminology of the German sociologist-philosopher Jurgen Habermas, a world of individuals and systems (economic and administrative), but not a lifeworld. The lifeworld missing in these conservative and liberal ideologies is the place where we communicate with others, deliberate, come to agreements about standards and norms, pursue in common an effort to create a valuable form of life—in short, the lifeworld is the world of community.

DEMOCRATIC COMMUNITARIANISM

I want to sketch a framework that escapes the ideological blinders of current American politics and highlights what is missing in much of our debate. As opposed to free market conservatism and welfare state liberalism, I want to describe another approach to our common problems which I will call—borrowing from Jonathan Boswell in *Community and the Economy: The Theory of Public Co-operation*—democratic communitarianism. Democratic communitarianism does not pit itself against the two reigning ideologies as a third way. It accepts the value and inevitability of both the market and the state, but it insists that the function of the market and the state is to serve us, not to dominate us. Democratic communitarianism seeks to provide a humane context within which to think about the market and the state. Its first principle is the one already enunciated in what I have said about community: it seeks to define and further the good which is the community's purpose. I want to offer four values to which democratic communitarianism is committed and which give its notion of the good somewhat more specificity:

1. Democratic communitarianism is based on the value of the sacredness of the individual, which is common to most of the great religions and philosophies of the world. (It is expressed in biblical religion through the idea that we are created in the image and likeness of God.) Anything that would oppress individuals, or operate to stunt individual development, would be contrary to the principles of democratic communitarianism. However, unlike its ideological rivals, democratic communitarianism does not think of individuals as existing in a vacuum or as existing in a world composed only of markets and states. Rather, it believes that individuals are realized only in and through communities, and that strong, healthy, morally vigorous communities are the prerequisite for strong, healthy, morally vigorous individuals.

2. Democratic communitarianism, therefore, affirms the central value of solidarity. Solidarity points to the fact that we become who we are through our relationships—that reciprocity, loyalty, and shared commitment to the good are defining features of a fully human life.

3. Democratic communitarianism believes in what Boswell has called "complementary association." By this he means a commitment to "varied social groupings: the family, the local community, the cultural or religious group, the economic enterprise, the trade union or profession, the nation-state." Through this principle it is clear that community does not mean small-scale, all-inclusive, total groups. In our kind of society an individual will belong to many communities and ultimately the world itself can be seen as a community. Democratic communitarianism views such a multiplicity of belonging as a positive good, as potentially and in principle complementary.

4. Finally, democratic communitarianism is committed to the idea of

participation as both a right and a duty. Communities become positive goods only when they provide the opportunity and support to participate in them. A corollary of this principle is the principle of subsidiarity, derived from Catholic social teaching. This ideas asserts that the groups closest to a problem should attend to it, receiving support from higher level groups only if necessary. To be clear, democratic communitarianism does not adhere to Patrick Buchanan's interpretation of subsidiarity, which projects a society virtually without a state. A more legitimate understanding of subsidiarity realizes the inevitability and necessity of the state. It has the responsibility of nurturing lower-level associations wherever they are weak, as they normally are among the poor and the marginalized. Applying this perspective to current events, at a moment when powerful political forces in the United States are attempting to dismantle a weak welfare state, democratic communitarians will defend vigorous and responsible state action.

Nothing in this argument is meant to imply that face-to-face community is not a good thing. It is, and in our society it needs to be strengthened. But the argument for democratic community—rooted in the search for the common good—applies to groups of any size, and ultimately to the world as a community. It is a political argument grounded on the belief that a politics based on the summing of individual preferences is inadequate and misleading. Democratic communitarianism presumes that morality and politics cannot be separated and that moral argument, painful and difficult though it sometimes is, is fundamental to a defensible stance in today's world.

3

The Limitations of Libertarianism

Thomas A. Spragens, Jr.

THE LIBERTARIAN PERSUASION

For much of its history the liberal tradition has included among its fellow travelers a cohort of political libertarians. These precursors of the libertarian persuasion can be found relatively early in the history of liberalism. For example, Bernard Mandeville provided in his *Fable of the Bees* (1714) a classic statement of the claim that unleashing the self-interested passions of individuals is the pathway to creating public benefits. The pure form of libertarian thought, however, was probably not codified until the 19th century, principally as a critique of efforts to subject the economic marketplace to more extensive democratic control. A classic example, and a milestone in the development of libertarianism, was Herbert Spencer's *Social Statics* (1850). Libertarian ideas continue to receive vital and influential expression today in the works of neoclassical economists who venture into political theory—such as Ludwig von Mises, Friedrich Hayek, and Milton Friedman—and moral philosophers who postulate an expansive conception of individual rights as their starting point, such as Robert Nozick.

In the popular political culture, libertarianism may be said to have its left-wing and right-wing versions. Leftist libertarians seek to maximize political and civil liberties. They are often members of the American Civil Liberties Union. Rightist libertarians want to maximize economic liberties and minimize the scope of government action. They include those who like to wear neckties that bear the profile of Adam Smith. For a variety of reasons stemming from class, interests, and ideology, leftist libertarians may not object to government regulation of the economy in the interest of fairness, whereas rightist libertarians may be willing to countenance governmental limits on individuals' sexual or artistic expression. The most consistent libertarians—including most of those who belong to the Libertarian party—espouse maximum individual freedom in all spheres of life.

The "ideal typical" logic of libertarianism includes both moral and prudential arguments. On grounds that are often not fully articulated, libertarians characteristically accord individual freedom preeminent moral status. This preeminence is often flatly stated in terms of putatively inalienable rights. For example, the very first words of Nozick's *Anarchy, State, and Utopia* are: "Individuals have rights, and there are things no person or group may do to them (without violating their rights). So strong and far-reaching are these rights that they raise the question of what, if anything, the state and its officials may do." It follows, then, that in any instance in which liberty conflicts with some other human value, liberty must be predominant. Milton Friedman suggests, in *Capitalism and Freedom,* that when "equality comes sharply into conflict with freedom, one must choose. One cannot be both an egalitarian, in this sense, and a liberal."

The absolute moral standing of individual freedom is in the view of libertarian theorists bolstered by prudential considerations. That is, the principal practical merit of unleashing individual self-interest is the economic prosperity that such a policy produces. A free market maximizes efficiency, engenders innovation, and optimizes gross national product (GNP). Reliance on private enterprise also decentralizes power and thereby thwarts majority or elitist tyranny. It permits the flowering of genius. It promotes social peace by creating a form of effective proportional representation in determining the allocation of resources. Conversely, relying on collective action or state authority is held to foster an inefficient and irrational allocation of productive resources. It opens the door to paternalistic oppression. It enfranchises free riders and special pleaders and stifles individual initiative. In A.V. Dicey's words, "State help kills self-help."

Based on these moral and prudential grounds, libertarians make three major polemical claims. First, they claim to be the proper heirs and interpreters of political liberalism. (For example, Friedman writes in the introduction to *Capitalism and Freedom,* that "the rightful and proper name . . . for the political and economic viewpoint elaborated in this book . . . is liberalism.") Second, they assert that maximizing individual freedom should be the appropriate normative goal of a good society. Third, they believe that norms are sufficient to guide public policy in a healthy liberal democracy.

CRITIQUING LIBERTARIANISM: AN OVERVIEW

My purpose here is to dispute each of these claims. Libertarian doctrine, I shall argue, narrows and distorts liberal theory. Libertarian norms are inadequate as a basis for a good democratic society. And libertarian strategies can in some domains be positively destructive of democratic institutions.

Before condemning libertarians for their inadequacies and distortions, it is only fair and also useful to acknowledge the value and strengths of their viewpoint. It should be conceded, for example, that respect for human liberty is essential to any adequate moral theory and certainly to any liberal theory. Both logic and experience suggest, moreover, that libertarians are on firm ground in claiming that productive economies must encourage and reward individual entrepreneurship. And the libertarian insistence that collective policies are often distorted by paternalistic impositions and special-interest extortions is to my mind incontrovertible. Libertarians thus make good allies whenever one is confronted by the *libido dominandi* of socialist intellectuals or the monopolizing practices of the American Medical Association. With all that has been said, however, doubts remain.

The fundamental intellectual defect of libertarianism lies in its tendency toward abstraction and simplism. It extracts from the numerous requisites and complexities of a good human life the single requisite of freedom, and it conceives of this sole requisite in a simplistic manner, even as it elevates it to normative hegemony. This central weakness manifests itself in two principal ways. First libertarian doctrine decontextualizes human freedom, and hence loses sight of the way that it interacts with, and indeed is dependent upon, other human values and social achievements. Second, it *defines freedom as nothing more than acquiescence to inclination, thereby losing sight of the real meaning and value of human liberty*. As a consequence, libertarians tend to collapse their social ethic into their juridical doctrine in a way that threatens the foundations of a successful liberal policy. In all of these respects, libertarianism departs from the more complex vision of traditional liberalism; and it promotes social policies that are sometimes deleterious of a good society.

DECONTEXTUALIZING FREEDOM

When libertarians isolate liberty from other elements of a satisfactory social existence and raise it to unquestioned normative supremacy, they are not being true to the best insights of the liberal tradition. In the mainstream of historical liberalism, *individual liberties are not the be-all and end-all of a good society*. Instead, they are associated with other social goods and obligations.

Specifically, among the other social goals that liberalism has sought are equality and community. Liberal equality has generally not been taken to imply complete equality of condition or a strictly need-based ethic of distribution. For one thing, that kind of procrustean egalitarianism would require morally dubious and practically costly constraints on the freedom that liberalism, as well as libertarianism, cherishes. But liberals have generally recognized that some attempts to mitigate the unfairness of nature and social inheritance are intrinsically proper in moral terms and necessary for the preservation of liberty and for the sustenance of a viable political community. As Rousseau properly insisted, democratic citizenship is incompatible with a situation in which some may buy their fellow citizens and others are forced to sell themselves. We should also remember that however much the authors of *The Federalist* embraced the importance of freedom and the decentralization of power, the object was not to maximize liberty per se but to attain the more complex goal of justice. "Justice," wrote Madison in The Federalist #51, "is the end of government. It is the end of civil society."

Despite some caricatures of their doctrines that have suggested otherwise, *liberals recognize the value of community and civic commitments.* Libertarians therefore distort the liberal vision of the good society when they neglect community as an important social goal, or when they grant it legitimacy only as an adventitious byproduct of self-interested individual contractual agreements. The word *community and the phrases common good, public good, general good,* and *the good of the people* figure prominently in John Locke's account of legitimate power. John Stuart Mill, in *Consideration on Representative Government,* decisively rejects the notion that a good society can be nothing more than a concatenation of private projects. In such a purely privatistic society, Mill writes,

> . . . a neighbor, not being an ally or an associate, since he is never engaged in any common undertaking for the joint benefit, is therefore only a rival. Thus even private morality suffers, while public is actually extinct. Were this the universal and only possible state of things, the utmost aspirations of the lawgiver or the moralist could only stretch to making the bulk of the community a flock of sheep innocently nibbling the grass side by side.

It is also characteristic of libertarians to be blind to the natural obligations of citizens to sustain the freedoms they enjoy. Perhaps misled by abstract and hypothetical philosophical claims about people being "naturally free," libertarians seem innocent of the fact that civil liberties are difficult and sophisticated accomplishments bestowed by societies upon their members, often at considerable cost in blood, treasure, and forbearance. It is, therefore, appropriate for thus-favored citizens of a free society to give something back, just as it may be necessary from time to time for them to defend their freedoms against outside depredations.

Milton Friedman typifies this libertarian failing when he complains that John F. Kennedy's inaugural admonition to "ask what you can do for your country" reduces individual citizens to subservient votaries of the state. But Friedman's denunciation of Kennedy's plea for public spiritedness is pusillanimous and based on a common libertarian misconception. It is pusillanimous because it rejects the genuine debt that citizens owe their country for the resources, laws, and institutions that nourish their lives, protect their liberties, and allow them to pursue happiness and to govern themselves. The inherent misconception derives from a simplistic social analysis that divides the world into governments and individuals— and then it collapses *country* into *government.* Kennedy's appeal was not for his listeners to send the Internal Revenue Service extra tribute or to grovel before their local sheriffs: it was for them to willingly contribute their abilities and energies to the general good through the myriad avenues of social service available to them.

Once again, it should be stressed that this libertarian penury of social spirit and narrowness of vision represents a distortion rather than a true reflection of mainstream liberalism. While he admonishes his readers to listen to Adam Smith, Milton Friedman and his devotees might ponder the words of their hero in *Wealth of Nations:*

> The wise and virtuous man is at all times willing that his own private interests should be sacrificed to the public interest of his own particular order of society—that the interests of this order of society be sacrificed to the greater interest of the state. He should therefore be equally willing that all those inferior interests should be sacrificed to the greater interests of the universe, to the interests of that great society of all sensible and intelligent beings, of which God himself is the immediate administrator and director.

However great his appreciation of the economic beneficence of the "invisible hand," Smith was in no way a licenser of privatism or selfishness.

OVERSIMPLIFYING FREEDOM

The libertarian insistence upon abstracting liberty from other values and from its complementary obligations engenders a moral simplism that is a pernicious misrepresentation of liberalism. This moral simplism is then compounded by the conceptual simplism with which libertarians interpret their own core value of liberty. *For when liberty is conceived too abstractly and simplistically, it becomes indistinguishable from mere license or capriciousness.* In such instances, the moral significance—let alone the moral priority—of liberty becomes questionable.

I do not want to embrace here the notion of "positive liberty" invoked by many critics of liberalism. All too often such appeals are used to justify paternalistic and tyrannical impositions on the grounds that one is simply being "forced to be free." Better here to agree with the libertarians that liberty always refers in some essential sense to freedom *from* outside interference and not to a so-called freedom *to* attain some specified end. But if liberty is to be a meaningful and worthy goal, it is equally important to keep in mind the point and context of the quest for freedom.

The clear tendency of libertarian thought is to define liberty in the broadest, simplest, and most straightforward terms. Liberty is, in this view, the freedom to do whatever one pleases. Whether what I choose to do is the product of conscientious reflection, habitual inclination, or sheer impulse is irrelevant. The only relevant question, morally and politically, is whether my inclinations are being impeded by others.

It is perhaps instructive to note that this very broad and indiscriminate concept of liberty places libertarians in the conceptual company of the political absolutists. Libertarian liberty is Hobbesian liberty: "absence of impediment." It is consonant with Sir Robert Filmer's definition of freedom as "a liberty for every one to do what he lists, to live as he pleases, and not to be tied by any laws." For Hobbes and Filmer, of course, such a definition opened the way for them to argue that freedom was neither a sound nor a realistic goal for civil society. Liberal theorists, perceiving that the legitimacy of the absolutist critique was facilitated by such a simplistic account of liberty, argued for a more complex conception that distinguished liberty from license and related it to law and rationality. Thus, Locke insisted, in his *Second Treatise* that even the state of nature was "a state of liberty yet . . . not a state of license"; and he explicitly rejected Filmer's definition, arguing that civil liberty properly understood was "to have a standing rule to live by, common to every one of that society, and made by the legislative power erected in it" and "a liberty to follow my own will in all things where that rule prescribes not, not to be subject to the inconstant, uncertain, unknown arbitrary will of another man."

When liberty is conceptualized as a mere "absence of impediment," it becomes incoherent as a general norm, morally unworthy, and potentially self-destructive. The absolutist theorists recognized these difficulties and traded upon them in their critiques of liberal aspirations. Libertarians have accepted the Hobbesian concept, but, sustained by an unwarranted optimism so common to their persuasion, seem innocent of the problems it creates. Succinctly stated, liberty as "absence of impediment" is an ungeneralizable norm because, wherever we associate, *one of us can be free of impediment only by wholly dominating another*. Liberty so conceived is morally unworthy because it accords its greatest privilege and protection to mere appetite. And liberty thus understood is likely self-undermining because it seems to invite descent into a Hobbesian state of nature in which chaos is terminable only through the establishment of a political force beyond the reach of the warring subjects.

The liberty so cherished and pursued by the liberal tradition, I would argue, is not this kind of aimless and arbitrary "absence of impediment." Instead, its essence is properly understood as autonomy—the independence of action proper to a rational being. *The liberal agenda is not the apotheosis of self-indulgence but the creation of a society in which people can be self-governing.* This is why Locke reaches out to associate civil liberty with lawfulness and rationality. And it explains why Condorcet, the prototypical liberal, makes Reason rather than liberty the political opposite of Authority in his epic of human progress. We are politically free, according to the best liberal account, not when our wills are utterly ungoverned—and possibly ungovernable—but when we are governed by laws of our own making. And such laws will perforce be constrained by the rationality that makes us human.

The propriety of conceiving liberal freedom as autonomy may best be seen by recalling the historical context in which liberalism emerged and by reflecting upon what its revolutionary heroes were doing. Liberals fought for free inquiry, free speech, free worship, free trade, freedom to associate, and freedom to choose one's own government. In each of these contexts, they were attempting to remove arbitrary and irrational restraints to the exercise of these activities; they were not seeking a franchise to do whatever they pleased. Moreover, they took as their role models rebels who had demanded autonomy, not license. Martin Luther's apologia was "Here I stand. I can't do otherwise." It was not "I'm staying here because I feel like it." Galileo wanted the freedom to pursue his studies wherever the evidence of his senses led him. The Physiocrats aimed to free production and trade from external and extraneous political forces that were invidiously discriminatory and economically irrational. The Founding Fathers sought to vindicate their right of self-governance in the face of arbitrary imperial impositions. These were all cases of attempts to be governed by the self-affirmed *nomos* proper to the activity at hand, whether it be religious belief, scientific inquiry, economic enterprise, or political governance. They represented objections to arbitrary and capricious behavior on the part of illegitimate authority, not claims of inviolability for lawless or whimsical behavior. Hence it distorts the very essence and point of liberty in the liberal tradition to use it as a justification for upholding the putative right of drunks to be on the highway or drug dealers to deal on the streets "absent of impediment."

UNDERMINING THE CULTURAL BASIS OF LIBERAL FREEDOMS

In addition to its moral and conceptual simplism, libertarian thought is guilty of empirical simplism in one important respect. Libertarians tend to assume that the behavioral norms appropriate for a liberal society are the same as the political norms appropriate for liberal governments. This is what I referred to earlier as the libertarians' tendency to collapse their social ethic and their juridical doctrine. The assumption is that *the ideal of political toleration and government neutrality entails a thorough social permissiveness and moral relativism.* A liberal regime has no right to evaluate its citizens' character and values, since these are presumed to be purely private and subjective matters. Individual liberty prevails across the board.

The reasons for this "don't worry, be happy" idea that a liberal polity and a libertarian culture go hand in hand are various and not always well articulated. One underlying premise may be an extension of the "private vice, public virtue" doctrine from economic affairs into all social interaction. The invisible hand is broadened from a disciplining mechanism for regulating economic pursuits into a magical force for transmuting base individual actions into socially beneficial outcomes. Another possible warrant for a libertarian social ethic is perhaps a tacit absorption of ethical "emotivism," a doctrine which construes moral judgments as merely expressions of taste that are impervious to rational criticism and hence on a moral par. Or perhaps this outlook is informed by a kind of "democratic" romantic individualism—whether it be Whitmanesque, Marcusean, or postmodern. Whatever the underlying rationale, the crucial idea is that maximum liberty is the proper standard, not only for a liberal polity but for a liberal culture as well.

This cheerful simplism is not sustained by most liberal theorists, who instead present a more complex and more persuasive account of the relationship between a polity and its culture. In this view, the functional relationship between cultural mores and political institutions is better understood as one of complementarity than one of symmetry or identity.

The liberal theorist who was most emotivist in his moral philosophy and most libertarian in his psychology was Thomas Hobbes. And that was precisely why his political prescriptions were eccentrically authoritarian from the standpoint of mainstream liberalism. Because Hobbes construed human reason to be devoid of moral content and interpreted human behavior to be relentlessly self-interested, he concluded that a strong sovereign power beyond popular control was a functional necessity. Moral anomie and universal avarice would produce social chaos unless a strong-arm government could dictate rules and knock heads.

James Madison, in Federalist Paper #55, disputed Hobbes's depiction of human nature, but he nevertheless pronounced himself in full agreement with Hobbes's logic. Human beings, he said, are not what those who see the world like Hobbes believe them to be; but if they were, something like a Hobbesian sovereign would be a necessity. "Were the pictures which have been drawn by the political jealousy of some among us faithful likenesses of the human character, the inference would be that there is not sufficient virtue among men for self-government, and that nothing less than the chains of despotism can restrain them from destroying and devouring one another."

In *Consideration of Representative Government,* John Stuart Mill expands upon the same theme. Governmental forms, he insists, "must be adjusted to the capacities and qualities of such men as are available." Only some forms of political culture are compatible with the demands of genuine representative government. Thus, "a people may prefer a free government, but . . . from indolence, or carelessness or cowardice, or want of public spirit [be] unequal to the exertions necessary for preserving it." Among other things, a free government can survive and prosper only if the people are willing to "cooperate actively with the law and public authorities in the repression of evil-doers." A people "more disposed to shelter a criminal than to apprehend him, who will perjure themselves to screen the man who robbed them . . . who pass by [street violence] because it is the business of the police to look into the matter . . . who are revolted by an execution but not shocked at an assassination" will require a government "armed with much sterner powers of repression than elsewhere." Likewise, where people's "passions are too violent, or their personal pride too exacting, to forego private conflict," their government "will require to be in a considerable degree despotic."

The example of Hobbes and the analyses of Madison and Mill together make the same point. Any functioning civil society requires some minimum of orderliness and adherence to basic norms of behavior that distinguish it from a state of war. These elements of restraint and civil morality must come from somewhere. A political society can therefore be open, free, and nonauthoritarian only when internalized norms or social suasion successfully restrain the human proclivity to dominate others or to aggrandize oneself at their expense. In places where these prepolitical restraints are unavailable, political authority must fill the vacuum. At the extremes, licentious societies produce—because they require—authoritarian sovereigns, while highly ordered societies may approach anarchy at the government level. Hobbes's eccentric liberal realism depicts one extreme as inevitable; Marx's romantic vision of the withering away of the state anticipates the other.

The most sophisticated libertarian theorists exhibit some awareness of this dynamic and the problems it creates. Hayek, for example, conjoins his political and economic libertarianism with a conservative Humean sociology. But most garden-variety libertarian ideologues and activists ignore the problems created by the requisite functional complementarity of social culture and political institutions. This theoretical lacuna can engender some practical dangers. A libertarian ethos and a libertarian social policy can undermine the self-restraints and the informal social norms that sustain a liberal polity. With apologies to Daniel Bell, we can call this problem the "cultural contradiction" of liberal society. And whereas liberal theorists generally recognize the problem, libertarians blithely accelerate the destructive dialectic.

The Limitations of Libertarianism, Part II

The argument thus far can be summarized as follows: Libertarianism as political theory suffers from multidimensional simplemindedness. It is morally simplistic in its elevation of the single norm of liberty to complete hegemony over other important norms of a good society. It is conceptually simplistic in its tendency to conceive liberty as the mere absence of impediment rather than as autonomy. And it is empirically simplistic in its failure to recognize that the political institutions of a free society are viable only when the social culture provides the necessary complements of civility and restraint. Libertarians stoutly defend what is a genuinely important half-truth. But when they insist that this half-truth tells the whole story, they distort liberal ideals and weaken liberal policies.

POLICY IMPLICATIONS OF LIBERTARIANISM: A SUMMARY OVERVIEW

Looking at the world through libertarian eyes is akin to donning heavily polarized lenses. What you see you see clearly, since it is brought into sharp relief by eliminating competing images. But what is screened out may still be very important. As the first portion of this article suggested, libertarian theory fails to "see" the legitimate role that moral equality, fellow feeling, and obligation play in a good democratic society. It also fails to acknowledge the complexity of the liberal good of individual autonomy. And it overlooks the dependence of a free society upon an orderly and civil citizenry. As a consequence, the libertarian vision proves to be of little help with regard to some social policies, and is positively harmful when it comes to some others.

DISTRIBUTIVE POLICIES

Libertarian obtuseness with regard to the need for moral equality and fellow feeling in a good society, for example, renders libertarian norms inadequate *vis à vis* distributive policies. It is not, as some theorists would

31

argue, that we can deduce definitive rules of distributive justice. In fact, demonstrating the impossibility of such rules is one of the strong suits of libertarian polemicists. But what they miss, in turn, is the fact that no real-world society—much less a good society—can cede all allocative determinations to the vagaries of the marketplace, however rational that might seem in purely economic terms. The bonds of any genuine civil association are not reducible to the haggling interactions of a bazaar. The members of a commonwealth, to use an appropriately suggestive term at this juncture, are not merely wholly independent entrepreneurs who jostle and compete with one another. They are fellow citizens in a common enterprise with goals that go beyond personal recompense and with terms of association that of necessity extend beyond "Those with the most toys win." These fellow citizens may not, in a contemporary pluralistic society, be partners "in every virtue and in all perfection," as Burke would have it. But they do have common purposes that transcend using each other as stepping-stones for individual economic accumulation. In order to associate in this more expansive manner, they must be in some sense civic friends. And in order to attain this form of relationship, they must regard each other with some measure of compassion and not stand upon a footing of gross inequality. So long as the life chances of a society's members greatly diverge because of forces beyond individual control, society will find itself both morally and practically obliged to temper socioeconomic inequalities with fair and prudent redistributive policies. Reasonable people can, and perennially will, differ over the proper form and extent of such measures. But these measures are an unavoidable component of sound social policy. And libertarian insistence upon our individual entitlement to market distributions or polemics about the mirage of social justice are misleading and utterly beside the point.

Robert Nozick unwittingly provides a good illustration of where libertarianism goes awry in this area in the process of one of his arguments against John Rawls's redistributive principles of justice. Suppose, he says, that a number of Robinson Crusoes were to discover each others' existence. Suppose further that their economic circumstances were markedly different. Could "the disadvantaged" Crusoes make a persuasive claim on the resources of "the better-off" Crusoes? Nozick says no. What is it then about the introduction of coexistence and social cooperation that would weaken the entitlement of the several Crusoes to their individually attained goods? Nothing, he answers, so long as it is possible to assign each Crusoe a share of the social product proportional to his marginal productivity. The market can do that. Hence, Nozick concludes, nothing about social cooperation makes his entitlement doctrine either morally unacceptable or practically infeasible.

Nozick's critique is invited by Rawls's claim that his principles of justice represent fair terms of social cooperation. And it in fact strikes home because Rawls's argument at this juncture adopts an economizing frame of reference and proceeds in a sloppy manner. Even as he demonstrates the incompetence of one of Rawls's lines of reasoning, however, Nozick exhibits the very conceptual inadequacies of libertarianism that incapacitate it as a reliable analyst of social association and its requisites. For his argument here turns on the assumption that the members of a civil association may properly be conceived of as Crusoe-like "miniature firms" who relate to each other only as economic competitors. No society could be constructed on such a proposition, and even if it could, it would be fragile and corrupt. Rawls may provide the wrong measure and bad reasons for redistributive policies, but Nozick misses the point altogether. A good society must constrain extreme inequalities and provide buffers against individual economic catastrophe—and not because no way exists to ascertain the relative economic value of individual contributions to cooperative modes of production. Rather, these redistributive measures are necessary to maintain moral equality, to express compassion for fellow citizens, and to reflect the broader prudential interdependencies that are part of any genuine civil association. "Miniature firms" may properly stand on their market "entitlement," but the friends, neighbors, and countrymen of a political society are joined in a common venture in which the prerequisites override these "entitlements."

CIVIC OBLIGATIONS

It is this same obtuseness regarding the bonds of civil association that lies behind libertarians' opposition to national citizen service. I am not here to recommend or defend any particular form of such service. It may, in fact, turn out that the practical difficulties of implementing such a project may render it unworkable. The question, however, is one of principle. From the libertarian perspective, any national service obligation represents a tyrannical imposition on the individual by the state. But once again that stubborn opposition derives from the "Robinson Crusoe/miniature firm" concept of membership in a political society. When we recognize the patent unreality and moral myopia of that concept, and when we reflect instead upon what real-world civic associations involve, we can see how something like a universal citizen service requirement would be morally justifiable and prudentially valuable.

To participate in any real-world civil association that has a history is to incur moral obligation. Even if the society in question is seriously flawed, each participant in its ongoing common life is in debt to all sorts of fellow citizens whom he or she has never met and cannot even name. The institu-

tions, the infrastructure, the very existence of a political order that is part
of what creates and sustains us—all are received as a patrimony that we
did not purchase and that we cannot in any coherent sense be said to
deserve.

As a member of the Duke University faculty, I can look out my office
window at a magnificent chapel that was built by Italian stonemasons
many decades ago. I also enjoy the beauty and shade of trees that were
planted and nurtured by people who never lived to see them reach matur-
ity. I teach in facilities that were built with the gifts of countless friends
and alumni of the university. As a North Carolinian, I can drive down
the lovely Blue Ridge Parkway that was provided for by a Depression-
era Congress and built by Works Progress Administration laborers. I can
recreate in state parks that were financed by taxpayers of years long past.
I have legal rights—the right to a jury trial and the right to vote—that
were fashioned by British lawyers centuries ago and established by American statesmen long since departed. As a citizen of the United States, I
enjoy all sorts of rights and privileges—both political and economic—that
were created through the labors of innumerable Americans and protected
with great personal sacrifice and suffering. I can say, as libertarians insist,
that I am a free person with rights that the state must respect. But if I take
that status to mean that I do not owe something to my country, then I
am a fool and an ingrate.

It is entirely appropriate, therefore, for my fellow countrymen to ask
of me some kind of service to the common cause. To make this request is
to do no more than what parents say they want when their children in-
quire what they can do to repay them: Just do the same for our grandchil-
dren. The record of my own generation in this regard, it must be said, is
altogether less than admirable. Cheered on by Reaganite libertarian re-
gimes, we have clearly taken more than we have given; and we are well
on our way to leaving our own progeny burdensome debts, a crumbling
infrastructure, and a deteriorating environment. The kind of argument I
made in the previous paragraph may come to seem like a joke to succeed-
ing generations as they struggle to dig themselves out from the ashes created by the bonfire of the vanities.

The narrow purview of the libertarian outlook also obscures a potentially significant by-product of a well-designed national service program.
For in addition to the direct social benefits produced by such a program,
there would be its contribution to a sense of common cause and civic
friendship among the participants. The abstract individualism of libertarian theory fails to comprehend that some strands of mutual understanding and a sense of the common good that transcends the powerful
divisions of section, race, ethnicity, and religion are both difficult to
achieve and essential for a successful democratic society. The minimal

civic bonding required to sustain a democratic polity does not occur automatically, as countless examples around the globe vividly attest. Some nurturance of this civic bonding is likely to be especially important in the years ahead, given that various forms of ethnic chauvinism are on the ascendant and given the increasing influence of a multiculturalist ideology that seems content to replace the motto "E pluribus unum" with "Separate but *really* equal."

FAMILY POLICY AND CREATING AUTONOMY

Libertarian norms are either unavailing or downright misleading in the domains of family policy and property ownership. The common difficulty here is the libertarian failure, noted earlier, to recall the context of the liberal concentration on freedom. Consequently, libertarians fail to conceive the crucial social purpose to be creating and protecting personal autonomy, rather than maximizing liberty *per se* or treating market outcomes as morally sacrosanct.

Libertarian doctrine is especially unhelpful in shaping good family policy. Its central tenet, after all, is that competent adults should be left as free as possible to pursue their self-interest as they define it. But the family is a mini-society devoted in significant measure to the nurturance of those who are neither adults nor fully competent. It could be said that families produce the crucial participants in the libertarian scheme (i.e., rational adults). But libertarianism has, for that very reason, almost nothing useful to say about how the task should be accomplished, nor how the larger society should comport itself toward those engaged in it. About all that a libertarian such as Milton Friedman can do is to admit that policies toward children fall into a narrow domain in which paternalism is legitimate; regarding this domain, however, he has nothing useful to say that can be derived from his principles. The general thrust of a libertarian culture, moreover, is in some respects deleterious to family success and the welfare of children. With its focus on the liberties of consenting adults, it tends to promote the progressive loosening of social constraints on sexual conduct. How adult behavior bears on the welfare of children does not figure prominently in libertarian concerns. Children are simply the by-product of some forms of consenting behavior; the rules and conventions governing their care are pushed beyond the scope of public concern into a black box labeled "private choices." If changes in sexual mores worsen the situation of the nation's children, libertarianism has no warning flags to raise and no counsel to give. Indeed, the ethos it creates is in part responsible for exacerbating the problem.

If the relevant policy norm were conceived as the creation and sustenance of citizen autonomy rather than the maximizing of liberty *simpliciter*, things would be approached differently and more productively. Public policy would be directed more toward the needs of those striving to achieve the autonomy level requisite for competent adulthood and less toward the whims of those who have already attained that status. First things first. However tolerant such a society might be regarding the right of individuals to follow their sexual preferences and their matrimonial proclivities, it would not hesitate to insist that these same individuals behave responsibly toward the dependents that their preferences and proclivities brought into the world. It would likewise not hesitate to use its resources to guarantee, (as far as it is feasible) each child an environment that is conducive to becoming an autonomous member of society. In short, the crafting of laws dealing with marriage, divorce, and child support; the shaping of tax policies; and the disposition of the society's resources would take on a different cast, in which the purpose of liberty was clearly understood to be the fostering of autonomy and not simply the removal of impediments to the inclinations of the already enfranchised.

PROPERTY RIGHTS AND THE GOOD SOCIETY

Understanding the point of liberty to be the achievement of autonomy also has a bearing upon social policies that relate to property rights and their role in a good society. Libertarian theory counsels the social embrace of whatever patterns of property ownership develop out of the free market. This counsel is justified on three principal grounds: efficiency, entitlement, and the decentralization of power. Leaving property distribution to the market allows the most productive allocation of resources; people should be permitted to own whatever they have acquired without violating others' rights; and leaving economic power in private hands prevents state or majority tyranny.

If abstract liberty is the highest goal, the combination of arguments holds together without a hitch. If, however, the goal is a society in which all citizens are free in the sense of autonomy, some soft spots begin to appear in the libertarian scheme. Leaving economic power to the winners in the marketplace does indeed keep us free from government tyranny, but it by no means secures individual autonomy. Concentrations of economic power in private or public hands, combined with the absence of property-holding by other members of society, thwarts autonomy. Hence, if a free and democratic society both depends upon and finds moral value in the creation of an independent, self-governing citizenry, *laissez-faire* is clearly not enough. A truly liberal perspective on private property is Jeffersonian, not Spencerian. A liberal society need not, and should not, abandon all determination of property rights to the confluence of astuteness, effort, private beneficence, and sheer luck that libertarians would make sacrosanct. Instead, consistent with the demands of efficiency and justice (and what libertarians call entitlement is not, as they themselves concede, necessarily grounded in moral desert), a liberal democracy should seek to decentralize economic power, that is, to diffuse property-holding as much as possible. The political value of liberal economics is its contribution to a society of free people; and that is not the same thing as a market society.

A property policy directed toward a goal of human freedom—i.e., a citizenry of autonomous individuals—would not countenance robber barons, company towns, or corporate domination in the name of abstract liberty. It would seek the contemporary equivalent of "40 acres and a mule." It would structure tax incentives to encourage employee shareholding and participation in corporate governance. It would recall the original purpose of the mortgage-interest deduction and reshape the provision to facilitate more extensive individual home ownership, instead of subsidizing the vacation homes of the wealthy. It would look with favor upon the conservative populist scheme of allowing public-housing tenants to acquire an ownership interest in their buildings, and so on. Needless to say, these are not the usual proposals of libertarians. But that is not because they value liberty too much: it is because they define it too narrowly and simplistically.

CIVILITY AND THE PUBLIC REALM

The third and final theoretical weakness of libertarian social theory discussed earlier was its failure to remember what most classical liberals understood well: that a liberal polity is dependent upon social sources of order and civility to function properly. In policy areas in which this dialectic of internalized restraint and public freedom is involved, libertarian counsel is therefore likely to be at best incomplete. In some cases, acquiescence in the libertarian ethos may directly undermine important liberal institutions.

The best example of this problem is the role that libertarianism plays in the deterioration of public spaces and public facilities. In effect, left-wing civil libertarianism and right-wing economic libertarianism conspire to batter the public realm from both sides. Right-wing libertarians deprive the public domain of sufficient revenue to perform its tasks. Left-wing libertarians undermine the authority and integrity of public enterprises. Then right-wing libertarians cluck their tongues that the real problem is that we "seek through government to force people to act against their own immediate interests in order to promote a supposedly general interest" (Friedman, *Capitalism and Freedom,* chapter 13). To which the answer is that a democratic society must have a vital public sphere, but that no public enterprise can succeed without adequate funding or without the capacity to defend the integrity of its purposes.

The libertarian contribution to the atrophy of the public realm can be illustrated through the hypothetical horror story of a single lower-class urban child. (This child is, of course, an apocryphal composite, but each element in the composite is based on actual situations.) The child lives with her mother (she receives no financial support from her father) in public housing, which is dangerous and unpleasant because some of the inhabitants are criminal or disturbed. She sleeps on the floor to avoid random gunfire from drug deals gone awry on the street. She travels on public thoroughfares where 10 percent of the cars are driven by people with alcohol in their veins. She avoids the public parks, which have been taken over by assorted unsavory characters. She uses the public library, but is frightened by the street people who use it as a combination home- less shelter and detoxification center. She attends a crumbling public school where learning is difficult because of poor discipline.

It would be silly, of course, to try to lay the full, or even the primary, responsibility for this sad litany at the feet of Milton Friedman or the American Civil Liberties Union. But the extent to which the libertarian impulse exacerbates these problems is nonetheless striking. Libertarian organizations or jurists have frustrated efforts to institute routine identi- fication checks that would push drug dealers and related brawls off the streets; opposed efforts to keep the inebriated off the highways by using random checkpoints; held it impermissible for city authorities to remove stoned squatters from the library; sought in the name of student rights to make it almost impossible to remove disruptive students from the class- room; and prevented public-housing authorities from screening known troublemakers from their projects.

Certainly, a free society must remain vigilant against majoritarian at- tempts to stifle freedom of speech and the freedom to associate. But it is equally certain that these rights should not be interpreted or applied in such an inanely wooden manner as to render the public domain chaotic and incompetent. Besides casting all public endeavor into disrepute, these excesses of libertarian fundamentalism work powerfully against the health, safety, and welfare of the very groups that sound democratic pol- icy should want most to protect. Both for moral and prudential reasons, I would argue, a decent and intelligent democracy should be most anxious to advance the life chances of relatively disadvantaged young people who are determined to become productive and law-abiding adults. Yet these are the very people whose lives are most damaged by the decay of public enterprises. The sons and daughters of neoclassical economists and ACLU attorneys can generally buy their own books, recreate at private clubs, and, if need be, attend private academies. But less fortunate children who want to get ahead in life are dependent upon the public schools, public parks, and public libraries; when these facilities crumble, they are the people who are most damaged—and so are the social mobility and basic fairness that should be the concerns of any good society.

CONCLUSION:
LIBERAL GOODS AND LIBERTARIAN DISTORTIONS

The limitations of libertarianism, then, originate in its oversimplification of the nature of human liberty and liberty's role in a good society. Libertarians conceive liberty as the absence of impediment rather than as the achievement of personal autonomy. They neglect the complementary liberal values of equality and fraternity. And they fail to remember that the freedoms of a liberal polity are made possible by habits of the heart that engender social order and civility. The practical result of this narrow doctrine, in turn, is the promotion of social policies that impoverish and cripple a liberal public regime. The ultimate outcome of an unrestrainedly libertarian public policy would be an unsafe society of strangers, in which inequalities were extreme; the wealthy hid behind walls defended by private security forces; public spirit and a sense of common purpose were nowhere in evidence; disadvantaged children were bereft of the resources and the environment necessary to escape their misfortunes; and the social bond between individual citizens was reduced to the cash nexus complained about by both Carlyle and Marx. What would be lost would be the hope of a genuinely liberal democracy: the complex achievement of a community of autonomous moral equals who enjoy their protected private domains as they pursue their common purposes.

Properly understood and properly pursued, there is nothing illiberal or antiliberal about communitarian ideals or policies. Instead, they represent an attempt to recover a valid and important dimension of liberal theory that libertarian distortions of liberalism have cast aside. As various allusions throughout the essay suggest, one need not abandon liberal texts for collectivist, socialist, or reactionary treatises to find a concern for community, for participation, for civic virtue, and for legitimate common enterprise. These concerns are well represented in the works of Locke, Mill, Madison, and even Adam Smith. Liberalism at its best has never fallen prey to the simpleminded individualism promulgated by libertarians. It has known what Reinhold Niebuhr reminded us of several decades ago:

"The community requires liberty as much as does the individual; and the individual requires community more than bourgeois thought comprehended. Democracy can therefore not be equaled with freedom. An ideal democratic order seeks unity within the conditions of freedom; and maintains freedom within the framework of order" (*The Children of Light and the Children of Darkness*, chapter 1).

4

A Moral Reawakening Without Puritanism

Amitai Etzioni

Are the new moral voices heard across the land those of meddling busy-bodies, or of reasonable, gentle, fellow Americans prodding one another to live up to their moral duties? Harbingers of moral reaffirmation, such as this journal, are encountering a chorus of libertarians. They fear that the moral resurgence threatens privacy, liberty, and other individual rights; the communitarian movement is accused of intolerance, of neopuritanism or worse: social engineering of the type that lost the day in Eastern Europe. A cover story in *Time* (on August 12) rails against the dangers of busybodies who "humorlessly [impose] on others arbitrary (meaning their own) standards of behavior, health and thought." The London *Economist* (on July 20, and reprinted by the *New York Times* on July 29) cautions against dangers associated with trying to legislate our social problems out of existence. Both labeled this new wave of American morality a form of puritanism. Both are half-right; if only they had made room for the other half of the story.

They are correct to point to a potential danger: that the new moral reawakening will turn into a witch-hunt in which a small number of American ayatollahs will impose their capricious moral perspective on the rest of the community through loyalty oaths, condemnations, and excommunications. There have been some attempts to remove books from libraries, to impose specific prayers on a few public schools, and to forcibly close abortion clinics. However, because the religious right is generally in retreat (televangelism has been rocked by a series of salacious scandals and the Moral Majority is an increasingly irrelevant minority), America is currently experiencing relatively little intolerance.

Indeed, the moral voices that have been raised recently are, by and large,

41

rather genial, and typically reflect the consensus of the community rather than the notions of isolated busybodies and moralizers. Community campaigns such as "Friends don't let friends drive drunk" are a case in point. Neighborhood watches, in which neighbors attend to one another's safety by minding one another's homes, continue to spring up across the country, and so on.

The examples given by those concerned that the new morality will revert to puritanism are sociological rubbish. They use one-of-a-kind (or fewer) incidents to claim nationwide trends. Thus, to demonstrate that America has become "the Punitive Society," the London *Economist* writes, "They [Americans] reprimand a neighbour for kissing her boyfriend goodnight on the steps of her house and so lowering the tone of the block (as happened recently in California)." While we are sure that sooner or later everything conceivable happens once or twice in California, this incident constitutes no pattern. Indeed, the storm of publicity that surrounded the event suggests just the opposite: the busybodies were widely reprimanded, and kissing in California and elsewhere continues unabated on doorsteps and quite a few other places.

The *Economist*'s other example of rising American punitiveness is that "if you lose your job you can sue for the mental distress of being fired" (no time and place is mentioned). While you can sue for practically any reason, you are extremely unlikely to win, on these grounds. Elsewhere, the *Economist* confuses matters of equity with punitiveness by suggesting that rent control and getting part of your spouse's income after divorce are punitive measures.

Other examples deserve more serious attention. To properly assess them, one must separate three categories that are often lumped together: new or renewed values fostered by members of the community upon one another, values that corporations impose upon their employees, and values that are underwritten by law.

THE MORAL VOICE OF THE COMMUNITY

The first and most important foundation for the reconstruction of the moral order of a community is the informal support that members accord to values they affirm. Thus, if New Yorkers on the Upper East Side do not pick up after their dogs, friends, neighbors, and even strangers will stare pointedly, remind, or even reproach the unmindful. This social pressure is sufficient to keep most members of that community from misbehaving. Similarly, in those suburbs that constitute communities, residents encourage one another to cut their lawns regularly, cover their garbage cans, and, increasingly, attend to their children. Nobody is excommunicated or exiled, let alone stoned, for failing to discharge a community duty. People are, however, made to feel appreciated when they act responsibly and uncomfortable when they do not.

To object to this mode of moral encouragement and attentiveness is to oppose the social glue that helps hold the moral order together. Relying on internalized values and consciences—expecting people to do what is right completely on their own—asks too much of individuals and disregards their social moorings and the important role that communities have in sustaining moral commitments. In effect, those who are so adamantly opposed to statism must recognize that communities require some ways of making their needs felt; these critics should welcome these gentle, informal, and—currently in America—generally tolerant voices of the community, especially given that the alternative is often state coercion, or anarchy.

Furthermore, it is important to recognize that the proper focus of the new morality, and what it censors or affirms, is *behavior*, not thoughts and attitudes. The "thought police" of the PC forces on campus, referred to by *Time* and others, that seek to suppress thoughts and verbal expressions that are not politically correct, should not be lumped together with those that are opposed to antisocial and immoral *conduct.*We may argue whether or not we wish to tolerate racial epithets, sexist slurs, even pornography. However, when it comes to harassment, pollution, and other behaviors that violate the community's values, its members have the right to speak up and state unequivocally: This is not to be done here.

Indeed, there is room for an additional distinction that William Galston ["Rights/Rightness," p. 7] highlights: the difference between tolerating most, if not all, verbal and other symbolic expressions versus refraining from expressing our displeasure with some of them. Thus, most communitarians would agree that there is little sense in calling in the police to suppress purely verbal expressions of prejudice and bigotry. But the community need not stand silent while bigots speak. Tolerance of free speech does not include freedom from counterspeech. Thus, if a white drunk shouts racist expletives on Brown's campus, charging him with a legal offense or arresting him is not the response of choice; a long line of other students telling him how despicable they find his utterances is probably a more effective, and surely a more legitimate, community response.

CORPORATIONS AND THEIR MORAL ORDER

The critics of the new morality point to corporations that use economic power to force their employees to behave. Some businesses, they say, are insisting that employees refrain from smoking, avoid drug abuse, lose weight, exercise, and so on. Many of these measures, however, are prudent and to us hardly smack of neopuritanism. Corporations that make it explicit before they retain new employees that the job entails, say, drug testing are leaving the choice up to the employee whether or not he or she wishes to join such a workplace. (Economic coercion enters here only if there are no other jobs to be had.)

More important, most of the conducts at issue have clear consequences for the public at large, and corporations may legitimately take the public interest into account. Smoking effects not merely the smoker but his or her coworkers. Drunken pilots endanger not only themselves, but the lives of their passengers, and so on.

More problematic is the question whether corporations may properly ban behavior that takes place off the job. These controls are generally appropriate only if the employee's private behavior affects his or her job performance. Recent studies show that consumption of alcohol impairs behavior as long as 24 hours after intake. Hence, pilots may well be expected not to drink for a given period before they come to work. Drugs that lead to unexpected bouts of hallucination or paranoia may be forbidden at any time, at least until we know more about the length of their effects.

Finally, there remains the question of the propriety of corporations curbing private behavior that only affects health-care costs. *Time* reported that Janice Bone had lost her job as a clerk at the Ford Meter Box Company because a test proved that she had been smoking away from work. Should corporations regulate this type of behavior? Probably not. In fact, this may be a good place to limit the reach of corporate morality. An important criterion for corporate intervention—protecting life and limb—is not met. If we go further down this road, there is no stopping. Most behaviors affect health costs, and if we endorse this kind of paternalism, corporations will soon insist that we go to bed early, floss and brush our teeth regularly, engage only in heterosexual intercourse with one partner, and meditate frequently to reduce stress. In short, when private behavior directly affects job performance or the public interest, business may step in. Otherwise, it should refrain from regulating the private affairs of its employees.

BY FORCE OF LAW

The London *Economist* is particularly troubled by America's alleged new proclivity to impose the new morality, or what it terms puritanism, by force of law. This, the *Economist* rules, is nothing more than an archaic form of Eastern European social engineering. Not only is this latter-day red baiting uncalled for, it is also misleading. A world of difference separates former Eastern European laws and American ones. Laws in the United States are democratically arrived at, not imposed by a tyrannical government. They are limited in scope and are neither omnipresent nor totalitarian; moreover, they are gently enforced: gulags, secret police, and torture chambers are conspicuously absent from the American scene.

Second, laws represent, in every society, a method of expressing social and moral values and of signaling conduct that the community considers proper or abhorrent—even when these laws are rarely enforced by fines, jail sentences, and other coercive means. Thus, we do not approve of adultery, and our laws used to say so, even if they typically went unenforced. Studies suggest that when the divorce laws were changed to "no fault," far from being viewed as a technical distinction or as a less costly way to deal with divorce, the new laws were seen by many as one more indication that the community was less troubled by divorce. For much the same reason, if we were now to repeal these laws, it would serve as a signal that we were restoring our respect for the family. It is important, then, to recognize the expressive power that law holds for the community's moral concerns.

Third, the law as a deterrent has its place in any moral order. Morality rests on the intricate interaction among three factors: individual consciences, social and community voices, and the state. Each one helps to sustain the others. Hence, while it is best to build up individual consciences and community voices, communities must also resort, on occasion, to the force of law. Without punishing those who do serious injury to our commonly held values—child abusers, toxic polluters, fathers who renege on child support, corporations who market unsafe drugs—no moral order can be sustained. We do not have to love the coercive side of the law, but we cannot fail to recognize its power as a last resort.

Finally, regarding the *Economist*'s insistence that we rely on incentives instead of laws, the empirical evidence that cash changes antisocial behavior is very thin indeed. Thus, while newly introduced programs such as Learnfare in Wisconsin (in which a family's welfare payment is cut if its youngsters are truant) are widely hailed by ideologues, social science studies have so far not been able to establish a clear benefit. The same holds true for programs that offer teenagers cash if they do not get pregnant. It is doubtful that one can persuade youngsters to control their impulses by throwing greenbacks at them.

We need not fear busybodies at the first signs of America's moral rejuvenation. Most of what we hear is the gentle voice of community members calling on one another to reaffirm their values and behave accordingly, a most welcome sound.

5

The Dangers of Soft Despotism

Charles Taylor

I would like to look by way of illustration at some familiar types of failure of the democratic process, and at their possible remedies.

FIRST DANGER: THE CENTRALIZATION OF POWER

The first is the familiar sense of citizen alienation in large, centralized, bureaucratic societies. The average citizen feels power to be at a great distance and frequently unresponsive to him or her. There is a sense of powerlessness in face of a governing machine which continues on its way without regard to the interests of ordinary people, who seem to have little recourse to make their needs felt. There seems to be no way that the ordinary citizen can have an impact on this process, either to determine its general direction, or to finetune its application to his or her own case. This effect is greater the more matters are concentrated in the hands of a remote central government, and the more bureaucratized the procedures of government are.

Centralized bureaucratic power does not mean, of course, that the government has things all its own way. Powerful lobbies intervene and affect its course. But these too are remote from the ordinary citizen and generally equally impervious to his or her input.

This is the situation Tocqueville warned about, and for which he suggested the following remedy. It consists of decentralized power, of having certain functions of government exercised at a more local level, where citizen mobilization to make an impact is a less daunting task.

But hypercentralization is not only a danger of the political system. It also affects the public sphere. Just as in politics, local concerns may impinge only with difficulty on the center; so the national debate may become concentrated in a small number of large-scale media that are impervious to local input. The sense becomes widespread that the debate on the major television networks, for instance, is shaped by relatively narrow groups or interests, and that its animators operate within a charmed circle which is very difficult to penetrate. Other views, other ways of posing the questions, other agendas cannot get a hearing.

THE NEED FOR A FLOURISHING PUBLIC SPHERE

Tocquevillian decentralization is necessary in the public sphere as well. And indeed, each can support the other. The fact that important issues are decided locally enhances the importance of local media, which in turn focus the debate on these issues by those affected.

But it is not just a matter of bringing certain issues down to the local level where the local debate can affect them. The national debate can be changed as well by effective local public spheres. The model which seems to work here is one in which smaller public spheres are nested within larger ones, in the sense that what goes on in the smaller ones feeds into and has an impact on the agenda of the national sphere. The public sphere of a regional society can have that kind of impact, provided the political life of this society itself has some significance for the whole—a good example of how political decentralization also facilitates the enlarging of the public sphere.

But there are other kinds of smaller spheres as well. An example of a type that has been significant for some western societies is provided by certain political parties and social movements. These can function as nested public spheres to the extent that their internal debate is open to the larger public. Then, depending on the significance of the party or movement politically, their inner debate can spill over and help to determine the national agenda. Some parties have had this function. But the most striking examples in recent decades are found in some of the "new social movements": for instance, the feminist movement (to the extent that one can speak of it in the singular), and ecological campaigns. These movements have not impacted on the political process the way lobbies usually do, mobilizing their efforts behind some agreed public stance and keeping their internal discussion to themselves. On the contrary, their internal debates have been out there for all to see, and it is as much through these as through their global impact that they have helped reshape the public agenda. That is why I want to speak of them as nested public spheres.

The model of public sphere which is emerging in this discussion is clearly different from the original 18th-century paradigm in at least two respects. That original model seemed to posit a unitary space, and I'm suggesting here a multiplicity of public spheres nested within each other. There is a central arena of debate on national policy, but it is not the public sphere analogue of a unitary state, but rather of a central government in a federation. Secondly, the clear boundary between the political system and the public sphere has to be relaxed. Some of the most effective nested public spheres are, in fact, political parties and advocacy movements, which operate in the gray zone between the two. In a modern democratic polity, the boundary between political system and public sphere has to be maximally porous.

That is, if we want this sphere to play its role in widening and expanding the public debate. If we think of it as a watchdog, limiting power, then the old model seems right. It is obviously easier for national networks, or prestigious papers with a national reputation, to take on the power-holders. For the purposes of this function, a sphere dominated by large and powerful units, maintaining political neutrality, can seem ideal. But it can be disastrous for a genuine national debate.

SECOND DANGER: A DIVIDED PUBLIC

Democratic decision making can also be impeded, even stymied altogether, by rifts within the political community. These can arise in a number of ways. One is a modality of "class war," in which the least favored citizens sense that their interests are systematically neglected or denied. In this regard, it is clear that the kind of solidarity expressed in most Western democracies in the various measures of the "welfare state," apart from their intrinsic justification, may also be crucial to the maintenance of a functioning democratic society.

Another kind of rift may arise when a group or cultural community feels itself to be unrecognized by the larger society, and becomes less willing in consequence to function on a basis of common understanding with the majority. This may give rise to a demand for secession, but even short of this it creates a sense of injury and exclusion, in which the requirement that all groups be adequately heard seems impossible to fulfill. In the climate of presumed exclusion, the said group will not consider its demands adequately addressed unless they are completely accepted. There is no simple way to deal with this kind of rift once it arises, but one of the major objectives of democratic politics ought to be to prevent them arising. This is another reason why ensuring that all groups have a bearing is of the utmost importance. This is not easy to achieve in our present era of "multiculturalism."

POLITICAL FRAGMENTATION

The effects of centralization and divisions can be exacerbated if they produce what I want to call political fragmentation. That is, if they impact on the political process and change its form. People can respond to a sense of exclusion by practicing a mode of politics which seems predicated on the belief that society is at best composed of mutually disinterested citizens, and is perhaps for the most part even malevolent in relation to the group in question. To the extent that the people concerned have already come to accept an atomistic outlook, which sees society as an aggregation of individuals with their life plans and denies the reality of political community, this reaction is all the more readily available. Or the response may be powered by a philosophic vision of exclusion—say, a Marxist view of "bourgeois" society as irretrievably divided by class war, or certain feminist views of liberal society as irremediably vitiated by patriarchy—such that any invocation of political community is made to appear a sham and a delusion.

The kind of politics which tends to emerge out of this sense of exclusion, whether grounded in reality or philosophically projected (and it is often a mixture of both), is one which eschews the building of coalitions on a broad range of policies around some conception of the general good. Its attempt is rather to mobilize behind the group's demands on a narrow agenda, regardless of the overall picture, and the impact on the community at large. Any invocation of the community good as grounds for restraint in this politics tends to be viewed with suspicion.

This is what I want to call political fragmentation, the breaking up of the potential constituencies for majority coalitions behind multifaceted programs designed to address the major problems of the society as a whole, into a congeries of campaigns around narrow objectives, each mobilizing a constituency determined to defend its turf at all costs.

The picture I am offering here is somewhat Tocquevillian, and yet it is significantly different from Tocqueville's. He apprehended a kind of vicious circle, in which citizen apathy would facilitate the growth of irresponsible government power, which would increase the sense of helplessness, which would in turn entrench apathy. But at the end of the spiral would lie what he called "soft despotism," in which the people would be governed by an "immense tutelary power."

Now Tocqueville's portrait of a "soft despotism," much as he means to distinguish it from traditional tyranny, still sounds too "despotic" in the traditional sense. Modern democratic societies seem far from this, because they are full of protest, free initiatives, and irreverent challenges to authority; and governments do in fact tremble before the anger and contempt of the governed, as these are revealed in the polls that rulers never cease taking.

SPECIAL-INTEREST POLITICS

But if we conceive Tocqueville's fear a little differently, then it does seem real enough. The danger is not actual despotic control, but what I am calling fragmentation, that is, a people less and less capable of forming a common purpose and carrying it out. This fragmentation comes about partly through a weakening of the bonds of sympathy, through a rift of one of the kinds described above, and partly also in a self-feeding way, through the failure of democratic initiative itself. Because the more fragmented a democratic electorate in this sense, the more they transfer their political energies to the promotion of their partial groupings, in the way I want to describe below, and the less possible it is to mobilize democratic majorities around commonly understood programs and policies. A sense grows that the electorate as a whole is defenseless against the leviathan state; a well-organized and integrated partial grouping may, indeed, be able to make a dent, but the idea that the majority of the people might frame and carry through a common project comes to seem utopian and naive. And so people give up. Already-failing sympathy with others is further weakened by the lack of a common experience of action, and a sense of hopelessness makes it seem a waste of time to try. But that, of course, makes it hopeless, and a vicious circle is joined.

Now a society that goes this route can still be in one sense highly democratic—that is, egalitarian—and full of activity and challenge to authority, as is evident if we look at the contemporary United States. Politics begins to take on a different mold, in the way I indicated above. One common purpose which remains strongly shared, even as the others atrophy, is that society is organized in the defense of rights. The rule of law and the upholding of rights are seen as very much the "American way," that is, as the objects of a strong common allegiance. The extraordinary reaction to the Watergate scandals, which ended up unseating a president, are a testimony to this.

In keeping with this, two facets of political life take on greater and greater saliency. First, more and more turns on judicial battles. The Americans were the first to have an entrenched bill of rights, augmented since by provisions against discrimination, and important changes have been made in American society through court challenges to legislation or private arrangements allegedly in breach of these entrenched provisions. The famous case of *Brown vs. Board of Education,* which desegregated the schools in 1954, is a case in point. In recent decades, more and more energy in the American political process is turning towards this process of judicial review. Matters which in other societies are determined by legislation, after debate and sometimes compromise between different opinions, are seen as proper subjects for judicial decisions in the light of the Constitution. Abortion is a case in point. Since *Roe vs. Wade* in 1973 greatly liberalized the abortion law in the country, the effort of conservatives, now gradually coming to fruition, has been to stack the court in order to get a reversal. The result of the growing importance of the courts has been an astonishing intellectual effort, channeled into politics-as-judi-cial-review, which has made law schools the dynamic centers of social and political thought on American campuses; and also a series of titanic battles over what used to be the relatively routine—or at least non-partisan—matter of senatorial confirmation of presidential appointments to the Supreme Court.

Alongside judicial review, and woven into it, American energy is channeled into interest or advocacy politics. People throw themselves into single-issue campaigns and work fiercely for their favored cause. Both sides in the abortion debate are good examples. This facet overlaps the previous one, because part of the battle is judicial, but it also involves lobbying, mobilizing mass opinion, and selective intervention in election campaigns for or against targeted individual candidates.

INABILITY TO FORGE CONSENSUS OR COMPROMISE

All this makes for a lot of activity. A society in which this goes on is hardly a despotism. But the growth of these two facets is connected, part effect and part cause, with the atrophy of a third, which is the formation of democratic majorities around meaningful programs which can then be carried to completion. In this regard, the American political scene is abysmal. The debate between the major candidates becomes ever-more disjointed, their statements ever-more blatantly self-serving, their communication consisting more and more of the now famous "sound bites," their promises risibly unbelievable ("read my lips") and cynically unkept, while their attacks on their opponents sink to ever more dishonorable levels, seemingly with impunity. At the same time, in a complementary movement, voter participation in national elections declines, and has recently hit 50 percent of the eligible population, way below that of other democratic societies.

Something can be said for, and perhaps a lot can be said against, this lop-sided system. One might worry about its long-term stability, worry, that is, whether the citizen alienation caused by its less and less functional representative system can be compensated for by the greater energy of its special-interest politics. The point has also been made that this style of politics makes issues harder to resolve. Judicial decisions are usually winner-take-all; you either win or you lose. In particular, judicial decisions about rights tend to be conceived as all-or-nothing matters. The very concept of a right seems to call for integral satisfaction, if it's a right at all; and if not, then nothing. Abortion once more can serve as an example. Once you see it as the right of the fetus versus the right of the mother, there are few stopping places between the unlimited immunity of the one and the untrammeled freedom of the other. The penchant to settle things judicially, further polarized by rival special-interest campaigns, effectively cuts down the possibilities of compromise.

We might also argue that it makes certain issues harder to address, those which require a wide democratic consensus around measures which will also involve some sacrifice and difficulty. Perhaps this is part of the continuing American problem in coming to terms with their declining economic situation through some form of intelligent industrial policy. And perhaps this has something to do with the underdeveloped nature of the welfare state in the U.S., in particular, the lack of a public universal-health scheme. These kinds of common projects become more difficult to enact where this style of politics is dominant. For they cannot be carried through by mobilizing a clearly defined constituency around a single, narrowly-focused front. They require rather the building of a wider alliance which can sustain a broader range of interlinked policies over time— the kind of politics practiced by social-democratic parties in a number of Western democracies. (Or for that matter, by their opponents: see the Thatcher counter-revolution for an example.)

TURNING A VICIOUS CIRCLE INTO A VIRTUOUS CIRCLE

How do you fight fragmentation? It's not easy, and there are no universal prescriptions. But we have seen that fragmentation grows to the extent that people no longer identify with their political community, that their sense of corporate belonging is transferred elsewhere or atrophies altogether. And it is fed, too, by the experience of political powerlessness. And these two developments mutually reinforce each other. A fading political identity makes it harder to mobilize effectively, and a sense of helplessness breeds alienation. Now we can see how in principle the potential vicious circle here could be turned into a virtuous circle. Successful common action can bring a sense of empowerment and also strengthen identification with the political community. Indeed, the debate around certain kinds of issues, which establishes certain common goals despite radical disagreements about the means, can help to make the sense of political community more vivid, and thus to some extent offset the tendency of deep political divisions to paint the adversary as the devotee of utterly alien values. The contrast is striking with, say, the abortion debate, where both sides readily can come to believe that their opponents are enemies of morality and civilization.

One of the important sources of the sense of powerlessness is that we are governed by large-scale, centralized, bureaucratic states. What can help mitigate this sense is decentralization of power, as Tocqueville saw.

And so in general, devolution, or a division of power, as in a federal system, particularly one based on the principle of subsidiarity, can be good for democratic empowerment. And this is the more so, if the units to which power is devolved already figure as communities in the lives of their members.

What this points to is a kind of equilibrium which a liberal political system should seek. It is a balance between the party-electoral system on one hand, and the proliferation of advocacy movements on the other which are not directly related, if related at all, to the partisan struggle. The first is the channel through which broad coalitions on connected issues can be built and can effect their purposes. When this atrophies, or functions badly, effective citizen action on a large number of issues becomes difficult if not impossible. But if the party electoral system were to be there alone, if the wide range of movements engaged in extra-parliamentary politics were to disappear, then the society would be badly blocked in another way. It would lack that network of nested public spheres which alone keeps its agenda open and provides a way into political efficacy for large numbers of people who would never make the same impact through the established parties.

In a sense, there needs to be not only a balance between these two, but a kind of symbiosis; or at least open frontiers, through which persons and ideas can pass from social movements to parties and back again. This is the kind of politics which liberal societies need.

6

Beyond Teledemocracy: "America on the Line"

James S. Fishkin

American politics is suffering from a near-fatal attraction: we are continually being drawn toward too simple a notion of democracy. Some of the obvious symptoms of this fascination are: the proliferation of primaries to select a president (the number increased from 17 to 39 from 1968 to 1992); the proliferation of referendums (the recent spate of state ballot initiatives was the largest since 1932); and the continuing reliance on polls to evaluate the standing of our political officials, from the president all the way down to local officeholders.

The fascination with direct democracy has brought power to the people, but under conditions in which the people have little opportunity or incentive to think about the power they exercise. It has, in short, brought us democracy without deliberation. This appeal of direct democracy is motivated, at least in part, by a false image of political community. When we think of direct democracy, we tend to conjure images of the New England town meeting or the Athenian assembly. But when direct democracy is transplanted from the face-to-face encounters of such small-scale settings to the institutions of the nation-state, it produces a very different phenomenon: it yields a democracy of atomized voters who receive most of their political information from the mass media and who lack the social conditions that would motivate and facilitate debate and reflection on the information they receive.

Consider the three conditions that make deliberation possible in the face-to-face context: First, political messages of substance can be exchanged at length. Citizens are not reduced to receiving ever-shrinking sound bites. Second, there are opportunities for citizens to reflect on these messages. They do not have to respond instantaneously, because they are members of a political community that permits ongoing debate and reflection. Third, the messages can be processed interactively. Citizens can exchange reactions, voice and receive rival arguments, and test their opinions against those expressed by others. These are the three essential elements of face-to-face deliberation. In most applications of direct democracy to the modern nation-state, one or more of them is likely to be absent. This does not mean that direct democracy is useless on a large scale, but it does mean that its application is seriously flawed. Later, I will suggest an alternative form of democracy that is appplicable to the large-scale and that fulfills all three of these conditions for face-to-face deliberation.

The mass appeal of instant direct democracy is dramatized by the centerpiece of H. Ross Perot's campaign: his proposal for "electronic town meetings" to "put the owners back in charge of their country." As he explained in nationally televised interviews, "We're supposed to have a government that comes from us. Today, we have a government that comes at us." Perot would give us a system that is even more plebiscitary than the one we have now. He hopes to break down the results of viewer call-ins by congressional district. "The Congress needs to understand what the people want," Perot says, "as opposed to what the lobbyists want, and in the electronic town hall, you have feedback by congressional district. People understand through detailed explanations what the issues are; they respond in terms of what they want. Congress knows what the people want, not what the lobbyists want, and we're back on track."

The pitfalls facing this kind of teledemocracy are illustrated by a recent experiment that was actually broadcast: "America on the Line," a prototype for a series on CBS that aired after the president's State of the Union message. CBS tabulated the instant reactions from hundreds of thousands of viewers to the president's address and to current issues in the campaign. About seven million people tried to call, and about 300,000 actually succeeded in getting their preferences registered on the air.

Those calling in offered a distorted picture of public opinion when compared to poll results that had been obtained from a representative sample, which were also announced on the program. For example, 53 percent of the "America on the Line" respondents said that they were "worse off" now than a year ago, while only 32 percent of the representative sample said so. Only 18 percent of "America on the Line" respondents reported being in basically the "same" economic situation as they had been a year ago, while 44 percent of the representative sample reported their economic status was unchanged. Furthermore, the geographical distribution of respondents suggested that the population of New York State was about twice that of California, when the opposite is true.

Despite the unrepresentative nature of the viewer respondents, the results were presented on the broadcast as the voice of the people with real political consequences. The anger of these citizens, Connie Chung speculated, "does not bode well for President Bush after the State of the Union."

The flaws in this "innovation" are not new. The problem is reminiscent of the *Literary Digest* fiasco of the 1930s, when millions of ordinary citizens responded in writing to the *Digest's* straw polls. As a result, the *Digest* predicted that Alf Landon would win by a landslide over Franklin Roosevelt in 1936. Clearly, without carefully constructing a sample, the sheer number of responses means nothing. Norman Bradburn, the director of the National Opinion Research Center at the University of Chicago calls such surveys SLOPs—self-selected listener opinion polls. SLOPs do not accurately measure opinion distribution because self-selected participation is skewed toward those who have some motivation for participating.

A deeper problem with "America on the Line" is the reliance on instantaneous, off-the-cuff responses of millions of ordinary citizens. This problem fully applies to scientific samples as well as to the program's self-selected sample. Public opinion polling has given us a kind of plebiscitary democracy, in which immediate reports of the public's surface impressions are given legitimacy as the voice of the people. The public gets only surface impressions on most issues because it has limited incentives and opportunities to acquire and think about political information. The situation has worsened as sound bites have shrunk, candidate appearances have become more orchestrated, and the techniques of advertising have increasingly acquired primacy as the filter through which our political discourse must pass. If all the minutes about the issues (rather than about the horse race) that were aired on the CBS Evening News during a recent presidential campaign from January to June (covering the entire primary process) were put back to back, they would add up to a little less than two hours. Note that the pregame show for this year's Super Bowl was two-and-a-half hours. Sound bites of presidential candidates averaged about nine seconds in 1988. Our political discourse is being reduced to messages that are more appropriate to fortune cookies and bumper stickers. Under these conditions, why should we pay so much attention to the unreflective first impressions of ordinary citizens?

Of course, "America on the Line" solicited viewer reactions after an hourlong message, the State of the Union Address. (In Perot's proposal, there would be detailed presentations on specific issues such as health care.) The difficulty is in the solicitation of immediate, off-the-cuff responses without a structure of incentives and opportunities that would lead to face-to-face debate and investment by voters in further information and deliberation. In "America on the Line," then, at least two of our three conditions were missing: we were given instantaneous responses without an opportunity for face-to-face debate.

Although the stimulating message was long, it is worth noting that even lengthy political messages have been transformed by the effort to produce sound bites—quotable snippets of dialogue that may have a television and newspaper half-life long after most of the rest of the speech has been forgotten. The quest for sound bites has so oversimplified our political rhetoric that great speechmaking and debate have come to be exemplified by such statements as "Where's the beef?" the Wendy's advertising slogan that Mondale adopted to stem the tide of Gary Hart in the 1984 campaign. The numerous nationally televised debates early in the primary season achieved low ratings (ranging from about 2 percent to 5.5 percent of the nation's viewing households), and were mostly productive of sound bites that focused on conflict and controversy (such as an attack on Tsongas for taking a position that left the door open to nuclear power and an assault on Clinton for alleged conflicts of interest because of his wife's law firm affiliation). Despite such debates, the effective discourse reaching the public remains the sound bite on the evening news and the paid political advertisement.

Polls, primaries, and referendums have brought us a shallow form of mass democracy. But a return to previous political structures would be politically unthinkable, because they were perceived to be grossly undemocratic. Therefore, efforts at democratic reform are enmeshed in a dilemma: it seems that we must choose between politically equal but relatively incompetent masses and politically unequal but relatively more competent elites. In the area of presidential selection, for example, at least the smoke-filled rooms of prereform days had the benefit of providing for "peer review" of candidates. On the other hand, primaries have brought the people into the process, but in a manner that gives them little opportunity for deliberation.

Imagine a new beginning to our season of presidential selection. Suppose we took a national random sample of voting-age citizens and transported them to a single site. We would then invite the major presidential candidates for several days of face-to-face questioning in small-group sessions. We would provide the citizens beforehand with briefing materials on the major issues facing the country. At the end of these deliberations, we would poll the citizens on their views of both the candidates and the issues.

Such an event would constitute what I have called a "deliberative opinion poll." An ordinary poll models what the public thinks—given how little it knows and how short its attention span is. A deliberative poll models what the public would think if it had a more adequate chance to think about the questions at issue. The point of an ordinary poll is descriptive and predictive. The point of a deliberative poll is prescriptive. It gives voice to the people under special conditions in which the people would have a voice worth listening to. The poll can be thought of as a sample of what the public's judgments would be in a hypothetical version of our society—one in which everyone had the same opportunity for thoughtful deliberation and interaction that the members of the sample would have. In order to make this more concrete, imagine that our experiment were repeated over and over until every member of the society had participated. Clearly, such a supposition represents only a philosopher's theoretical experiment. But however hypothetical it may be, we can see that it would offer a superior form of democracy—one that is based on thoughtful, face-to-face questioning of the candidates and deliberation on the issues. Furthermore, practical interest in such an experiment stems from the fact that while the deliberative society that the sample represents is hypothetical, the actual experiment need not be. It is an eminently practical kind of event to hold at the beginning of the presidential selection season. In fact, my proposal for such an event was announced and nearly broadcast by PBS this political season. While the January 1992 event fell through for lack of funds, a serious effort will begin early for 1996.

A successful demonstration of the idea could have a major effect on the presidential selection system by turning the "invisible primary" into a deliberative event. The "invisible primary" is the period before the first official events when candidates jockey for position and for credibility with the media and potential donors. Given the role of momentum in the invisible primary, a change in the way candidacies are launched could determine the results.

For example, the Florida Democratic Party Straw Poll, which represents party activists in one Southern state, played a major role this year in Clinton's early rise, just as it played a major role in Jimmy Carter's emergence before the Iowa caucuses in the 1976 campaign. Instead of an event like the Florida straw poll, which is both unrepresentative of the country and undeliberative, we would have an event that is both representative of the entire country in all its diversity and deliberative on the issues. Instead of candidates repeating standard stump speeches, we might imagine a process in which they were forced to respond in depth on the issues, with sustained follow-ups.

New innovations are necessary if we are to create a public voice for the expression of the will of the people. The recommending force of a deliberative opinion poll at the beginning of the process could have a major effect on all that follows. Instead of forcing us to choose between bringing power to the people (as exemplified by primaries, referendums, and such programs as "America on the Line") and bringing deliberation to the process (as in the "peer review" of elite smoke-filled rooms), we could bring power to the people and, at the same time, allow the people an opportunity to think about the issues in question. They could debate face-to-face, exchange political messages of length and substance, and reflect on the results before being polled. Such a situation would fulfill all three of our conditions for face-to-face dialogue in a manner adapted to the large-scale nation-state. Such an experiment might also produce a voice of "we the people" that would be worth listening to.

7

Social Justice: A Communitarian Perspective

Philip Selznick

In this essay I seek to reaffirm, and to clarify if I can, the communitarian commitment to social justice. I shall try to do so by showing how our understanding of community makes social justice a moral imperative.

Communitarians look to the experience of community for moral guidance and promise. In doing so we should draw on the whole of that experience, the dangers and deficits of community as well as the benefits and ideals. We should take account of egoism as well as altruism; and we should recognize that some forms of altruism may limit the reach of community and tarnish its ideals.

Our chief prescription—the main lesson we draw for the United States today—is the need for enhanced responsibility. As we observe the weakening of institutions, the blurred line between liberty and license, the widespread preference for short-run gains, we see the need for more extensive responsibility in every aspect of personal experience and social life.

I do believe we have hit the right note. I am troubled, however, by a selective concern for personal responsibility, personal virtues, personal morality. While these themes are music to the ears of conservative writers and politicians—whose main concerns are crime, illegitimacy, and similar offenses, and who see immorality as a lower-class evil appropriately addressed by punitive measures—they pay little attention to the responsibilities of the affluent, or of business leaders. Most important, the moral responsibilities of the community as a whole are only dimly perceived and given short shrift.

There is plenty of truth in the conservative critique of modern culture. Communitarians do not shrink from recognizing that truth. We have

61

joined in calls for more responsible parenting, more discipline in schools, and safe streets and homes. But we part company with conservatives insofar as we look to collective as well as personal responsibility; and insofar as we understand that collective responsibility includes obligations of care for the vulnerable and the disadvantaged.

Furthermore, communitarians need to appreciate the close connection between personal and collective responsibility. *Personal responsibility is most likely to flourish when there is genuine opportunity to participate in communal life.* These conditions require substantial investment by the community and its institutions. At the same time, how much the community invests, and what kind of investment it makes, will depend on the prevalence of a sense of personal responsibility for the common good.

Let us not confuse responsibility with compassion. The communitarian ethos is not mainly about sympathy or benevolence. It is about meeting our obligations as responsible parents, children, citizens, officials, and economic actors. These obligations are eased by love, and supported by love, but they arise and persist even where love is absent or hard to sustain. At bottom, responsibilities arise from social involvements or commitments. Our lives touch others in many ways, for good or ill, and we are accountable for the consequences—accountable to ourselves as well as to others. Accountability and obligation give a tough-minded spin to concepts of community and responsibility. They also point us toward social justice as a foundation of community, and as a communitarian imperative.

In what follows I review four basic principles of social justice: equality, mutuality, stewardship, and inclusion. All are expressions of the morality of community.

EQUALITY

Communities are best understood as frameworks within which diverse interests are served and ordinary life goes forward. This pluralistic image of community is evident in Amitai Etzioni's idea that community is "a community of communities," or, as I have put it, a "unity of unities." These phrases are meant to capture a remarkable feature of communal life. A flourishing community builds upon and is nourished by other unities, notably persons, groups, practices, and institutions. These constituent unities characteristically claim respect and protection. Although boundaries may be blurred, for example between family and school, each has its own special functions, values, and needs. *Hence what we prize in community is not unity of any sort at any price but unity that preserves the integrity of the parts.* The unity of community is, ideally, a federal unity.

This conception has fateful implications for communitarian doctrine and social policy. Most important is a postulate of moral equality. The federal principle to which I have referred guarantees the dignity of the community's fundamental constituents, who are individual persons. This understanding of community bridges Biblical and Enlightenment thought. All persons have the same intrinsic worth. They are unequal in many ways—in talents, in contributions, in authority, in power, in valid claims to rewards and resources. But no person's well-being is inherently more worthy of consideration than any other's. Everyone who is a person is equally an object of moral concern.

A corollary not well understood, especially among critics of communitarian thought, is that community presumes separateness as well as integration. To be sure, people need strong communities if they are to develop and flourish as fully realized persons. Nevertheless every person is unique, separate, and morally autonomous. This separateness creates what John Rawls calls "an inviolability founded on justice that even the welfare of society as a whole cannot override." This idea does not require us to think of people as disaggregated or "abstract." Individual persons are not necessarily detached from their social contexts; they are not necessarily arm's-length participants in contracts of limited obligation; they do not necessarily believe that all their choices should be autonomous. They are likely to be socially embedded, socially implicated, even socially encumbered. Yet they do make choices; they struggle against authority; and they sometimes cast off their received identities. There is nothing objectionably "individualistic" in recognizing these facts, or in treating the well-being of individual persons as the criterion by which we judge policies and practices.

It is widely recognized, at least implicitly, that moral equality is at the heart of justice. Even among young children, experienced injustice is closely tied to a compelling sense of moral equality, often accompanied by loud demands for its vindication. "Why don't I count as much as my brothers? Not fair!" Indeed an arbitrary judgment, insofar as it violates the principle of equal justice, is at bottom an offense to the moral equality of litigants, citizens, or other members of the relevant community.

From the standpoint of *social* justice, the most important threat to moral equality is social subordination. Although moral equality does not require social equality—communitarians are hardly egalitarian—we recognize that significant differences in wealth, income, and education tend to create and reinforce beliefs that affluent people are inherently more worthy than their disprivileged brethren. Social justice requires eternal vigilance against this caste principle, and against the invidious discrimination it breeds.

I want to stress the concept of *invidious* discrimination. In the United

States this idea has been obscured and mystified—indeed very roughly handled—in debates about affirmative action and equal opportunity. Classification by race may be distasteful, often arbitrary, and ultimately undesirable. However if such classification serves a legitimate moral and public purpose, such as overcoming prejudice and opening opportunities, it is not necessarily invidious; it does not impose a caste principle. Even very weak forms of affirmative action, let alone preferential hiring or promotion, require institutions to "know the race" of those entitled to enhanced opportunity. Such programs may deny to some people benefits they might otherwise have. But they are not thereby demeaned or degraded; they do not suffer invidious discrimination. Despite some rhetorical overreaching, in the slogan that the Constitution is color-blind, that document need not be read as requiring our governments to turn a blind eye to the most wounding reality of American life.

We cannot vindicate moral equality—and thereby do justice—if we do not remedy the most important effects of domination and impoverishment. Social justice requires a regime in which everyone's basic needs for life, health, liberty, and hope are respected and addressed. Therefore we must be committed to a baseline equality of condition, that is, a social minimum of nurture and opportunity. This can and should be conditional. It may well require a reciprocal exercise of personal responsibility with respect to work, education, and deferred gratification; and the level of the baseline will necessarily reflect the level of prosperity in the community as a whole. Moreover, inequality as such is not the issue. There is no question of requiring those who have more to help those who have less *just because they have less.* The obligation is owed to people who suffer or are degraded because they are oppressed and impoverished; to people who are in danger of being despised and excluded—that is, rejected as objects of moral concern.

MUTUALITY

I turn now to an aspect of community that is poorly understood yet bears closely on justice. When we think of community, what comes most easily to mind is the experience of belonging, especially belonging based on a shared history and identity. But belonging by itself may produce a caricature of community, such as a family in torment, just as voting, without more, can produce a caricature of democracy.

The moral benefits of belonging are real enough—rootedness, humility, loyalty, piety. Not less important, though routinely overlooked in discussions of communitarianism, are the moral bonds of civility. Piety celebrates a shared faith, culture, and history. Civility protects diversity, autonomy, and conflict, which are presumed to be prevalent and beneficial. Compared to piety, the norms of civility are more impersonal, more rational, and more inclusive. Civility and piety are competing and complementary principles of moral integration; each is an important foundation of community. (For more on civility and piety, see my book, *The Moral Commonwealth,* ch. 14.)

I do not mean to suggest that the experience of belonging is irrelevant to justice. Belonging is a mainstay of justice, above all because it generates demands for moral equality. However, to explain the need for justice, and the workings of justice, we must focus attention on a different aspect of communal life, which we may call mutuality.

Mutuality arises from all the ways people are knit together by interdependence, reciprocity, and self-interest. Its connotations include harmony, sharing, and commonality, as when we speak of mutual interests, mutual aid, mutual obligations, and mutual friends. Mutuality also invokes the distinctive moralities of negotiation, contract, and association, especially trust, good faith, and reliance. It thereby creates the moral infrastructure of cooperation. Thus mutuality finds moral imperatives in diversity as well as identity; in self-regard as well as altruism; in pervasive competition, not preordained harmony; in civility, not piety.

We may need to be reminded that any community draws much of its sustenance from the pervasive facts of interdependence and reciprocity. These very practical conditions account for the voluntary and rational components of community. If people do not need each other, if little or nothing is to be gained from exchanging benefits and cooperating for common purposes, community is not likely to emerge or endure. Think how difficult it is to sustain community among affluent neighbors who can easily afford to pay for the conveniences of everyday life and therefore have no need for help, no need to incur obligations to neighbors. Think of the changes that occur, even among the affluent, when children need playmates or when serious threats to the safety of a neighborhood must be addressed.

We may readily admit that the bonds of community are largely emotional and nonrational. Yet rationality is by no means excluded. It would be strange indeed to think of participation in communities as irrational or self-destructive. This is so in part because we expect communities to be settings within which people *can be rational* about their interests, purposes, and connections. Rationality is enhanced because participation in communities is mediated by participation in families, localities, networks, and institutions. This social fabric does much to preserve autonomy and good sense. Thus the demands of community are not opposed to rational judgment and personal autonomy. On the contrary, any radical abridgment of these values will corrupt or even destroy community.

These thoughts suggest we should be open to theories that find well-springs of morality, justice, and community in the rational pursuit of self-interest. As a communitarian I have no problem with the idea that self-preservation and self-enhancement are reliable if limited sources of moral ordering. No one acquainted with the realities of civic participation and institutional life will fail to recognize the role of self-interest in underpinning reciprocity, cooperation, and fidelity to obligation.

Of course *raw* self-interest and *destructive* conflict must be tempered by strategies of protection and cooperation. The prime demand is for justice, which adjudicates controversies, settles claims of right, restrains domination, and curbs arbitrary power. Justice speaks civilly to the inevitable diversity of passions and interests. As it does so it brings to bear principles of fairness and of mutual obligation. Justice emerges as a response to practical urgencies; under appropriate conditions we can expect it to eventuate in ideas and practices that express deeper understandings and more comprehensive ideals.

The quest for justice encourages a subtle but significant move from raw, narrow, short-term self-interest to broader, more prudent, more long-run conceptions of what rationality requires. As one "neo-Hobbesian" moral philosopher, David Gauthier, has put it, "justice, the virtue of the self-interested, also curbs self-interest." This is a gateway to communitarian ideas.

I have gone on at some length about the significance of mutuality for the theory of community in order to correct some misunderstandings about the place of rationality and self-interest in communitarian thinking. Now let us review, very briefly, some of the conclusions we may draw for social justice from the experience of mutuality.

Restraining Domination

Mutuality presumes rough equality in the free play of exchange, association, interest, and power. This condition is threatened by the viruses of domination and exploitation. Enter social justice, whose chief office is to protect the weak against the strong. This it does by strengthening the rule of law and by correcting imbalances of social power, especially gross inequalities of wealth, education, and opportunity.

For communitarians the main tenets of pluralism are very congenial. Social power must be dispersed and balanced—but not fragmented. Therefore we seek a richly textured civil society, which has many benefits, including limiting the power of the state. It is often forgotten, however, that civil society depends vitally on law, which is part of government. Furthermore, we need effective government to secure public goods, such as environmental protection, basic science, and much else that is lost if we rely on market mechanisms alone. And we should be sensitive to the potential for abuse of power by all leaders, private as well as public.

Equality of Opportunity

When we embrace equality of opportunity as a principle of social justice, we acknowledge the value, within a moral community, of open competition for self-regarding ends. Whatever opportunities there are should be open to all without regard to social origins, including class, race, creed, ethnicity, or gender. Thus equality of opportunity vindicates moral equality. It has the vital but limited objective of overcoming prejudice and systematic subordination while maintaining the legitimacy of differential rewards.

In its elementary form equality of opportunity does not speak to *all* special advantages. A person born into affluence is privileged, but not necessarily because society recognizes an intrinsic moral or social superiority. Nor is the principle violated if some people are luckier than others. When barriers of caste and stigma come down, the door is open to merit but also to good fortune, manipulation, and aggressive competition.

A more robust view of equal opportunity would offer more positive support. A modern opportunity-centered educational system allocates special resources to children of poor families and provides a variety of programs to encourage and sustain hope and self-respect. Thus understood, equal opportunity is not tied to ascription and stigma. It offers a larger vision in which every individual is free to become, and effectively able to become, a fully realized person.

Equal opportunity invites meritocracy, in which advancement depends wholly on ability and achievement. But meritocracy can undermine community. When everyone has the same chance to succeed, no one can take refuge behind oppression and discrimination. No one can save self-esteem by claiming lack of opportunity. If a person's worth is bound up with achievement it is easy to suppose that high achievers are inherently more worthy than others.

We must conclude, therefore, that a society committed to moral equality needs to offer something more than the opportunity to seek reward through merit. It must find ways of upholding the ultimate worth of persons without regard to differences of talent, effort, or character. To truly embody a communitarian vision, the principle of equal opportunity must be embedded in a larger vision of social justice.

Controlling Externalities

To take community seriously is to take responsibility for the consequences of what we are and do. This was a central theme in John Dewey's communitarian liberalism. In more current jargon, we are responsible for the "externalities" we produce when we engage in autonomous and self-regarding conduct. Negative externalities are the costs we impose on the community, such as a degraded environment, or the health care needed because of personal recklessness or negligence. We are also responsible for producing positive externalities, that is, for contributing to good outcomes. The communitarian movement should be in the forefront of efforts to encourage concern for externalities, on the part of corporations as well as individuals. This is not a rejection of autonomy, or of self-interest. On the contrary, those values are presumed. The question is how they are put into practice.

Richesse Oblige

From the standpoint of social justice, benefits as well as rights incur responsibilities. People who gain most from the social and economic order, and from the benefits of community, have correspondingly greater obligations than those who get less, and especially those who get the least. This principle is rich with implications for political participation and economic policy. We expect affluent and well-educated voters to take more account of the public interest than people for whom bread-and-butter issues must be paramount. And social justice is at least friendly, and more than friendly, to the policy of progressive taxation. Although progressive taxation is redistributive, it is not a repudiation of unequal resources and rewards. Rather, it is a demand for responsible participation by those who gain most from the contributions of all.

STEWARDSHIP

Stewardship is the exercise of comprehensive and dedicated responsibility for a valued practice, institution, resource, relationship, or group. From a religious perspective, those who hold power are required to be God's delegates and trustees, steward's of His dominion. More generally, stewardship binds social power to moral ideals. The idea is to do justice by chastening power and vindicating interests, especially interests closely tied to the steward's control.

This principle is more demanding, and more distinctively communitarian, than reciprocity, the reconciliation of interests, or even giving to each his due. The responsibilities of stewardship go beyond mutuality. They call for a deeper commitment to selected objects of moral concern.

Stewardship is most familiar to us in demands for environmental protection. Environmentalists have fought hard to substitute an ideal of stewardship for the unbridled exploitation of nature. Whereas "exploitation of resources" once had a positive ring, as a call to progress, today we are more ready to accept a moral bond between humanity and nature. This bond, and the stewardship it creates, serves the interests of future generations. It is, therefore, a vital aspect of social justice.

The principle of stewardship is at the heart of recurrent calls for corporate responsibility. Are corporate leaders responsible for the well-being of an enterprise, or only for the gains of shareholders? Do they have multiple responsibilities or only a single concern? Does profitability require *maximizing* returns on investment, especially short-term returns? The virtues of a market economy are plain enough, but they do not justify a flight from responsible conduct. The interests of employees, customers, communities, and other stakeholders, as well as the long-run prosperity of the enterprise, must be faithfully and responsibly considered. This calls for an expanded conception of fiduciary responsibility—an ethos of stewardship.

INCLUSION

In a thriving community people want to be treated as members; and they aspire to full membership. Therefore inclusion is a major principle of social justice. The most important ways of being included—of participating in community—flow from the basic continuities of life: procreation, child-rearing, kinship, friendship, and work. Religion and politics are distorted if those continuities are weak, or absent, or if they are excessively demanding. The underlying truth is that community brings people together, not as manipulated or mobilized "masses," but in ways that sustain the wholeness and soundness of personal life.

Two aspects of inclusion are especially important:

Work

For most people of working age, the most important road to belonging and self-respect is a decent and steady job. Therefore full employment must be a lodestar of communitarian policy. A jobless underclass is wholly unacceptable, and the poor need more than money. They need effective participation in social life. They need jobs, education, and opportunities for service.

Cultural Diversity

The greatest challenge to inclusion—indeed the most important problem for communitarian thought and policy—is the tension between universalist and particularist ideals. Universalist concepts of tolerance, impartiality, the rule of law, and human rights are by no means alien to the spirit of community. They reflect a quest for community that looks outward rather than inward. A crucial step is the embrace of strangers. As we move from the "we" of affinity to the "we" of humanity, more and more people are perceived as of the same kind, sharing a common identity and fate. In this way, the enlargement of community—in nation-building for example—offsets primordial ties of family, tribe, religion, and locality. This broader perspective is decisively reinforced by moral progress, that is, by the ability to understand and the competence to uphold soundly based conclusions of moral and social theory. Among these are universalist principles of equality, respect, and concern.

At the same time, communitarians recognize and defend the virtues of particularism. These virtues include loyalty and piety, especially accepting responsibility for children, parents, and others to whom we owe special obligations. Particularism arises from the experience of connectedness, which makes us aware that we are implicated selves, bound up with lives that we have created and that have created us.

Most people flourish, morally and psychologically, if they have strong and stable attachments to specific families, communities, and ways of life. This accounts for the persistent pull of culture, including recurrent pleas for authenticity and rootedness; and for the backlash that occurs when these needs are ignored or unmet.

There is a dark side, to be sure. Particularism has often promoted arrogance, bigotry, exclusion, and worse. To correct and restrain these evils we rely on universalist norms of tolerance and equality. Nevertheless, the human worth of particular attachments—to family, locality, religion, language, and tradition—cannot be ignored, or easily dismissed.

Our problem is to reconcile these competing perspectives. We must respect diversity without allowing its claims to override those of basic humanity and justice. There can be no set rule for striking such a balance. Too much depends on specific histories and contexts. Nevertheless, some guidelines can be helpful:

First, we can reject the extremes of radical multiculturalism, which would fragment society, and of cultural imperialism, which is indifferent or hostile to local sources of identity and authenticity.

Second, we can recognize that particular attachments are often compatible with, and indeed may help preserve, more comprehensive unities. If people feel that their cultural origins and distinctive identities are respected, they can more readily give their loyalty to a larger "community of communities."

Third, each perspective must accept some limits. Advocates of universal human rights should limit their claims, especially enforceable claims, to baseline imperatives, such as rejection of genocide, torture, ethnic cleansing, and murder or imprisonment of political opponents. Such essentials should not be confused with fully elaborated ideals of justice and democracy. The latter are more likely to reflect distinctively Western values, and may well be insensitive to cultural diversity.

And finally, we can be more sensitive to the interplay of critical and conventional morality. Because critical morality looks to the authority of reason, it is often identified with universalist ideals. But reason and reflection, properly understood, are empirical as well as theoretical; they rely on facts as well as arguments. Critical morality can readily appreciate, on the basis of reflection and experience, the moral worth of special obligations and the implicit truths in convention and tradition. This sensitivity is wholly compatible with the idea that parochial experience is not self-justifying, not morally final, not an unqualified good. We must always be ready to criticize a particular culture, including our own, from within in the light of its own premises, and from without in the light of other experiences and more comprehensive interests.

8

A Precarious Balance: Economic Opportunity, Civil Society, and Political Liberty

Ralf Dahrendorf

As this essay will show, the countries of the First World are currently faced with a perverse set of choices. To remain competitive in growing world markets, they have to take measures that damage the cohesion of civil societies. If they are not prepared to take such measures, they will have to resort to restrictions on civil liberties and political participation, restrictions that will amount to a new authoritarianism. At least this appears to be the quandary. The overriding task of the First World in the decade ahead is to maximize—to the extent possible—wealth creation, social cohesion, and political freedom, realizing that the promotion of any one of these goals may only be achieved at the expense of the others. This task may be impossible; but one can get close to it. And realistically, getting close may be all that a project for social well-being can hope to achieve.

PART I: IN DEFENSE OF THE FIRST WORLD

At its best, the First World was not a bad place in which to live (past tense intended). Did anyone ever call it the First World, or was the name merely a reference to the unmentionable Second World of communist oppression that has now all but disappeared, and the Third (later also the Fourth) World of destitution, disease, and despondency? Whatever the motive, let us not dismiss the First World too easily. At its prime, it combined three social virtues:

- economies that not only offered a decent life to many but which were set to grow and to open up opportunities to those not yet prosperous;

- societies that had taken the step from status to contract, from dependence to individualism, without destroying the communities in which people lived;
- polities that combined respect for the rule of law with those opportunities for political participation and for choosing governments that we have come to call democracy.

One may well ask when and where such wealthy, civilized, and enlightened countries existed. It is a considerable temptation to hide behind acronyms and refer to what is often called the OECD world, the membership of the Organization for Economic Co-operation and Development. But let me overcome the temptation and name names. The United States of America in the period from Roosevelt to Kennedy (if not to quite the same extent before and after) is one example. Tens of millions of people from all over the world dreamed of living in America, and millions went to great lengths to get there. (Immigration rates are not the worst index of social well-being.)

This migration logic applies to other countries as well. The United Kingdom has long had a more even balance of emigration and immigration—except for the Irish, for persecuted Jews, and later for people from the poorer colonies—than the United States. But for long periods of this century it certainly belonged in the First World as here defined. So did parts of the former British Empire, the "temperate Commonwealth" as some call it in geographically correct—if politically incorrect—language: Australia, New Zealand, Canada, and a few other bits and pieces around the world. Then there are smaller European countries to mention: Switzerland, Sweden, and the other Scandinavian states. By the 1950s, when the Organization for European Economic Cooperation (which meant, above all, reconstruction) was turned into the OECD, most of Western Europe had become part of the "happy few."

Their characteristics were, to repeat, economic opportunity, civil society, and political liberty. However, it would be testing the benevolence of the reader beyond the permissible to leave such a smug statement without qualification. In fact, three major qualifications have to be added before a serious discourse becomes possible. Each of these qualifications could warrant an essay of its own, but I will summarize them here.

Far From Perfect

First of all, the First World in its heyday was flawed. All of its members excluded some individuals from the benefits of their achievements, and even from opportunities. The history of the United States is one long sequence of battles for inclusion—from the Civil War to the Civil Rights campaigns to today's underclass. For the most part, the battles could be fought within the institutions of the country, which is worth noting. Moreover, they were fought not just by the excluded groups themselves; they had allies, in the Supreme Court for example. But U.S. society was never even nearly perfect in terms of economic opportunity, social inclusion, or political participation. To the present day (to mention just one of many shocking facts) the U.S. president is probably elected by no more than 15 percent or so of those who, by law, are entitled to vote.

The American imperfections may be more stark and visible, but those of the United Kingdom, Australia, Switzerland, or Sweden are no less important. Economic inequality meant that, for many, the promise of citizenship remained unfulfilled. The social conflicts of a hundred years ago were fierce. It took decades of internal struggles—class struggles as they were correctly called at the time—to assert the basic equality of all human beings in society. It also took two modern wars; horrible though it is to say this, there is no greater social equalizer than a modern war in which entire populations are involved. It was not an accident that the Second World War was called a "total war."

These wars, to be sure, were not fought by the great democracies among themselves. They set civilized and not (not yet?) quite civilized countries against each other, those that had made it in terms of universal opportunity, and those that had not quite made it. I stress this point intentionally, and will even add a general thesis: The greatest risk to peace emanates from countries on the way from the old cycle of poverty, dependence, and illiberty to the life chances here described as those of the First World. When opportunities are held out for people but are not yet there to grasp, when economic development accelerates but social and political development lag behind, a mixture of frustration and irresponsibility develops that breeds violence.

Such violence can be individual and undirected, but it can also become collective and directed against apparently happier neighbors, more successful strangers in one's midst, or both. While it is likely that economic development coupled with political democracy and a civil society will generate both an internal sense of tolerance and peaceful international relations, the road that leads to such a state is full of pitfalls and temptations. *Imperial Germany and the Industrial Revolution* (to quote Thorstein Veblen's title of 1915) is only one example. Whenever a formerly traditional country embarks on this road, the rest have good reason to be apprehensive (as well as hopeful). But, as I will now show, this warning is not said to condemn the rest of the world to poverty.

Citizenship and Inequality

The second qualification of my initial thesis about the First World is that civil society—citizenship—is incompatible with privilege for the few. This holds not just at home—in a given country, where privilege is by the same token a denial of the citizenship of others—but internationally, too. As long as some people are poor, and moreover are condemned to remain poor because they live outside the world market altogether, prosperity everywhere remains an unjust advantage. As long as some people have no rights of social and political participation, the rights of the few cannot be described as legitimate. Systematic inequality—as opposed to comparatively incidental inequality within the same universe of opportunity—is incompatible with the civilized assumptions of the First World.

This is not simply a moral statement, but also presents a fundamental problem. Take immigration, which illustrates the problem. To obstruct the free movement of people is, in principle, unacceptable for free countries. Yet one appreciates that Switzerland, for example, would put the quality of life of its citizens at risk if it allowed everyone who wanted to settle there to do so on equal terms. So what does that country do? It allows some people in because they can make a useful contribution by, for example, enabling the locals to avoid disagreeable jobs; but it turns these "guest workers" into second-class citizens who cannot vote and who can be sent "home" on short notice. Most, however, are not allowed in at all; and to implement such a policy, a whole machinery of control must be set up not only at the borders but also within the country. The humiliating experiences of asylum-seekers in many countries of the First World are an indictment of the latter's claims to civilization. Yet there is no simple answer to the predicament.

Rather, there is only one answer, and it is not simple. It is the universalization of the benefits of the First World—what has come to be called development. Others are more qualified than I to express a view on this vast set of issues. We now know for sure, if we did not know before, that economic and social development is as much a matter of internal effort as it is of external assistance. We also know that large countries, notably in Asia but also in Latin America, have embarked so successfully on the road of economic development that the old First World is beginning to regard them as threats. When people speak of the Third World these days they mean, very largely, Africa; and by Africa they do not mean Tunisia or the liberated South Africa. Thus development can, and does, happen.

However, it is not only a precarious, but also a long process. Arguably, it takes humanity through the most threatening period of its history. The so-called population explosion; the dangers of military aggression, aggravated by the wide diffusion of lethal weapons; militant *integrisme*, or less precisely "fundamentalism," both of which emphasize the rule of faith rather than the rule of law; protectionism with regard to goods as well as to people—these and other evils are all possible and all too often real by-products of the early phases of development. They will be with us for generations to come. And yet the process is necessary, not because of any hidden hand of history—such Hegelianism is far from my Popperian way of thinking—but because the very values of an enlightened and civilized society demand that privilege be replaced by universal entitlements, if not ultimately by world citizenship then by citizenship rights for all human beings in the world.

Eternal Flux

Add to the above two qualifications a third one, and the seemingly bright picture with which I began looks more overcast still. Actually, the third qualification has a great deal to do with Karl Popper, or with Herakleitos long before him: "panta rhei"—everything is in flux. Nothing lasts, not even the blessings of prosperity, civil society, and democracy. For good reason did I use the past tense when I referred to the achievements of the United States, the United Kingdom, and even Switzerland and Sweden. At times, one has a sense that the great age is over. At minimum, the great age is seriously under threat. Thus, having set the wider scene, it is these threats to the First World that I want to concentrate on in the body of this paper. I will then turn to a few modest recommendations for combatting their effects, and perhaps their causes.

PART II: GLOBALIZATION—ITS CONSTRAINTS AND ITS CHOICES

It would be possible to consider economy, society, and polity separately; in fact this has often been done. Economic growth is uppermost on government agendas in the OECD world, and their advisers—civil servants as well as professors—help them focus on the issue to the exclusion of all others. Will deregulation do the trick? Is inflation, after all, a helpful lubricant? How do taxes have to be levied to stimulate rather than to impede growth? Extreme proponents of "economism"—economics as a political ideology—either ignore or decry social factors. Was it not a prime minister who said that "there is no such thing as society" because she wanted to encourage individuals to fend for themselves? As for society, the dissolving, disintegrating quality of modern societies has been a theme for a century. Anomie, suicide, crime, the collapse of the family, the loss of religion—these were themes long before "community" became a correct word again. And so far as the polity is concerned, democracy has been in crisis as long as anyone can remember such a thing as political science. Governability was certainly an issue in the 1970s. But long before that, scholars and politicians were aware of the link between the economy, society, and polity, wondering why people turned against democracy when unemployment hit and the stock market collapsed.

Such allusions may help avoid the fallacy of historical uniqueness—though the opposite fallacy that history keeps on repeating itself is no less risky. There is, however, a case for saying that in the OECD world, economic, social, and political well-being are intertwined in a new and vexing manner. The reason is probably, in one word, globalization. It has become hard, and for most impossible, to hide in this world. All economies are interrelated in one competitive marketplace, and everywhere the entire economy is engaged in the cruel games played on that stage. There is no getting away from it, and the effect of globalization is felt in all areas of social life.

"Global"-ization?

The skeptic will no doubt raise his or her eyebrows: Is this really so? And why should it be so? Moreover, what exactly does globalization mean? The skeptic would win, as of 1995, a good part of the argument. Globalization is, so far, by no means total. Whole economies, including that of China, are more national than global (though part of their national success is due to their global involvement). Economic regions are forming to provide common markets or free trade areas (though this may be a response to the new productive forces of globalization rather than their refutation). Within countries, important activities such as the provision of health services or of nursery and primary education—if not education in general—seem removed from global competition (though it cannot be an accident, or a mere fad, that the values of a globalizing economy have entered these services). It would certainly be possible to make a case for the imperfections of globalization at this point, though whether or not this would also be an argument against its force is another matter.

Why should globalization have happened at all, and why now? The obvious answers are probably the best. Whether the end of the Cold War is cause or effect may be a moot question; certainly the Soviet bloc countries were economically no longer viable. One reason was that the concept of country, or nation, lost a good part of its economic meaning. This was a result of the emergence of transnational entities that found it surprisingly easy to combine a degree of adjustment to local needs with the advancement of worldwide strategic planning, direction, and profit making. Add to this the two related "revolutions" of information technology and financial markets, and an economic scene emerges the likes of which the world has never seen before. It is unique not only in terms of movements of money, but also in terms of services (such as booking airplane tickets). In the end, even terms of production and conventional physical boundaries begin to lose all meaning. Politics, technology, market pressures, and organizational innovations all conspire to create, in important areas of economic activity, a wholly new space that anyone—any company, any nation—ignores at their peril.

What then does such globalization mean? The most important answer is to the question not asked: What does it *not* mean? There has never been—as Michel Albert reminded us in his *Capitalism against Capitalism*—just one economic culture, even among the market economies. We have long sensed that Japan is different from the United States, and Germany from the United Kingdom. The differences are quite profound, even if they are badly understood. The rest of the world keeps on pressing Japan to open up its markets when one cause of their inaccessibility is the people's ingrained tastes and another, let us face it, the Japanese language. The United Kingdom and Germany speak much the same language of economic policy, yet the United Kingdom's textbook capitalism and Germany's textbook corporatism create very different attitudes, especially since in the first case the textbook is one of economics and in the second, one of political science.

Such cultural differences will not disappear. To what extent they will continue to be national may be an open question. There is a certain cultural plausibility, after all, to the regions that are beginning to form: those of Europe, the Americas, and East and Southeast Asia. (It is also apparent that certain countries do not obviously belong, such as the United Kingdom in Europe and, perhaps increasingly, Japan in Asia.) Whatever these emerging regional structures will be like, the basic presumption remains that reactions to globalization will differ despite the fact that the global marketplace requires some of the same virtues from all. Indeed, if it were not for such differences, the question raised in this paper would lose its meaning. Balancing economic growth, civil society, and political liberty is a universal task, but it would be foolhardy to assume that everybody will tackle it, or even try to tackle it, in these terms. For those who will, the assumption is that the goal can be approximated without losing out in the global marketplace.

The Universal Demands of the Economy

What then are the inescapable conditions of globalization? What, in other words, must be done everywhere if companies, countries, or regions do not want to condemn themselves to backwardness and destitution? To use the fashionable word, economic actors need, above all, "flexibility." The word is intended to convey something desirable, though for many it describes the price they have to pay. Also, the word has so many connotations that it is hard to pin down any particular meaning. Yet without considerable flexibility, companies cannot survive in the world market.

Flexibility means in the first instance the removal of rigidities. Deregulation and less government interference generally help create flexibility; many would add a lighter burden of taxation on companies and individuals. Flexibility has increasingly come to signify the loosening of the constraints of the labor market. Hiring and firing become easier; wages can move downwards as well as upwards; there is more and more part-time and limited-term employment; workers must be flexible also and are expected to change jobs, employers, and locations of employment. The concept of flexibility brings to mind Schumpeter's idealized figure of the entrepreneur and his "creative destructiveness." Flexibility also means the readiness of all to accept technological changes and respond to them quickly. In marketing terms, it is the ability to move in wherever an opportunity offers itself, and also to move out when those opportunities are exhausted. The story is familiar enough, as is its accompanying language of structural adjustment, efficiency gains, competitiveness, and seemingly unending increases in productivity.

Yet choices remain. At least they are choices in theory; in practice they are just as likely to be brought about by circumstances, traditions, and irresistible pressures. One choice is between a low-pay and a high-skill economy. In practice, most countries will combine both in some ways, but there are important differences of emphasis. Low-pay economies find their place in the world market by undercutting others. Their products are cheaper, and their workers are poorer. One sometimes hears arguments that this is the only road to success; but the evidence is that such extreme economism is simply a mistake. A high-skill economy can also create a competitive advantage. This is the case not only because high skills advance the frontiers of technology, but also because certain quality products and product qualities require a skill input. Indeed, there even comes a point at which one highly skilled person, who costs less than five low-paid ones, produces the same effect. The United States seems to move in the direction of low pay, whereas Japan opts for high skill; the United Kingdom prefers low pay and Germany high skill.

One other point must be emphasized that concerns incomplete globalization. Despite the enormous force of the global marketplace, there is and always will be privileged access to markets. Even without explicit protectionism, the Japanese phenomenon exists everywhere to a greater or lesser extent. People will "buy American" in the United States, "buy German" in Germany, and even "buy British" in the United Kingdom if there are British products on the market. Regional trade arrangements are about extending these privileged markets. "Buy American" then means

"buy NAFTA-American," and "buy European" replaces national rally-
ing calls. In classical economic terms, such regionalism introduces inflex-
ibility; people will probably call it predictability, or security. The point
should be borne in mind.

However, the options alluded to here are minor variations on the major
theme of globalization. The forces of globalization are strong everywhere
and bring with them pressure for greater flexibility, with all the implications listed earlier. By choosing one or the other variant, companies—
even countries, for many of the choices invite government action—can
take the edge off certain effects or give additional emphasis to others; but
one thing they cannot do is opt out of the global marketplace. Even the
attempt to stay in an older socioeconomic age to serve the political purposes of dictators will not work for any length of time, as the examples
of Myanmar or Cuba, and probably soon the Democratic People's Republic of Korea, show.

PART III: CIVIL SOCIETY UNDER PRESSURE

The term "civil society" is more suggestive than precise. It suggests, for
example, that people behave towards each other in a civilized manner; the
suggestion is fully intended. It also suggests that its members enjoy the
status of citizens, which again is intended. However, the core meaning of
the concept is quite precise. Civil society describes the associations in
which we conduct our lives, and that owe their existence to our needs and
initiatives rather than to the state. Some of these associations are highly
deliberate and sometimes short-lived, like sports clubs or political parties.
Others are founded in history and have a very long life, like churches or
universities. Again others are the places in which we work and live—
enterprises, local communities, the family, etc.

The crisscrossing network of such associations—their creative chaos, as
one might be tempted to say—makes up the reality of civil society. It is a
precious reality, far from universal, itself the result of a long civilizing
process; yet it is often threatened, by authoritarian rulers or by the forces
of globalization.

Globalization threatens civil society in a variety of consequential ways.
The social effects of economic responses to the challenges of globalization
have become the subject of public and scholarly attention, especially in
the United States. This is no accident. North America is the home of
modern civil society, where threats to its strength are most acutely felt.
Suddenly Tocqueville's world, indeed that of the *Federalist* authors, appears to be crumbling; *The Disuniting of America* is the new theme, accompanied by fear, violence, and versions of fundamentalism. It is small

consolation that the United States is not alone in this predicament. The following sketchy catalog of pressures on civil society draws from European as much as U.S. experience, and is at least in part applicable to other OECD countries as well.

Globalization, Inequality, and Civil Society

Economic globalization appears to be associated with new kinds of social exclusion. For one thing, income inequalities have grown. Some regard all inequalities as incompatible with a decent civil society; this is not my view. Inequality can be a source of hope and progress in an environment that is sufficiently open to enable people to make good and improve their life chances by their own efforts. The new inequality, however, is of a different kind; it would be better described as inequalization, the opposite of leveling. It builds paths to the top for some and digs holes for others, creating cleavages. The incomes of the top 10 to 20 percent are rising significantly, whereas the bottom 20 to 40 percent are watching their earnings decline. Robert Reich and others have made this observation the starting point of their search for remedies, though even the U.S. Labor Secretary has not been able to do much to reverse the trend. This systematic divergence of the life chances of large social groups is incompatible with a civil society.

The process is aggravated by the fact that a smaller but significant set of individuals seems to have fallen through the net of citizenship altogether. The concept and the phenomenon of the underclass are much discussed. (Not everybody likes the term, which is clearly misleading if one considers it in terms of class theory. The socially excluded are not a class; they are at most a category of people who have many different life stories.) Though some of them manage to get out of the predicament, many are in a position in which they have lost touch with the "official" world, with the labor market, the political community, and the wider society. Figures vary as to the size of the underclass, but most OECD countries now have in their midst what William Julius Wilson called "the truly disadvantaged"—would-be citizens who are non-citizens, an indictment of the rest of us.

Many of the truly disadvantaged are not just economically excluded, but also excluded as "strangers" by virtue of race, nationality, religion, or whatever distinguishing marks are chosen to provide excuses for discrimination, xenophobia, and often violence. Declining social groups, such as the 40 percent whose real incomes have been falling for 10 years or more, are breeding grounds for such sentiments. Borders, including social boundaries, are always particularly noticeable for those closest to them. A wave of "ethnic cleansing" is not confined to war zones like Bosnia-Herzegovina, but threatens to engulf us all.

What does this have to do with globalization? As far as the new inequality—the increasing divergence of those near the top and those near the bottom—is concerned, it takes us back to the low-pay/high-skill alternatives. On the one hand, countries that have taken the low-pay route have produced a large group of "working poor." On the other hand, high-skill countries begin to get accustomed to a significant group of long-term unemployed. Some people are—awful as it is even to put this on paper—simply not needed. The economy can grow without their contribution. Whichever way you look at them, they are a cost to the rest, not a benefit.

This experience has now hit middle-class individuals and families as well. While their problems may be milder for the individuals, they are more acutely felt by the nation as a whole. The latest wave of efficiency gains has reached, especially in large companies, all the way to the once hailed echelons of middle management. Such trends document a fundamental change in the world of work. No one would argue that there is not enough work to be done, but work at decent rates of pay is increasingly hard to come by. It is a privilege, not a realistic aspiration for all. Manufacturing and many services are following agriculture into a stratosphere of productivity in which half or fewer of those employed in the past can now produce twice as much output or more. What remains is a strange assortment of ill-paid personal-service jobs, numerous forms of hidden unemployment—some called "education," others "self-employment"—and, in Europe, long-tern unemployment for at least 5 percent, and probably soon 10 percent, of the population of employment age.

I have not offered here any probing thoughts about the conditions under which civil societies thrive. However, some simple analysis will make clear the tension created by growing inequality. Poverty and unemployment threaten the very fabric of civil society. Civil society requires opportunities of participation which in the OECD societies (if not universally) are provided by work and a decent standard of living. Once these are lost by a growing number of people, civil society goes with them.

Globalization, Flexibility, and Civil Society

Let me move on to another set of social issues associated with economic globalization. Flexibility may be the opposite of rigidity, but it is also the reverse of stability and security, necessary components of civil society. One may fairly debate *how much* stability and security are needed to preserve civil society, but the economic response to globalization is intrinsically inimical to both stability and security. Uprooting people becomes a condition of efficiency and competitiveness; in addition, the dismantling of the welfare state is on the agenda everywhere.

Such developments may not be all bad; they are to some extent unavoidable. But the pendulum is swinging far in the opposite direction. The
dual effect is the destruction of important features of community life and
a growing sense of personal insecurity for many. Inner cities tell a shocking part of the story, aggravated by the tendency to erect suburban shopping centers at the expense of downtown markets and department stores.
On the employment side, limited-term contracts—like part-time work—
are fine for a while, notably for the young and the able-bodied and perhaps for childbearing women; but people, even children, do get older, and
discovering at the age of 55 (and sometimes earlier) that one is no longer
needed is enough to turn many into bitter activists.

Add to such phenomena the return of Social Darwinism under the
pressures of globalization, and the concoction becomes even more lethal.
At times one detects strange similarities, at least in Europe, between the
end of the nineteenth and the end of the twentieth centuries. Then as now,
people had been through a period of rampant individualism—
Manchesterism then, Thatcherism now. Individuals were set against each
other in fierce competition and the strongest prevailed—or rather those
who prevailed were described as the strongest, regardless of the qualities
that led them to their success. Then, as now, there was a reaction. Around
1900, it was called collectivism. Today, this is a badly discredited word.
However, the new vogue has a similar objective; it is called communitarianism.

Perhaps the most serious effect of adopting the values that go with
flexibility, efficiency, productivity, competitiveness, and profitability is
the destruction of public spaces and the decline of the services that go
with them. The prevailing carrot-and-stick philosophy has overlooked
and then attacked noneconomic motives—motives that lead people to do
things because they are right, or because people have a sense of duty, a
commitment. Introducing pseudoeconomic motives and terms into public
spaces robs these of their essential quality. A national health service, universal public education, basic income guarantees under whatever name—
all become victims of an economism that is running amok. Small wonder
that commuter transport, environmental protection, and public safety
suffer in the process.

This gloomy picture is not the whole story, of course. Many people are
better off than ever before. They have more choices not just of dishwasher
fluids and television channels but of education and leisure pursuits. They
live longer. They grumble, but perhaps they should, if it helps them to do
something about the objectionable things they see. (Readers of Albert
Hirschman will have noticed more than a trace of *Exit, Voice and Loyalty*
in these comments.) Yet there can be little doubt that the economic challenges of the global marketplace have not helped civil society. One analyt-

ical footnote may help put flesh on this assertion and also provide a link to the issues of political liberty to which we must turn.

I have spoken of the underclass, of the marginalized, and of people giving voice to their concerns. Why is there no massive movement to defend civil society? Where is the twentieth century equivalent of the labor movement of the late nineteenth century? It does not yet exist, and likely never will. For reasons that antedate the challenges of globalization, individualization has not just transformed civil society, but social conflicts too. Many people may suffer the same fate, but there is no unified and unifying explanation of their suffering, no enemy that can be fought and forced to give way. More importantly, and worse still, the truly disadvantaged and those who fear to slide into their condition do not represent a new productive force, nor even a force to be reckoned with at present. The rich can get richer without them; governments can even be reelected without their votes; and GNP can rise and rise.

Individualized conflict is by no means easier to handle—to regulate—than organized class or other struggles. On the contrary, it means that people have no sense of belonging or commitment to the society, and therefore no reason to observe the law or the values behind it. It seems hard to dispute the observation that social disintegration is associated with a degree of active disorder. Young men, and increasingly young women—as well as many who are not so young—see no reason to abide by prevailing rules that for them are the rules of others. They opt out of a society that has already pushed them to the margin. They become a threat. Those who can afford it pay for protection. Those who cannot afford protection become victims. A sense that something has gone badly wrong—a sense of anomie (Durkheimians might say) or lawlessness and deep insecurity—is spreading.

PART IV: TEMPTATIONS OF AUTHORITARIANISM

The condition of global competitiveness coupled with social disintegration is not favorable to the constitution of liberty. Freedom and confidence go well together—confidence in oneself, in the opportunities offered by one's environment, and in the ability of the community in which one lives to guarantee certain basic rules—the rule of law. When such confidence begins to crumble, freedom soon turns into a more primordial condition, the war of all against all. Who thrives in a such state of anarchy? The warlord, the impostor, the speculator, the jester if he is lucky enough to find a protector—but not the citizen, for he no longer exists. Everyone else becomes a victim. People do not like the prospect, especially if they had once been citizens. They begin to doubt the wisdom of the fathers of their constitutions if liberty leads to anomie. They look for a way out, for authority.

It is important to turn dramatic, metaphorical language into precise analysis. We must also consider the political approach of non-OECD countries. Competitiveness no longer means that Europe and North America just have to keep up with Japan, their fellow-OECD member. There are new players, notably in Asia, who are not yet, and perhaps never will be, OECD members. Hong Kong, Taiwan, and other countries with a Chinese business class began the change towards increasing the number of serious world players. They were soon joined by the Republic of Korea and Thailand. Then China itself followed suit. From little more than 5 percent of world exports in 1980, the Asian tigers and dragons plus China moved up to nearly 15 percent by 1994; since the mid-1980s the GNP of these countries has been growing at almost three times the rate of the OECD countries.

More importantly, the new Asian economies, or at least their political spokesmen, show no sign of emulating European ways. *The Asia That Can Say No* is the title of a book by the Malaysian prime minister, Dr. Mahathir Mohammed, that sets out a "policy to combat Europe and America." (The title is adapted from the earlier Japanese best-seller by Shintaro Ishihara, *The Japan That Can Say No.*) Dr. Mahathir's thesis is simple and it has often been propounded by Senior Minister Lee Kwan Yew of Singapore and other spokesmen of Singapore's government. It is that Asia can compete with anyone in world markets without abandoning its values. No bricked-up inner cities, no underclass, no drugs, and no crime for Asia! Social cohesion—some say Confucianism—will remain the moral basis of life, and will not interfere with economic growth. Indeed, such values may contribute to growth.

And how are the dreaded Western values supposed to be kept out? By strong government, is the answer. Authoritarianism is not totalitarianism. Law-abiding citizens who assiduously attend to their own affairs and otherwise live inoffensive private lives need not fear the wrath of their leaders. The permanent and total mobilization of all by the state that characterizes totalitarian régimes will not happen. Among other things, it would be incompatible with a successful modern economy. But those who criticize government for its unaccountable power, those who use their freedom of speech to expose nepotism, those who dare put up alternative candidates in elections—these people are in trouble. The limits of civic freedom are tightly drawn.

Is this, then, the alternative with which modern societies are faced: one choice being economic growth and political freedom without social cohesion, and the other being economic growth and social cohesion without political freedom? And is the "Asian" alternative both viable and acceptable to Westerners? More and more people in the OECD world think so. Many in business like the Asian model, and conservative politicians from Margaret Thatcher to Silvio Berlusconi agree. Asian values have become the new temptation, and political authoritarianism with them. Abandon the U.S. model, suggests the new wave, and look to Asia for a new model of how economic progress can be combined with social stability and conservative values.

A Look at History

The story is not as new as it sounds. Under different names it has accompanied modern economic development for over a century. After all, Imperial Germany was a case of a combination of the industrial revolution with an authoritarian régime. But we must not forget that it took a long and murderous century for Germany to grow out of this fallacy.

For countries that embrace modern economic ways before their societies have become civil and their polities democratic, the temptation of authoritarianism is great indeed. (The same is actually true for countries that attempt the economic and political transition from the tyranny of a leader or a party to an open society at the same time.) In the early stages, the creation of a market economy invariably requires sacrifices from the people subjected to it. It requires what is called delayed gratification, or—in economic terms—savings (investment before consumption). People will have to work hard for low wages and tolerate miserable working and living conditions before their countries manage to turn the corner and join the developed world. Such sacrifices are rarely if ever made voluntarily. Even Max Weber's thesis of the usefulness of Calvinism—an early analogue to today's Confucianism—begs the question of whether it was religious beliefs or authoritarian governments that made people forgo the fruits of their labor. It is hard to think of an example where ascetic values were not reinforced by strong secular powers.

But for the most part, the situation did not last. Capitalism itself changed, to be sure, from saving to spending and on to borrowing. As it progressed, however, society and politics also changed. Increasingly (so the West would like to believe) people demand a share of the wealth they produce; they also want to be masters of their own lives. They want to travel and watch television and choose their own neighbors. They want to have a say in their affairs, the vote, the right to form associations, the ability to tell a government to go away. Civil society and political liberty seem to follow economic development if they do not precede it. But do they always?

The test of history rarely yields unambiguous results for such large theories. Still, this particular one is being tested every day in Asia, and particularly in Japan. There are signs that Japan will go down the Western route, *mutatis mutandis,* which is one reason why Asian leaders criticize it almost as much as the United States. But theories can be wrong; once again there is no inexorable march of History. It is possible that a new Asian—essentially Chinese—balance will be found that combines world competitiveness in economic terms with a social cohesion that is traditional rather than civil, and with authoritarian political régimes. It is also possible that such an example will affect European leaders and voters, and that a growing number will wish to go down a similar route at the risk of abandoning some of the cherished rights and liberties of the European and North American tradition. The temptations of such authoritarianism are considerable. They are likely to arise in many policy areas. To mention but a few potentially popular positions:

- Integrating the young into society is no longer easy. Where families fail, schools cannot succeed. Labor markets are not exactly waiting for newcomers. Many young people begin to drift and to embrace antisocial behavior. People want to see them disciplined. Someone should be able to tell them what to do, people may say, and to punish them if they do not obey.
- Punishment is also the main demand of those who speak incessantly about law and order. The caning of an American youth (who was charged with vandalizing cars) in Singapore has led to official protests but much private gloating in the West. The cane, it is said in pubs around Europe, should be brought back. The police should be given greater powers. Life in prisons should be really hard. The death penalty should be reintroduced.
- The welfare state must be reformed and that cannot be done without hardship. But such hardship, people think, should hit first the scroungers who live on other people's money without contributing anything themselves. If people do not want to work, they must be made to do so, or not get anything. Parents who do not look after their children must, if necessary, be forced to do so.
- All too often liberty has become license. The behavior of people in public is, some people think, disgusting. Unkempt men drinking beer in public places, half-undressed girls cavorting about, no one paying respect to the elderly or the infirm—all of this is not surprising, perhaps, in view of the media and the tabloids; but it still must be stopped.
- The invasion of foreigners simply cannot go on. In state schools local children have become a minority, and teachers offer prayers in several religions. Somehow this mess must be sorted out again, and England

returned to the English, Germany to the Germans, France to the French, etc.

It would be only too easy to go on. Nor are these the most extreme demands for change. One could probably quote a respectable academic author to give reasons for every one of them. They all add up to the demand for a régime that is less tolerant, one that enforces values at the risk of violating civil rights as we have come to know them, and one that cannot simply be removed by an election. It would be an agreeable side effect, in the view of the supporters of the above positions, that such a government could guarantee economic competitiveness without having to listen to disgruntled trade unions, or to special-interest groups from Greenpeace to animal-rights campaigners, or to local environmentalists, or indeed to political parties, which are unpopular whatever their persuasion may be.

It is not easy to assess the strength of authoritarian sentiments of this kind in the OECD world. Not everything said by a businessman or a taxi driver in a moment of exasperation amounts to demands for a régime change. There are signs that some of the solutions hinted at will be promoted by perfectly law-abiding democratic forces. Some suspect that law and order will dominate the political agenda to such an extent that perpetrators are bound to face harsher treatment (whatever that means precisely). It would not be surprising to see the death penalty reintroduced in countries that abolished it for good reasons. Certainly, the time of adjustment to global competitiveness—with its economic cost for many, social disintegration with the attendant discomforts and pains, and lack of confidence in traditional political parties and leaders—tests the ability of democracies to promote change without violence and without violation of the rule of law. One wonders who the first OECD leader is going to be who gets up and says: "Give me 10 years, and I promise the trains will run on time again!"

PART V: SOME MODEST PROPOSALS

While we wonder about risks, we must not forget to think about solutions. We want prosperity for all, and that means acceptance of the needs of competitiveness in global markets. We want civil societies that hold together and provide the basis of an active and civilized life for all citizens. We want the rule of law and political institutions that allow change as well as critical discourse and the exploration of new horizons. These three desires are not automatically compatible. The challenges of globalization require responses that threaten civil society. The onset of anomie gives rise to the temptation of authoritarianism, which is more tempting to some based on the perceived success of the Asian model. So what can be done to preserve a civilized balance of wealth creation, social cohesion, and political freedom?

One feature of the Popperian approach to problems is that it shuns comprehensive solutions. Whoever claims to have the answer to every question answers none. Total solutions will aggravate rather than improve matters. This means, however, that viable answers are bound to look woefully inadequate in comparison to the dimension of the problem. The six suggestions that I propose to discuss briefly, to give some substance to the analysis, all fall into this category. They are beginnings, no more.

Social GNP

We must change the language of public economics. It is remarkable how unquestioningly we have adopted in public discourse the concept of "economism," even though many leading economists have moved away from it. For governments, let alone for international organizations, GNP growth is still the primary obsession. Sometimes politicians are surprised if growth remains "jobless" (and hence voteless); even with growth of 3 percent, few new jobs are created and opinion polls continue to show the government in a dim light. Something is missing. Some call it the "feel-good factor."

The inventors of GNP accounting, great men like Samuelson or Arrow, speak of the limitations of this yardstick as much as its uses. In response, others have tried to develop supplemental yardsticks. In a recent book, Partha Dasgupta contrasts destitution (his main subject) with "well-being," even "social well-being." He, as well as Amartya Sen before him and Meghnad Desai after him, tried to introduce measures for aspects of well-being not included when we speak of gross national product—measures of human rights for example, or of democracy. Clearly, wealth is more than per capita GNP. Whether we want to spend much time and energy to produce one complex measure of wealth, or well-being, may be an open question. The answer is probably no. But governments and international organizations should be encouraged to add other information every time they produce GNP figures, such as information about trends in inequality, measurable opportunities for people, and human rights and liberties. A proper wealth and well-being audit should take the place of a single simple and often misleading figure. This will bring much-needed attention to the relative health of civil society and political freedom of nations and, at least from the perspective of language, balance these important concerns with that of economic growth.

Linking School and Work

The new world of work makes it imperative that proper provisions be made for young people to pass through a phase of vocational training that is closely related to real jobs and ends up in a period of regular employment. The nature of work is changing. Increasingly, a single career for life is the exception rather than the rule. Over a lifetime, people will have been in and out of work, employed full-time or part-time, in training and retraining. In some ways the experience of women will become the general norm, to the chagrin of many young men. Such changes have many implications—for example entitlements must not be tied to particular jobs.

More importantly, however, this whole transformation can work only if everyone has, at an early stage, gained some experience of the labor market. Education does not solve all problems; young people understandably ask where it is leading them. But education linked to employment at the critical age—16 to 19, or so—provides a basis of experience and of motivation that can sustain people through a lifetime of changes. Conversely, if the early opportunity to encounter the uses of education and the constraints of the labor market is missed, much if not all is lost. We should look at the best practices in this area and try to apply them more generally. By providing training and preparation for the job market, a nation prevents the perpetual creation of an underclass, the existence of which threatens civil society.

Reaching Out to the Underclass

The truly disadvantaged—the underclass—present an almost unmanageable problem. Clearly, just offering opportunities to those who have fallen through the net is not enough. People will not take such chances without much more inducement. Many have become indolent and accustomed to a life at the margin. Everything that can be done to include the excluded underclass must be done.

Yet the more critical task is, in the words of the British parliamentarian and reformer Frank Field, to cut the supply routes to tomorrow's underclass. We may not be able to do enough for those already excluded, but we must prevent another generation from having the same dismal experience. In part, vocational training for all may do the trick. Possibly some form of universal national service would aid the integration of all into the values of a changing society. Community building through housing and the creation of public spaces might also help.

The issue clearly needs further exploration. But turning public attention from the remedial to the prospective, from helping today's underclass to preventing the emergence of tomorrow's, would itself help. Advocating international conferences is always a bit of a copout; but some agency or other would surely find it attractive to try to bring together expertise and imaginative thought on this subject. It is crucial that we find ways to provide these individuals with the economic opportunities that are necessary to fulfill the promise of citizenship that the OECD countries offer.

Sustaining Local Communities

Globalization means centralization. It individualizes and centralizes at the same time. Intermediate agencies—indeed, civil society—are to some extent obstacles on the path to globalization. There is a sense in which competitiveness in world markets helps destroy communities. But this does not have to be the case. It is possible to counteract the simultaneous pressures towards individualization and centralization by a new emphasis on local power. The word "local" is deliberately chosen. Nations within nations—such as Wales, Quebec, or Catalonia—do not have the same effect. They may contribute to a general sense of belonging, but as a principle of social and political organization they divide and produce unhelpful rigidities. (The so-called Europe of Regions is, from this point of view, at best an irrelevance and at worst a mistake.)

Local communities, on the other hand, can provide a practical basis for vocational training, for small and medium-sized businesses, for personal involvement and participation, for strengthening the public domain—in short, for civil society—without detracting from economic imperatives. Some countries like Switzerland, and some parts of Germany have much experience in this regard; France and Britain, on the other hand, have suffered from ignoring the potential of local power. As always, there is no general blueprint for sustaining local communities, but some form of political identify, from revenue-raising powers to elected mayors, undoubtedly helps.

Stakeholder Involvement

Local power is but one factor in the wider concept of stakeholder economy. Some economists, notably in the United States, do not like the concept. They think that shareholders are the only stakeholders and that the actions of shareholders keep businesses on the straight and narrow. Leaving vast cultural differences—as well as the fact that most shareholders nowadays are institutions—aside, the point about stakeholders is that (contrary to shareholders) they cannot put their interest in companies up for sale. The workforce, the local community, banks, and even suppliers and buyers are, as it were, stuck with the companies to which they are committed. This can be regarded as an undesirable rigidity only in an inhuman world in which it does not matter whether firms are bought or sold, taken over, merged, extended, reduced, or closed as long as the shareholders get a maximum yield for their investment. In truth it does matter.

What is more, competitiveness is not increased by lack of commitment, especially if companies choose to go down the high-skill rather than the low-pay route. Reliability and predictability have their own value in business relations across the globe. Recognition and involvement of stakeholders is the practical answer. This can be brought about in many ways, from work councils for employees to the involvement of banks in investment decisions, from business participation in school boards to the activity of local chambers of commerce. Moreover, organized stakeholder relations are only a part of the story; it is attitudes that matter, an awareness of connections, and a commitment to concerns that, in the end, serve most people best. Civil society will be buttressed by this new commitment to the stability and security of communities.

A Positive Role for the State

Little has been said in this essay about the role of governments. Acceptance of the fact that in the global marketplace the actors are transnational companies, and a preference for the creative chaos of civil society, seem to leave governments out. Yet they clearly are not out of the picture. Nor are they simply the guardians of the rules of the game, as some liberal theorists would have it. At the very least, governments set the tone for the economy and for society more generally.

Beyond that, governments have a special responsibility for the public domain. Public services require by definition government involvement in funding and administration. Much depends on how such involvement is expressed, both in terms of the value placed on service as a human activity and in terms of the organization of public services. It is quite possible that some OECD countries have gone further in using the public service model than they can afford, or even than is good for the quality of service. It is also possible that in reacting to the experience, some have introduced so-called business values into the public sphere to a point at which both the intended service and the general readiness for commitment suffer. A new balance must be found. Health care is quite likely to provide the main example, given its importance for individuals, its cost, and its location on the borderline between global economic constraints and local or even national opportunities. Reassessing the role of the state is now more important than ever, when the authoritarian approach seems to be gaining favor in some circles.

This list leaves out many matters that need consideration. Above all it leaves undecided the critical question of the institutional—one might almost say, the geopolitical—response to the challenges of globalization.

Regional blocs of some sort may be where the world is headed. The cultural debate on Asian vs. European values, which underlies the project of universal development, points to the possible significance of such blocs. It is, however, a key part of European—or perhaps OECD—values never to lose sight of the truly universal nature of the project for the next decade. We are talking about prosperity for all, civil society everywhere, and political freedom wherever people live. This means that in the end we must be concerned not with privileged regions but with one world and its appropriate institutions.

II

RIGHTS AND RESPONSIBILITIES

9

Rights and Responsibilities

Dallin H. Oaks

I propose to speak about rights and responsibilities and their relation to law and the legal profession. I will suggest that we have tried to promote too many societal goals through rights and have given too little attention to responsibilities. After discussing some of the strengths and weaknesses of the rights approach and the responsibilities approach, I will suggest some ways that law and the legal profession can promote the voluntary fulfillment of responsibilities.

In the vocabulary of the law, a right signifies a claim enforceable by law. This kind of right cannot exist without law. In this sense, a person with a right can always compel action or inaction by someone. Lawyers thrive on rights. The enforcement of rights provides employment for the legal profession. In relation to rights, a lawyer functions as a popular champion—a gladiator or enforcer. No wonder lawyers like rights.

Responsibility connotes duty or obligation. In one sense, responsibility is just the duty side of someone else's right. That kind of responsibility is enforceable. I speak of a different kind. I refer to an obligation or duty that, as a practical matter, is not enforceable by legal processes. Such responsibilities include those that are owed to one's conscience and to one's God, and many that are owed to one's fellow beings, to one's community, and to a host of other groups. These kinds of responsibilities are the rent we pay for the privilege of living in a civilized society. They include such familiar virtues as tolerance, trustfulness, benevolence, patriotism, respect for human and civil rights, participation in the democratic process, and devotion to the common good.

There are important differences between rights and responsibilities. "Rights" is a lofty term, enshrined in the consciousness of Americans. The best known and most highly revered portion of our Constitution is the Bill of Rights. A person who can put needs or desires in terms of rights captures the high ground of moral discourse.

Responsibilities are necessities we respect, but we rarely stand up and cheer for them. In contrast to rights, which can be enforced, responsibilities can only be encouraged. Not many members of the legal profession like to preach or listen to a sermon on responsibilities. The best such sermon I have encountered is Elliot L. Richardson's speech at an American Bar Association meeting just after the Watergate tragedy, published in the *Buffalo Law Review.* He commented that "the drumbeat accompanying the steady forward march of rights during the past decade" has been so insistent "that the voice of obligations has scarcely been heard." He then gave this brilliant summary of the relationship between rights and responsibilities—or obligations, as he calls them:

> Obligations in any case, transcend rights: the full extent of my obligation to respect my neighbor's right to worship as he pleases cannot be spelled out in any court decree. Obligations embody a moral, and not merely a legal, command. And yet, it seems to me, we increasingly tend to behave as if the minimum required by the law were the maximum required of us. . . . In the case of civil rights, the law can enforce their observance but not their respect. Indeed, where there is true respect for other people—the awareness that each is a unique, sacrosanct individual equal in dignity to every other human being—there is an awareness of obligation which is higher and more sensitive than any requirement of the law.

The English legal philosopher A.J.M. Milne makes a strong case for the primacy of responsibilities as a rational matter. Indeed, he asserts in *Freedom and Rights* "that in any joint activity or enterprise, responsibility takes priority over justice." This is because justice is highly individual and takes no account of the common enterprise and the problems of a group as a whole. Since no group enterprise can prosper unless it is advanced by its participants, a member of a group "can never be entitled to insist on doing or having done anything which weakens or undermines the common enterprise." Consequently, Milne concludes that "while it is rational to be just, it is more rational to be responsible and to interpret justice from the wider perspective of responsibility. It is the higher of the two standards of rationality at the level of social morality. . . ." He later concedes that this test of rationality is an appropriate guide to policy only when a group is homogenous and fundamentally united on values.

Milne's insistence on the superior rationality of responsibility provides a corrective for current overemphasis on the enforcement of rights as a means of promoting worthy social goals. I am trying to contribute to that corrective in this lecture. Such an effort is needed. With the definition of new rights, we have tended to ignore old responsibilities. As a result, the responsibilities approach is now neglected and the rights approach is overburdened.

For example, modern legal discourse has much to say about the rights of children and little to say about the responsibilities of parents. I am dubious about how much we can really help children by defining and enforcing their rights. I think we may do more for children by trying to reinforce the responsibilities of parents, natural and adoptive, even when those responsibilities are not legally enforceable. We might start by reducing our enthusiasm for 'no-fault' divorces in the case of marriage partners who are parents. In many such cases we should encourage the parents to keep their marriage together for the sake of interests larger than their own rights, convenience, and desires.

There is a social interest as well as an individual interest in marriage. Professor Bruce C. Hafen expounds the constitutional implications of that fact in his brilliant article in the *Michigan Law Review*. I quote:

> [T]he individual and the social interests are so intertwined in family cases that meaningful analysis of the competing interests is rendered impossible by current civil liberties approaches that always give the individual interest a procedurally exalted priority over the social interest. Great need exists for a method of constitutional analysis that will allow for explicit consideration of the social interest in domestic relations.

Another example concerns current laws against discrimination. I wonder whether we can realistically expect to accomplish much more effective enforcement by more extensive use of legal process. Instead of exploring new ways to enforce non-discrimination *rights,* we might be more effective by exploring new ways to win hearts to the proposition that each of us has a *responsibility* to treat persons on their own merits as children of God, whatever their race, creed, color, sex, or national origin.

I seek to promote responsibilities as a worthy alternative to efforts to promote social goals exclusively through the enforcement of rights. By this means, I seek to contribute to a better balance between what John A. Howard, in his address "Education and Freedom," has called "the human impulse to pursue one's own course" and what he calls "the necessity to modify one's conduct according to the needs of the group."

An example will illustrate the legal profession's relative concern with rights and responsibilities. About twenty-five years ago, a group of distinguished lawyers under the leadership of Dean Jefferson B. Fordham of The University of Pennsylvania Law School proposed that the American Bar Association establish a Section of Individual Rights. While the ABA was studying the proposal, the proponents added the word "Responsibilities" as a political concession in the interest of balance. No one had any

objection to this addition, but, according to Dean Fordham, the proponents devoted very little thought to what the Section could do under the
heading of individual responsibilities because they were preoccupied with
individual rights.

Even after the name was changed, the formal proposal was devoted
exclusively to explaining the importance of individual rights. The only
mention of responsibilities pertained to how rights would be secured, as
in the statement, "[W]e of the organized Bar have a tremendous responsibility as such in the field of individual rights." The other submissions to
the Board of Governors and the discussion that led to approval in the
House of Delegates reflect the same emphasis. The new Section's statement of purpose is almost exclusively devoted to the promotion of individual rights. There are passing references to the "correlative nature of
both rights and duties" and to the "recognition and enforcement of individual rights and duties," but no explanation of responsibilities as a free-
standing concern of the Section.

I have been a member of the Section of Individual Rights and Responsibilities since its founding. I am proud of its impressive list of achievements
in respect to rights, but I am sorry that it has done little or nothing about
responsibility. To cite another measure, the *Index to Legal Periodicals*
does not index anything under the heading "responsibility" and this
heading is merely a cross-reference in the *Current Law Index* and the
Legal Resource Index.

One legal educator has suggested why the legal profession does well
with rights and poorly with responsibilities. I refer to Cornell Law School
Dean Roger C. Cramton's provocative essay, *The Ordinary Religion of
the Law School Classroom,* which discusses the fundamental value assumptions of legal education. One value assumption is what Dean Cramton calls the law school's "instrumental approach to law and lawyering."
Under this approach, law is nothing more than "an instrument for achieving social goals." The goals are, of course, those of the client. The lawyer
need not be concerned with selecting goals or with the value questions
associated with them, because the lawyer is simply the skilled craftsman
who works out the *means* by which predetermined goals are to be
achieved. This kind of focus on means gives primacy to a law student's
recognizing and enforcing *rights* and strips away his or her concern for
values and responsibilities. The result reminds me of the doctor who told
an educator that medical science would soon perfect a means to sever the
human mind from the rest of the body and, with appropriate support
systems, "keep the brain alive indefinitely with no connection to the
heart." As Cullen Murphy recounts it in his article in *Change,* the educator replied, "That's really not new, we've been doing that in our college
for years."

Although lawyers unquestionably relate more readily to rights than to responsibilities, there are at least two compelling reasons why the American Bar Association needs a Section that is actively involved with both. First, the enjoyment of rights cannot endure without the voluntary fulfillment of responsibilities. Morris Janowitz, in *The Reconstruction of Patriotism—Education for Civil Consciousness,* reminds us that a democracy needs patriotic citizens alive to their duties as well as to their rights. We need reminding. Our generation values the right to vote over the duty to vote, and the right to a trial by jury over the obligation to serve as a juror. No society is so secure that it can withstand continued demands for increases in citizen rights and decreases in citizen obligations.

Civic responsibilities, like honesty, self-reliance, participation in the democratic process, and devotion to the common good are basic to the governance and preservation of our country. Any person who is concerned with preserving the force of law and the enforceability of individual rights should be profoundly concerned about the civic responsibilities upon which the legal order is based. "It is widely recognized," Janowitz declares, "that effective citizenship rests on a rigorous and viable system of civic education which informs the individual of his civil rights and obligations." The Atlantic Council has given educators a proper reminder that they cannot afford to be neutral concerning such "civic values."

Another reason for lawyer concern with responsibilities is that some of the goals we seek to achieve by the enforcement of rights may be achieved more effectively and at lower cost by the encouragement of responsibilities. Rights necessarily entail public enforcement. Responsibilities as defined here require only private persuasion and initiative. As a private remedy, responsibilities are subject to all of the limitations of voluntary action. But rights are also limited. The enforcement of rights is limited by the resources of government and by the will of government officials. The effectiveness of a rights approach therefore will ebb and flow with the fashions of different administrations and with the fortunes of the economy and its impact on public budgets.

The rights approach also has some side effects that should be counted among its costs. The subject of side effects reminds us of what has been called the first rule of modern packaging: One bag of groceries, when consumed, will produce two bags of trash. One side effect of the rights approach concerns the person who must act to achieve the goal. This approach uses compulsion, whereas the responsibilities approach uses persuasion. Using coercion to enforce rights may embitter the person who is compelled to act. In contrast, the use of persuasion to fulfill responsibilities may ennoble the actor, who sees himself as having responded to a higher impulse.

In a 1978 article in *The Public Interest,* Nathan Glazer has noted other effects of the judicial enforcement of rights, such as in welfare programs and in educational, penal, and mental institutions. A rights approach reduces the power and authority and, correspondingly, the responsibilities of administrators. It gives primacy to the theoretical knowledge of the lawyer-enforcers over the practical or clinical knowledge of the defendant-administrators.

To cite another cost, the rights approach is subject to internal contradictions that may impair its utility. Individual rights and individual freedom are both worthy goals. Unfortunately, the more government seeks to enforce rights, the more it interferes with freedom. The more it assures one individual's freedom, the less it is able to enforce another individual's rights. This tendency is all too apparent in the current controversy over prayer in the public schools and in a multitude of circumstances involving laws against discrimination. The achievement of one goal for one person often impairs the goal of another. The responsibilities approach has no such contradiction since it subjects freedom to persuasion rather than coercion. Though less effective for achieving a goal in an individual case, the responsibilities approach inevitably imposes less cost on competing goals. The irony that one worthy goal can be attained only at the expense of another worthy goal reminds us of the aphorism, as it appears in P. Dickson's *The Official Rules,* that "[P]roblems worthy of attack prove their worth by hitting back."

What can the legal profession and the law do to encourage the voluntary fulfillment of responsibilities? How can we strengthn the common sense of obligation, so that voluntary action will become a more effective means of attaining worthy goals? The most powerful instrument of conversion to any proposition is the power of example. The legal profession's most powerful sermon on responsibilities is its voluntary compliance with obligations that are unenforceable, especially when a lawyer's fulfillment of public responsibility is done at the expense of his or her private interest. So it is with professional obligations to work pro bono publico on matters such as legal services for the indigent, the improvement of the profession, or the administration of justice. Many lawyers fulfill such responsibilities admirably, but their example goes unheeded because it is unnoticed. In an article published in *The California Law Review,* Notre Dame Dean Thomas L. Shaffer said of another effort to improve the profession, "Too many candles are under too many bushels." The profession should increase the power of its positive examples by making them more visible. And we should also recognize and work to overcome the fact that too many lawyers devote little or no time to their professional responsibilities. On this subject, too many lawyers fall back on the old maxim that "nothing is impossible if you don't have to do it yourself."

I believe that the public influence and standing of lawyers would also be enhanced if they were seen as professionals who would prevent or mediate controversies rather than concentrate on enforcing rights. In his 1984 annual message to the American Bar, Chief Justice Burger suggested that the entire legal profession "has become so mesmerized with the stimulation of the courtroom contest that we tend to forget that we ought to be healers—healers of conflicts." This plea—that lawyers be healers as well as warriors—is, in substance, a plea for lawyers to be concerned with their own and their client's responsibilities as well as their rights.

We can also encourage the responsibilities approach by strengthening the position of institutions that promote moral development, including the content and observance of responsibilities. I refer to family, to church, to educational institutions, to community organizations, and to educational media programs that are concerned with moral development. If we can improve the performance of these institutions, we will increase the extent to which worthy social goals can be attained through voluntary action.

I illustrate this point by reference to the role of the family. Recent legal and social developments have cast doubt on the value our society places on the family. At the same time, the family is generally conceded to be our most effective instrument for the development of moral values. In view of that fact, our laws and social priorities should be seeking to strengthen families, instead of contributing to or acquiescing in their decline. Professor Hafen argues that the value-instilling functions of the family are vital to our moral education. I quote him:

> The commitments of close kinship and marriage represent the last modern vestiges of Status as a source of duty. Much of what family members especially marital partners "owe" one another cannot be enforced in a court of law; yet the sense of family duty has an uncanny power to produce obedience to the unenforceable in ways that defy Adam Smith's assumption that self-interest is man's dominant value. In this way, the family tradition is a prerequisite to successful individual tradition. Through the commitments of marriage and kinship both children and parents experience the need for the value of authority, responsibility, and duty in their most pristine forms.

For the reasons cited by Hafen, any forces that weaken the family or the practice of individual responsibility in family relations diminish the sense of responsibility and the vital work ethic in our society as a whole. Conversely, by strengthening the family and its role as a teacher of moral values, we encourage the fulfillment of responsibilities in society as a whole. The legal profession should be enlisted, and the laws should be shaped to strengthen the family. We should do the same for other institutions and efforts that strengthen our common sense or responsibility, such as the teaching of civic virtues in schools, community organizations, and the media.

The content of the law can also encourage the fulfillment of responsibilities, even without making them legally enforceable. I cite two examples from United States Supreme Court opinions recognizing the constitutional rights of parents in respect to their offspring. The first, *Pierce v. Society of Sisters,* gives voice to the familiar concept that rights are accompanied by responsibilities: "[T]hose who nurture [a child] and direct his destiny have the right, coupled with the high duty, to recognize and prepare him for additional obligations." In this formation, the rights and responsibilities of parents seem to be equivalent, as if they existed together or not at all. More recently, in *Lehr v. Robertson,* The Supreme Court expressed a different idea, suggesting that, at least concerning the father of an illegitimate child, the existence of the right depends on the prior fulfillment of the responsibility. In rejecting an unwed father's claim to a constitutional parental right to a two-year-old child whom he had not reared or supported, the Court declared that "the rights of the parents are a counterpart of the responsibilities they have assumed." Making the existence of a right dependent on the prior fulfillment of a responsibility in some instances would surely contribute to restoring the status of responsibilities in our way of thinking.

We have tried throwing money at problems and throwing regulations at problems. I suggest we should now try throwing preachments at some problems. It may even be desirable to afflict responsible parties with the power of a good example. I suggest that it is time our leaders and our teachers turned down the volume on what we *deserve* and tried to tune us in to how we can *serve.* As President John F. Kennedy said in a famous line that is honored in memory but ignored in practice: "Ask not what your country can do for you. Ask what you can do for your country."

One of the glories of our free society is the way it protects the interests and worth of the individual against the overbearing preferences of the majority. None of us would have it otherwise. Yet there is truth in John Howard's observation that the "fixation in our thinking about the importance of rights, however well intentioned," is probably one of the reasons for the unsatisfactory performance of some organizations. Why? As Howard observes, "[t]he very concept of rights inclines people to focus on their own well-being and to demand their due, instead of focusing on the well-being of all humanity."

Dr. Ben C. Fisher, in his lecture "The Challenge of Secularism to Christian Education," is surely right in reminding us that our hope for a "unifying principle by which men might dwell together in peace" lies not in acts that affirm the autonomy of the individual but in acts that glorify the brotherhood of man. We cannot raise ourselves by adding to our inventory of individual rights. The fulfillment of individual rights depends on the fulfillment of individual and group responsibilities. If we are to raise ourselves and all mankind, we must strengthen our common commitment and service in the cause of responsibility for the welfare of others and the good of society at large.

10

"Absolute" Rights: Property and Privacy

Mary Ann Glendon

A man's home is his castle. That maxim (traditionally attributed to Sir Edward Coke) was Marvin Sokolow's defense when he was hauled into a Queens County court by his landlord after his downstairs neighbors had complained about the noise above them. They claimed that their peace and quiet were being destroyed by the Sokolow children, ages two and four. The landlord sought to evict the Sokolows on the basis of a clause in their lease providing that no tenant shall make, or permit any members of his family to make, "disturbing noises," or otherwise interfere with the "rights, comforts or convenience of other tenants."

In rendering his decision, Judge Daniel Fitzpatrick went right to the heart of the matter. "The difficulty of the situation here," he said, "is that Mr. Sokolow's castle is directly above the castle of Mr. Levin." The judge sympathized with the Levins, a middle-aged working couple who cherished a quiet evening at home after a grueling day in Manhattan. He was understanding about the Sokolows' predicament as well. The judge opined that "children and noise have been inseparable from a time whence the mind of man runneth not to the contrary." He took a dim view, however, of Mr. Sokolow's claim that "this is my home, and no one can tell me what to do in my own home." The judge pointed out the obvious fact that modern apartment-house living brings us into a kind of "auditory intimacy" with our neighbors. Apartment dwellers in urban America are in a different relation with each other than lords and ladies living in an age "when castles were remote, separated by broad moors, and when an intruder had to force moat and wall to make his presence felt within."

Though he rejected the notion that Mr. Sokolow had the right to do anything he wanted in his home, the judge did not accept the equally extreme position of the landlord and the Levins that, under the lease, *any* disturbing noise provided grounds for throwing a family out of its apartment. Neither the property interest claimed by the tenant nor the contract language relied on by the landlord could be treated as giving rise to absolute rights. Both were subject to evaluation in the light of reason, and in that light the judge found that the noise made by the Sokolows was neither excessive nor deliberate. Noting that the Christmas season was approaching ("a time for peace on earth to men of good will"), Judge Fitzpatrick announced his solution to the problem: "They are all nice people and a little mutual forbearance and understanding of each other's problems should resolve the issues to everyone's satisfaction."

Nice people all over the United States, like Mr. Sokolow and his neighbors, often deploy the rhetoric of rights as though they and their particular interests trumped everything else in sight. So far as property is concerned, few of us have not maintained at one time or another that "it's mine and I can do what I want with it"—whether the "it" is a flag, a backyard, or our own bodies. If a neighbor complains about our stereo, our noisy party, or our late-night piano practicing, our automatic reaction is apt to be that we have a right to do as we please in our own homes.

In these sorts of situations, like Mr. Sokolow, we often try to clinch the argument by appealing to the ancient property rights of Englishmen, and by invoking these rights in the strongest possible way. Yet this careless manner of speaking cannot be blamed on our English legal inheritance, nor even on the American frontier mentality. Neither in England, nor even in Canada (where conditions were historically more similar to ours) is the idea of property or the discourse of rights so extravagant.

The exaggerated absoluteness of our American rights dialect is all the more remarkable when we consider how little relation it bears to reality. There is a striking discrepancy, as the *Sokolow* case illustrates, between our tendency to state rights in a stark unlimited fashion and the common-sense restrictions that have to be placed on one person's rights when they collide with those of another person. On any given day, in courtrooms all over the nation, harried judges use a chastened, domesticated concept of rights when they handle garden-variety disputes. Landlords' contract rights do not extend to evicting tenants for any disturbing noise; but tenants cannot make as much noise as they wish in the enclosed space that belongs to them.

Property, historically the paradigmatic right in England and the United States, has always been subject to reasonable regulation, despite the excited rhetoric that often attends its assertion. How then can we explain the persistence of absoluteness in our property rhetoric, and in our rights rhetoric in general? To find the beginnings of an answer, we must go back to the first great "moment" in the history of rights, when property became the template from which other American rights were cut.

Property acquired its near-mythic status in our legal tradition, in part, because the language and images of John Locke played such a key role in American thinking about government. To show that property rights were "natural" and prepolitical, Locke postulated a "state of nature" in which "every Man has a Property in his own Person," and in the "Labour of his Body, and the Work of his Hands." When a man "mixed" his labor with something by removing it from its natural state, Locke argued, he made the acorn—or the apple, or the fish, or the deer—his property, "at least where there is enough, and as good left in common for others." The same was true, Locke said, for his appropriation of land by tilling, planting, and cultivating. After spinning this famous tale, Locke went on to his next proposition—namely, that the essential reason human beings submit to government is to safeguard their "property." In a move that was to have great significance for Americans, he announced that he would use the word *property* to designate, collectively, *Lives, Liberties, and Estates.* According to Locke, the preservation of property, in this capacious sense, is "the great and *chief end"* for which men come together into commonwealths.

Locke's property theory entered into a distinctively American property story. It was mediated and reinforced in this respect by William Blackstone's lectures on law that were much more widely read and consulted in the United States than in England. Whereas for Locke property had been a means to an end (constitutional monarchy), it was for Blackstone a good in itself. And what a good! "There is nothing which so generally strikes the imagination and engages the affections of mankind," Blackstone wrote, "as the right of property; or that sole and despotic dominion which one man claims and exercises over the external things of the world, in total exclusion of the rights of any other individual in the universe." In this apostrophe to property, we find no *ifs, ands,* or *buts.* A property owner, Blackstone tells us, rules over what he owns, not merely as a king, but as a despot. Property rights are absolute, individual, and exclusive.

The strong property-rights talk of Locke and Blackstone was in the air at the right moment to fuse with certain political factors that helped to make property the cardinal symbol of individual freedom and independence in the United States. Chief among these factors was the uneasiness felt by the framers of our Constitution concerning the potential threat posed to property rights by popularly elected legislatures. As Jennifer Nedelsky has put it, the Founding Fathers took property as the "central instance of rights at risk in a republic governed by popularly elected legislatures."

From the very beginning, the absoluteness of American property rhetoric promoted illusions and impeded clear thinking about property rights and rights in general. The framers' efforts to directly and indirectly protect the interests of property owners did not, and were not meant to, preclude considerable public regulation of property. The Fifth Amendment expressly recognized the federal eminent domain or "takings" power. In the 19th century, the takings authority was liberally invoked, especially at the state level, to promote economic development, and notably to aid railroads in acquiring land. Furthermore, traditional flexible legal limitations on the rights of owners (such as the broad principle that one should not use one's property to inflict harm on others) were routinely applied in the capillaries of private law.

Despite many limitations on property rights in practice, the paradigm of property as a specially important, and very strong, right continued to exert a powerful influence on the law. From the latter years of the 19th century up to the 1930s, the Supreme Court repeatedly invoked property rights (in an expansive form) to strike down a series of progressive laws that, taken together, might have served to ease the transition here, as similar legislation did in Europe, to a modern mixed economy and welfare state.

While the Supreme Court was thus according a high level of protection to the interest of owners of productive property, courts at the state level were diligently using the law of trespass to erect a protective shield around another kind of property: the family home. Legal historian Aviam Soifer has written that "the rhetoric surrounding legal doctrine from the middle to the end of the nineteenth century tended to reinforce [beliefs of most white male Americans that they were] entirely free to contract for, hold, and devise property as they saw fit."

The heyday of the absolutist property paradigm in American *law* came to an end more than 50 years ago when the Supreme Court, under heavy pressure to uphold the economic and labor legislation of the Depression and New Deal period, repudiated several earlier cases in which it had sacrificed progressive legislation on the altar of a broad notion of "property."

Nevertheless, the paradigm persists in popular discourse and still occasionally receives lip service even from the Supreme Court. The Court's now-common subordination of property to other rights makes it all the more remarkable that property continues to cast its spell and to entrance the minds of legal scholars as well as laypersons. In America, when we want to protect something, we try to get it characterized as a right. To a great extent, it is still the case that when we *especially* want to hold on to something (welfare benefits, a job) we try to get the object of our concern characterized as a property right.

There are Lockean echoes in the efforts of many persons on both the left and right of the American political spectrum to link "property" with liberty and independence. Each camp, of course, has a different understanding of property. Since land ownership can no longer serve to provide the majority of citizens with a protected sphere, jobs and their associated benefits (especially pensions) are the principal bases for whatever economic security most middle-class people possess. Welfare benefits have become the meager counterpart for a large part of the poverty-level population. As the importance of employment and social assistance for status and security came to be appreciated, Thurman Arnold, Charles Reich, and other legal theorists began to try to reconceptualize jobs and welfare as new forms of property. In the 1960s reformist lawyers launched a campaign to persuade the Supreme Court that welfare benefits, Social Security, and government jobs should be treated as property for constitutional purposes. This effort had only limited success in a series of cases that established that one could not be deprived of welfare benefits and certain other statutory entitlements without an opportunity to be heard. Conservative lawyers, for their part, have had equally modest success in trying to convince the Court that the takings clause should accord more protection to the type of property that interests them—the wealth produced by the free operation of market forces.

Much of the attention the Supreme Court once lavished on a broad concept of property, including the freedom of contract to acquire it, it now devotes to certain other liberties that it has designated as "fundamental." Remarkably, the property paradigm, including the old language of absoluteness, broods over this developing jurisprudence of personal rights. The new right of privacy, like the old right of property, has been imagined by the Court and lawyers generally as marking off a protected sphere that surrounds the individual. Indeed, much of the old property rhetoric has simply been transferred to this new area, and the Court has reexperienced familiar difficulties in working out principled limitations on a right that seemed for a time to have no bounds.

Though the "preferred" rights change from time to time, American legal discourse still promotes careless habits of speaking and thinking about them. Mr. Sokolow spoke for many of us when he claimed that no one could tell him what not to do in his own home. He must have known perfectly well that he could not print dollar bills, raise chickens, commit mayhem, or even have a late-night jam session in his Queens castle. When he spoke as he did, he was not speaking the language of the Founders. Still less was he speaking the language of the early colonists, who accepted much official (and officious) intrusion into their personal lives. The frontier offered more scope, perhaps, for the illusion of absoluteness, but the circumstances of those who opened the West were also conducive to a vivid awareness of human vulnerability and interdependence. Where then does this tough talk come from? Why do we Americans habitually exaggerate the absoluteness of the important rights we legitimately claim?

The starkness of some of the language in the Bill of Rights has helped to legitimate intemperate arguments made by those who have a particular attachment to one of the rights framed in such terms. But stark constitutional formulations alone cannot explain our fondness for absolute rights talk. For property rights appear in the Constitution only in an oblique and implicitly qualified form: "No person . . . shall be deprived of . . . property, without due process of law; nor shall private property be taken for public use, without just compensation." In the case of property, it was not the Fifth Amendment but the Lockean paradigm, cut loose from its context, that became part of our property story as well as of our rights discourse. Blackstone's flights of fancy about property as absolute dominion stuck in American legal imaginations more than his endless boring pages on what property owners really might and might not do with what they owned.

However, neither Lockean rights rhetoric as mediated by Blackstone nor constitutional language can account directly or fully for the illusions of absoluteness that are promoted by American rights talk. Another key piece of the puzzle is the pervasiveness of legal culture in American society. The strong language that Mr. Sokolow and the rest of us so frequently use is remarkably similar to a certain type of lawyers' talk that has increasingly passed into common parlance. A large legal profession, whose most visible members habitually engaged in strategic exaggeration and overstatement, was already having a substantial effect on popular discourse in Alexis de Tocqueville's day. The rank and file of the legal profession, it is true, spend the greater part of their professional lives in the humdrum business of adjusting one person's rights with another's. But we are not only the most lawyer-ridden society in the world, we are also the country in which the lawyer's role is the most adversarial. The careful, precise, professional jargon of the workaday office lawyer appears in popular discourse mainly in caricature ("whereas hereinbefore provided"), while the highly colored language of advocacy flows out to the larger society on the lips of orators, statesmen, and flamboyant courtroom performers. Courtroom law talk, it should be noted, rests on an assumption that is not generally to be commended in civil conversation: that when each of two disputants pushes his or her version of the facts and theory of law to the ethically permissible limit, some third party will be smart enough to figure out from the two distorted accounts what probably happened and how the law should be brought to bear on the case.

What's wrong with a little exaggeration, one might ask, especially in the furtherance of something as important as individual rights? If we always took care to note that rights are qualified, would we not risk eroding them altogether? Well, no. In the first place, no one can be an absolutist for *all* our constitutionally guaranteed rights, because taking any one of them as far as it can go soon brings it into conflict with another. Second, the rhetoric of absoluteness increases the likelihood of conflict and inhibits the sort of dialogue that is increasingly necessary in a pluralistic society. In the common enterprise of ordering our lives together, much depends on communication, reason giving, and mutual understanding. Even the legal profession is beginning to question the utility and legitimacy of the traditional strategic adoption of extreme positions by lawyers. Lawyers, as well as clients, are reckoning the social cost of our unique brand of adversary litigation. How ironic it would be if the American legal profession became more sophisticated about alternative methods of dispute resolution, yet the old hardball litigators' talk lingered on in the rest of society and continued to make it difficult for neighbors and family members to deal with the frictions inherent in everyday living.

Claims of absoluteness have the further ill effect of tending to downgrade rights into the mere expression of unbounded desires and wants. Excessively strong formulations express our most infantile instincts rather than our potential to be reasonable men and women. A country in which we can do "anything we want" is not a republic of free people attempting to order their lives together.

Absoluteness is an illusion, and hardly a harmless one. When we assert our rights to life, liberty, and property, we are expressing the reasonable hope that such things can be made more secure by law and politics. When we assert these rights in an absolute form, however, we are expressing infinite and impossible desires—to be completely free, to possess things totally, to be masters of our fate and captains of our souls. There is pathos as well as bravado in these attempts to deny the fragility and contingency of human existence, personal freedom, and the possession of worldly goods.

The exaggerated absoluteness of our American rights rhetoric is closely bound up with its other distinctive traits: a near-silence concerning responsibility and a tendency to envision the rights bearer as a lone autonomous individual. Thus, for example, those who contest the legitimacy of mandatory automobile seat-belt or motorcycle-helmet laws frequently say: "It's my body and I have the right to do as I please with it." In this shibboleth, the old horse of property is harnessed to the service of an unlimited liberty. The implication is that no one else is affected by the exercise of the individual right in question. This way of thinking and speaking ignores the fact that it is the rare driver, passenger, or biker who does not have a child, a spouse, or a parent. It glosses over the likelihood that if the rights bearer comes to grief, the cost of medical treatment, rehabilitation, and long-term care will be spread among many others.

Fortunately, Americans are both better and smarter than our current political rhetoric makes us out to be. Many signs are appearing on the political landscape of a significant constituency for candor, moderation, and adequate complexity in public deliberations. The appearance of *The Responsive Community,* and the interest it has already provoked, is one of them.

11

Permissible Paternalism: In Defense of the Nanny State

Robert E. Goodin

Paternalism is desperately out of fashion. Nowadays notions of "children's rights" severely limit what even parents may do to their own offspring, in their children's interests but against their will. What public officials may properly do to adult citizens, in their interests but against their will, is presumably even more tightly circumscribed. So the project I have set for myself—carving out a substantial sphere of morally permissible paternalism—might seem simply preposterous in present political and philosophical circumstances.

Here I shall say no more about the paternalism of parents toward their own children. My focus will instead be upon ways in which certain public policies designed to promote people's interests might be morally justifiable even if those people were themselves opposed to such policies. Neither shall I say much more about notions of rights. But in focusing upon people's interests rather than upon their rights, I shall arguably be sticking closely to the sorts of concerns that motivate rights theorists. Of course, what it is to have a right is itself philosophically disputed, and on at least one account (the so-called "interest theory") to have a right is nothing more than to have a legally protected interest. But on the rival account (the so-called "choice theory") the whole point of rights is to have a legally protected choice. There, the point of having a right is that *your choice in the matter will be respected, even if that choice actually runs contrary to your own best interests.* It is that understanding of rights which leads us to suppose that paternalism and rights are necessarily at odds, and there are strict limits on the extent to which we might reconcile the two positions. Still, there is some substantial scope for compromise between them.

Those theorists who see rights as protecting people's choices rather than promoting their interests would be most at odds with paternalists who were proposing to impose upon people what is judged to be *objectively* good for them. That is to say, they would be most at odds if paternalists were proposing to impose upon people outcomes which are judged to be good for those people, whether or not there were any grounds for that conclusion in those people's own subjective judgments of their own good.

Rights theorists and paternalists would still be at odds, but less so, if paternalists refrained from talking about interests in so starkly objective a way. Then, just as rights command respect for people's choices, so too would paternalists be insisting that we respect choices that people themselves have or would have made. The two are not quite the same, to be sure, but they are much more nearly the same than the ordinary contrast between paternalists and rights theorists would seem to suggest.

That is precisely the sort of conciliatory gesture that I shall here be proposing. In paternalistically justifying some course of action on the grounds that it is in someone's interests, I shall always be searching for some warrant in that person's own value judgments for saying that it is in that person's interests.

"Some warrant" is a loose constraint, to be sure. Occasionally will we find genuine cases of what philosophers call "weakness of will": people being possessed of a powerful, conscious present desire to do something that they nonetheless just cannot bring themselves to do. Then public policy forcing them to realize their own desire, though arguably paternalistic, is transparently justifiable even in terms of people's own subjective values. More often, though, the subjective value to which we are appealing is one which is present only in an inchoate form, or will only arise later, or can be appreciated only in retrospect.

Paternalism is clearly paternalistic in imposing those more weakly-held subjective values upon people in preference to their more strongly held ones. But, equally clearly, it is less offensively paternalism thanks to this crucial fact: at least it deals strictly in terms of values that are or will be subjectively present, at some point or another and to some extent or another, in the person concerned.

THE SCOPE OF PATERNALISM

When we are talking about public policies (and maybe even when we are talking of private, familial relations), paternalism surely can only be justified for the "big decisions" in people's lives. No one, except possibly parents and perhaps not even they, would propose to stop you from buying candy bars on a whim, under the influence of seductive advertising and at some marginal cost to your dental health.

So far as public policy is concerned, certainly, to be a fitting subject for public paternalism, a decision must first of all involve high stakes. Life-and-death issues most conspicuously qualify. But so do ones that substantially shape your subsequent life prospects. Deciding to drop out of school or to begin taking drugs involves high stakes of roughly that sort. If the decision is also substantially irreversible—returning to school is unlikely, the drug is addictive—then that further bolsters the case for paternalistic intervention.

The point in both cases is that people would not have a chance to benefit by learning from their mistakes. If the stakes are so high that losing the gamble once will kill you, then there is no opportunity for subsequent learning. Similarly, if the decision is irreversible, you might know better next time but be unable to benefit from your new wisdom.

EVALUATING PREFERENCES

The case of paternalism, as I have cast it, is that public officials might better respect your own preferences than you would have done through your own actions. That is to say that public officials are engaged in evaluating your surface preferences, judging them according to some standard of your own deeper preferences.

Public officials should refrain from paternalistic interference and allow you to act without state interference, only if they are convinced that you are acting on:

- relevant preferences;
- settled preferences;
- preferred preferences; and, perhaps,
- your own preferences.

In what follows, I shall consider each of those requirements in turn. My running example will be the problem of smoking and policies to control it. Nothing turns on the peculiarities of that example, though. There are many others like it in relevant respects.

It often helps, in arguments like this, to apply generalities to particular cases. So in what follows I shall further focus in on the case of one particular smoker, Rose Cipollone. Her situation is nowise unique—in all the respects that matter here, she might be considered the prototypical smoker. All that makes her case special is that she—or, more precisely, her heir—was the first to win a court case against the tobacco companies whose products killed her.

In summarizing the evidence presented at that trial, the judge described the facts of the case as follows:

> Rose . . . Cipollone . . . began to smoke at age 16, . . . while she was still in high school. She testified that she began to smoke because she saw people smoking in the movies, in advertisements, and looked upon it as something "cool, glamorous and grown-up" to do. She began smoking Chesterfields . . . primarily because of advertising of "pretty girls and movie stars," and because Chesterfields were described . . . as "mild." . . .

> Mrs. Cipollone attempted to quit smoking while pregnant with her first child . . . , but even then she would sneak cigarettes. While she was in labor she smoked an entire pack of cigarettes, provided to her at her request by her doctor, and after the birth . . . she resumed smoking. She smoked a minimum of a pack a day and as much as two packs a day.

> In 1955, she switched . . . to L&M cigarettes . . . because . . . she believed that the filter would trap whatever was "bad" for her in cigarette smoking. She relied upon advertisements which supported that contention. She . . . switched to Virginia Slims . . . because the cigarettes were glamorous and long, and were associated with beautiful women—and the liberated woman. . . .

> Because she developed a smoker's cough and heard reports that smoking caused cancer, she tried to cut down her smoking. These attempts were unsuccessful . . .

> Mrs. Cipollone switched to lower tar and nicotine cigarettes based upon advertising from which she concluded that those cigarettes were safe or safer . . . [and] upon the recommendation of her family physician. In 1981 her cancer was diagnosed, and even though her doctors advised her to stop she was unable to do so. She even told her doctors and her husband that she had quit when she had not, and she continued to smoke until June of 1982 when her lung was removed. Even thereafter she smoked occasionally—in hiding. She stopped smoking in 1983 when her cancer had metasized and she was diagnosed as fatally ill.

This sad history contains many of the features that I shall be arguing makes paternalism most permissible.

RELEVANT PREFERENCES

The case against paternalism consists in the simple proposition that, morally, we ought to respect people's own choices in matters that affect themselves and *by and large only themselves.* But there are many questions we first might legitimately ask about those preferences, without in any way questioning this fundamental principle of respecting people's autonomy.

One is simply whether the preferences in play are genuinely relevant to the decision at hand. Often they are not. Laymen often make purely factual mistakes in their means-ends reasoning. They think—or, indeed, as in the case of Rose Cipollone, are led by false advertising to suppose—that an activity is safe when it is not. They think that an activity like smoking is glamorous, when the true fact of the matter is that smoking may well cause circulatory problems requiring the distinctly unglamorous amputation of an arm or leg.

When people make purely factual mistakes like that, we might legitimately override their surface preferences—the preference to smoke—in the name of their own deeper preferences—to stay alive and intact. Public policies designed to prevent youngsters from taking up smoking when they want to, or to make it more expensive or inconvenient for existing smokers to continue smoking when they want to may be paternalistic in the sense of running contrary to their own manifest choices in the matter. But this overriding of their choices is grounded in terms of their own deeper preferences, so such paternalism would be minimally offensive from a moral point of view.

SETTLED PREFERENCES

We might ask, further, whether the preferences being manifested are "settled" preferences or whether they are merely transitory phases people are going through. It may be morally permissible to let people commit euthanasia voluntarily, if we are sure they really want to die. But if we think that they might subsequently have changed their minds, then we have good grounds for supposing that we should stop them.

The same may well be true with smoking policy. While Rose Cipollone thought smoking was both glamorous and safe, youngsters beginning to smoke today typically know better. Many of them still say that they would prefer a shorter but more glamorous life, and that they are therefore more than happy to accept the risks that smoking entails. Say what they may at age sixteen, though, we cannot help supposing that they will think differently when pigeons eventually come home to roost. The risk-courting preferences of youth are a characteristic product of a peculiarly daredevil phase that virtually all of them will, like their predecessors, almost certainly outgrow.

Insofar as people's preferences are not settled—insofar as they choose one option now, yet at some later time wish that they had chosen another—we have another ground for permissible paternalism. Policymakers dedicated to respecting people's own choices have, in effect, two of the person's own choices to choose between. How such conflicts should be settled is hard to say. We might weigh the strength or duration of the preferences, how well they fit with the person's other preferences, and so on.

Whatever else we do, though, we clearly ought not privilege one preference over another just because it got there first. Morally, it is permissible for policymakers to ignore one of a person's present preferences (to smoke, for example) in deference to another that is virtually certain to emerge later (as was Rose Cipollone's wish to live, once she had cancer).

PREFERRED PREFERENCES

A third case for permissible paternalism turns on the observation that people not only have multiple and conflicting preferences but also preferences for preferences. Rose Cipollone wanted to smoke, but judging from her frequent (albeit failed) attempts to quit, she also wanted not to want to smoke. In this respect, it might be said, Rose Cipollone's history is representative of smokers more generally. The U.S. Surgeon General reports that some ninety percent of regular smokers have tried and failed to quit. That recidivism rate has led the World Health Organization to rank nicotine as an addictive substance on a par with heroin itself.

That classification is richly confirmed by the stories that smokers themselves tell about their failed attempts to quit. Rose Cipollone tried to quit while pregnant, only to end up smoking an entire pack in the delivery room. She tried to quit once her cancer was diagnosed, and once again after her lung was taken out, even then only to end up sneaking an occasional smoke.

In cases like this—in which people want to stop some activity, try to stop it, but find that they cannot stop—public policy that helps people implement their own preferred preference can hardly be said to be paternalistic in any morally offensive respect. It overrides people's preferences, to be sure. But the preferences which it overrides are ones which people themselves wish they did not have.

The preferences which it respects—the preference to stop smoking, like preferences of reformed alcoholics to stay off drink, or of the obese to lose weight—are, in contrast, preferences that the people concerned themselves prefer. They would themselves rank those preferences above their own occasional inclinations to backslide. In helping them to implement their own preferred preferences, we are only respecting people's own priorities.

YOUR OWN PREFERENCES

Finally, before automatically respecting people's choices, we ought to make sure that they are really their own choices. We respect people's choices because in that way we manifest respect for them as persons. But if the choices in question were literally someone else's—the results of a post-hypnotic suggestion, for example—then clearly there that logic would provide no reason for our respecting those preferences.

Some people say that the effects of advertising are rather like that. No doubt there is a certain informational content to advertising. But that is not all there is in it. When Rose Cipollone read the tar and nicotine content in advertisements, what she was getting was information. What she was getting when looking at the accompanying pictures of movie stars and glamorous, liberated women was something else altogether.

Using the power of subliminal suggestion, advertising implants preferences in people in a way that largely or wholly by-passes their judgment. Insofar as it does so, the resulting preferences are not authentically that person's own. In consequence, those *implanted preferences* are not entitled to the respect that is rightly reserved for a person's authentic preferences.

Such thoughts might lead some to say that we should therefore ignore altogether advertising-induced preferences in framing our public policy. I demur. There is just too much force in the rejoinder that "wherever those preferences came from in the first instance, they are mine now." If we want our policies to respect people by, among other things, respecting their preferences, then we will have to respect all of those preferences with which people now associate themselves.

Even admitting the force of that rejoinder, though, there is much that still might be done to curb the preference-shaping activities of, for example, the tobacco industry. Even those who say, "They're my preferences now" would presumably have preferred, ahead of time, to make up their own minds in the matter. So there we have a case, couched in terms of people's own (past) preferences, for severely restricting the advertising and promotion of products—especially ones which people will later regret having grown to like, but which they will later be unable to resist.

CONCLUSION

What, in practical policy terms, follows from all that? Well, in the case of smoking which has served as my running example, we might ban the sale of tobacco altogether or turn it into a drug available only by prescription to registered users. Or, less dramatically, we might make cigarettes difficult and expensive to obtain—especially for youngsters whose purchases are particularly price-sensitive. We might ban all promotional advertising of tobacco products, designed as it is to attract new users. We might prohibit smoking in all offices, restaurants, and other public places, thus making it harder for smokers to find a place to partake and providing a further inducement for them to quit.

All of those policies would be good for smokers themselves. They would enjoy a longer life expectancy and a higher quality of life if they stopped smoking. But that is to talk the language of interests rather than rights and choices. In those latter terms, all those policies clearly go against smokers' manifest preferences, in one sense or another. Smokers want to keep smoking. They do not want to pay more or drive further to get their cigarettes. They want to be able to take comfort in advertisements constantly telling them how glamorous their smoking is.

In other more important senses, though, such policies can be justified even in terms of the preferences of smokers themselves. They do not want to die, as a quarter of them eventually will (and ten to fifteen years before their time) of smoking-related diseases; it is only false beliefs or wishful thinking that make smokers think that continued smoking is consistent with the desire not to avoid a premature death. At the moment, they may think that the benefits of smoking outweigh the costs, but they will almost certainly revise that view once those costs are eventually sheeted home. The vast majority of smokers would like to stop smoking but, being addicted, find it very hard now to do so.

Like Rose Cipollone, certainly in her dying days and intermittently even from her early adulthood, most smokers themselves would say that they would have been better off never starting. Many even agree that they would welcome anything (like a workplace ban on smoking) that might now make them stop. Given the internally conflicting preference here in play, smokers also harbor at one and the same time preferences pointing in the opposite direction; that is what might make helping them to stop seem unacceptably paternalistic. But in terms of other of their preferences—and ones that deserve clear precedence, at that—doing so is perfectly well warranted.

Smoking is unusual, perhaps, in presenting a case for permissible paternalism on all four of the fronts here canvassed. Most activities might qualify under only one or two of the headings. However, that may well be enough. My point here is not that paternalism is always permissible but merely that it may always be.

In the discourse of liberal democracies, the charge of paternalism is typically taken to be a knock-down objection to any policy. If I am right, that knee-jerk response is wrong. When confronted with the charge of paternalism, it should always be open to us to say, "Sure, this proposal is paternalistic—but is the paternalism in view permissible or impermissible, good or bad?" Thinking along the lines sketched here, I think we will find that paternalism proves perfectly defensible much more often than not.

12

Finding a Place for Community in the First Amendment

Roger L. Conner

Does the First Amendment permit communities to ban loud and unseemly noises in downtown streets? Or must free speech be protected within a public forum, regardless of the volume and no matter the harm done to the community? This legal question frames a bitter controversy between street preachers and downtown merchants in a small South Carolina town, and unless cooler heads prevail, the courts will be forced to choose between the right of merchants to be free of unwanted noise and the right of preachers to deliver the Word of God in their chosen manner. But in the heat of the "either/or" debate, both sides have neglected the needs of a healthy and unpolarized community: tolerance for others, and public spaces to foster such tolerance.

The setting is Beaufort, South Carolina, a quiet coastal town of 13,000. Beaufort's history dates back to Spanish exploration in 1520 and attempted settlements by French Huguenots in 1562. The town was spared during Sherman's March during the Civil War thanks to early occupation by Union troops, and its collection of antebellum homes and storefronts has been designated a national historic landmark. It has a history of tolerance and cooperation. The local synagogue dates back to 1908. The rabbi and Catholic priests are full partners in an ecumenical ministry to the local hospital and nearby Paris Island military base. Beaufort's tranquil setting has been used as a venue for such movies as *The Big Chill*, *The Prince of Tides*, and *The Great Santini*.

The downtown business districts of most small American towns are dilapidated and virtually abandoned, victims of strip shopping centers and huge discount stores built on the edges of town. Beaufort is an exception, thanks in large part to a recent, multi-million dollar reinvestment campaign spearheaded by local residents. Thirty-seven buildings and storefronts have been renovated and 45 new shops opened in the past five years alone. Downtown is, once again, a meeting ground for the residents of Beaufort, especially on Saturday when the farmer's market operates.

Beaufort is connected to another bit of southern history: itinerant street preachers. The Reverend Karl Baker, a local businessman and preacher, runs a school for street preachers. The Reverend Mr. Baker specializes in the craft of shouting. He teaches his students to pick an object about 75 feet away and aim their voices right at it. To project, speak from the diaphragm, not the throat; slow the words down, enunciate. "You must be loud to reach people," he says.

As business in downtown Beaufort began to pick up, the Reverend Mr. Baker and his students began to turn up every Saturday in considerable numbers to thunder messages like "Unless you're born in God's spirit and washed in Christ's blood, you'll bust hell wide open." Their most intense rhetoric was saved for women in slacks and shorts ("whores and fornicators"), "wicked merchants" (who "would rather you go to hell than give your life to Jesus"), Catholic priests and rabbis ("false prophets"), and Christmas shoppers.

THE COMMUNITY'S INTERESTS

The central business district, located on Bay Street, is a three-block-long, crowded lane of two-story buildings which create something of a natural amphitheatre. A practiced orator with a loud voice can effectively occupy the entire downtown commercial district. When the preachers are in full voice, asserts Billy Rhett, owner of a local art gallery, it is not possible to carry on a conversation, and customers flee out the back door rather than put up with the constant din. Rhett and other store owners feel their very economic survival is at stake, since "local customers won't come downtown on Saturdays now."

Under a barrage of complaints from merchants, residents, and even the local clergy, city officials worked out a compromise: no more than one hour of preaching each Saturday, rotating weekly between six locations. Tensions continued to build, however. Some residents gathered to taunt and yell back. The ministers were denied access to a favored grassy strip by its owner, one of the objecting merchants. The Reverend Mr. Baker was sprayed with a garden hose.

On August 31, 1991, Mr. Baker descended on Beaufort with more than twenty preachers gathered from all over the state, who held forth for more than three hours in a single location (near the entrances of two stores whose owners were denounced by name in the sermons). Emotions ran so high that the state ACLU director called it a "potentially violent situation" and death threats were reported.

By happenstance, a short news article from Maryland came to the attention of the Beaufort city attorney at about this time. It described a Maryland Supreme Court decision upholding a state law aimed at anti-abortion street preachers in Hagerstown, Maryland. Six weeks later, the City Council adopted an identical ordinance, which made it illegal to "willfully" make "unseemly and loud" noises in public places.

At this stage, the ministers went to state ACLU director Steven Bates, who advised them that the controversy should be settled in court rather than through further negotiation with the powers-that-be in Beaufort. The court "is a more appropriate avenue for addressing the disputes of this nature than for the city to apply local law," he wrote. However, he continued, because the ordinance appeared to be neutral on its face, it would be necessary for the preachers to provoke actual arrests, in order to create the basis for a court challenge. The Reverend Mr. Baker announced the contents of the letter to the local newspaper, explaining that Bates was "telling us to go ahead and test it, and that's what we're going to do."

Hoping to defuse the controversy, the police chief paid a call on The Reverend Mr. Baker, offering to issue two warnings so that any potential violator could lower his voice and avoid arrest. Mr. Baker responded that he "must challenge the ordinance . . . be sure the handcuffs are put on correctly."

What followed was a game of tit for tat. Preachers who violated the ordinance were initially fined. When they persisted, the local judge threatened jail. Then the preachers refused to pay the nominal fines, effectively forcing the judge's hand. Once consigned to jail, Mr. Baker refused to work as required by local law and was briefly transferred to the state prison as punishment.

Orin Briggs, the lawyer for the defendants, offered a compromise to be mediated by the judge to halt the escalation. The preachers would voluntarily limit the duration of their preaching if the city would stop all arrests. However, on discovering that mediation could lead to a "permanent solution," which would prevent "a ruling on whether [the noise ordinance] is constitutional," the ministers bailed out and called Patrick Flynn, Clinical Law Professor at the University of South Carolina Law School and board member of the state ACLU. Flynn agreed to take the case, to the U.S. Supreme Court if necessary. The Beaufort ministers then fired Briggs, went back to jail, and a legal fight to the finish was on.

The South Carolina Supreme Court recently affirmed the criminal convictions, and an appeal to the U.S. Supreme Court is planned. The ministers have also asked a federal district court judge to intervene with a civil suit asking for damages against the merchants for "conspiracy" to violate the preachers' civil rights, and an injunction against the city.

THE RIGHT TO PREACH LOUDLY

The preachers see this as a simple case. "It is our First Amendment right" to preach loudly, said one preacher, regardless of the effects on the merchants, other residents, or the economic viability of the downtown area. They see street preaching as an anti-establishment tradition with deep American roots—Roger Williams, the founder of Rhode Island, was imprisoned for his passionate street sermons which mixed religion and politics. One defendant, Thomas Anderson, conceded that the noise he was making was so loud that nearby businesses could have considered it "too much to take." Another testified that it would be within his rights to "stand on a public sidewalk immediately adjacent to a church, every Sunday [morning] and shout at top volume," even if he created "disruption to the church."

In its briefs, the city countered with the right of store owners to be spared unreasonably loud speech on the street in front of their shops, based on Supreme Court rulings that hold that the First Amendment collides with the right of privacy when the speech is inescapable. The "captive audience" doctrine, as it is known, has been cited to uphold, for example ordinances which prohibit demonstrations in front of homes in residential neighborhoods.

The ministers answered that a commercial area is a "public forum." "The First Amendment requires that society tolerate some inconvenience in public forums to protect the values of free expression." And "the interests of downtown merchants in their businesses which are by choice located in a public forum and invite the public to come cannot be equated with the privacy rights of individuals in their homes in residential neighborhoods."

Even if the loud speech is held to invade the privacy interests of the merchants, the ministers' brief continued, an "extreme invasion" of the privacy interests is required to tip the balance against speech. "It must 'rise far above public inconvenience, annoyance or unrest' " (citing *Edwards vs. South Carolina*, 372 U.S. 229 [1963]) to the level that "substantial privacy interests are being invaded in an essentially intolerable manner." Mere assertions that the loud preaching "affected their (merchants') concentration" or "affected their ability to carry on 'normal' conversation" is not "a sufficient invasion of the merchants' privacy interests to justify abridging plaintiffs' free speech rights."

The vagueness of the prohibition on "willfully" making "unseemly and loud" noises invites selective enforcement, the ministers added. The annual downtown Christmas parade makes more noise than all of them combined, yet no one called the police. (Would it make a difference if the city had passed the ordinance in response to noisy civil rights protesters rather than street preachers?)

A PLACE FOR RESPONSIBILITY?

This controversy illustrates some of the problems associated with the contemporary rhetoric of rights in the United States. Newspaper and TV reporters have produced dozens of articles and shows since the controversy erupted. Everyone saw the clash of the preachers' First Amendment rights versus the privacy rights of the merchants, but was blind to the failures of responsibility on both sides.

How common it has become in America for people to exercise their rights to the absolute limit, without regard for the effect on others. Yet, how can we hope to function in a multi-racial, multi-ethnic America without a more generous dose of mutual respect and self-restraint? And how can we change the prevailing attitudes until, when faced with self-centered behavior, we respond with the language of responsibility?

The Beaufort ministers earnestly believe that they have been directed by God to disturb people. Yet, a bit of civility is not inconsistent with their calling. In a conversation after a CNN interview, one of the ministers explained to me how he had avoided conflicts in communities outside Beaufort: not preaching in a single location for more than 15 or 20 minutes, never blocking an entrance, asking permission to use private property, and shifting to a different storefront each time in business districts which he visited frequently.

On three separate occasions, the ministers found common ground with the merchants, which permitted high-volume preaching at limited times and places, only to renounce the agreement in favor of vindicating their rights in court. Rather than strike a compromise that would allow for restricted preaching, the ministers pushed for an all-or-nothing decision.

Did the city live up to its responsibilities? Responsive communities are characterized by diversity and tolerance, being especially careful to avoid symbolic acts which have the effect of telling minority factions "you are not a part." The preachers believe, rightly or wrongly, that downtown merchants encouraged hecklers and were directly responsible for the infamous garden hose incident. While the merchants contend that it is in the best interests of the city to provide a downtown area attractive to shoppers, the preachers point out it is also in the city's best interests to ensure a cooperative and inclusive atmosphere. The ordinance adopted by the city council—a total ban—reinforced bitter feelings among the preachers. "They have a country club mentality and they are redoing the town and its image," Mr. Baker said bitterly. "They despise some of us rednecked country preachers and don't want to include us in that."

The strategy of forcing disputes into court by provocative tactics and extreme rights assertions is not without cost. Setting aside for a moment the waste of money and civic energy, Beaufort's proud tradition of tolerance has been strained beyond the breaking point.

Today, in place of tolerance, there is fear; in place of generosity there is anger. A boycott of all the pay phones—owned by Mr. Baker—is in effect. Catholics are wondering how many of their neighbors believe in the Papist conspiracies being screamed about from the streets. Jews are resentful that one of the two shops which has been targeted every week for nine months is Lipsitz's, the only Jewish family business in the downtown area. The street preachers feel that the police and city council are doing the bidding of wealthy, society types who view the "little people" with disdain.

As framed before the courts, the legal arguments will turn on a choice between the privacy rights of merchants and the speech rights of the preachers. While the lawyers are enthusiastically adding to the edifice of First Amendment law, something different is going on in Beaufort. A rare community asset—a downtown which invites frequent encounters from which feelings of civic friendship and human connection can grow—has become a powerful symbol of division.

13

Aids Prevention vs. Cultural Sensitivity

Ronald Bayer

It has become a matter of conventional wisdom, repeated in almost talismanic fashion, that acquired immunodeficiency syndrome (AIDS) prevention programs should be culturally sensitive—sensitive to the particular values of a particular community. It is time to examine the validity of this received wisdom and to make clear that the call for cultural sensitivity entails a number of perspectives, some of which are obvious and uncontroversial, some of which are not so obvious, and some of which are simply false. In the end it will be clear that the most demanding conception of cultural sensitivity is incompatible with the goals of AIDS prevention.

Two arguments are typically made on behalf of the centrality of cultural sensitivity. The first is pragmatic and instrumental; the second is ethical and political.

The pragmatic-instrumental claim is expressed forthrightly by Collins Airhihenbuwa and colleagues:

> The cultural pluralism prevalent in the United States warrants the development of culturally appropriate HIV/AIDS education programs that are sensitive to the cultural values and beliefs of different ethnic groups. Cultural diversity is evident in the different languages, cultural practices, and beliefs regarding illness and health seeking behavior. Thus it may be more effective to develop and implement health education programs that are adapted to a community's existing practices and beliefs rather than try to change them to fit the program.

In short, AIDS prevention efforts that are not culturally sensitive will be ineffective. They will fail to promote, support, and sustain the behav-

ioral modifications that are the *sine qua non* of AIDS prevention. They
will fail because they will not reach their intended audience, will not be
understood by those who are reached, and will not be accepted by those
who understand. They may, indeed, provoke outright opposition.

The second claim on behalf of cultural sensitivity, less often made explicitly but nevertheless of central importance, is ethical and political. The
basic principle of ethics—that individuals should be treated with respect
and that their dignity should not be violated—is by extension applied to
cultures. Cultural sensitivity is thus required of us by the ethics of pluralism. A failure to respect the cultural integrity of others is almost always
characterized as an imposition of the values of the dominant and powerful
on the subordinate and marginal. Writing about the "politics of recognition," Charles Taylor has captured the essence of this claim: "Just as all
must have equal civil rights, and equal voting rights, regardless of race and
culture, so all should enjoy the presumption that their traditional culture
has value." And so the insistence on cultural sensitivity is premised on
an egalitarian ethos, on the ethos that should inspire public policy in a
multicultural democratic society.

Harlon Dalton employs the concept of neocolonialism to oppose those
who act without regard to cultural sensitivity: "When we want help white
America is nowhere to be found. When, however, *you* decided that we
need help you are there in a flash, solution in hand. You then seek to
impose that solution on us, without seeking our views, hearing our experiences or taking account of our needs and desires."

What, then, is meant by cultural sensitivity? It is important to distinguish three very different ways in which the concept is used: the semantic,
the instrumental, and the principled. The first two uses are rooted in the
pragmatic arguments, the last in ethical and political ones.

AN AWARENESS OF LANGUAGE

The semantic conception of cultural sensitivity underscores the importance of conveying AIDS prevention messages in a form that makes the
content understandable—that uses the linguistic and stylistic characteristics of those to whom the message is addressed. Failure to understand the
complex ways in which language and culture filter prevention messages is
a recipe for failure in AIDS prevention.

It is important to understand the ways in which language is used not
only because in different cultures different words may be used to describe
the same behaviors or things, but because the same words may have different meanings. As Vickie Mays has written, "For gay men this has meant
the extensive formulation of 'safer sex' interactions in which low-risk sex-

ual behaviors are promoted using vernacular common to the gay male community."

According to the semantic conception of cultural sensitivity, then, what is demanded is that the universalistic and uniform messages of AIDS prevention be packaged in a way that is appropriate for diverse target audiences. This conception of cultural sensitivity raises few problems from the perspective of public health. Indeed, it is the decade-long efforts on the part of those who oppose the use of "street language" that exemplify the hobbling of AIDS prevention messages in the United States. The imposition of restraints on the Centers for Disease Control and Prevention by Congress and the White House and the subsequent imposition of restraints on local and community AIDS prevention programs have represented a profound burden on the public health mission in the face of AIDS.

INSTRUMENTAL CONCERNS

The second conception of cultural sensitivity is instrumental. This conception underscores the importance of understanding the cultural context of sexual, drug-using, and procreative behavior, with the goal being to facilitate the transformations of those behavioral norms that foster the transmission of human immunodeficiency virus (HIV) infection.

This conception of cultural sensitivity finds repeated expression in the literature on women and ethnic minorities. In writing about African-American female adolescents, Gina Wingood and Ralph DiClemente note the importance of a research agenda that "can identify the cultural, gender, and psychosocial influences within the African American community [because] understanding, modifying and harnessing these forces can transform them [into] powerful agents toward reducing the risks of HIV infection." Janet McGrath and her colleagues, focusing on Ugandan women, note, "Because Baganda women have limited ability to reduce their risk of HIV infection due to prevailing cultural values with respect to sexual behavior, policymakers are faced with the dilemma of how to alter the sexual norms and values of a cultural group." In discussing African-American men, Larry Icard and his colleagues speak of "socio-politically appropriate and culturally sensitive interventions that can overcome" the cultural barriers to AIDS prevention. Finally, and more bluntly, Merrill Singer writes of "us[ing] culture therapeutically to both reach participants and to assist them in making behavioral or other changes" and of "attempting to redefine certain cultural values."

Not only is the instrumental conception of cultural sensitivity compatible with the goals of public health, it seeks to advance them with a solid grounding in cultural studies and analysis. In so doing, it reflects the insights of "social marketing," which has sought to harness the understanding derived from commercial advertising for the ends of social betterment. In pursuit of public health goals, social marketing must identify and overcome what Robert Manoff has called cultural "resistance points" so that "awareness" may be converted into "practice."

PRINCIPLED CULTURAL SENSITIVITY

The principled conception of cultural sensitivity represents a radical departure from the other two, since it would prohibit those interventions that violate the cultural norms of those to whom they are directed. The foundations for this conception are respect for the cultural integrity of those to whom public health efforts are directed and the moral claims of pluralism. It is in this strong sense of cultural sensitivity that a profound clash between the goals of public health and the demand that interventions respect groups' cultural integrity becomes clear. Indeed, the clash is inherent in the broadly understood ends of AIDS prevention, which require fundamental changes in sexual and drug-using behavior and the norms that inform and structure such behavior.

Four brief examples will serve to underscore the fissure between the norms of public health and the demand for cultural sensitivity in the principled sense of the term.

1. In the 1970s an exuberant sexuality took hold among urban middle-class gay men, one that fostered a multiplicity of sexual encounters, often with anonymous partners. At least initially, calls for sexual restraint provoked a strong reaction from some gay men, who saw in them an aggressive assault on their freedom. Reflecting this view, Michael Lynch wrote, "Gays are once again allowing the medical profession to define, restrict, pathologize us. . . . So we have a disease for which supposedly the cure is to go back to all the styles that were preached at us in the first place." Needless to say, those were not the only voices heard in the gay community. Dr. Joseph Sonnabend asserted, "There can be no equivocation. Promiscuity is a considerable health hazard." Larry Kramer's widely read "1,112 and Counting," published in 1983, appealed to gay men to alter their sexual behavior at a time when the number of AIDS cases was but a pale portent of what was to come.

In the face of conflict within the gay community, should public health officials have remained silent, respectful of the culture of promiscuity, or should they have done much more than they did to challenge the norms that encouraged deadly behavior?

2. Many public health officials, and almost all AIDS activists, have

called for the provision of condoms and condom education to high school students, for whom sexual activity poses a risk of HIV transmission. Efforts to undertake such programs have been endorsed by those who adhere to liberal secular values, but fiercely resisted by political conservatives and, most importantly, by many working-class and lower-middle-class parents. Bolstered by the Roman Catholic Church and by fundamentalist Protestants, some groups have viewed condom programs as an assault on parental prerogatives and the values of their own communities. They have sought to defend their moral and religious views of appropriate sexual behavior for their children against the forces of secularism. As a member of the New York City School Board asserted, "There is no way in this city, in these United States, that someone is going to tell my son that he can have a condom when I say he can't."

In the face of such opposition, was it the obligation of public health officials to seek to protect the youth whose lives were placed at risk by their sexual behavior, or were they obliged to respect the culture of the parents who so opposed them? The fact that it is the AIDS Coalition to Unleash Power (ACT-UP) that has often been in the forefront of condom distribution efforts on school grounds, even when school or health department officials have been reluctant, noncommittal, or timid, demonstrates that the challenge to cultural sensitivity may come not only from the authorities but from AIDS activists imbued with a sense of misison.

3. From the mid-1980s on, an increasing number of public health experts have argued that needle exchange programs could play an important role in inhibiting the spread of HIV infection. That those associated with the Reagan and Bush administrations and with law enforcement would oppose such efforts is not surprising. More troubling, even startling, was the fierce opposition of the leadership of the African-American community—ministers, physicians, politicians—who saw needle exchange programs as one more experiment visited on powerless African-Americans or as a threat to whatever fragile efforts existed to prevent drug abuse. Such efforts were denounced as genocidal. Summarizing the imbroglio surrounding a proposed needle exchange program in New York City, Harlon Dalton wrote:

> In fairness it cannot be said that New York City's health commissioner simply disregarded the issue of whether free needles would encourage addiction. Rather, after thoughtfully considering the issue, he concluded that the risk was minimal. The rub is that most African-American critics of needle exchange rejected that conclusion. Given this disagreement over a matter of fundamental importance to the African-American community, to proceed anyway looks a lot like indifference or disrespect.

Should public health officials have acceded to the concerns of the African-American community, respecting its culturally informed weighing of the risks and benefits of needle exchange, or should they have pressed vigorously to challenge the cultural resistance to such efforts and the political forces that gave it expression? When they failed to overcome that opposition, should they have acknowledged defeat and attempted conciliation, or should they have proceeded to impose needle exchange programs by exercising their political power and authority, hoping that the opposition to needle exchange would either splinter or wither? Should ACT-UP have given up its vigorous efforts to establish illicit exchange programs in light of the opposition of the African-American community?

4. Those committed to inhibiting the heterosexual transmission of HIV infection have come to recognize the necessity of a fundamental change in the culturally embedded imbalance of power between men and women. Indeed, the literature on AIDS prevention has increasingly asserted that the empowerment of women is essential if heterosexual transmission is to be limited. Such empowerment is necessary if women are to gain control over the conditions under which they engage in sexual intercourse. In short, AIDS prevention is viewed as requiring a rupture in the cultural norms that define women as subordinate to men—that define the very nature of their relationshiops with their sexual partners.

WHEN SENSITIVITY KILLS

In each of these four cases, it is clear that acceding to the demands of cultural sensitivity, in the principled sense of the term, not only is *not* a prerequisite for effective public health practice, but would be inimical to the goals of AIDS prevention. Certainly it is necessary to recognize cultural differences as prevention efforts are fashioned, to recognize that communities are not monolithic and that cultural conflicts may occur within them. Crucial, too, is an understanding of the cultural barriers to AIDS prevention. In the face of such barriers it is desirable to reach for understanding, to persuade, even to hector. But diktat and ukase are to be avoided. In the case of the more powerful social groups, persuasion is preferable to fiat because of the capacity of such groups to politically thwart the efforts of those committed to AIDS prevention. In the case of social and ethnic minorities, as well as those whose beliefs place them beyond the mainstream, impositions from above can cause humiliation and provoke resistance that would be counterproductive to the goals of public health.

But in the end, no strategy for effective AIDS prevention can be limited by the demand that cultural barriers to behavioral change always be respected. There is an irony here: the demand for cultural sensitivity in the semantic and instrumental senses—the two weakest senses—raises few problems from the perspective of public health; yet the demand for cultural sensitivity in the principled and strongest sense, the sense that compels us to think carefully about the political and moral warrant for public health intervention, is ultimately incompatible with the goals of AIDS prevention. Homilies about cultural sensitivity must be replaced by a forthright acknowledgement that we cannot seek radical behavioral and normative change while adhering to a dictum that serves principally to protect the status quo.

14

A Gangsta's Rights

Roger L. Conner

A hallmark of the U.S. Constitution is that fundamental rights extend even to those people whom many would consider the least deserving—perhaps especially to such people. But in California, a court has interpreted this principle so broadly as to prevent communities from reigning in those who make their neighborhoods unlivable.

The case in question grew out of an innovative tactic, pioneered by Los Angeles District Attorney Gil Garcetti and *pro bono* lawyers from the law firm of Latham & Watkins. The strategy is to obtain injunctions that prohibit gang members from engaging in certain activities. The efforts have been so effective that they have been duplicated throughout the state. In San Jose, for example, residents of the Rocksprings neighborhood were constantly in fear of two violent street gangs. Gang members staked out their turf with graffiti, loud music, and urine. Gunshots and drug deals were commonplace, and car windows were frequently smashed. So in 1993, the city attorney brought a civil action to have six key gang members declared public nuisances. California District Court Judge Robert Foley sided with the district attorney and issued an injunction prohibiting the gang leaders from activities that harassed and intimidated the entire community. According to San Jose City Attorney Joan Gallo, arrests in the targeted area dropped by 72 percent in two years, and many gang-related problems were largely eliminated. As one enjoined gang member remarked, "There's nothing for me to do anymore."

But then the American Civil Liberties Union (ACLU) brought suit—and won. In *The State of California v. Carlos Acuna, et al.*, the California Court of Appeals vacated the injunction and adopted the ACLU's contention that gang members have a right to the tools and tricks of their trade. The three-judge panel held that activities such as carrying crowbars and chains, possessing "slim jims" and spray paint, engaging motorists in traffic, and climbing trees to maintain lookouts, are all constitutionally protected. The court also maintained that gang members have a right to gather together for such purposes in public places. Apparently uncompelling was the trial court's determination that, as a group, gang members used these actions as a direct means of intimidation, assault, theft, vandalism, drug dealing, and other crimes.

The California Supreme Court has agreed to review the ruling and many California jurisdictions are deeply worried about the outcome. Injunctions represent a breakthrough strategy in the effort to undermine youth street gangs. The *Los Angeles Times* reported that a civil order in Burbank dissolved a gang-run drug ring entirely. In Panorama City, gang activity was reduced by 70 percent. The Los Angeles County Sheriff noted that in the six months after an injunction took effect, Norwalk police, who had been summoned to a gang-plagued neighborhood an average of eight times a day, were called only *once a month* on gang-related incidents.

The injunctions, by preventing gangsters from flaunting their gang affiliation and congregating in specified public areas, directly attack the sense of collective impunity that drives gang activity. They thus give the community the leverage it needs to face down threats of violence and rebuild a culture of respect. And while supporters admit that civil orders must be only one part of a wider anti-gang effort—an effort that would include education, youth diversion, community policing, and traditional law enforcement—they are powerful preventive tools.

DEFINING A NUISANCE

The ACLU's lawyers insist that it is impermissible for a court to issue a civil order to prohibit gang members from any act that is not expressly illegal. "The issuance of injunctions makes some activities criminal that would not otherwise be criminal," said Amitai Schwartz, the ACLU lawyer challenging the San Jose order. "It's a shortcut for law enforcement [and] an end run around constitutional protections." The Court of Appeals agreed: an individual may be forbidden from illegal acts like dealing drugs, but not from anything that is ordinarily legal. In other words, gang members cannot be prohibited from brandishing heavy chains or crowbars, even when such weapons constitute an implicit threat to anyone who fails to show proper compliance.

The city attorney had countered that any activity that constitutes a public nuisance *is* a crime. The California Penal Code defines a public nuisance as "anything which is injurious to health, or is indecent, or is offensive to the senses, or an obstruction to the free use of property, so as to interfere with the comfortable enjoyment of life or property by an entire community, or by any considerable number of persons." The appellate court opinion in *Acuna* cited this definition but, adopting the ACLU's reasoning, narrowed the meaning of the word "anything" in the statute to apply only to "criminal activity" as defined by other statutes. Thus, the court held, any activity that could "have legitimate non-criminal purposes . . . may not be judicially enjoined."

It is this holding that most perplexes critics of the ruling. For, in fact, the law is filled with many examples of otherwise lawful acts that are enjoined because, in context, they amount to unreasonable behavior. Abusive spouses are ordered to stay a certain distance from their victims, though walking is itself hardly criminal. Playing music, yelling, and applauding are enjoined when an establishment's noise level consistently disturbs its neighbors, though at a stadium rock concert these activities are legal and encouraged. Other examples abound.

BALANCING THE FIRST AMENDMENT

The ACLU has also used the *Acuna* case to get the courts to broaden the range of association protected by the First Amendment. It is the position of the ACLU that the First Amendment's protection of expression includes all personal association. The San Jose injunction infringes on this right, lawyers argue, by prohibiting gang members from congregating on the four square blocks they call their turf—where, incidentally, not one of them lives. Adopting this view, the California appeals panel stated that "non-criminal associational conduct cannot be enjoined solely on the basis of [gang] membership."

The U.S. Supreme Court has repeatedly rejected such an interpretation, however, maintaining that the Constitution does not create a right to associate for social purposes. Only association that is directly linked to expressive purposes, such as petitioning the government, is constitutionally protected. In *The City of Dallas v. Stanglin,* for instance, the high court ruled against a dance hall owner who claimed that restricting 14- to 18-year-olds from his club late at night violated their associational rights. Furthermore, in *Bailey v. City of National City,* the court upheld a police department policy that caused an officer to be fired for his "continuous associations" with a known felon. The ruling was based on the grounds that, absent some significant expressive component, laws regulating social relationshiops are not subject to First Amendment scrutiny. In other words, for Constitutional purposes, gang membership is not the equivalent of joining the NAACP or the Republican Party.

This is not to deny the fact that these injunctions can walk fine constitutional lines at times. Some judges have prohibited wearing gang insignia and displaying gang signs. While the First Amendment extends to all, "fighting words" have never been protected. The California high court should thus permit civil orders in this area when a trial court judge finds that, as a matter of fact, colors and signs are used to intimidate others in the community.

In an era of mandatory minimum sentences and high incarceration rates, civil injunctions provide a viable alternative to criminal convictions—a way for the community to intervene in wayward kids' lives before the trouble gets too serious. Moreover, by making it difficult for gangs to operate, injunctions make it harder for gangs to recruit impressionable youngsters in the first place. The ruling in *Acuna* has left Rocksprings residents afraid that they will be forced once again to keep their children indoors at all times, to return home themselves before dark, and to face violent retaliation for cooperating with police. It is the right of these citizens to the peaceful enjoyment of their homes and streets that deserves protection, and not some ersatz right to operate an intimidating gang.

III

COMMUNITARIAN POLICY

15

A Liberal-Democratic Case for the Two-Parent Family

William Galston

WHY LIBERAL DEMOCRATIC SOCIETIES NEED STRONG FAMILIES

I am here chiefly concerned with a traditional issue: the role of the family as a *moral* unit that transmits (or fails to transmit) the beliefs and dispositions needed to support oneself and to contribute, however modestly, to the community. This moral concern is linked to a broader political thesis. A healthy liberal democracy, I suggest, is more than an artful arrangement of institutional devices. It requires, as well, the right kinds of citizens, possessing the virtues appropriate to a liberal democratic community. A growing body of empirical evidence developed over the past generation supports the proposition that the stable, intact family makes an irreplaceable contribution to the creation of such citizens, and thus to promoting both individual and social well-being. For that reason, among others, the community as a whole has a legitimate interest in promoting the formation and sustaining the stability of such families.

As in many other spheres of American life over the past generation, family relations have witnessed a tremendous expansion of individual rights and liberties. In the process, some long-festering problems have been addressed. But these gains have not come without costs, many of which have been borne by America's children. It is time, I suggest, to put the family at the center of our thinking about social policy, and children at the center of our thinking about the family. As we do so, we discover that a discourse of responsibilities supplements the language of individual rights.

Responsibility is a two-way street. The liberal democratic community has a wide range of responsibilities to families: not to tax away the money they need to raise children; to ensure that full-time work provides a non-poverty family income; to decrease as far as possible the current tension between family and work; to increase supportive services available to families experiencing severe stress; and to nurture rather than undermine the network of intermediary associations ("civil society") within which families function best.

I have discussed policy implications of these community responsibilities elsewhere (see "Putting Children First," published by the Progressive Policy Institute and co-authored with Elaine Ciulla Kamarck). My focus here is on the *responsibilities of parents to their children and to the community*, among which are: to make every effort to *stay married;* to *acknowledge or establish paternity;* to *contribute adequately to their children's financial support;* to *refrain from activities such as substance abuse that harm their children;* and to *involve themselves in their children's education and socialization.*

To say that the community ought to take a legitimate interest in parental discharge of these responsibilities is to leave open the possibility that this interest may assume the form of law. James Childress distinguishes between policies that "express" community and those that "impose" community. There can be little doubt that, whenever a meaningful choice exists, it is preferable to create moral incentives for socially desirable behavior rather than to employ directly coercive measures. *But in family policy as elsewhere, this choice is not always available. The law—the moral voice of the state—must sometimes command as well as cajole.* The hope is that over time, this legal demonstration of community commitment will evoke a higher level of normative internalization and voluntary compliance.

At some point, legal demands may jeopardize a liberal democracy's dedication to a wide sphere of individual freedom. What begins as the expression of legitimate community interest can become inappropriate and counterproductive meddling. State action must therefore be justified in light of widely shared public purposes, and the line separating such public purposes from personal moral preferences must be vigilantly safeguarded.

THE DECLINE OF THE AMERICAN FAMILY

Surveys conducted throughout the 1990s demonstrate the public's belief that America is in the grip of "moral decay." The public's prime explanation of moral decay: the breakdown of the family. These worries are hardly the product of an overheated public imagination. Last year, nearly one-third of all infants were born out of wedlock. For black infants, that figure was about two-thirds. Divorce trends paint an equally alarming picture. From 1940 to 1960, the U.S. annual divorce rate was essentially stable. From 1960 to 1985, by contrast, it skyrocketed by 250 percent. If current trends persist, at least 40 percent of marriages undertaken today in the United States will end in divorce. So when we talk about the "breakdown of the family" and its consequences for children, family breakup is even more significant than is the failure of families to form in the first place.

To be sure, similar trends may be observed in virtually every advanced industrialized country except Japan. But it has proceeded farther in the United States. Even today, French and (West) German divorce rates are actually lower than were U.S. rates in 1960, and Swedish rates, popularly believed to be stratospheric, are, in fact, less than one-half those of the U.S. As Constance Sorrentino of the Bureau of Labor Statistics summarizes the situation, "Based on recent divorce rates, the chances of a first American marriage ending in divorce are today about one in two; the corresponding ratio in Europe is about one in three to one in four."

We have known for some time about the economic consequences of family breakdown. As David Ellwood of Harvard University observes, "The vast majority of children who are raised entirely in a two-parent home will never be poor during childhood. By contrast, the vast majority of children who spend time in a single-parent home will experience poverty." According to Ellwood, eighty percent of children growing up in two-parent families experienced no poverty whatever during the first ten years of their lives, while only twenty-seven percent of the children in single-parent households were so fortunate. Conversely, only two percent of children in two-parent households experienced persistent poverty (seven years or more), while a full twenty-two percent of children in single-parent households literally grew up poor. It is no exaggeration to say that *the best anti-poverty program for children is a stable, intact family.* Conversely, family disintegration is a major reason why after a decade-long economic expansion—the poverty rate among children is nearly twice as high as it is among elderly Americans.

If the economic effects of family breakdown are clear, the non-economic effects are just now coming into focus. While scholars over the past generation have disagreed over the consequences of divorce, work done during the 1980s has on balance reinforced the view that children of broken families labor under major non-economic disadvantages. Writing recently in the *American Enterprise,* Karl Zinsmeister summarizes this emerging consensus: "There is a mountain of scientific evidence showing that when families disintegrate, children often end up with intellectual, physical, and emotional scars that persist for life. . . . We talk about the drug crisis, the education crisis, and the problems of teen pregnancy and juvenile crime. But all these ills trace back predominantly to one source: broken families."

In 1981, John Guidubaldi, then president of the National Association of School Psychologists, picked a team of 144 psychologists in thirty-eight states, who gathered long-term data on 700 children, half from intact families, the other half children of divorce. Preliminary results published in 1986 showed that the effects of divorce on children persisted over time and that the psychological consequences were significant even after correcting for income differences. The results also indicated that during grade-school years, boys were significantly less able than were girls to cope with divorce, in large measure because divorce almost always means disrupted relations with the father rather than with the mother. Boys need on-the-scene fathers and are highly vulnerable in their absence.

The problems engendered by divorce extend well beyond vanishing role-models. Children need authoritative rules and stable schedules, which harried single parents often have a hard time supplying. As Guidubaldi puts it, "One of the things we found is that children who had regular bedtimes, less TV, hobbies and after-school activities—children who are in households that are orderly and predictable—do better than children who [did] not. I don't think we can escape the conclusion that children need structure and oftentimes the divorce household is a chaotic scene."

The results of the Guidubaldi study have been confirmed and deepened by Judith Wallerstein's ten-year study of sixty middle-class divorced families. Among her key findings published in *Second Chances: Men, Women, and Children a Decade After Divorce:*

- "Divorce is a wrenching experience for many adults and almost all children. It is almost always more devastating for children than for their parents. . . .
- The effects of divorce are often long-lasting. Children are especially affected because divorce occurs during their formative years. What they see and experience becomes a part of their inner world, their view of themselves, and their view of society. . . .
- [A]lmost half the children entered adulthood as worried, underachieving, self-deprecating, and sometimes angry young men and women. . . .
- Although boys had a harder time than girls, suffering a wider range of difficulties in school achievements, peer relationships, and the handling of aggression, this disparity in overall adjustment eventually dissipated. . . .
- Adolescence is a period of grave risk for children in divorced families; those who entered adolescence in the immediate wake of their par-

ents' divorces had a particularly hard time. The young people told us time and time again how much they needed a family structure, how much they wanted to be protected, and how much they yearned for clear guidelines for moral behavior. . . ."

Although Wallerstein's work has been criticized as resting on an unrepresentative sample, a recent study of 10,000 British children by Andrew Cherlin, Lindsay Chase-Lansdale, and Kathleen Kiernan found that 23-year-olds whose parents had divorced had a 39 percent higher risk of serious mental-health problems. Cherlin takes issue with the intensity of the damage Wallerstein describes, but not with the basic thrust of her findings.

Given the profound psychological effects of divorce, it is hardly surprising that recent studies confirm what many teachers and administrators have suspected for some time: *the disintegrating American family is at the root of America's declining educational achievement.* There is nothing new about this proposition. Ever since James Coleman and his coauthors published their seminal study nearly a quarter century ago, research has consistently indicated the importance of family background for student achievement. An overwhelming body of data suggests that the "hidden curriculum of the home," which consists largely in the development of language skills, is directly related to children's later success in school.

Untangling just what it is about family structure that makes for high or low educational achievement is a difficult task. Family economic status is clearly important; children from poor families consistently do less well than do children from non-poor families. Still, income is not the whole story. After controlling for income, significant differences in achievement remain between children from single-parent families and those from intact families—especially for boys.

To summarize: Evidence indicates that from the standpoint of the psychological development and educational achievement of children as well as their economic well-being, the intact two-parent family is generally preferable to the available alternatives. It follows that a prime purpose of sound family policy is to strengthen such families by promoting their formation, assisting their efforts to cope with economic and social stress, and retarding their breakdown whenever possible. This "prime" purpose is not the only purpose: Family policy must also seek to ameliorate the consequences of family breakdown for children while recognizing that some negative effects cannot be undone.

To avoid misunderstanding, I want to make clear that *a general preference for the intact two-parent family does not mean that this is the best option in every case.* That proposition would be absurd. Nor does it mean that all single-parent families are somehow "dysfunctional"; that proposition would be not only false, but also insulting to the millions of single parents who are struggling successfully against the odds to provide good homes for their children. The point is that at the level of statistical aggregates and society-wide phenomena, significant differences do emerge, differences that can and should shape our understanding of social policy.

Nor, finally, should the endorsement of the two-parent family be mistaken for nostalgia for the single-breadwinner "traditional" family of the 1950s. Setting aside all other variables, it cannot be doubted that much of the surge of women into the workforce in the past three decades has come in response to economic stress. As inflation-adjusted hourly wages have fallen in response to international competition and stagnant productivity, only increased female labor force participation has enabled families to maintain their purchasing power. For better or worse, the new reality for most American families is that two earners are now needed to maintain even a modestly middle-class way of life—and that many of their marginal economic gains are being eroded by work-related expenses. The economic benefits are counter-balanced, however, by a sense of increasing stress brought about by decreased time available for family life. The point of a policy that takes its bearings from the two-parent family is not to turn the clock back, but rather to enable such families to deal more effectively with the economic and social challenges of the 1990s.

Having entered these disclaimers, I want to stress that my approach is frankly normative. The focus is on what must be a key objective of our society: raising children who are prepared intellectually, physically, morally, and emotionally—to take their place as law-abiding and independent members of their community, able to sustain themselves and their families and to perform their duties as citizens. Available evidence supports the conclusion that on balance, the intact two-parent family is best suited to this task. *We must then resist the easy relativism of the proposition that different family structures represent nothing more than "alternative lifestyles"*—a belief that undermined the Carter administration's efforts to develop a coherent famil policy and that continues to cloud the debate even today.

In taking this position, I associate myself, not just with scholarly evidence, but also with the moral sentiments of most Americans. Over the past few years, Barbara Whitehead has conducted one-on-one and focus-group discussions with a cross-section of middle-class parents. Her overall finding: "Our national debate on the family is being conducted in two separate languages. The first is official language, spoken by experts and opinion leaders in politics, the media and academia. The second is family language, spoken by ordinary middle class families." "Official" language speaks mainly of economics and public policy; "family" language focuses on culture and values. Official language is self-consciously relativistic; family language is unabashedly judgmental:

> In the official debate, . . . the remembered past is almost always considered a suspect, even unhealthy, guide for the present or the future. . . . these memories harken back to what the official language is pleased to term the "mythical" or "nostalgic" family of the past—a sentimental fiction that blinds us to the real challenges of modern life. But the mothers and fathers I met do not hesitate to look back at their own childhoods. And in a majority of cases, they report that, compared to today, families then were stronger, children better off, and neighborhood and community life far more support-ive of family well-being. In the official language, the family isn't getting weaker, it's just "changing." Most parents I met believe otherwise.

The reasons for this belief are not hard to identify. Most Americans are neither moral fanatics nor moral experimentalists. They are tolerant of individual and group differences, and they don't want to impose their views on others. But they do have moral views, strongly held and deeply rooted in America's cultural heritage. And they regard many family changes of the past generation as violations of these convictions.

With regard to the family, these views go roughly like this: A primary purpose of the family is to raise children, and for this purpose families with stably married parents are best. *Sharply rising rates of divorce, unwed mothers, and runaway fathers represent abuses of individual freedom,* for they are patterns of adult behavior with profoundly negative effects on children.

The character of the family, these Ameicans believe, is the key to raising children successfully. Families have primary responsibility for instilling such traits as discipline, ambition, willingness to abide by the law, and respect for others—a responsibility that cannot be discharged as effec-tively by auxiliary social institutions such as public schools. This respon-sibility entails a sphere of legitimate parental authority that should be bolstered—not undermined—by society. It requires personal sacrifice and delay of material and emotional gratification on the part of parents. But this responsibility can be fulfilled, even in the face of daunting odds. Generations of Americans have shown that economic and social hardships are compatible with strong families raising competent children—and that such families are the key to overcoming these hardships.

This, then, is the core of average Americans' moral understanding of the family. But these same Americans do not, for the most part, see con-temporary society as supportive of this understanding. On the contrary, they see their efforts to transmit moral values to their children counter-acted by many of our society's most powerful forces. They are experienc-ing what might be termed a "cultural squeeze."

Two principal objects of parental concern are rampant materialism and the dominance of the media. As these parents express it, reports Whitehead:

> They are losing the struggle to pass on their family values to their children—losing it to an aggressive and insidious consumer culture. In their eyes, their children are no longer acquiring an identity at home as much as they are attempting to buy one in the marketplace.

Other evidence suggests an even broader indictment: of a society that seems unable to control drugs, that cannot even guarantee their children's physical security in school and on the way to it, that fails to reinforce discipline and high standards, that emphasizes instant gratification over working for the future, that flaunts transitory sexuality at the expense of lasting commitment.

For all these reasons, I suggest, *we must reject the moral relativism characterizing much "official" discussion of the family.* We should reject, as well, the thesis that questions of family structure are private individual matters not appropriate for public discussion and response. After all, the consequences of family failure affect society at large. We all pay for systems of welfare, mental and physical disability, criminal justice, and incarceration; we are all made poorer by the inability or unwillingness of young people to become contributing members of society; we all suffer if our society is unsafe and divided. There is a fundamental distinction between social institutions and practices that affect only the consenting parties to them and those that affect everyone else. Whenever institutions and practices have such pervasive consequences, society has the right to scrutinize them and, where possible, to reshape them in light of its collective goals.

This suggests that from a moral viewpoint, there is a deep difference between families with children and those without them. Families without children may be regarded as consensual arrangements that touch the vital interests of their immediate members only, and principles of individual freedom and choice may be most appropriate. By contrast, families with children are engaged in activities with vast social consequences. Moral categories such as duty, continuing responsibility, and basic interests come into play in addition to, and as restraints on, freedom of choice. Society may then be justified in treating these two types of families quite differently in the structure of the law and policy.

THE RETURN TO RESPONSIBILITY: DIVORCE LAW REFORM

One prime candidate for this strategy of differentiation is the law of divorce. To begin with, because of the shattering effects of divorce on children, it would be reasonable to introduce "braking" mechanisms that require parents contemplating divorce to pause for reflection. I also believe that we could reconsider the availability of no-fault divorce in cases involving minor children.

Of course, such reforms will not always—perhaps not usually—succeed in warding off divorce. It is then necessary to turn to phase two—the reform of procedures affecting the economics of divorce for families with children. For these families, the divorce revolution of the past generation has worked out badly. On average, the income of the custodial parent (usually the mother) and minor children falls by 30 percent immediately after the divorce.

This situation is made even worse by the fact that non-custodial parents (usually fathers) do not always fulfill their financial responsibilities. Even after the limited federal and state reforms of the 1980s, the child support system is a mess. More than one-third of all absent fathers simply ignore their legal obligation to support their children, and many others pay only a fraction of what they owe. The average annual contribution of those who do pay is only $2,300, and many use delays or arbitrary reduction in support payments to achieve other bargaining objectives vis-a-vis the custodial parent. If the system were made less discretionary and more uniform, a major source of uncertainty, conflict, and distress for custodial parents would be removed.

The fundamental norm that should guide our efforts is this: The responsibility of biological parents for their children does not cease simply because of divorce, separation, or out-of-wedlock birth. To give voice to—and to enforce—this basic moral proposition, our society should create a far more uniform and straightforward method of child support. Among the major steps toward reform:

- Society would commit itself to identifying every child's father and mother. In the future, the Social Security numbers of both parents would appear on each child's birth certificate.
- All absent parents would be expected to contribute a portion of their income, which would vary with the number of children they fathered (or bore).
- Payments would be collected by employers, just like Social Security taxes, and remitted to the federal government, which would then send the money directly to custodial parents. All absent or non-custodial parents would be included, not just delinquents. Failure to pay would be an offense comparable to tax evasion.

These and other reforms will require fundamental changes, not just in what we legislate, but in how we think as well. As Mary Ann Glendon, a leading American student of the law of divorce, has observed in *Abortion and Divorce in Western Law*, "When almost three-fifth of all divorces in the United States involve couples with minor children, it is astonishing that our spousal support law and marital property law treat that situation as an exception to the general rule." She goes on to recommend a set of guidelines for divorces with children:

> A "children first" principle should govern all such divorces. . . . the judges' main task would be to piece together, from property and income and in-kind personal care, the best possible package to meet the needs of the children and their physical custodian. Until the welfare of the children had been adequately secured in this way, there would be no question or debate about "marital property". All property, no matter when or how acquired, would be subject to the duty to provide for the children.

COERCION AND THE MORAL VOICE OF THE LAW

I offer divorce law reform as an illustrative example of what a turn toward a responsibility-based family policy would mean. By becoming parents, individuals assume certain responsibilities, among which Glendon's "duty to provide for the children" bulks large. And because the failure to fulfill this duty entails such negative consequences for children and for the community, society has a right—indeed, a responsibility to take an active interest in its fulfillment.

It would be wonderful if a simply hortatory expression of that interest—society's collective moral voice—were sufficient to achieve general compliance. But our experience gives us little warrant for believing this to be the case. Indeed, mandatory declarations—laws with teeth—are typically needed to convince citizens that the community is serious about its professed standards of responsibility. From drunk driving to racial discrimination, vigorous enforcement backed by sanctions has proved essential in changing behavior.

To say that social responsibility must sometimes begin with a measure of public coercion is not to say that it must always remain there. The post-Brown history of U.S. race relations offers some grounds for hoping that, over time, changed behavior can lead to changed belief—that is, to a genuine internalization of previously external norms. Laws such as the Civil Rights and Voting Rights acts have turned out to be schools for a new and widely shared understanding of a more equal citizenship for all.

But—to repeat—the force of these laws rested on more than the moral norms they articulated. Without the demonstration of deep seriousness in the form of the coercive power of the state, few if any changes in public attitudes would have occurred.

Thus, to return to the matter at hand, I do not doubt that the coercive features of the family proposals I have advanced will arouse deep misgivings in many quarters. Forcing individuals to discharge their responsibilities is not a prospect that anyone can regard with equanimity, let alone satisfaction. But the alternative seems to be a society in which one group of citizens can inflict grave damage on a second group and then force a third group to bear the collective costs. The long-term prospects of a community unwilling to act forcefully against such abuses cannot be regarded as bright.

16

How Therapists Threaten Marriages
William J. Doherty

Soon after her wedding Marsha felt something was terribly wrong with her marriage. She and her husband Paul had moved across the country following a big church wedding in their home town. Marsha was obsessed with fears that she had made a big mistake in marrying Paul. She focused on Paul's ambivalence about the Christian faith, his avoidance of personal topics of communication, and his tendency to criticize her when she expressed her worries and fears. Marsha sought help at the university student counseling center where she and Paul were graduate students. The counselor worked with her alone for a few sessions and then invited Paul in for marital therapy. Paul, who was frustrated and angry about how distant and fretful Marsha had become, was a reluctant participant in the counseling.

In addition to the marital problems, Marsha was suffering from clinical depression: she could not sleep or concentrate, she felt sad all the time, and she felt like a failure. Medication began to relieve some of these symptoms, but she was still upset about the state of her marriage. After a highly charged session with this distressed wife and angry, reluctant husband, the counselor met with Marsha separately the next week. She told Marsha that she would not recover fully from her depression until she started to "trust her feelings" about the marriage. What follows is how Marsha later recounted the conversation with the counselor:

Marsha: "What do you mean, trust my feelings?"
Counselor: "You know you are not happy in your marriage."
Marsha: "Yes, that's true."
Counselor: "Perhaps you need a separation in order to figure out whether you really want this marriage."
Marsha: "But I love Paul and I am committed to him."

Counselor: "The choice is yours, but I doubt that you will begin to feel better until you start to trust your feelings and pay attention to your unhappiness."
Marsha: "Are you saying I should get a divorce?"
Counselor: "I'm just urging you to trust your feelings of unhappiness."

A stunned Marsha decided not to return to that counselor, a decision the counselor no doubt perceived as reflecting Marsha's unwillingness to take responsibility for her own happiness.

Two aspects of Marsha and Paul's case stand out. First, the couple saw a counselor who was not well-trained in marital therapy. Any licensed mental health professional can dabble in marital therapy, but most therapists are far more comfortable working with individuals. When marriage problems are formidable or the course of treatment difficult, these therapists pull the plug on the conjoint sessions (involving both spouses) in favor of separate individual therapy sessions. Often they refer one of the spouses to a colleague for separate individual therapy, with this rationale: "You both have too many individual problems to be able to work on your relationship at this point." Of course, the couple is living together in this relationship seven days a week and has no choice but to "work on it" continually.

The unspoken reason for this shift in treatment modality, especially if it occurs early in the marital therapy, is generally that the therapist feels incompetent with the case, especially in dealing with a reluctant husband who is not therapy-savvy and says he is there only to salvage his marriage. This husband lacks a personal, psychological agenda. When he gets turfed off to another therapist to do his "individual" work, he balks, thereby confirming to his wife and her therapist that he is unwilling to work on his own "issues" and thereby do his part to save the marriage. The marriage is often doomed at this point, an iatrogenic effect of poor marital therapy.

The second noteworthy feature of Marsha and Paul's case is the strong individualistic and anti-commitment orientation of the therapist. Like most psychotherapists, she viewed only the individual as her client. She perceived no responsibilities beyond promoting this individual's immediate needs and agenda. The therapist not only ignored obligations to other stakeholders in the client's life, but also did not give proper weight to the role that sustained commitments play in making our lives satisfying over the long run. No doubt the therapist viewed herself as "neutral" on the issue of marital commitment. But, as I pointed out in *Soul Searching: Why Psychotherapy Must Promote Moral Responsibility*, claiming neutrality on commitment and other moral issues in American society means that the therapist likely embraces the reigning ethic of individualism. There is nothing neutral about asking a newly married, depressed woman, "Are you happy in your marriage?" and urging her to trust her frightened and confused feelings. No self-respecting therapist would urge a suicidal patient to "trust your feelings about how worthless your life is," but many well-regarded therapists play cheerleader for a divorce even when the couple has not yet made a serious effort to understand their problems and restore the health of their marriage. Therapist-assisted marital suicide has become part of the standard paradigm of contemporary psychotherapy.

A postscript to this case: Marsha talked to her priest during this crisis. The priest urged her to wait to see if her depression was causing the marital problem or if the marital problem was causing the depression—a prudent bit of advice. But a few minutes later, the priest brought up the possibility of an annulment if the marriage was causing the depression. Marsha was even more stunned than she had been by the therapist.

Some marriages, of course, are dead on arrival in the therapist's office, in which case the therapist's job is to help with the healthiest possible untangling for all involved parties, especially the children. Some marriages are emotionally and physically abusive, with little chance for recovery. Some marriages appear salvageable, but one of the parties has already made up his or her mind to leave. I am not suggesting that the therapist harangue the reluctant spouse or urge an abused wife to keep her commitment in the face of debilitating abuse. Divorce is a necessary safety valve for terminally ill marriages, and in some cases, divorce is what morality demands. (I think of a woman who discovered her husband and co-parent was a pedophile, and he would not seek treatment.) My critique focuses on the practice of therapists, many of whom lack good skills in helping couples, and who philosophically view marriage as a venue for personal fulfillment stripped of ethical obligation, and similarly view divorce as a strictly private, self-interested choice with no important stakeholders other than the individual adult client.

HOW DID WE GET HERE?

Marriage counseling (now termed "marital therapy" in the profession) was born in the 1930s and 1940s in an era of worry about the viability of modern "companionate" marriages. The early marriage counselors were mostly gynecologists, educators, and clergy. Of course psychiatrists treated many distressed married people, but did not see their primary responsibility as assisting the marriage. It was not until the 1950s that marriage counselors began to work with both spouses together in one session. Prior to then, it was considered inappropriate treatment, and even unethical, to have both partners in the sessions, because this would destroy the powerful one-to-one psychological transference dynamics deemed necessary for successful treatment of the individual problems that were feeding the marital problems.

During the 1950s and early 1960s, "conjoint" marriage counseling became more widespread as therapists began to appreciate the power of working on relationship patterns directly in the session. The American Association of Marriage Counselors grew in numbers as credentialed psychotherapists joined clergy who specialized in marriage counseling. Interestingly, marriage counseling as a professional activity developed independently of "family therapy," which grew out of psychiatry's experiments with family treatment for mental health disorders. (Only in the 1970s did the associations of marriage counselors and family therapists merge into the American Association for Marriage and Family Therapy.)

Prior to the U.S. cultural revolution of the late 1960s and 1970s, many marital therapists saw their task as saving marriages. Divorce was seen as an unequivocal treatment failure. There was little recognition of spouse abuse and the ways in which a stable but destructive marriage can undermine spouses' emotional health and create domestic hell for children. The individual tended to get lost in the marriage. Early feminist critics of marital therapy were quick to point out how this treatment approach could be dangerous to a woman's health. Women were often held responsible for the problems, since family relationships were supposed to be their forte, and women were implicitly encouraged to follow the then-popular cultural value that parents should stay together for the sake of the children. In addition, some clergy counselors added a religious rationale to the support of stable marriages, to the dismay of critics who saw this as making people feel guilty before God for salvaging their mental and physical health from a toxic marriage.

Research and professional literature on marital therapy burgeoned during the 1970s, during the era of skyrocketing divorce rates. Sobered by feminist critics and enamored with the 1970s cult of individual fulfillment, marital therapists largely rejected the "marriage saver" image. The 1980s brought a wealth of research studies on marital communication, marital distress, and effective treatment techniques. Marital therapists who were trained in these new techniques viewed themselves as performing a form of mental health treatment that not only helped marriages but also the individual well-being of the spouses. But on the value of preserving marital commitment if possible, the field was mostly "neutral"—which means embracing a contractual, individualist model of commitment. A decision about divorce became just like any other lifestyle decision such as changing jobs; the therapist's job entailed simply helping people sort out their needs and priorities.

As therapists during the 1970s and 1980s experienced their own divorces and those of colleagues, they increasingly saw divorce as a bonafide lifestyle option and a potential pathway to personal growth. The self-help books written by therapists reflected this positive orientation to divorce. In the term coined by Barbara Dafoe Whitehead in her book *The Divorce Culture,* therapists followed the popular culture in embracing the "expressive divorce" as an enlightened way to start a new life when the old marriage was in disrepair. Although they were concerned for a couple's children, most therapists believed that children would do fine if their parents did what was best for themselves. I term this "trickle down psychological economics," which works for the children just as well as the other trickle down model has worked for the poor in American society.

WHERE WE ARE TODAY

The 1990s have witnessed marital therapy become mainstream as more professionals practice it, more couples seek it out, and some insurance companies pay for it. National political leaders make no apologies for having benefited from marriage (and family) therapy. The decade of the 1990s has also seen a movement back towards espousing the value of marital commitment and the therapist's role in promoting it. This was first seen in Michele Weiner-Davis's early 1990s work on solution-oriented therapy for highly distressed couples. "Divorce Busting" is what she titled her training workshops, and later her popular book. She and others began to take a deliberately pro-marriage stance, much to the dismay of established leaders in the field. Having come to a "middle" point of encouraging neither divorce nor staying together, many leaders in marriage therapy saw this new pro-marriage stance as a conservative backlash against feminism and emancipated individualism. If marriage and divorce are primarily lifestyle choices, and if a bad but stable marriage is destructive for all involved, why should therapists be in the business of saving marriages?

In the 1990s—a decade of backlashes and counter-backlashes—there has also been an assault on the use of the term "marriage" among scholars and practitioners. The critique is that "marriage" marginalizes cohabiting couples and especially gay and lesbian couples. Most marital therapists, when giving professional presentations, use the term "couples therapy" or "couples counseling." The list of presentations at national conferences of marriage and family therapists contains multiple references to "couples" and scant references to "marriage." I have no doubt that the profession of marriage and family therapy (now credentialed in 37 states as an independent mental health profession) would take a different name if it were being created in the late 1990s. "Family" is still okay, as long as a variety of family structures are included in the definition, but "marriage" is out because it is not inclusive.

This trend away from using the word "marriage" is unfortunate, because the term "couple" carries no connotations of moral commitment and lifetime covenant. My daughter and her boyfriend were a "couple" during their summer after high school, but the relationship did not survive their going to different colleges. Is this relationship morally equivalent to Marsha and Paul's, or to a long-married couple with children? Even if we use the term "committed couple" or "committed relationship," we beg the question of how deep and permanent the commitment. Rather than lower the bar for marital commitment by abandoning the term "marriage," why not expand the definition of marriage to include gay and lesbian couples who wish to make a permanent, moral commitment to each other? Why not make the marriage umbrella larger without sacrificing its essential values, instead of folding the umbrella and watering down the precious moral dimension of this unique, for-better-or-for-worse human relationship?

GIVING COMMITMENT ITS DUE

My own work has offered a communitarian critique of the individualist ethic of psychotherapy in the United States. Although the focus of this article is on marital therapy as a treatment modality, I believe that all psychotherapy for individuals who are married is, in part, marital therapy, even if only one spouse participates. This is because issues of personal need versus marital bonds and obligations are inevitably present in individual therapy. Furthermore, I am convinced that there is widespread and invisible harm done to marriages by many individual-oriented psychotherapists. Consider the following example:

Monica was stunned when Rob, her husband of 18 years, announced that he was having an affair with her best friend and wanted an "open marriage." When Monica declined this invitation, Rob bolted from the house and was found the next day wandering around aimlessly in a nearby woods. He spent two weeks in a mental hospital for an acute, psychotic depression, and was released to outpatient treatment. Although he claimed during his hospitalization that he wanted a divorce, his therapist had the good sense to urge him to not make any major decisions until he was feeling better. Meanwhile, Monica was beside herself with grief, fear, and anger. She had two young children at home, a demanding job, and was struggling with lupus, a chronic illness she had been diagnosed with 12 months earlier. Indeed, Rob had never been able to cope with her diagnosis, or with his own job loss six months afterwards. (He was now working again.)

Clearly, this couple had been through huge stresses in the past year, including a relocation to a different city where they had no support systems in place. Rob was acting in a completely uncharacteristic way for a former straight-arrow man with strong religious and moral values. Monica was depressed, agitated, and confused. She sought out recommendations to find the best psychotherapist available in her city. He turned out to be a highly regarded clinical psychologist. Rob was continuing in individual outpatient psychotherapy, while living alone in an apartment. He still wanted a divorce.

As Monica later recounted the story, her therapist, after two sessions of assessment and crisis intervention, suggested that she pursue the divorce that Rob said he wanted. She resisted, pointing out that this was a long-term marriage with young children, and that she was hoping that the real Rob would reemerge from his mid-life crisis. She suspected that the affair with her friend would be short-lived (which it was). She was angry and terribly hurt, she said, but determined to not give up on an 18-year marriage after only one month of hell. The therapist, according to Monica, interpreted her resistance to "moving on with her life" as stemming from her inability to "grieve" for the end of her marriage. He then connected this inability to grieve to the loss of her mother when Monica was a small child; Monica's difficulty in letting go of a failed marriage stemmed from unfinished mourning from the death of her mother.

Fortunately, Monica had the strength to fire the therapist. Not many clients would be able to do that, especially in the face of such expert pathologizing of their moral commitment. And equally fortunately, she and Rob found a good marital therapist who saw them through their crisis and onward to a recovered and ultimately healthier marriage.

This kind of appalling therapist behavior occurs every day in clinical practice. A depressed wife of a verbally abusive husband who was not dealing well with his Parkinson's Disease was told at the end of the first, and only, therapy session in her HMO that her husband would never change and that she would either have to live with the abuse or get out. She was grievously offended that this young therapist was so cavalier about her commitment to a man she had loved for 40 years, and who was now infirm with Parkinson's Disease. She came to me to find a way to salvage a committed but nonabusive marriage. When I invited her husband to join us, he turned out to be more flexible than the other therapist had imagined. He too was committed to the marriage and needed his wife immensely.

These illustrations should not be dismissed as examples of random bad therapy or incompetent therapists. They stem from a pervasive bias among many individual-oriented therapists against sustaining marital commitment in the face of a now-toxic relationship. From this perspective, abandoning a bad marriage is akin to selling a mutual fund that, although once good for you, is now a money loser. The main techniques of this kind of therapy are twofold: a) walk clients through a cost-benefit analysis with regards to staying married—what is in it for me to stay or leave? and b) ask clients if they are happy and if not, then why are they staying married? If those questions yield what appears to be an irrational commitment in the face of marital pathology, as the therapist believed to be true for Monica, then the therapist falls back on pathologizing the reasons for this commitment. It takes extraordinary conviction to weather such "help" from a therapist.

These therapist questions and observations are value-laden wolves in neutral sheep's clothing. The cost-benefit questions in particular brook no consideration of the needs of anyone else in this decision. I was trained in the 1970s to dismiss clients' spontaneous moral language ("I don't know if a divorce would be fair to the children") by telling them that if parents take care of themselves, the children will do fine. And then I would move the conversation back to the safer ground of self-interest. That's how most of us learned to do therapy years ago, and it's still widespread practice.

A COMMUNITARIAN APPROACH TO MARITAL THERAPY

The first plank in a communitarian platform for marital therapy would be for therapists, both those who work only with individuals and those who work with couples, to recognize and affirm the moral nature of marital commitment. This stance moves therapists beyond the guise of neutrality, which in fact covers an implicit contractual, self-interested approach to marital commitment. Divorce, from a communitarian perspective, is sometimes necessary when great harm would be caused by staying in the marriage. Particularly in the presence of minor children, the decision to divorce would be akin to amputating a limb: to be avoided if at all possible by sustained, alternative treatments, but pursued if necessary to save the person's life.

The second plank affirms that personal health and psychological well-being are indeed central dimensions of marriage and important goals of therapy. There is no inherent contradiction between emphasizing the moral nature of marital commitment and promoting the value of personal satisfaction and autonomy within the marital relationship. These moral and personal elements together define the unique power of marriage in contemporary life.

The third plank is that it is a fundamental moral obligation to seek marital therapy when marital distress is serious enough to threaten the marriage. We need a cultural ethic that would make it just as irresponsible to terminate a marriage without seeking professional help as it would be to let someone die without seeing a physician.

The fourth plank holds that promoting marital health should be seen as an important part of health care, because we now know the medical and psychological ravages of failed marriages for most adults and children. And the health care system should support this kind of treatment as an essential part of health care, instead of regarding marital therapy as an "uncovered benefit."

The fifth plank concerns the importance of education for marriage and early intervention to prevent serious marital problems. We need a public health campaign to monitor the health of the nation's marriages and to promote community efforts to help couples enhance the knowledge, attitudes, values, and skills needed to make caring, collaborative, and committed marriage possible. There are many well-tested courses and programs in marriage education across the country that can fill this need. Information about these courses and programs needs to be disseminated.

The sixth plank asserts that therapists should help spouses hold each other accountable for treating their spouse in a fair and caring way in the marriage. Although commitment is the linchpin of marriage, justice and caring are essential moral elements as well. A communitarian approach to marital therapy would incorporate feminist insights into gender-based inequality in contemporary marriages. It would be sensitive to how women are often expected to assume major responsibility for the marriage and the children, and then are criticized for being over-responsible. When a husband declines to do his fair share of family work on the grounds that "it's not my thing," the therapist should see this as a cop-out from his moral responsibilities, not just as a self-interested bargaining position with his wife. Communitarians promote more than marital stability; they promote caring, collaborative, and equitable marital unions that are good for the well-being of the spouses as individuals.

The seventh plank is based on the prevalence of therapist-assisted marital suicide. We need a consumer awareness movement about the potential hazards of individual or marital therapy to the well-being of a marriage. Consumers should be given guidelines about how to interview a potential therapist on the phone, with questions such as "What are your values about the importance of keeping a marriage together when there are problems?" If the therapist responds only with the rhetoric of individual self-determination ("I try to help both parties decide what they need to do for themselves"), the consumer can ask if the therapist has any personal values about the importance of marital commitment. If the therapist hedges, then call another therapist. (Look elsewhere too if the therapist says that marriages should be held together no matter what the consequences.) Consumers should also be aware that many therapists who primarily work with individuals are not competent in marital therapy and thus are likely to give up prematurely on the marital therapy and the marriage itself. It is best to see a therapist who has had special training in working with couples.

Many therapists are now reconsidering their approach to marital commitment. They have been entranced by a cultural mirage about what constitutes the good life in the late 20th century, and they are beginning to rehink their ill-begotten moral neutrality in the face of disturbing levels of family and community breakdown. A communitarian critique and reformulation of marital therapy can point the way to a new kind of marriage covenant that views moral responsibility, sustained commitments, and personal fulfillment as a garment seamlessly sewn, not a piece of Velcro designed for ease of separation.

17

Residential Community Associations: Community or Disunity?

Daniel A. Bell

Champions of civil society from Alexis de Tocqueville to Robert Putnam contend that intermediary associations between the family and the state generally have favorable effects on the polity at large. Associations such as churches, community centers, labor unions, and PTAs are said to break down social isolation and allow people to cooperate and to discover common interests that may otherwise have gone unnoticed. They are, in Tocqueville's words, "large free schools" where citizens "take a look at something other than themselves." In them, political interests are stimulated and organizational skills enhanced, thus countering the disposition to give precedence to personal ends over the public interest and leading to a broader notion of public-spiritedness.

Of course not all intermediary associations are said to produce desirable consequences of this sort. Tocqueville himself made a distinction between "American" associations that allow for and encourage independent behavior and "French" associations that are tyrannical within themselves, thus producing passive and servile behavior instead of training members in the use of their energies for the sake of common enterprises. Along these lines many civil society theorists argue that in an overall authoritarian context, associations will reproduce hierarchical relationships within themselves and reinforce political apathy, whereas in a democracy, citizens tend to freely and equally associate within groups, developing participants' taste for collective benefits, and eventually forging a sense of common purpose in the wider political community.

Senator Bill Bradley expresses a similar viewpoint in the Spring 1995 issue of *The Responsive Community:* "Civil society . . . is the sphere of our most basic humanity—the personal, everyday realm that is governed by values such as responsibility, trust, fraternity, solidarity, and love. In a *democratic* civil society such as ours we also put a special premium on social equality—the conviction that men and women should be measured by the quality of their character and not the color of their skin, the shape of their eyes, the size of their bank account, the religion of their family, or the happenstance of their gender."

The problem with this view is that a *liberal* democratic society also gives people a right to freely associate in communities not governed by such virtues as fraternity and social equality. If people want to form hierarchical and exclusivist communities such as, for example, the Mormon church, they have a right to do so. And even if certain civic associations do allow members to freely and equally participate in the internal life of the community, there is no reason to expect that outsiders will be the beneficiaries of what can be termed "internal democracy." As Yael Tamir puts it, "the reality is that one necessary feature of group life is drawing a distinction between insiders and outsiders, and development of loyalty to the former at the expense of the latter. . . . Associations may foster among their members feelings of respect and reciprocity but they often promote self-interested behavior towards outsiders." Such is the price of living in a liberal society—only a tyrannical regime would try to force people to join communities governed by a particular set of virtues meant to forge an attachment to the overall political community.

But what if associations in civil society begin to seriously undermine attachment to the polity at large, maybe even to erode the bare minimum of social cohesion and trust needed to promote social justice and sustain the democratic process? Unfortunately, this is more than a theoretical possibility in view of the worrisome social and political implications arising from a relatively new type of civic organization known as "Residential Community Associations" (RCAs). Almost unnoticed by academics and government officials, more than 32 million Americans—one in eight—live in homes and condominiums as members of over 150,000 RCAs, a number that may exceed 50 million by the year 2000. This essay will look at the political implications of these private communities.

WHAT ARE RESIDENTIAL COMMUNITY ASSOCIATIONS?

A residential community association is a form of communal home ownership that developers adopted in the early 1960s as land suitable for traditional suburban homes became more expensive. Instead of building single-family homes surrounded by large private yards, developers turned to a more economical way of building a new kind of suburban home at prices most middle class families could afford. The concept was first pioneered in such planned communities as Radburn, New Jersey. Smaller individual lots were built and supplemented by common areas for recreation and other activities, areas owned and managed by the residents themselves. New housing in all regions is increasingly RCA housing, but they are most common in the suburban areas of California, Florida, New York, Texas, and Washington, D.C. As of 1990, 61 percent were classified as condominium associations (typically located in multi-family, multi-story buildings) and 35 percent as homeowner associations (detached single-family homes or townhouses with common areas.)

RCA developments have three distinct legal characteristics: common ownership of facilities used by all residents (e.g., swimming pools, parking lots, parks) who are assessed fees to pay for these facilities and for private services such as police protection, snow removal, and garbage collection; mandatory membership in a non-profit homeowner association; and the requirement of living under a set of private laws drawn up by the developer (known as "covenants, conditions, and restrictions," or CC& Rs) and enforced by fellow residents elected to a board of directors. It is the latter characteristic that has drawn the most controversy thus far.

PROTECTION OR PATERNALISM

CC&Rs are put into place on the assumption that most homeowners prefer to forsake some private property rights to the group in exchange for protection against unwelcome change, such as a depreciation of property values or a deterioration in the neighborhood's aesthetic appearance. But some CC&Rs are also said to impinge upon quite intimate areas of the residents' private lives. The CC&Rs can empower the association's board of directors to decide what color homeowners can paint their house or condominium, how many people can spend the night in a home, how often homeowners must mow their lawn, and whether to allow household pets, day-care centers, satellite dishes, commercial vehicles, or basketball hoops. Some community associations have even banned political signs, prohibited the distribution of newspapers, and forbidden political gatherings in the common areas. Evan McKenzie, author of *Privatopia: Homeowner Associations and the Rise of Residential Private Government*, reports some particularly egregious cases:

- In Ashland, Massachusetts, a Vietnam War veteran was told that he could not fly the American flag on Flag Day. The board backed down only after the resident called the press and the story appeared on the front page of a local newspaper.

- In Monroe, New Jersey, a homeowner association took a married couple to court because the wife, at age 45, was three years younger than the association's age minimum for residency. The association won in court, and the judge ordered the 60-year-old husband to sell, rent the unit, or live without his wife.
- In Santa Ana, California, a 51-year-old grandmother received a citation from her condominium association for violating an association rule against "kissing and doing bad things" while parked one night in the circular driveway. She acknowledged kissing a friend good night, but retained an attorney and threatened legal action. A press report quoted her as saying, "Somebody, or a group, has decided to invade my privacy. And it just doesn't feel right to say, 'Let them get away with it.'"

Such rigid enforcement of rules against people's use of their own homes has led an increasing number of residents to file lawsuits against association board members. Critics also advance the charge that CC&Rs are often of questionable legitimacy because residents can be tricked into buying a home unaware of the accompanying restrictions on personal freedom. In addition, the whole process is denounced by some for having a number of antidemocratic features: CC&Rs initially put into place by developers can sometimes only be changed with great difficulty (e.g., by a unanimous consent rule); association board members entrusted with enforcing CC&Rs are not elected according to a one person one vote principle (most significant, renters living in residential community associations are disenfranchised, since voting within RCAs is based on ownership, not residence); and few eligible voters even bother to participate in association elections.

The fact remains, however, that RCA residents generally seem happy with their lot, and the lack of interest and participation in the internal workings of homeowner associations can plausibly be interpreted as an indication that the system works to the satisfaction of most people. If the concern is to protect the interests of *residents*, many of the problems are potentially corrigible. Robert Jay Dilger, author of *Neighborhood Politics: Residential Community Associations in American Governance*, notes that laws can be passed to ensure that potential buyers are given the opportunity to fully understand CC&Rs and other RCA-related documents and to make it easier for RCA members to terminate or modify CC&Rs (e.g., by a majority vote or a two-thirds vote). In California a new law was passed that requires two parties involved in a legal dispute in a homeowners association to try to resolve the conflict through nonbinding mediation or arbitration before they file a lawsuit. Relatively noninterventionist regulations of this sort can minimize the number of lawsuits and the harassment of residents by RCA board members.

RELINQUISHING YOUR RIGHTS—CAN YOU DO THAT?

But there still remains the legal question of whether some association convenants violate constitutional rights. In the case of *City of Ladue v. Gilleo* in June 1994, the U.S. Supreme Court unanimously declared as unconstitutional a Ladue, Missouri city ordinance that banned all residential signs. The court ruled that the ordinance violated a property owner's right to freedom of speech. If *Ladue* is used to challenge the constitutionality of an RCA's restrictive covenant that bans residential signs, this case may also apply to community associations. The court may find that RCAs operate as *de facto* local governments rather than as private associations—recall that the actions of an individual or an entity can violate constitutional rights only if those actions constitute "state action"—and RCA advocates worry that many other CC&Rs could thus conceivably be struck down as unconstitutional. CC&Rs that allow associations to enter an owner's unit for the purpose of inspection or maintenance may be found to violate the right to privacy. A guideline regulating holiday lights may violate an owner's freedom of religion. Restrictions on the colors of paint permissible may be said to violate an owner's freedom of expression. And so on.

But even if the Supreme Court holds RCAs to the same standards as local governments, the whole restrictive covenant regime need not be called into question in view of the fact that local governments themselves are permitted regulations that, for example, restrict the exterior color and architectural style of homes and businesses in the interests of aesthetics and community stability. Nonetheless, some RCA groups and state governments are already taking precautionary measures against the possibility of an unfavorable judgment. Some CC&Rs are being modified to allow for temporary political signs and, at the government level, the state of California has passed several laws to control the content of the original governing documents and thus protect homeowners from abuses.

Whatever the outcome on the legal front, one suspects that many social critics will still find it hard to believe that millions of Americans actually prefer to live in an environment tightly regulated by CC&Rs. Evan McKenzie, for example, notes disapprovingly that RCA boards "exercise power over members . . . in vital areas of concern, in that their decisions govern what individuals do in the privacy of their own home and what they do with the physical structure of the house and its surroundings. Their actions touch on what is perhaps the most basic human drive: the desire to exercise control over our immediate environment."

But is it really the case that the most basic human drive is "the desire to exercise control over our immediate environment?" If many Americans genuinely prefer to accept restrictions on individual freedom for the sake of owning a home in the context of a stable and prosperous neighborhood, should the state "force them to be free?" As University of Virginia School of Law Professor Clayton Gillette puts it, "There seems something anomalous about arguing for protection of groups such as orthodox Jews or the Amish when their cultures conflict with majoritarian norms while opposing similar license for those who seek residence in artificially pastoral settings free from technologies that they deem unsightly or who live in such fear of crime that they literally wall themselves off from the outside world." If the only concern, in short, is to protect the interests of RCA *members,* extensive governmental (or judicial) regulation of the internal workings of RCAs does not seem justified. There is little evidence that most members value individual autonomy—defined as a desire to maintain the maximum feasible amount of *ongoing* control of one's immediate environment—as an essential human interest. Thus it would be difficult to assert that RCA members view CC&Rs as a serious threat to their "desire to exercise control."

Unlike the Amish and orthodox Jewish communities, however, RCAs are large in number and have the potential to significantly affect the lives of *nonmembers.* And once we take into account the impact of RCAs on nonmembers and the attendant implications for political life in America, a more worrisome story emerges.

COMMUNITIES OR PRIVATISTIC ENCLAVES?

RCAs seem to exemplify many of the characteristics of civic associations celebrated by Tocqueville and his intellectual heirs. They are generally small in size (the average association has approximately 150 units), well-organized, and provide most members with the opportunity for participation in local public affairs. One might thus be led to expect that RCAs foster norms of generalized reciprocity and social trust that contribute to the benefits of associational life, such as those described by Robert Putnam in his now famous article "Bowling Alone": "better schools, lower crime, faster economic development, longer lives, and more effective government."

Not surprisingly, RCAs are in fact promoted on the grounds that they provide all the benefits of village democracy. As the Urban Land Institute put it in one of their studies, "The home association is an ideal tool for building better communities . . . The explosive growth of our cities, their trend to giantism, and the high mobility of their residents are rapidly destroying a sense of community among individuals in America . . . The best possible way to bring about—or to revive—a grassroots sense of community is for homeowners to control nearby facilities of importance to them and through this to participate actively in the life of their neighborhoods." On this view, participation in RCA governance encourages people to become more knowledgeable about local political affairs, to view the world from the perspective of the neighborhood as a whole, thus broadening the participants' sense of self and developing habits of public-spiritedness that spill over into the larger political world.

The reality, however, is almost the inverse of the myth. As both Dilger and McKenzie document, instead of functioning as facilitators of civic virtue, RCAs allow and encourage "citizens" to act as privatized individuals who participate in public affairs only for the most narrow of self-interested reasons, with profoundly detrimental consequences for the public at large.

Some of the consequences are indirect, not necessarily the effects of conscious political decision making. RCAs give middle and upper income city residents the opportunity to leave the urban setting, either literally as in a move to a new suburban community or in the functional sense of moving to a fortified condominium in a gentrified downtown neighborhood. This amounts to, McKenzie argues, a gradual secession of the well-off that would leave the city stripped of much of its population and resources, exacerbating the social and economic problems of the city and the cleavage between rich and poor. As a warning on the likely effects of RCA housing, McKenzie invokes the voice of Charles Murray: "I am trying to envision what happens when 10 or 20 percent of the population has enough income to bypass the social institutions it doesn't like in ways that only the top fraction of 1 percent used to be able to do. . . . The Left has been complaining for years that the rich have too much power. They ain't seen nothing yet." Murray predicts that cities will come to be viewed in much the same way mainstream America views Indian reservations today, as places of squalor for which the successful would acknowledge no responsibility.

Perhaps this grim diagnosis of the future could be avoided if RCAs served as forums for lively political exchanges and debates, with members learning to think about common purposes and eventually entering the political realm with a certain amount of civic virtue and concern for the less well-off. As mentioned previously, however, few members actually participate in RCA meetings (though, as Dilger notes, RCA member turnout at general membership meetings is higher than the turnout rate for all adults at local government elections). According to a California survey most RCA members collectively participate in their association's business only when they feel threatened by its decisions or the actions of outsiders. More worrisome, political activity seems to take the phenomenon of NIMBY (Not In My Back Yard) to new heights. Consider the following examples:

- RCA members in California mobilized with the aim of opposing a proposal to build a second high school for the city of Redlands near their homes. Dilger notes that 29 out of 30 speakers at a local government public hearing identified themselves as members of RCAs, and they were unanimous in their view that building the high school at the proposed site would increase traffic, litter, criminality, loitering, drug use, and noise in and around their neighborhoods, thus adversely affecting their property values and their neighborhood's aesthetic appearance. The local school board was apparently impressed by these arguments and subsequently announced that the new high school would be built in a location where there were few RCAs to contend with.
- RCA members in Indiana sought to prevent the creation of a group home for developmentally disabled individuals within their subdivision. Covenants that governed the subdivision restricted the use of lots within the subdivision to "single-family or two family dwellings," and while the state had enacted a statute invalidating restrictive covenants that prohibited the use of "property as a residential facility for developmentally disabled or mentally ill persons," association members went to court and won. The state statute was struck down because it was said to violate the contract clause of the state constitution, insofar as it applied to preexisting restrictive covenants. (The court considered such covenants to be issues of private concern, rather than of public policy.)

It is unlikely that participating in this kind of local politics teaches the "lessons" that Tocqueville had in mind. Instead of being "schooled" in civic virtue and increasing commitment to the good of the overall society, participants learn to act *in opposition* to the interests of the wider community and to evade their responsibility for a fair share of the burdens (e.g., housing the mentally ill) that political communities normally undertake.

Critics point to another manifestation of RCA politics, one with similar negative effects on nonmembers. Local government officials and even state legislatures are facing increasing demands from RCA members for tax reimbursements for the provision of local services such as snow and ice removal, street lighting, and the collection of garbage. RCAs argue that since they pay for their own services through their homeowner associations, why should they pay property taxes for duplicating public services that they do not need? The problem, as McKenzie explains, is that for RCA members "tax equity" means that they would provide for their own private parks and private streets, from which the public could be excluded, while members would still make use of outside services such as public parks and streets, for which they would not have to pay. And one may add that RCA members in all likelihood would expect federal disaster relief aid if, say, severe floods or earthquakes hit their local communities.

Nonetheless, the issue of double taxation is gathering steam among those who live in RCAs. In Naugatuck, Connecticut, according to McKenzie, an organized RCA contingent made double taxation an issue in a local election and claimed to have "turned the town around from being completely Democratic controlled to Republican controlled. . . . We were a force to be reckoned with." In New Jersey, a law was recently approved requiring all cities to reimburse RCAs for the cost of providing for their own snow removal, street lighting, and trash collections. On an even larger level, a nationwide RCA voting bloc is a possibility. As Dilger explains, "Another tax equity issue involves the national government. It allows taxpayers to deduct their property taxes from their taxable income when determining national tax liability. . . . To promote tax equity, RCA members want the national government to allow them to deduct from their taxable income the portion of their assessment fees used to pay for services that are provided by their local government to other residents in their community."

The consequences of greater political participation by RCA members are predictable: for members, a decreasing sense of loyalty and commitment to the national community and the local communities in which their RCAs are located; for nonmembers, a decreasing tax base to provide for public services; and for the nation as a whole, greater alienation from the political system and an increasing gap between rich and poor.

NEITHER NATURAL NOR INEVITABLE

If the above diagnosis is at least partly correct, the United States needs to pay more attention to the baleful effects of RCAs on the public sphere. Whereas extremist forces among certain ethnic groups may be a more visible cause for worry—for example, Diane Ravitch worries about the possibility that "if all we have is a motley collection of racial and ethnic cultures, there will be no sense of the common good. Each group will fight for its own particular interests, and we could easily disintegrate as a nation"—in actual fact RCA mobilization constitutes a far more serious long-term threat to the public good. They are more numerous, more powerful, more wealthy, and potentially better organized than any marginalized ethnic group can ever hope to be now or in the foreseeable future.

So what can be done to make RCA growth a matter of public debate and concern? First and foremost, it is important to emphasize that the development of RCAs is not "natural." They are scarcely existent in the rest of the industrialized world. But in the United States, the national and local governments facilitate the formation and expansion of RCAs. Developers make contributions to local politicians who then provide municipal assistance of various kinds (e.g., infrastructure, public regulation of the land surrounding RCAs) that help to keep development costs as low as possible. Sales are promoted by having transportation (especially freeways) near RCAs. And most explicitly, the Federal Housing Administration helps by advocating RCA construction in its own publications and by providing developers with federal mortgage insurance and hence assuming much of the risk should RCA projects prove to be unprofitable.

Thus one can question whether or not public authorities should continue to promote the construction of RCAs as opposed to, say, insuring loans for modernizing older homes or for building more cooperative housing. On another level, local governments could use their zoning powers to make entry-level housing more affordable by encouraging developers to build smaller lot sizes and placing public parks and other recreational amenities within walking distance of these homes. Zoning can also be used to help promote home construction in relatively heterogenous settings (with a mixture of social classes, cultural groups, and residential and commercial uses). Some urban planners propose that RCAs themselves can be reorganized around principles more beneficial to the polity at large—for example, covenants that favor mixed-income homeowners and mixed-use neighborhoods. Perhaps the granting of favorable zoning decisions and mortgage subsidies to relatively civic-friendly RCAs can be raised as a public issue.

The statement (by historian Kenneth Jackson) that "no agency of the United States government has had a more pervasive and powerful impact on the American people over the past half-century than the Federal Housing Administration" may be a slight exaggeration. But there is no doubt that more public scrutiny must be brought to bear on the social and political implications arising from the FHA's administrative preferences and the zoning authority delegated to local governments. It is an area of public policy that demands our attention.

18

When Redistribution and Economic Growth Fail

Senator Dan Coats

America's most aggressive cultural diseases—family breakdown, decaying civic institutions, rising crime, addiction, and illegitimacy—seem virtually immune to politics. They have resisted $5.4 trillion in government spending and have turned generations of public policy reformers into cynics and pessimists.

On the left, the traditional response has been cash transfers, now discredited by a culture of dependence. On the right, the hope has been for a rising economy to lift all boats. But Reagan-era prosperity produced 18.4 million new jobs without making a significant dent in the underclass. Economic opportunity, we have found, is an empty concept in neighborhoods where 90 percent of children lack a father, entry-level jobs are dismissed as "chump change," and young men (on good evidence) don't expect to live past their 20th birthday.

Economic redistribution and economic growth have both shown their limits. "What is wanted," argues social critic Irving Kristol, "is a black John Wesley to do for the 'underclass' what Wesley did for the gin-ridden working class in 18th century britain. Reformation has to be on the agenda, not just relief." It should be added that Wesleys are needed for every race, because the underclass problem does not discriminate.

This theme was taken up by President Clinton in a speech to high school students in suburban Virginia. "Don't you believe," he asked, "that if every kid in every difficult neighborhood in America were in a religious institution on weekends—a synagogue on Saturday, a church on Sunday, a mosque on Friday—don't you really believe that the drug rate, the crime rate, the violence rate, the sense of self-destruction would go way down, and the quality and character of this country would go way up?"

REFORM, COMPASSION, AND MEANING

It was a founding principle of the modern, liberal state that society must change if we ever hope to change individuals. It is the dawning truth of our time that this principle is precisely backwards. Individuals must change if we ever hope to change our society. Matters of behavior and character—the value men and women place on life and property, the commitment they show to marriage, the sacrifices they make for their children—have assumed a central place in America's debate on social policy.

If, to confront urgent social problems, reformation must be on the agenda, the direct role of government is nonexistent. Government can feed the body, but it cannot touch the soul. That delicate work is performed by certain kinds of private institutions and religious charities. By any objective measure most private and religious organizations are more effective, efficient, and compassionate than government programs, for at least three reasons.

First, private organizations have the freedom to require changed behavior in return for help. Once criticized as paternalistic, these groups actually assert the essential connection between responsibility and human dignity.

Second, their approach is personal rather than bureaucratic. The literal meaning of "compassion," as historian Marvin Olasky points out, is "suffering with." These groups understand that serving those in need is not primarily a function of professional background but of individual commitment.

Third, religious organizatins often provide an element of moral challenge and spiritual renewal that government programs cannot duplicate. Robert Woodson Sr., a community activist in Washington, D.C., observes, "People, including me, would check out the successful social programs—I'm talking about the neighborhood-based healers who manage to turn people around—and we would report on such things as size, funding, leadership, technique. Only recently has it crystallized for me that the one thing virtually all these programs had in common was a leader with a strong element of spirituality. We don't yet have the scales to weigh the ability some people have to supply meaning—to provide the spiritual element I'm talking about. I don't know how the details might work themselves out, but I know it makes as much sense to empower those who have the spiritual wherewithal to turn lives around as to empower those whose only qualification is credentials."

A vivid contrast between government and private approaches is found in Washington, D.C., just blocks from the Capitol. The Gospel Mission, run by the Reverend John Woods, is a homeless shelter that offers unconditional love but accepts no excuses. Residents are required to take random drug tests. If they violate the rules, they are told to leave the program.

The success of the mission, however, comes down to something simple: It does more than provide a meal and treat an addiction—it offers spiritual renewal. One addict who came to Reverend Woods after failing in several government programs observed, "Those programs generally take addictions from you, but don't place anything within you. I needed a spiritual lifting. People like Reverend Woods are like God walking into your life. Not only am I drug-free, but more than that, I can be a person again."

The Gospel Mission has a 12-month rehabilitation rate of 66 percent, while a once-heralded government program just three blocks away rehabilitates less than 10 percent of those it serves. The privately run religious program achieves this success while spending one-twentieth of that spent by the government program.

In a period of "compassion fatigue" and frustration over counter-productive social spending, institutions like the Gospel Mission duplicated around the country, are a source of hope beyond anything the government can offer. The measure of our compassion as a nation is the manner in which we celebrate, accommodate, and promote the work carried out by private and religious institutions and caring individuals. They should be invited to participate in the renewal of our society.

FAMILIES AND REAL ROLE MODELS

The aforementioned themes provide the foundation for "The Project for American Renewal," a 19-piece policy initiative I have launched with Empower America Co-Director Bill Bennett. Along with emphasizing the primacy of private and religious organizations in the provision of social welfare, the Project also addresses "Fathering, Mentoring, and Family."

There is overwhelming empirical evidence linking broken homes with social pathologies. Seventy percent of prison inmates were raised in single-parent households, and the number of single-parent families in a neighborhood is closely associated with that community's violent crime rate. Nearly three-fourths of children from single-parent families will live in poverty, and children from fatherless households are also more likely to abuse drugs, suffer physical and sexual abuse, and perform poorly in school.

Public policy can choose either to respect the role of parents and mentors, or to adopt an official neutrality that translates into the suffering of children. Taking the first approach requires a serious reordering of government priorities, in at least two ways:

First, we should communicate a clear, public preference for marriage and family in matters such as public housing, the tax code, family planning, and divorce law. Rewarding intact families is not, as some argue, a form of discrimination; it is a form of self-preservation.

Second, in the absence of fathers and families, children need more than funding and programs—they need mentors and examples. Precisely because we have a crisis in fatherhood, we need to be creative in providing children with models of responsible male behavior.

The Project for American Renewal also reaches one other important level of American life that lies between a distant government and isolated individuals: the community. When it is healthy, a community includes strong neighborhoods, successful businesses, vital churches, effective schools, and active voluntary organizations. These institutions encourage cooperation, build trust, and confront social problems before they become large enough for politics or the police. Local grassroots organizations infuse a community with its warmth, train its people to be good citizens, and make its neighborhoods seem smaller, more human, and more manageable.

"The point of curbing government," says Republican strategist William Kristol, "is not simply to curb it for curbing's sake (though there is merit in that). The point is to enable the strengthening of civic institutions, the reinvigoration of institutions from the family up through voluntary and civic and religious institutions to communal institutions. We must curb government and strengthen civic institutions."

Woodson makes the point that every social problem, no matter how severe, is currently being defeated somewhere, by some religious or community group. This is one of America's great, untold stories. No alternative approach to our cultural crisis holds such promise because these institutions have resources unavailable from government—love, spiritual vitality, and true compassion. It is time to publicly, creatively, and actively take their side in the struggle to recivilize American society.

Editor's note: The following is a sample of the bills introduced by Senator Coats:

- *The Character Development Act* (S.1203) would give school districts three-year demonstration grants when they agree to work with community groups to develop mentoring programs.
- *The Family Housing Act* (S.1204) would set aside 15 percent of public

housing units for families headed by two individuals who are legally married.

- *The Adoption Assistance Act* (S.1206) would offer a $5,000 refundable targeted tax credit for adoption, available in full to families earning less than $60,000 and in part to families earning between $60,000 and $100,000.
- *The Maternity Shelter Act* (S.1214) would provide $50 million in vouchers which could be used by women at private and religious maternity group homes.
- *The Compassion Credit Act* (S.1216) would create a $500 tax credit for taxpayers who provide home care for individuals in need, including the homeless, battered women, abused women with children, hospice care patients (including AIDS and cancer patients), and unmarried pregnant women.

19

What Makes a Good Urban Park?

Peter Katz

Everyone has a favorite park, or should. Mine is Washington Square in the heart of San Francisco, bordering the legendary coffeehouses and bookstores of North Beach. First laid out around 1850, the park's design is mostly open with a simple looping walkway. The subtle ripples and rolls of the park's topography give me a sense of how the city's hills and valleys once must have looked. In and around the park, neighborhood life flourishes. Lining its edges are half a dozen restaurants, various offices and townhouses, a church, post office, theater, hotel, bakery, and an Italian social club. Regulars claim sunny benches to read and chat. Elderly Chinese residents practice the graceful movements of Tai Chi. Schoolchildren play frisbee. Commuters disembark from buses which stop alongside the park. Lunchtime picnics are daily events on the sprawling lawn.

Unfortunately, most small urban parks—particularly those in downtowns—fail to deliver the sort of civic experience that can be enjoyed in Washington Square. Such parks are the victims of strapped city budgets, the latest theories on crime prevention, and the nervous tinkerings of overzealous designers.

Ultimately, these assaults can be traced back to a larger cause—the disinvestment in cities that resulted from America's postwar flight to the suburbs. Though the money needed to build and maintain urban parks left town, the people who needed them most remained. By the seventies and eighties, when downtown land values soared along with the gleaming new highrises, it became even harder to realize the idea of a true public realm at the heart of our cities. Many once-proud parks like New York's Bryant Park and Los Angeles's Pershing Square fell on hard times. Lack of funds led to lower standards of maintenance and security, which in turn led to crime, drug dealing, and the use of parks as havens by the homeless.

But people's need for parks didn't go away. A new form of quasi-public space was invented by the private sector to meet the needs of downtown workers. Generous plazas such as those facing New York's Park Avenue and Avenue of the Americas were provided by property owners, often in exchange for increased building height. While such spaces provided a dramatic setting for the modernist boxes of corporate America, the experience at ground level was sometimes less than appealing. The combined forces of wind, weather, and the airfoil effect of many of the heroic towers rendered the wide-open spaces below virtually unusable for much of the year.

Enter the atrium as a way to tame the extremes of climate. In cities such as Montreal, Minneapolis, Atlanta, and Houston, an elaborate system of climate-controlled interior courtyards, gardens, lobbies, and passageways enable workers to park, walk to their offices, go to lunch, run errands, and work out at the health club without ever having to set foot on a city street. These not-quite public spaces offer two essential elements that many city parks fail to provide: safety and a clean, well-maintained environment.

But, like the proverbial sidewalks that in many places "roll up at five o'clock," these private corporate domains shut down not long after the close of business each day, forcing after-hours city dwellers out into the now second-class public realm of the street. Once-vital downtown streets are now largely deserted as restaurants and merchants have moved indoors to capture the lucrative daytime trade.

More troubling than the lack of downtown street life is the erosion of the intimate and longstanding connection between democracy and the public realm. Many popular movements have been played out in the town square—Czechoslovakia's Velvet Revolution in Wenceslas Square and the student demonstrations in Beijing's Tiananmen Square. But free speech and soapboxes wouldn't stand much of a chance in the corporate plazas and shopping malls of today. Uniformed security patrols would likely whisk an offending citizen away long before a sympathetic crowd could ever form. Legal questions about private ownership versus public use have been debated in the highest courts. Special booths for pamphleteers in many airports attest to the awkward compromises resulting from such court decisions.

Even more important than such legal issues are the issues of public versus private "character." While many of the corporate plazas of the sixties and seventies assumed the function of public parks, albeit poorly, the newest generation of "real" city parks, closely patterned after their corporate predecessors, suffer many of the same shortcomings.

MAKING A CITY PARK WORK

What then defines a "good" park, a true urban public place? My own criteria for a successful urban park can be counted on one hand:

A Park Should be Nearby for Everyone

Public open space, such as a square or "commons," should be at the center of a neighborhood—no more than a five minute walk for most residents. Public buildings, shops (a corner store at minimum), and a transit stop should be part of the center, too. Smaller parks should be scattered throughout the neighborhood so that no one is more than a three-minute walk from a park.

A Public Park Should Look and Feel Truly Public

Being bounded by streets or sidewalks on all sides is one sure way to communicate publicness. The presence of civic buildings and monuments also reinforces this public character. Conversely, spatial relationships get confusing when private houses or buildings *back* up to a park, without a clear public zone in between. This ambiguous edge fosters conflict between those who live next to the park, and others who come from the surrounding area. A better approach would be for houses to *front* the park, so that porches, front yards, and streets define the edge between public use and private enjoyment.

Parks Should Be Simple and Not Overdesigned

Trees, grass, some walkways, and a bench—these are the basics of my ideal park. Unfortunately, in many new parks it's hard just to find a clear patch of grass where one can sit in the sun, or a meadow large enough to set up a volleyball net. A park can have a strong identity and implied use—for example, active versus passive recreation—but it should also have enough of the basics to satisfy the needs of a broad range of users.

A Park Should Retain or Enhance the Natural Contours of the Land

In densely settled areas, it's hard to get a sense of how the terrain looked before it was built over. I'm particularly aware of this in my own hilly city of San Francisco. I feel that too many new parks, both here and in other cities, are terraced and bermed beyond recognition. The legendary Olmsteds (whose designs include New York's Central Park) moved a lot of earth too, but they did so in such a way that the land looked as natural as when they started.

A Good Park Should Allow You to Both See and Walk Through It

Part of this relates to issues of safety, but this principle also applies to the earlier point about overdesign. In many new parks, I often feel like a victim of planning, forced to navigate an obstacle course just to walk through. By contrast, many older parks offer a simple network of walkways, providing a variety of routes for those who are just passing through. Such fleeting moments in an otherwise hectic day may be the only time that some city dwellers get to experience the pleasures of a park—to smell the flowers, so to speak.

After years of neglect and misdirection, there may at last be some rays of hope for the design of future urban parks. New York's renovated Bryant Park and Boston's Post Office Square have been runaway successes among a new generation of parks, largely because their designs respect the basics outlined here. They are effective models that can and should be emulated in other cities. Less successful by my standards are Los Angeles's redesigned Pershing Square and San Francisco's new Yerba Buena Gardens. While welcome contributions to the public realm of their respective cities, these parks seem overdesigned and cluttered to the point of dysfunction.

As planners, designers, citizens, and local governments take a renewed interest in public spaces, I offer them all a bit of advice before they get back to their drawing boards: Go out and take a walk in a *good* park. Look at the elements that cause it to work so well. Talk to the people who use it and find out what features they value most. And while you're there, don't forget to smell the flowers.

20

The Loss of Public Space

Fred Siegel

We have come to the end of our national romance with cities and the public spaces that define them. At their best our cities were engines of innovation, their streets the setting for the creative disorder that inspired our artists and economists. But the same streets that once inspired our largely urban common culture now too often induce fear as even the most innocent experiences become fraught with potential danger. It was surely a milestone of decline when some cities had to give up their long-standing campaigns to teach children to "Cross at the green, not in between," because the corners were dominated by drug dealers. "Cities," says Mayor Michael White of Cleveland, "are becoming a code name for a lot of things: . . . for crumbling neighborhoods, for crime, for everything that America has moved away from."

What unnerves most city dwellers, however, is not crime per se but rather the sense of menace and disorder that pervades day-to-day life: the gang of toughs on the corner exacting their daily tribute in the coin of humiliation, the "street tax" paid to drunk and drug-ridden panhandlers, the "squeegee" men shaking down motorists waiting for a light, the threats and hostile gestures from the mentally ill who live in the parks, the provocations of pushers and prostitutes plying their "trade" with impunity, and the swirling masses of garbage left by pedlars and panhandlers and open-air drug bazaars on uncleaned streets. These are the visible signs of cities out of control, cities that can't protect either their spaces or their citizens. "When you take your child to a public playground and find a mental patient has been using the sandbox as a toilet," writes liberal columnist Lars-Erik Nelson, "it's normal to say, 'Enough, I'm leaving.' "

Nelson is by no means alone. Recent polls show that 43 percent of Boston, 48 percent of Los Angeles, and 60 percent of New York would like to leave the city. A 1989 Gallup poll found that only 19 percent of the country wanted to live in cities.

Fearing the return of nineteenth-century urban conditions, those who can afford to flee do so, sorting themselves into suburbs and leaving the cities to the poor. They move into areas organized by homeowners' associations, private governments that stand beyond the reach of cities and their experiments in civil liberties. Thirty million Americans belong to such community associations, 80 percent of which administer territory as well as buildings. In return for the bastion such communities erect against the pathologies of the metropolis, residents agree to a "covenanted conformity" that dictates everything from the size of their mailboxes to the type and number of visitors permitted. These shadow cities generally establish "one-dollar-one-vote governments" that recreate the preindustrial dictum of "all power to the property holders."

Even those who remain in the cities migrate away from the problems they associate with disordered public space. Oscar Newman's "defensible space principles," which William H. Whyte has decried as "the fortressing of America," are now so fundamental to design that they are sometimes written into zoning regulations. Cities that revitalize their downtowns are creating controlled spaces deliberately separated from the street. The Motion Picture Corporation of America (MCA), for example, built City Walk, a 100 million-square foot shopping and entertainment center in the ethnically mixed, middle-class San Fernando Valley. Billed as a "an exact replica of Venice Beach and Sunset Boulevard" minus the menace, graffiti, and homelessness, the mall tries to recreate the variety and unexpected pleasure of street life before "the fall."

From Los Angeles to Chicago to Miami, communities are trying to achieve some small measure of the security that even poor neighborhoods once took for granted and that now comes only with "private police" and "convenanted communities." Those who can't or won't leave are increasingly turning public space into a potent political issue.

Recent elections in San Francisco and Los Angeles revolved around public space and safety. San Francisco Mayor Art Agnos was defeated in 1991 by a relatively unknown challenger named Frank Jordan, who campaigned against the growth of graffiti, trash, and aggressive panhandling. Jordan, a former police chief, criticized Agnos for allowing homeless encampments in the parks, and he proposed that the homeless be put to work cleaning off graffiti.

The 1993 Los Angeles mayoral race cut to the underlying assumptions behind the politics of public space. In a race without an incumbent, maverick Republican Richard Riordan campaigned against disorder, using a mailer with an unflattering picture of a homeless man on the front and proposals on panhandling and graffiti within. Democratic candidate Michael Woo responded that the urge for order was a disguised call for conformity:

> my goal has never been to turn Hollywood Boulevard into an antiseptic, artificially sanitized area . . . Hollywood Boulevard will be an exciting, diverse and exotic place. Homeowners will see kids with ghetto blasters . . . I don't want to drive out the eccentric and interesting people, who are no harm to anyone else. I want to encourage real street life on Hollywood Boulevard.

Though Los Angeles is overwhelmingly Democratic, twice as many voters thought graffiti should be a new mayor's first priority as thought health care or the environment should, and Woo thus lost by seven points to Riordan. People prefer not to choose between the antiseptic and the antisocial but our contemporary cities often force them to.

How can we explain the unparalleled social breakdown of public space during a period of both peace and prosperity? Poverty per se is not a good answer. New York, as Senator Moynihan points out, was a far poorer but far more tranquil city fifty years ago. The breakdown has proceeded apace regardless of the phase of the business cycle. Nor is it primarily a matter of Reagan-Bush policies. New York, for instance, boomed in the 1980s, and minority income grew apace even as the breakdown continued unabated. In his justly acclaimed article for the *American Scholar*, "Defining Deviance Down," Senator Moynihan uses Durkheimian functionalism to describe the mechanisms of accommodation to growing levels of violence and pathology. We can as a society, he argues, accept only so much deviance. The excess gets defined away until the pathological is routinely accepted as unavoidable—at least for those who can't or don't flee. But except for a reference to family disintegration, important as that is, he doesn't explain the source of the breakdown in public conduct.

We have, over the past quarter-century carried out a great experiment in what Herbert Marcuse understood as radical desublimation. In that experiment zealous reformers of various stripes tried to eliminate the tension between individual desire and communal conscience solely in favor of desire, on the grounds that the release of tension would move us "beyond all known standards . . . to a species with a new name, that shall not dare define itself as man." In that new and higher state there would be no need for either self-control or social coordination since, much in the manner of the free market for goods and services, the free market in morals was to produce growth, albeit of the personal and self-expressive kind.

But since there is no such thing as a self-regulating market in morals, instead of an equilibrium we have a downward spiral. An unparalleled set of utopian policies has produced the unprecedented dystopia of day-today city life. Particularly damaging were those policies concerning the concept of victimless crime, the deinstitutionalization of the mentally ill, the decriminalization of public drinking, and the de facto decriminalization of drugs.

VICTIMLESS CRIME

Jane Jacobs, whose 1961 book *The Death and Life of Great American Cities* set the terms of how public space has been discussed ever since, argued that "lowly, unpurposeful and random as they may appear, sidewalk contacts are the small change from which a city's wealth of public life may grow." She further claimed that "The tolerance, the room for great differences among neighbors . . . are possible and normal only when the streets of great cities have built-in equipment allowing strangers to dwell in peace together on civilized but essentially dignified and reserved terms."

In the late 1960s and early 1970s, some of the "built-in equipment" was systematically dismantled. The movement to decriminalize what were known as victimless crimes—crimes in which none of the consenting adults directly involved has either cause or desire to press for legal action—was caught up in the new Vietnam-era version of the old argument that "you can't legislate morality." The moral authority of American institutions and the force of conventional norms were shattered by the cultural conflicts which broke out over Vietnam and racial injustice. Traditional authority and conventional morality were equated with authoritarianism or worse.

The need for a modicum of order, for instance, became entangled with the need to redress racial wrongs. Too often the discretionary authority to police public drunkenness or loitering had been used to harass racial minorities and gays and lesbians. In *Coates v. Cincinnati,* for instance, the Supreme Court struck down a loitering statute of long-standing provenance typical of other cities. The court argued that it was unconstitutional to outlaw "loiterers" who by congregating might "annoy" others, because enforcement "may entirely depend on whether or not a policeman is annoyed." The statute, they concluded, was an "invitation to [racially] discriminatory enforcement."

The argument for "victimless crimes" had a venerable pedigree. Jeremy Bentham, one of the founding fathers of modern liberalism, had in the early nineteenth century described drunkenness and fornication as "imaginary offenses," "acts which produce no real evil but which prejudice, mistake, or the aesthetic principle have caused to be regarded as offenses . . . " The more immediate motivation came from reformers like anthropologist Ruth Benedict who had an enormous influence on post-World War Two liberalism." "Abnormals," she wrote, "are those who are not supported by the institutions of their civilization . . . " A wiser and more mature society, she argued, would incorporate the widest range of personality types possible by becoming less judgmental, less willing to treat different types of behavior as deviant or shameful. Benedict's call was taken up by "Situationists," social scientists who argued that invidious distinctions were often made based on a misunderstanding of how marginalized people, often racial minorities, were forced by their circumstances into less-than-admirable actions. Going a step further, others used labeling theory to assume that "criminal laws by definition create criminals."

Edwin Schur, the leading proponent of decriminalizing "victimless crimes," spoke for many of his fellow sociologists, then at the peak of their since-shattered self-confidence, when he argued that social science research demanded reform. "As empirical data and realistic analysis replace misinformation and stereotyped thinking," he wrote, "neither the long-standing existence of a criminal statute nor a majority adherence to the norms and values it seeks to uphold is likely to be accepted as sufficient justification for maintaining it." Moreover, he insisted, past support for these laws rested on hypocritical moralizing, "misinformation . . . and . . . unsubstantiated assertions of the 'horrible consequences' likely to follow from decriminalization . . . "

Then, in an argument parallel to that of the anti-anticommunists, Schur turned the tables on the proponents of "traditional morality," by arguing that the cure was worse than the disease. "Proscribed behaviors [don't] necessarily constitute social problems," he argued. "Social problems are simply conditions about which influential segments of the society"—the uptight white middle class—believe "something ought to be done." The problem lay in the constricted morality of the white "squares" who attempted to impose their values on others through police action.

The intellectual bullets forged by anthropologists and sociologists were fired by police chiefs and legal reformers. These law enforcement professionals argued with considerable evidence that policing vice was inherently corrupting and that maintaining civility by arresting drunks and crazies conflated "real police work" with social work. If vice and other minor offenses to civility were decriminalized, the police chiefs and lawyers argued, the police could concentrate on major crime. The 1967 Task Force Report of the President's Commission on Law Enforcement and Administration of Justice captures what shortly became the conventional wisdom of numerous books, articles and reports: "Only when the load of law enforcement has been lightened by stripping away those responsibilities for which it is not suited will we begin to make the criminal law a more effective instrument of social protection."

What went wrong? First off, the reformers, in straining to be "hip," often trivialized the collateral consequences of the behavior they sought to decriminalize. "That prostitution tends to encourage derivative kinds of criminal activity can hardly be denied," wrote sociologist Gilbert Geis, "any more than it can be denied that kissing may lead to illegitimate births." The reformers' ideological equation had only two variables in simple inverse relation: individual rights versus state power. It was as if an economist wrote about commercial interactions of a chemical company without considering such externalities as pollution.

In New York City, where decriminalization was carried the furthest, not even running a red light remained a crime. Even though three percent of the people hit by cars in New York are already lying in the road, traffic tickets were "defined downward" in an effort to unclog the courts. Even serious traffic violations became merely civil offenses so that no warrants were issued. Fully one quarter of citations are now ignored; this invites, says Detective Chief Mario Selvaggi, "contempt for the law."

In practice "victimless" disorders can soon flood a neighborhood with serious, "victimizing crime." There is, as the New York Transit police learned under Chief William Bratton, a "seamless web" between low-level disorders and violent crime. Roughly 2 of 13 fare beaters, Bratton points out, have outstanding warrants, often for felonies. The decriminalizers got it exactly backwards: by failing to police small disorders we didn't free up the cops, rather we freed up would-be criminals at great cost to the vitality of our streets and cities.

DEINSTITUTIONALIZATION

When New York Governor Mario Cuomo was asked recently about the problems of violent mental patients on the streets of New York City his answer, in the words of Lars-Erik Nelson, was that "it's not true . . . or if it is true, it's not his fault, he's powerless." Or in Cuomo's own words: "The Constitution says you cannot lock up a person just because he's a nuisance, urinating in the street." How about changing the law? "Suppose you had a law you could lock up anyone who is endangering his health," Cuomo objects. "I could come to you and say you're drinking, you're smoking, I've got to lock you up." In what he defines as a zero-sum game between individual rights and state power, Cuomo argues that the patient's liberty interest must be paramount.

This conclusion is the essential claim of the deinstitutionalization movement, on which sociologist Erving Goffman exercised enormous influence. Goffman argued that mental hospitals were responsible for most of the symptoms of their patients. He argued further that he knew of no supposedly psychotic misconduct that had no precise analogue in the everyday conduct of psychologically healthy people.

In the "Billy Boggs" affair, when a homeless schizophrenic fought for her right to live and defecate on the streets, the American Civil Liberties Union (ACLU) played the Goffmanesque game. Did Billy Boggs urinate on the sidewalk? So did cabdrivers. Did she tear up or burn the money she had begged? This was a symbolic gesture similar to the burning of draft cards during Vietnam. And on it went. Billy Boggs, whose real name was Joyce Brown and who had grown up in a loving family and received social security checks she never bothered to cash, was described by her NYCLU attorneys as a "political prisoner," a victim of social indifference and Reagan's housing policies. And the NYCLU sucessfully sued to keep Boggs on the streets.

Freed from the clutches of New York City hospitals, wined, dined, and reclothed at Bloomingdales, Boggs was hustled on to talk shows and the Ivy League lecture circuit. But when the spotlight faded she was within weeks back on the streets, screaming, defecating, and destroying herself. In a series of publicized incidents, she was arrested for fighting, harassing passersby, and drug offenses. As former civil rights hero Charles Morgan put it, the ACLUers had become "ideologues frozen in time."

The fight for deinstitutionalization initially aimed to free those people who, made passive by many years of often unjust and unnecessry incarceration, posed little threat to society. Following this victory, however, the newly established community care system failed to continue providing calming psychotropic drugs and other types of assistance, and many mental patients moved from the back wards to the back alleys and eventually to the main streets.

For civil libertarians devoted to the abstract concept of freedom, this was not the problem with the new system. Paul Friedman, an early director of the NYCLU Mental Health Law Project, worried, on the contrary, that "because the deprivation of liberty is less in community-based treatment than in total institutionalization . . . the resistance against state intrusion will be less and the lives of many more people may be ultimately interfered with . . . "

The well-being of the patients didn't worry the civil libertarians. Said project founder Bruce Ennis, "I'm simply a civil libertarian, and in my view you don't lock people up because they've got a problem . . ." He added, "It's never been very important to me if there is or is not mental illness. My response would be the same." ACLU lawyers, he candidly admitted, "are doing what they think is right in terms of civil rights, whether it's good for the patients or not."

The full meaning of this mix of principled ignorance and militant anti-consequentialism manifested itself in the Larry Hogue case. In and out of mental institutions and generously provided with a $3,000 monthly Veteran's Administration (VA) check, Hogue in the mid-1980s began terrorizing parts of Manhattan's Upper West Side. Arrested more than 40 times, Hogue has never been convicted of a felony. He has, however, chased people down the street with a club threatening to murder them, set numerous fires (including fires under cars), repeatedly strewn garbage all over sidewalks, defecated in the back seat of a car after first threatening to kill its owner and then breaking into the auto by smashing part of a marble bench into the auto's window, masturbated in front of children, lunged at terrified women with a knife, and run about screaming with burning newspapers.

Though local community groups made a concerted effort to see Hogue incarcerated or institutionalized, people like Hogue can only be institutionalized under current New York State law if they present an immediate threat to themselves or to others. The staff at Manhattan State Hospital told community leaders that "Hogue is more violent than you think," but that they were "unable to hold him because of his rights." The official story of Hogue is that while he behaves wildly while on the crack he buys with his VA check, he's perfectly fine when off drugs, and mental health authorities thus have no choice but to release him. Researcher Heather MacDonald, however, has discovered the real reason Hogue is so quickly released: mental health authorities can't control him and want to get rid of him as quickly as possible. According to Dr. Michael Pawel, a psychiatrist who has treated Hogue, no one wants to deal with an unruly patient who isn't going to get better. Said Martin Begun of the New York City Department of Mental Health, Mental Retardation and Alcoholism Services, "We are operating with a mental health system created in the 1960s and 1970s on the basis of assumptions that are no longer applicable in the 1990s."

WHAT CAN BE DONE?

Several steps can be taken to counteract the excesses of past urban policies and reclaim public spaces for urban citizens:

Limited Institutionalization

Upon learning that Larry Hogue was about to be released once again, a New York panhandler who had been intimidated by him responded, "We'd all be better off if he were committed." He's right. Society should institutionalize the most dangerous of our mentally ill, who are also often drug dependent and homeless. Taking away someone's liberty is a very serious matter that should be done only with extreme reluctance. But there are some cases where both the patient and the society would benefit. For the most seriously sick, notes psychiatrist E. Fuller Torrey, the right to be psychotic "is an illusory freedom, a cruel hoax perpetrated on those who cannot think clearly by those who will not think clearly."

Carefully Tailored Anti-Begging Ordinances

Municipalities can pass laws designed not to ban panhandling, which the courts have tended to regard as protected speech, but to restrict its time, manner, and place. Carefully crafted laws restricting aggressive panhandling, where the action overwhelms the words, are on the books in 11 cities, and are likely to withstand legal challenge. Passed because aggressive panhandlers were driving people from the downtown streets, Seattle's law prohibits "intimidation" and "obstruction." Similarly, restrictions of begging in front of ATM machines and in confined spaces like subways and buses have also been upheld. Modern anti-begging laws, writes Robert Teir of the American Alliance for Rights and Responsibilities (AARR), are aimed at specific harmful conducts, not an individual's status.

BIDs and Decentralized Public Space Management

Business Improvement Districts (BIDs) are localized, self-assessing tax districts designed to reclaim public space from the sense of menace that drives shoppers and eventually store owners and citizens to the suburban malls. BIDs sweep the streets, augment police patrols, upgrade transportation, and generally promote downtowns. Thirty-eight states have passed enabling legislation and there are about 1,000 BIDs around the country.

A nongovernmental variant of public space management is offered by consulting firms for "sick spaces," like The Project for Public Space. Traditionally, architects have approached the design of plazas aesthetically. The Project associates, instead, approach the problem anthropologically, with an eye toward making the space hospitable. For example, movable chairs in public areas facilitate conversation and cordiality in a way that fixed park benches do not. The Project's microscopic methods have succeeded in reviving a number of "dead" or drug-ridden spaces, such as Bryant Park in mid-town Manhattan.

Community Cops, Courts, and Prosecutors

Community policing is now so popular and widespread as to require little comment. Less well accepted are the attempts to supplement community policing with community courts and community prosecution teams, both of which are aimed at giving neighborhoods some say in their own law enforcement. At some point this kind of localism may prove threatening to civil liberties. For now, it is forcing police departments and judges to set their priorities more responsibly. Community organizations in the Bronx, for example, pressured the police and judges to look upon the prostitution that was destroying their neighborhood as something more than a "victimless crime."

CONCLUSION

There is, it is true, no going back to an older concept of community that was too often racially exclusive, but there is growing support for a reassertion of common standards of public behavior. And "unlike previous calls for public order," writes Robert Teir of the AARR, which often came from racially homogeneous upper classes, current demands for public civility "come from people of all races wanting to walk streets or ride buses without feeling under constant siege by others asserting their 'right to be offensive.' " Teir's point is sustained by Antonio Pagan, a Puerto Rican city councilman representing the Lower East Side of Manhattan. "The people asking for the laws to be enforced," he says, "are the minorities themselves." Pagan is disdainful of the constant attempts to "cheapen the discussion" by past references to racially discriminatory enforcement. Civil libertarians, he argues, "try to turn it into a black-white issue to avoid the issue" of the social breakdown afflicting our neighborhoods.

The transformation Pagan represents is encapsulated in the story of an African-American tenant activist: Mrs. Jones (a pseudonym) has lived in Red Hook Houses, the biggest single public housing project in New York, for 36 years. She and her husband raised six kids there. When they first arrived there were five-dollar fines for small violations of project rules. Minor vandalism, littering, loitering, keeping dogs in apartments, playing on the growing grass all brought fines. The absence of due process gave management enormous discretionary authority that it sometimes abused. Like many tenants, she resented the arbitrary manner in which these fines were sometimes imposed by the white manager.

As a tenant leader she fought to strip the manager of his authority to levy fines, something she now regrets. Those small rules, she says, once set the civil tone for housing projects now overwhelmed by crime and violence. Much else has happened to drive the breakdown, but Mrs. Jones argues that the revival has to begin by restoring the standards of behavior she and her neighbors once shared. She now mourns the loss of legitimate authority. She says she never wanted to undermine authority in general, just its racially arbitary forms.

Her conclusions, I would suggest, are shared by an overwhelming majority of urbanites who recognize that the very heterogeneity of city life imposes "a premium on moral reliability" and a longing to see a new ideal of urbanity emerge.

21

Rebuilding Urban Communities

Senator Bill Bradley

Dedicated individuals in every city have built communities for themselves by inventing new tools. With little help and less encouragement from government, they have had to recombine and reinvent government programs intended for completely different objectives in order to make them do some good. I'd like to point to urban community-building and initiatives that would promote it, a package of bills that will take the tools invented at the community level, and use the power of government constructively to make those tools available to every community where there is the will and imagination to make them work—tools for creative communities to get self-improvement.

NEIGHBORHOOD RECONSTRUCTION CORPS

In East Harlem, Dorothy Stoneman started YouthBuild in 1978 to give young people both basic education and marketable vocational skills. While getting their high school equivalency diplomas, they have rehabilitated hundreds of abandoned buildings to create affordable housing. Other programs, such as developer James Rouses's Enterprise Foundation, have shown in Baltimore, Detroit, Miami, and other cities that local companies are willing to participate in rebuilding the cities in which they prosper.

To combine the idea of improving job skills with the idea of asking private companies to help build an economically healthy community, I have developed the Neighborhood Reconstruction Corps. This demonstration would provide federal funds to match private investments in light-infrastructure projects for public entities. For example, if a local company was willing to put up money to help repaint an inner-city school, or to refurbish a neighborhood center, some money would be available but only if an important condition was met: the project must employ a Neighborhood Construction Corps, a corps of disadvantaged workers who would be organized and trained for light construction by a community-based organization. The first idea might come from a company that realizes its own profit depends on clean, modern roads and good schools and housing. Or the initiative might come from the community-based organization that first assembles a Neighborhood Reconstruction Corps and then seeks out companies that want to undertake projects. Everyone must work together—the private business that will put up at least half the money, the local government or school system, and the community-based non-profit—and if they do, the government will be there to help.

COMMUNITY SCHOOLS

One of the great outrages of our cities is that the one public building that is part of every neighborhood and every family's life—the school—bolts its doors tight every afternoon at 3:30 or 4:00 and every Friday for 48 hours. During that time, kids whose parents are not home often have no safe place to go and no one to help them with homework, sports, or the basic questions about growing up. The dedicated people of the community, who want to be a part of raising the community's children, have no place to come together and help. But if we look at what a few dedicated people have done, we can find an answer. In Newark, New Jersey, it's the Boys and Girls Club of Newark. In East Orange, New Jersey, a local YMCA is transforming itself into a "safe haven" for young people after school. And in Washington, D.C., it's a former executive named Kent Amos, who gave up his career to give his full attention to the 50 or more kids who come to his home every afternoon for help with homework and other activities.

Meanwhile, the school buildings, with their gyms and libraries, their nurses offices and auditoriums, are shuttered. Later this year, I hope to join Senator Danforth (R.-Missouri) in introducing Community Schools. It will provide basic funds to open the schools after hours for purposes the community chooses. It might be a safe place for homework, or an athletic program, or a parenting program for young mothers. Kids need two things during their free time: a place and a mentor. This bill will give both, in communities where there is the kind of commitment that Kent Amos and others have demonstrated in Washington, D.C. But now a caring community can affect hundreds of thousands of kids, not just 50.

COMMUNITY CAPITAL PARTNERSHIP

Most of us take basic financial institutions for granted. We have savings and checking accounts, our bank lends our money to businesses in our communities, and we borrow ourselves when it comes time to buy a home or we have an inspiration to start a business. But in most American cities, the only financial institution they know is the check-cashing cubicle, which charges up to 5 percent just to cash a government check and takes the money back out of the community. People who want to save have nowhere to go, and businesses have no access to capital. Within the 165 square miles that make up the areas most affected by the Los Angeles disturbances, there are 19 bank branches, as compared to 135 check-cashing establishments.

Over the last 20 years, Shorebank of Chicago has shown the world that a financial institution that is committed to community development can lead a community back from the brink of economic and social decline. Since 1973, it has made $340 million available in development financing, mainly for the purchase of rehabilitation of housing units in Chicago's South Shore neighborhood.

Shorebank is more than just a bank. Through its various subsidiaries and affiliates, it has been an active force in the revitalization of the South Shore. Shorebank has used a subsidiary, City Lands Corporation, to make high-risk loans for housing development. It has used a non-profit affiliate, the Neighborhood Institute, to help disadvantaged residents achieve their GEDs, start up small businesses, and train for jobs available in the community. It has used its depository institution, South Shore Bank, to make loans to people seeking to renovate apartment buildings and establish small businesses that generate jobs in the community.

The bank now boasts of over $211 million in deposits, almost half of which come from residents of the South Shore community. We often hear about how banking institutions take money in the form of deposits from economically-distressed areas and reinvest them in other areas. Shorebank shows how assets from the community can be put to work for the community!

Another home-grown project dedicated to the benefits of capital and savings is New Community Corporation in Newark, New Jersey. New Community Corporation was formed in the wake of the Newark riots of 1967. Over the last 25 years, it and its subsidiaries have developed over 2,500 housing units, 25,000 square feet of office space, and an $11-million extended care facility. New Communtity has also built a $15-million shopping center, which contains Central Newark's only major grocery store built since 1967.

New Community's founder, Monsignor William Linder, testified recently before Congress: "I have seen bank branch after bank branch close because the bank did not find serving our community profitable. There was always the same trend. Managers were frequently changed, service became poor, the facility was always dirty. Frankly, no one in authority cared about our community."

But instead of giving up hope, Monsignor Linder and others started a credit union. He now presides over a credit union with about $1.7 million in assets that provides basic banking services to community residents. Last year, New Community's credit union made 165 loans, mainly to poor residents of Newark's Central Ward. Basic banking services like check cashing, consumer loans, and savings acounts are taken for granted by a lot of people, but in places like the Central Ward of Newark they have become scarce and prized commodities. Like Shorebank, New Community, in its own way, has recreated opportunities for its community.

The bill I've introduced commits the federal government to efforts like those taken in Shorebank in Chicago or New Communities in Newark. It increases the amount of funds authorized in various government programs for the benefit of community development financial institutions, and expands the number of institutions that are eligible for the funds. It creates a new program specifically designed to help institutions like New Community—community development financial institutions—grow into community development banks like Shorebank, and it helps institutions like Shorebank expand their services.

ENTREPRENEURSHIP TRAINING

When we confront our fears about the city, we have to start with our assumptions about the people who live there, particularly young black men. But here is another view of the young people of the inner city: "They confront risk daily; they are resilient, intuitive, creative and observant; and they have learned to take great initiative within a stifling environment, just to survive." To Steve Mariotti, a former Detroit auto executive, these were the characteristics of a successful entrepreneur. With help from private foundations, he started the National Foundation for Teaching Entrepreneurship. Where others looked at these same kids and saw only their deficits and their problems, Steve saw their strengths. And he was right. By working in schools and settlement houses with kids as young as six and up to the age of 24, he taught people about the value of money, and about how to use their instincts and skills to grow in the long run, not just to survive in the short run. In 1990, the Foundation graduated 225 young entrepreneurs, who started 152 businesses, including retail clothing firms and food and catering businesses.

The Foundation for Teaching Entrepreneurship is just one program that might benefit from my Entrepreneurship Training Program for urban residents young or old. The bill authorizes $85 million in grants to community colleges and community development corporations in economically-distressed central cities to develop an entrepreneurship curriculum and train urban residents for self-employment. It also provides $150 million in guarantees of loans made by community development corporations, community development loan funds, community development credit unions, and community development banks to finance small business start-ups by graduates of such self-employment training programs.

FIFTEEN-MONTH HOUSES

As essential as investment, capital, and infrastructure are, they are not family. They are not children. And nothing is more vulnerable than children to the pressures of the city. Raising children is a 24-7-365-20 proposition: 24 hours a day, seven days a week, 365 days a year, for 20 years. Young mothers often do not realize this, and with the pressures of the city—the economic pressures, drugs as a commonplace of life, crime and guns—it is more difficult for them to provide that steady hand than it is for many other parents. That's why I think Fifteen-Month Houses make sense.

Yet a few people have stepped in to build communities that set children on a sound course through life by caring for them in the most important fifteen months of life: the last trimester of pregnancy and the first year after birth. In Los Angeles, Bea Stolzer and an organization called New Economics for Women put together everything they could find, including low-income tax credits, local housing development credits, Community Reinvestment Act credits, and welfare system funds, to build Casa Loma, a residence for 110 single-parent families and senior citizens, with child-care space, family services, and vocational programs. In New York, the Bronx Parent Association has developed a 12-18 month residential program—La Casita—to serve pregnant women and women with young children. It provides initial evaluation of enrollees for psycho-social needs and substance-abuse problems, counseling, on-site medical services, job training, parenting classes, on-site day care, and a one-year follow up.

From these home-grown initiatives, I have come up with the idea of Fifteen-Month Houses, and later this year I will introduce a bill authorizing $250 million to establish residential programs for low-income and young mothers during the third trimester of the mother's pregnancy and the first year of life. The program must provide the mother with health and substance-abuse screening or treatment, and education in parenting.

For the child, the program must include cognitive stimulation as well as immunizations and other care. The Robert Wood Johnson Foundation recently completed a study showing that if children are provided not just healthy care during the first year of life, but also systematic cognitive stimulation, behavior problems will be reduced later, they will progress more quickly in education later, and the burden on the school to remedy problems from early in life will be correspondingly reduced. Fifteen-Month Houses will be intended to provide that safe and stimulating year to the most vulnerable children.

INDIVIDUAL DEVELOPMENT

Another reality of city life that we have to face up to is government's failure to lift people out of poverty. The average income in Newark, New Jersey, is about $9,000 a year. The average income for New Jersey overall is three to four times that. While cities have gotten poorer, government has been engaged in an endless debate about whether traditional welfare programs give people too much income, discouraging work—or too little. While this debate is important, it misses a key point: traditional welfare programs that support income and spending can never, by themselves, lift people out of poverty. You can no more spend your way out of poverty than you can borrow your way out of debt. To become economically self-sufficient requires at least some assets—a house, a savings account in case of an emergency, even an education counts as an asset. Poor people are much poorer in assets than in income. For example, African-American families with monthly incomes below $900 have an average net worth of about *$88*. That includes everything—furniture, a car, savings, the value of a pension. The average net worth for white familes earning only two to three times as much is *more than $50,000*.

For middle-class people, the government encourages and heavily subsidizes the development of assets. Interest paid on home mortgages is tax-deductible. Pensions are tax-deferred, and Individual Retirement Accounts are encouraged. Meanwhile, poor people live in neighborhoods where there are no banks; without a pension or a down payment on a home, they cannot take advantage of the many ways our government helps people develop assets. If they are on welfare, they cannot even save $2,000 or so to buy a car and get to a job without being penalized by welfare. Indeed, in Milwaukee, Wisconsin two years ago, a young single mother named Grace Capitello managed to save $3,000, making clothes and toys for her daughter instead of buying them and by scrimping at the grocery store. For her efforts, she was charged with fraud by the county and ordered to turn over all her savings. Fortunately a judge understood.

Throwing out the case, he complained, "I don't know how much more powerfully we could say it to the people in our society: 'Don't try to save'—than we were by this action."

From the creativity of Grace Capitello comes the idea for the Assets for Independence Act. This bill would not only allow poor people to save without penalty, it would encourage it. It would allow anyone with income up to twice the poverty line—or about $22,000 for a family of four—to establish an Individual Development Account (IDA) and contribute up to $2,000 a year, the same as in an Individual Retirement Account. This account could be used for only four purposes: to buy a first home, to pay for college education, for retirement, or to start a small business. To reward savings, the program would provide funds to community-based non-profits to match the savings in an IDA, up to a total of $2,000. This bill would authorize $200 million to establish a broad demonstration of this revolutionary concept.

INCREASING MOBILITY

The most striking characteristic of American central cities today is their isolation. Once the hub of their regions, the center of commerce, jobs, and culture, inner-cities are now isolated socially, culturally, and economically. Outsiders look in, through movies like *Boyz 'N the Hood,* at a world with its own values, its own language, and its own icons of popular culture. But all the talk in Washington about the "culture of poverty" diverts our attention from the very simple fact of isolation from jobs. It is not news that a central city like Newark lost 80,000 jobs between 1970 and 1988. But these cities are nestled in metropolitan areas that were creating far more jobs than were lost, including many entry-level jobs with modest skill requirements. Mobility strategies could connect entry-level jobs with the people who need them through creative transportation.

Unfortunately, those jobs were in the suburbs. To say that an urban resident can't get an entry-level job until the city revives in total is to say that a generation will be wasted, as politicians of all races give excuses and bureaucrats twiddle their thumbs and push paper. In 20 large metropolitan areas of America, more than 75 percent of the jobs created in the 1980s were outside of the central city. And in six areas, including Chicago, Cleveland, and Detroit, every single new job created—100 percent of the net job growth—was in the suburbs.

In southeast Chicago, residents of the Le Clair Court housing project concluded that the barrier between Le Clair residents and jobs was simply transportation. Most Le Clair residents don't own cars, and bus transportation to a suburban job means getting up three hours before work and returning home well after dark. With the help of a creative young manager named Theresa Prim, they scraped together $250,000 from foundations to buy five 20-person vans, and began to talk to suburban businesses about their desperate need for entry-level workers. They concluded that if people had good jobs, they would pay six dollars a day for transportation to those jobs. Now fares paid by workers or employers cover almost half the cost of the Accel Transportation project. The vans are full. And many Le Clair residents soon buy a car to get to their new jobs, opening a spot in the van for someone new. Besides transportation, the program includes job counseling and conflict resolution for workers who are not used to suburban jobs and employers who are not accustomed to hiring inner-city residents and often must overcome their own ingrained impulses on issues of race.

I have not given up hope that we can draw more jobs to the cities, but we can no longer put all our hopes in that strategy. We know where the jobs are, and we know that in good economic times, companies have a hard time filling those jobs. In 1987 and 1988, companies in northern New Jersey were desperate for workers and began to run their own vans into Newark. But when the economy turned down, companies quickly cut this cost, and urban workers were cut off before they developed a permanent attachment to the work force.

My "Mobility for Work" initiative is intended to build a lasting connection between urban workers and suburban jobs by helping projects like Accel Transportation get going. At only $15 million, it is the least expensive component of this urban initiative, but one with the most possibilities. Everything is interconnected. For example, when city dwellers return to their communities in the evening with real earnings from jobs, banks and retail businesses will emerge to serve them, creating more jobs in the community and starting a cycle of prosperity. Some urban residents might move out to the suburbs, closer to the jobs, or some businesses might be drawn back to the city, once they overcome their prejudices about inner-city minority workers. This is a demonstration program, with a rigorous evaluation at the end to determine the effects of this new strategy.

22

The Libertarian Conundrum: Why the Market Does Not Safeguard Civil Rights

Alan Wolfe

Here is a quick quiz, designed to see if the reader is familiar with the twists and turns of contemporary legal theory. What position would someone committed to the University of Chicago brand of law and economics—which holds that legal rules ought to be fashioned to facilitate the self-interest of individual parties—take on the burning issue of affirmative action? The somewhat surprising answer is that he would be *for* it, so long as the quotas and goals designed to encourage minority hiring were voluntarily promulgated by private firms or individuals.

This brief example gives as good an introduction as any other to the way Richard Epstein thinks about civil rights laws. Affirmative action is such a contentious issue because it brings into direct conflict two moral goods: the imperative of overcoming past discrimination and the belief that innocent individuals living in the present should not pay a price for the sins of others who lived in the past. What is interesting about Epstein's treatment of this issue is that *both* moral positions are bypassed; indeed all moral positions, save for the sanctity of individual freedom, are bypassed. Every question for Epstein turns on the issue of who is to regulate what. Private individuals ought to regulate themselves through the contracts they establish with each other. If they want to bind themselves to hiring quotas, that is their business. If they do not want to, that is also their business. The only rule here is that the state cannot adopt an affirmative action program because its actions are not voluntary and contractual.

AN ATTACK ON INTELLECTUAL COMPLACENCY

In *Forbidden Grounds: The Case Against Employment Discrimination Laws*, Epstein proposes to abolish the laws that attempt to prohibit discrimination in hiring. He does not advocate this position timidly. Nor does he expect his position to be an influential one. The Supreme Court would never adopt his position even if the Republicans had remained in power until the end of the century. (Chief Justice Warren Burger wrote the first important affirmative action decision; Chief Justice William Rehnquist has never urged repeal of the Civil Rights Act of 1964.) Epstein is not writing to influence policy directly. "Consensus may be indispensable for ordering political life," he writes, "but it is dangerous for intellectual work." Writing as an intellectual, Epstein is determined to show the rest of us how wrong-headed, counter-productive, and confused we are if we believe that employment and anti-discrimination laws—not only the 1964 Civil Rights Act, but laws that ban discrimination against the handicapped, the elderly, people with AIDS, or, for that matter, people with blue eyes—ought to be allowed to override the private wishes of two parties to a contract.

Let it be said right from the start that Epstein's attack on intellectual complacency is welcome. And it is welcome not only because every position, no matter how justifiable, ought to be subject to debate. For the truth is that the regulation of discrimination is a far more complex matter than we sometimes picture it, and Epstein has indeed found soft places to attack. Can we really expect that anti-discrimination laws will protect all workers irrespective of how old they become? Even if we should want to protect everyone's job irrespective of old age—a goal I for one do *not* share—what will be the costs of resulting discrimination against the young? If so, ought every firm to have the same proportion of workers as the population of the country, the state, or the local neighborhood? If a small firm that has some minority workers but fewer than we would like is forced to go out of business because of the costs of improving its racial balance, is the overall goal of racial justice served or harmed? Is pregnancy a disability? Should men and women compete on the same sports teams? In the same sports? If they compete on different teams, what is the difference between such practices and the doctrine of "separate but equal" invalidated by *Brown v. Board of Education*? It ought not be surprising that the achievement of any morally desirable goal presents complications. The failure of advocates of anti-discrimination laws to acknowledge such difficulties gives critics such as Epstein something of an open field in uncovering holes in the way we think about discrimination.

Yet aside from winning an occasional debating point, Epstein does not, in the end, make a convincing case that laws against discrimination ought to be repealed. His book, rather, has the same unanticipated consequences as many of the laws he examines, for in setting out to convince the reader that the Civil Rights Act of 1964 was a mistake, he reopens the wounds that only healed once we as a society fashioned a consensus on the importance of abolishing discrimination—a consensus that, in the more contentious 1990s, seems unfortunately to have weakened a great deal. Epstein ought to be thanked by those who believe in legislation against discrimination for returning us to those less complicated times when eliminating discrimination seemed so simple a moral command. In so doing he reminds us that, although we may disagree on the question of affirmative action, we rarely disagree—Epstein of course is the exception—with the idea that society took a giant step forward when it outlawed arbitrary and invidious discrimination.

THE MORAL CLAIMS FOR ANTI-DISCRIMINATION LAWS

There are two major reasons why we ought to deny individuals the freedom to conclude contracts that are premised on prejudice. The first is that private individuals, given enough freedom, are capable of doing lasting harm to others, harm so pernicious that the social and moral costs of regulating them are far less than whatever economic costs—if there are significant economic costs—result. The second is that the very values so admired by Epstein, especially the freedom of the individual, is a social value, made possible, and reinforced, by the culture, symbols, and norms of the society in which such values are appreciated. Private practices that weaken the symbolic or cultural framework of society weaken everything, including the ability of private individuals to engage in those very practices.

What caused anti-discrimination laws in the first place? The conventional answer is fairly clear. As a result of slavery, African-Americans were brought to this country against their will and their fundamental humanity was brutally denied. Even a war to free the slaves did not bring about true freedom, for the South established the system of Jim Crow in which blacks were treated as separate and less equal than whites. The Jim Crow system was upheld by the Supreme Court in *Plessy v. Ferguson* (1896), but a series of legal battles whittled away that precedent until, finally, the Court in 1954 upheld the claims of "simple justice." *Brown* established the national consensus that then made possible the passage of the Civil Rights Act of 1964. Although national policy in the wake of that

act has been fractured, the result of the Act was a significant decrease in
the amount of racism in American society.

EXCESSIVE GOVERNMENT TO BLAME

Epstein challenges every step in this story, but for my purposes here,
only one of his many points needs to be examined. Jim Crow, Epstein
claims, was *not* a result of private racism or discrimination but represented one more needless and obnoxious example of governmental interference in the private affairs of individuals. The South's failure to grant
full membership to African-Americans was a failure of the market, not
the state. Southern whites wanted integration, in this account, at least
those businessmen rational enough to want to serve every customer they
could. But the losers in the economic struggle were not powerless; controlling state legislatures, they forced the adoption of racial segregation
precisely to limit the economic power of those whose practices would
have produced a modern, and integrated, social fabric throughout the
South.

Epstein goes further. He points out that *Plessy* was decided only nine
years before *Lochner v. New York*, the case that overturned New York
State's efforts to regulate the number of hours that bakers could work.
Both these decisions are generally considered reactionary ones, among
the worst in the history of the Supreme Court. Not so, Epstein argues.
For *Lochner* could have provided a more appropriate vehicle for dealing
with discrimination than *Plessy*. Laws that call for segregation are one
more example of the inappropriate police powers of the state. Just as the
court was right to abolish a law telling employers how many hours their
workers should work, it would have been right to overturn a law telling
employers only to hire whites (or African-Americans). It is as if the
wrongs committed by private individuals are never laid on their own
shoulders, so long as some form of governmental action can be found,
which, in the modern world, is always possible.

DOES THE MARKET ENCOURAGE OR DISCOURAGE DISCRIMINATION?

But one need not develop a history counter to the one offered by Epstein
to see why private individuals discriminate. If there are occasions when
discrimination may be irrational, there are other occasions on which it is
rational. Hence Epstein—who is far more committed to rationality as he
understands it than to any position on discrimination—argues at some

points in his book that markets *will* encourage discrimination, and that this is as it should be. Spot markets, in which individuals come together to make a quick transaction only to depart, do not encourage discrimination because the individuals involved have so little to do with each other. But the employment contract is another matter entirely. This is a long-term commitment, one that welcomes a person into a firm, its culture, and its already-present employees. Because large firms with many members have diverse tastes, imposing a single preference on everyone will always cause friction. Hence "the temptation to discriminate, which makes little sense in a world of spot transactions and perfect information, makes a great deal more sense in a world of continuous relationships in which the costs of the legal system are often high and sometimes prohibitive." Voluntary markets will often be segregated markets, in which different firms do things in different ways in response to different customers, clients, or employees.

Epstein wants us to believe that "self-interested businessmen will be loath to practice discrimination when it hurts the bottom line" *and* that "the partition of the market into specialized and well-defined niches should increase the satisfaction of all customers." His economic history and theory contradict each other. If we listen to his history, we must conclude that the South would have abolished discrimination if only the state had stayed out and let the market rule. But if we listen to his economic theory, we must conclude that a market system will invariably result in segregated practices. It seems as if Epstein wants to be on both sides of the issue, turning the argument one way or another—but in all cases concluding that the state should stay out.

On this point, I think his economic theory is superior to his history. Markets do encourage a kind of "natural" segregation, and there is no reason in theory why such segregation cannot work to the persistent disadvantage of a group, solely on the basis of that group's skin color. Moreover, as Epstein is the first to suggest, such segregation is more likely to be thorough, not in the purchasing of soft-drinks and lunches, but in the finding and keeping of jobs that put food on the family table.

Finally, as once again his economic theory says, the individuals who are members of the group that experiences segregation from the dominant markets will themselves be denied the opportunity to maximize their own self-interest. The point would need to be made, except that Epstein makes it himself, that not all segregation is the result of what the state does. (Although Epstein never discusses the matter, boycotts by private individuals and firms that were tempted to break Jim Crow's strictures were a common feature of *economic* life in the South). If the market, for whatever reason, segments and divides by race, but if the elimination of racial barriers will enhance profits by maximizing customers or clients, then the market needs to be regulated in order to make the market function effectively. *In short, even within the terms of rational self-interest, there are perfectly good reasons why we might want a Civil Rights Act roughly like the one passed by Congress in 1964.* Indeed the lack of such a policy encouraged highly irrational economic behavior, which was not stopped until government put an end to it. As this example shows, Epstein tends to reason from his conclusions backwards to his analysis. This is not only unfortunate, it also stands in contrast to the way the Chicago School of Economics once offered surprising, if usually somewhat outrageous, theories.

For all the rigor offered by the law and economics approach, *Forbidden Grounds* stands on shifting grounds; if one argument against outlawing discrimination does not work, Epstein simply finds another. If discrimination is not found, the market is doing its job. If discrimination is found, the market is doing its job. There is nothing wrong with discrimination. At the same time, efforts to eliminate it will fail. One can find all these arguments in Epstein's book, even though some of them stand in tension with others. Such are the problems with a book that is far more interested in marshalling evidence for its conclusion than in persuading the reader that the conclusion might have some validity.

THE CRITIQUE OF PRIVATE UNIVERSITIES

Another, and more serious, example of Epstein's tendency to shift ground involves his thoughts on affirmative action in universities. Epstein, as I showed earlier in this essay, wants to tone down the war over affirmative action by granting it to those who want it and by exempting those who do not want it. Yet when he turns to universities, especially the elite universities, he clearly does not like what has been done in the name of affirmative action. (He joins those who argue that the politicalization of race, class, and gender will destroy what makes great universities great.) But on what basis can Epstein criticize what private universities do? One could hardly imagine a better example of a private market operating with minimal government regulation than America's elite universities. If they are far too politicized for Epstein's tastes, such is the way markets in ideas, faculty, and students work.

Moreover, the strongest arguments against affirmative action are made by those who support the Civil Rights Act of 1964, not those who oppose it. Not only was the possibility of affirmative action foreseen by the advocates of the 1964 law, it was repeatedly denounced by them. The 1964 Act strives toward, even if it cannot quite achieve it, the principle of color-blindness. If one rejects that principle, one has no strong basis on which to oppose affirmative action. Epstein is more consistent when he argues in favor of affirmative action. But this just makes his comment about the private universities seem gratuitous and out of keeping with the logic and argumentation of his book.

The same principle holds true for the argument against an active government trying to reform people's moral character. As Andrew Kull demonstrates in his important book *The Color-Blind Constitution,* the problem with race-conscious policies is that they enable the judiciary to craft public policy actively. Conservative pessimists, those who do not think government can or should do much to reform society, should prefer an explicit statement by the Supreme Court that the Constitution must be color-blind, a statement that the Court has never given, Kull argues. If Congress were to listen to Epstein and to repeal the Civil Rights Act of 1964, we would likely have an even more active judiciary—and therefore an even more active government. The conservative position should be that Congress did not go far *enough* in 1964 in insisting on color-blindness. What could be more conservative—or more cognizant of individual freedom—than a law which forbids discrimination both as a way of perpetuating racism *and* as a way of correcting for it?

Epstein stands proudly outside the mainstream. One reason he does is that most people look at the realities of inequality and discrimination rather than at hypotheticals that seem self-serving. In real life, discrimination is caused by both economic and political behavior, which means that efforts to eliminate it have to be two-pronged. In reality, if not in Epstein's book, those who are harmed by discrimination will use whatever branch of government they can to ease the harm; if it is not Congress, it will be the courts. In the real world, private and public depend on each other, the latter defining the scope of the former, the former establishing the priorities of the latter. It is because reality counts in any intellectual debate that so many individuals, who disagree over so much else, nonetheless find consensus in the Civil Rights Act of 1964. Those who would, as Epstein does, condemn such laws as "a new form of imperialism that threatens the political liberty and intellectual freedom of all" simply have not persuaded very many people that their point of view ought to be taken seriously. As Epstein would surely acknowledge, there are winners and losers in every market. Epstein is one of the losers in the marketplace of ideas about discrimination.

A STATE WITHOUT SYMBOLS?

"Given the limits of our knowledge," Epstein writes in the conclusion of his book, "I believe that the best way to take into account the full range of symbols, good and bad, noble and vain, is for the legal system to *ignore* them all—mine and yours alike." One wonders exactly how the legal system will do this. What symbols will it use to abolish symbols? In what language, using what words, and appealing to what unifying principles will we agree to allow everyone to go his own way? Who will establish the consensus that we ought not to seek consensus? "Symbols are, in a sense, too important and too volatile to be either the subject of, or the justification for, direct government regulation," Epstein writes.

On the contrary. Because symbols are both important and volatile, government will always be in the symbol business. There is, indeed, no more important task facing government than to reinforce—and if necessary regulate—what bonds Americans hold in common. In America, we lodge our most powerful symbols in a document called the Constitution. If we follow Epstein's arguments in favor of symbolic neutrality, we would have to repeal, not only the Civil Rights Act of 1964, but the Constitution itself. Epstein's views on symbols, if taken seriously, would put him well to the right of strict constrictionists such as Robert Bork. They want the symbols to have one meaning only. Epstein seems to be saying that symbols should have no meaning at all.

The absurdity of what Epstein says about symbols can be illustrated by asking what would be necessary to create a regime in which the principles of the law and economics approach would apply. We would, first of all, seek to create a set of rules that make the pursuit of self-interest the major value of our society. Then we would create a set of institutions, which we would call markets, the main mechanism for reaching those goals. Finally we would, when practices conflict, give preference to those practices that most contributed to the pursuit of profit. One can like or dislike such a regime; Epstein likes it, while I dislike it. But surely we can agree that such a regime would be filled with symbols sanctioned by some political authority. A free-market system would compel us to recognize the powerful symbol of the market; there can, in other words, be a free market in everything but symbols themselves. A government that upheld freedom of contract would not be symbolically neutral. In situations of conflict, all those symbols reinforcing individual freedom would be chosen over all those seeking to abolish racial discrimination. It is never a question of symbols versus no symbols, always a question of which ones we value.

DISREGARDING THE COMMUNITY

There is no question that there can be too much governance, just as there is no question that social conformity can be stifling. We would surely not wish to live in a society that so insisted on only some symbols that those for whom other symbols were important would be treated as pariahs. The trick of finding ways in which different people can live together is working out those things that must be held in common as well as those in which diversity can and should flourish. Epstein's symbolic neutrality helps us little, and not only because there is no such thing. It solves the problem of trying to balance the individual and the social by avoiding the problem entirely.

It is surprising that, in a period characterized by Arthur Schlesinger, Jr. as "the disuniting of America," a writer like Epstein would agree so much with the advocates of race, class, and gender consciousness he so thoroughly attacks. For, like them, Epstein encourages sub-communities to flourish at the expense of the larger community that makes them possible. We have, in America, two intellectual movements that tend to be hostile to the importance of community, one from the left and one from the right. Those who believe that the claims of particular ethnic groups for their own history, language, and culture should take precedence over national symbols and identities are not all that different from libertarians such as Epstein, with the exception that the latter seeks freedom for individuals rather than the groups to which they belong. The world of law and economics—an academic offshoot of the libertarian conservatism that flourished in the 1970s—has this much in common with the leftist multiculturalism that flourished in the 1980s: both posit entities who care primarily about themselves, choosing with whom and on what terms they will deal. The law and economics perspective is one more symptom—one more symbol, if you wish—of the degree to which Americans are losing a sense of their obligations to the society of which they are a part.

Americans at the moment are bitterly divided over whether the U.S. went too far, or not far enough, in the civil rights policy that followed the 1964 Act. Should gender have been included in the bill when it was gratuitously offered by the bill's opponents to defeat the legislation? Ought the executive branch and the courts to have been so determined to shift to race-conscious policies? Was the Americans with Disabilities Act a good idea? Epstein views the debates over these issues as so impassioned and irreconcilable that we ought to bypass them entirely. But it is the existence of such debates, more than the way they are resolved, that makes democracy a system worth having. We would be less of a society if we were not allowed to argue over such issues because the market took care of them for us. If we were ever tempted to build a society on Epstein's principles, we would not only be intellectually poorer, we would also be telling relatively powerless groups that they would have no recourse against unfair and discriminatory treatment. Some ways of making life simpler ought to be avoided.

Someone from the law and economics perspective could have written an important book about legislation that seeks to regulate discrimination. There is little doubt, at least in my mind, that the language of rights, including the language of civil rights, is both essential to the good society but destructive of community if asserted in such a way that everything else must give way before it. Our national preoccupation with race, and the harms caused by racism, would be improved by any realistic and original effort to understand these things anew. The trouble with *Forbidden Grounds* is that seeking such an understanding is not one of its major objectives. It knows where it wants to go and will use any route to get there. As a result, the important national dialogue currently taking place, one that is trying to find a way of healing our racial wounds, will not include Richard Epstein.

23

Drug Abuse Control Policy: Libertarian, Authoritarian, Liberal, and Communitarian Perspectives

Mark Kleiman

The three major theoretical perspectives that drive the American political debate—libertarian or small-government conservatism, rights-and-welfare liberalism, and authoritarian conservatism—seem unable to make sense of drug abuse control policy. The phenomenon of drug abuse is not fully consistent with their underlying models of human behavior and society; policy prescriptions that fit libertarian, liberal, and authoritarian preconceptions thus fit the real world only as a 42 long suit fits a man who is actually a 44 regular: that is, imperfectly. It remains to be seen whether a communitarian account of the topic can be made to fit any better.

THE LIBERTARIAN FANTASY

The libertarian approach to the topic was best expressed, perhaps, by a colleague to whom I was once introduced as a student of drug abuse control policy. "But there shouldn't be any such policy!" he exclaimed.

If individual human beings are in all circumstances the best stewards of their own welfare, and if civil society plus minimal governments suffice to facilitate their cooperation and to restrain them from violating one another's rights, then no intervention in private "lifestyle" choices or in the economic activity of production and promotion that serves and shapes those choices could improve average well-being. This is the libertarianism of Mill.

If each individual has a natural right to shape his or her own life constrained only by the rights of others, then intervention, except to punish transgression, is unjustified, even if it would by some measure improve welfare. Again, it is assumed that the ability of the criminal and civil laws to control "boundary crossing" is unaffected by the extent to which the members of the community in question are inclined to theft, violence, and recklessness, or prone to act on impulse. This is the libertarianism of Nozick.

A RATIONAL ADDICT?

Drug-taking poses a problem for any theory based on rational self-command. Drug-taking tends, more frequently than most other consumption activities, to exceed rational control. The tendency to excess inherent in drug-taking is reflected in our language; to describe a compulsive over-worker as a "workaholic" or to call someone with an insatiable desire to rule a "power junkie" reflects the belief that drug-taking is the archetype of bad habits, the mother of all addictions. The less drug-taking reflects the settled beliefs of drug-takers about what is good for them, the weaker the case on strictly utilitarian grounds against interfering with drug users' behavior, or that of those who sell and encourage drug use.

For the hard-core libertarian, for whom non-interference is a matter of principle rather than a theorem about welfare maximization, the mere observation that many drug-takers wish they weren't constitutes no argument for intervention. Only proof of harm to others would suffice. But is that proof hard to furnish? Grant for the purposes of argument that most of the crimes committed by users of illicit drugs are the result of their prohibition. However, the frequency of alcoholic assault and drunken driving stands as testimony to the power of intoxicant use to harm others, and the impotence of the criminal and civil laws to deter those too drunk to reckon the consequences.

AN ARGUMENT FOR GOVERNMENT INTERVENTION

The plausibility of minimal government as an adequate check on the tendency of individuals to harm one another depends on a population sufficiently respectful of boundaries and adequately in command of themselves to be deterred by the threat of lawsuit or prosecution. A regime that permits drug-taking *ad libitum* may therefore find it impossible to be as laisser-faire in other domains as it would prefer to be.

But, someone will point out, not all drug-taking is compulsive and not all drugs provoke users to aggression or negligence. Of course not. Neither does every campfire not doused with water become a forest fire. Drug-taking is not inevitably damaging; it is merely risky, to drug-takers and others, to an extent varying from drug to drug, from user to user, and from circumstance to circumstance. But that suggests that some degree of intervention—varying by drug, by user, and by circumstance—will be desirable to protect users and others from bad habits and intoxicated misbehavior: demanding exactly the sort of detailed intervention the libertarian most hopes to avoid.

The disjunction between libertarian theories and the facts of drug abuse is so great that the libertarian, small-government strain that runs through much of American conservative thinking on economic issues has had almost no influence on the stance conservative office-seekers take toward the drug problem. Politicians who oppose governmental intervention in virtually every other sphere find that, in this one instance, they must rise above principle and join with the authoritarians in demanding tougher drug laws.

THE AUTHORITARIAN INCONSISTENCY

A policy area in which individual freedom contradicts itself would seem to be a happy hunting ground for authoritarian conservatives. Drug-taking illustrates the inadequacy of individual pleasure-seeking as a guide to the good life or as a social binding force, and thus, apparently, the need for traditional values, enforced as needed by a benevolent government.

Yet authoritarians, too, find drug abuse a hard problem to embrace. After all, total abstinence from the use of psychoactive drugs is not in fact the traditional practice of most American subcultures. Tobacco-growing—that is, the production of the drug nicotine—was the economic basis of the Jamestown Colony; the Boston Tea Party and the Whisky Rebellion testify to the traditional importance of caffeine and alcohol.

TRADITIONAL FAVORITES

This would not pose a problem if the traditionally accepted drugs were clearly less hazardous to their users and others than more recent, illicit additions to the recreational pharmacopoeia: cannabis, the opiates, cocaine and the amphetamines, and the psychedelics. But, alas, there seems to be no such tendency. Although the damage done by caffeine is still being investigated, nicotine outstrips all of the currently illicit drugs in damaging the health of its users, and alcohol accounts for most of the country's intoxication, and most of its drug-related violence and negligence. Between them, they dwarf cocaine in the damage done to the unborn. Partly the preponderance of harms done by legal drugs reflects the success of prohibition in diminishing consumption of illegal drugs, but on purely pharmacological grounds it seems unlikely that alcohol and nicotine would be singled out for lenient treatment.

Thus authoritarians find it easy to support public measures to suppress drug abuse as long as the drug involved is not alcohol or tobacco. This resembles favoring maritime policies that do not deal with either the Atlantic or the Pacific.

With respect to illicit drugs, authoritarians have a simple message: "Drug-taking is bad. Don't do it. If we catch you doing it, we will punish you with loss of driving privileges, loss of property, loss of job, and loss of liberty; even, or perhaps especially, if your drug-taking does not harm you or anyone else, because successful drug-takers pose a special threat to traditional values." This formula has attracted overwhelming political support; the "war on drugs" is a winning issue for authoritarian conservatives.

Those authoritarian conservatives who like to paint themselves as "strict constructionists" of the Constitution and advocates of its interpretation according to "original intent" ought to have a problem with the extent of federal intervention in what would have appeared to the original framers of the Constitution as a matter for the police power of the states. The powers to regulate interstate commerce and to implement international drug control conventions do not obviously form the basis for federal criminal jurisdiction over someone who grows marijuana or gathers peyote buttons for personal consumption. The sight of a federal official actively campaigning for the passage of a state referendum, as "drug czar" William Bennett campaigned for the repeal of Alaska's marijuana decriminalization, ought to raise federalist hackles. That such objections are rarely heard may indicate, as liberals have often argued, that "strict construction," "original intent," and "federalism" are mere pretexts obscuring other motives, or simply that the drug issue has the political power to overcome ideological consistency.

A LOSING BATTLE

The main embarrassment to authoritarians in drug policy is practical rather than theoretical. Authoritarian policies, pursued with increasing vigor for more than a decade now, do not seem to be working very well.

Despite tens of billions of dollars spent trying to seal the borders, cocaine prices are near their all-time low and cocaine imports near their all-time high. Surveys indicate that the self-reported number of cocaine users has passed its peak, but cocaine-related visits to hospital emergency rooms just set another record. Heroin, too, is making a comeback after almost two decades of quiescence.

It turns out to be substantially easier to announce that one is opposed to drug-taking than to craft public policies to reduce the damage it does. As with most other policies, but perhaps more so than average, drug abuse control policy is subject to the law of unintended consequences. No matter how simple in concept, drug abuse control measures in practice involve substantial feats of "social engineering" of exactly the kind that authoritarian conservatives join their libertarian brethren in deploring.

A policy of announced hostility toward drug-taking and drug-takers will tend to make the remaining drug-takers worse off, and more dangerous to others, than they would otherwise have been. Moreover, it leads citizens and their representatives to shy away from the part of drug abuse control policy that involves providing services to drug-takers to help them quit, moderate their behavior, or better integrate themselves into the broader society (for example, through employment).

Just as authoritarianism is led to make too sharp a distinction between alcohol and the illicit drugs, it is virtually forced to make too little distinction among the "controlled substances." Speaking and acting as if marijuana and cocaine were comparably threatening leads to poor resource allocation at best, but careful distinctions are exactly what an appeal to traditional values cannot provide.

Thus authoritarian conservatives are left with no policy at all toward the drugs sold legally by large corporations, because such a policy would involve either taxes or regulations on commerce, both of which authoritarians, like libertarians, deplore. And while they have no problem in principle with policies to restrict the supply of illegal drugs, in practice their approach seems to work badly. This is partly because, in deference to their nativist strain, authoritarians over-concentrate their supply-control efforts on overseas crop eradication and border control.

THE LIBERAL QUANDARY

Just so, say the rights-and-welfare liberals. We could have told you as much. Of course a policy based on establishing a governmental preference for one lifestyle choice over another, backed by coercion and directed primarily at the poor, was certain to fail. Drug abuse is a disease that requires a public health approach. Those suffering from it must be treated, and the social conditions—poverty and deprivation—that breed this disease must be changed, just as the swamps that breed mosquitoes must be drained to prevent yellow fever.

Less married to the sovereign and infallible consumer than the libertarians and less married to traditional practices than authoritarians, liberals have no difficulty in recognizing that some consumption choices, especially those made with the persuasive help of large corporations, may not be in the best interest of the consumer. Tobacco-smoking is the most obvious example, with liberals leading the charge for higher taxes and tighter regulations. It seems likely that liberals also will lead the way toward tightening the current policies toward alcohol, which are insanely lax. Unlike the illicit-drug problem, smoking and, increasingly, alcohol abuse are not seen by liberals as mere epiphenomena of poverty and discrimination, but as independent problems that deserve, and can benefit from, attention in their own right.

JUST ANOTHER LIFESTYLE OPTION?

The liberals' problem is, or ought to be, with the illicit drugs. Taxes and regulations to prevent the distribution of unsafe consumer products obviously fit the liberal ideology with no stretching. But the direct application of coercive pressure on individuals to force them to choose one way of life over another conflicts with the commitment to governmental neutrality with respect to personal choice that liberals share with libertarians. If drug use is harmful only some of the time (rather than always evil, as the authoritarian believes), then a consistent liberal should be against it only some of the time. A liberal should no more delight in denouncing and punishing drug-users as a class than in denouncing and punishing unwed mothers as a class. And yet it seems hard to ignore the authoritarian claim that disapproval and intolerance are powerful modes of shaping behavior, or the evidence that the choice between using cocaine and not using cocaine is not the same as the choice between jogging and not jogging. Thus what to do with drug-users poses a problem for the rights-and-welfare liberal.

SINGLING OUT THE DISADVANTAGED

This is especially true when it comes to those drug-users whose drug-taking is most obviously harmful to others: those who steal or deal to support their habits. A focus on harm reduction would lead a liberal to want to concentrate on these drug-users, and to be willing to use coercion as well as offers of treatment to induce them to end a practice so damaging to their neighbors as well as to themselves. But of course stealing to support a habit is more characteristic of poor drug-takers than of more affluent ones. A policy of singling out drug-using offenders from other drug-users will thus tend to single out socially disadvantaged ethnic groups and the poor for unwanted attention. This smacks of "blaming the victim," that unforgiven sin against the liberal spirit. Harassing the underclass crack-smoker while ignoring the middle-class cocaine-sniffer is not a policy likely to appeal to the liberal impulse; a court in Minnesota was even persuaded to void a legislative distinction between crack and cocaine powder on the grounds of racially disparate impact.

Even drug dealers are largely persons of marginal social status and limited legitimate opportunity; once they are caught, they become first criminal defendants, and then prisoners. All of these are groups whose rights and interests liberals pride themselves on defending against an unfeeling social system and the wrath of the majority. The slow judicial repeal of the Fourth Amendment's protection against arbitrary search and seizure leaves all good liberals queasy. The fact that young African-American males are overrepresented among the street cocaine dealers whose work subjects them to the greatest probability of imprisonment makes things even worse for the liberal who wants to support drug law-enforcement. If raising the price of tobacco by taxation is a good way to reduce nicotine addiction, it seems logical that raising the price of heroin by putting heroin dealers in prison should be a good way to reduce heroin addiction; but liberals are reluctant to use prison cells as a primary tool of social policy. The liberal aversion to punishment makes the enforcement side of drug policy hard to swallow, just as the conservative aversion to governmental generosity creates a lack of enthusiasm for treatment.

THE LIBERAL DEFECTORS

Just as many office-seekers who are libertarian in principle make an exception for drug laws, overwhelming numbers of liberal politicians have decided not to be on the "wrong" side of the public fury against drug dealers. Some have simply kept their principled objections to themselves, fought rearguard actions against the excesses of the drug way, and argued against increased enforcement expenditure in the name of a "balance" between enforcement on the one hand and education and treatment on the other. Others have joined the full-throated hullabaloo against the drug lords, competing with authoritarians in inventing new offenses and imposing long and mandatory minimum sentences.

So we have libertarians with a consistent theory that fits the facts of drug abuse so poorly as to be a non-starter as a basis for policy, the authoritarians with a half-baked approach for the smaller half of the problem, and the liberals desperately hoping that the problem can be solved by giving (treatment, advice, and opportunity) and not (much) punishing, especially of poor and minority users and dealers. We also have a set of policies that perform poorly.

What might a communitarian approach to drug policy be?

A COMMUNITARIAN APPROACH

Let us start with its assumptions. It would reject both the authoritarian notion that all use of non-traditional psychoactives is evil per se and the libertarian one that the drug problem is a mere figment of the authoritarian imagination. It would acknowledge that since tastes are socially constructed and to some extent manipulated for economic gain, free consumer choice—allowing people to have what they think they want—is only a provisionally desirable goal.

A communitarian drug policy would acknowledge that maintaining security for individuals and institutions against theft, assault, and disorder is possible without intolerably intrusive levels of enforcement only if the vast majority of the population is inclined to honesty, nonaggression, and self-control; consequently, public action to ensure the character of the people may be justified and even necessary. It would neither glory in nor shrink from the task of imposing costs on those whose behavior is damaging to others. It would recognize that, for those who have lost control over their own behavior or never learned to regulate it, help and coercion are necessarily intermixed.

On a practical level, a drug policy along communitarian lines would pay far more attention to alcohol and tobacco than the current approach does. This would mean using taxation and regulation to reduce the incidence of cigarette smoking, almost all of which is compulsive in nature and harmful to health out of proportion to any benefits it confers. Taxation, negative advertising, and efforts to create new norms and social roles (for instance, the designated driver) would help limit alcohol consumption, but communitarians might be willing to further link rights and responsibilities by making drinking, like driving, a licensed privilege subject to withdrawal for misbehavior (drunken driving, drunken assault, repeated drunken mischief).

With respect to the illicit drugs, communitarians would notice that most of the public health benefits of drug prohibition are provided by the prohibition itself, and that, beyond a symbolic minimum the primary goal of drug law-enforcement should be to minimize the unwanted side effects of prohibition—violence and theft. This implies that exerting control over a relatively small number (2–3 million) of frequent hard-drug users who also are active criminals is essential, both because they commit much of the crime and because their demand supports the illicit markets that generate so much urban violence, both directly and by financing the purchase of firearms by young men inclined to use them. Since most people who finance heavy hard-drug habits by theft or drug dealing are on probation or parole when not in prison or jail, the best way to reduce their drug-taking is to require abstinence as a condition of probation or parole, with frequent, random drug tests and swift, certain, and progressively serious, but not draconian, jail terms for violations. Contrary to the myth of the addict helpless in the grip of his drug, most can and will comply.

A communitarian policy would thus acknowledge the libertarian goal of personal freedom, the authoritarian concern for character, and the liberal desire to protect rights and promote welfare. Would it work better than existing policies? Or perhaps we should rather ask: could it possibly do worse?

24

Inner-City Crime: What the Federal Government Should Do

John J. DiIulio, Jr.

The front-page story in the March 12, 1992, edition of *The Philadelphia Inquirer* was aptly entitled "Living Civilly in an Urban Hell." Its author, Matthew Purdy, told of the plight of a working inner-city mother named Irma Thomas:

> On a block of Susquehanna Avenue in Philadelphia there is Irma Thomas' stubborn oasis and nothing else. Inside her house, all is order. Three children sit at the kitchen table doing homework. Their tests and report cards are displayed proudly on the wall. . . . In their living room, Thomas grills her children in their only defense against frequent gunfire on the street: "Drop and Roll." . . . Thomas, 26, lives in a Philadelphia Housing Authority house, between two other homes that have been vacant for about 10 years, open to drug users, arsonists, and rodents. "We're forgotten about, down here," she said.

Over the last decade, there have been hundreds of newspaper, magazine, and television stories of this kind. But the Irma Thomas story struck a deep chord in me. My sister and I grew up minutes from where Ms. Thomas and her children live. But we did not live in fear of being murdered, mugged, and extorted. We were not in public housing, but the modest row home in which we lived still had a government lien on it from the days of the Great Depression when most of the family was on public relief. Financially, we lived from week to week, but my parents were not reluctant to sent us to school or let us go out to play for fear that drug dealers and gang members would prey on us. Instead of abandoned buildings, the neighborhood had plenty of small businesses—grocery stores, barber shops, hardware stores, pharmacies. We did not suffer from any sort of crime-induced depression of our neighborhood economy.

Today, I live in a solidly middle-class suburb of Philadelphia. Children in my neighborhood hear birds chirping at night, not gunfire. I do not have to worry about the crime and disorder that plague Irma Thomas, her family, and her decent, aspiring, law-abiding neighbors. Practically speaking, their plight is not my plight. I can avoid what they cannot escape; I can drive past the inner-city streets where they must walk and cope. I can lump the socio-economically disadvantaged together with the criminally deviant, label them an "underclass," and forget about them.

For the hard fact is that most of the serious crime in my region is concentrated in the types of inner-city neighborhoods where Irma Thomas lives. Any argument that I should care about inner-city crime out of enlightened self-interest will not hold water. There is no evidence that crime from poor and minority inner-city neighborhoods has spilled over into other places. For example, the Federal Bureau of Investigation's (FBI) Uniform Crime Report showed that in 1990 Philadelphia's total crime rate was about twice that of the four surrounding suburban Pennsylvania counties that ring the city, and its violent crime rate was over three times that of those counties. Forty-two percent of all violent crimes in Pennsylvania occurred in Philadelphia, which contained only 14 percent of the state's population.

The same picture holds true nationally. America's crime problem has been, and continues to be, an inner-city problem, one that is inextricably linked to the poverty and isolation of the minority citizens who live in these places. In December 1969, the National Commission on the Causes and Prevention of Violence declared that violent crimes are "chiefly a problem of the cities of the nation, and there violent crimes are committed mainly by the young, poor, male inhabitants of the ghetto slum." What was true in 1969 is doubly true in 1993. There is, to be sure, a good deal of crime outside the nation's inner cities. But the incidence of predatory street crime is highest on the streets of what were known as yesteryear's ghettos—today's "underclass" neighborhoods.

There are liberally thousands of statistics that make this point. For example, the Bureau of Justice Statistics (BJS) has reported that rates of violent crime in cities are about 92 percent higher than those in rural areas, and the rate of household crime (burglary, larceny, motor vehicle theft) is about 50 percent higher in the cities than in the suburbs. Most city crime is concentrated in poor, minority, inner-city neighborhoods. Of all Americans, inner-city African-American male teenagers and young adults from low-income families are at greatest risk of being victimized by serious crime.

In short, like most Americans, I am no more likely to be a victim of predatory street crime than I am to suffer from the poverty, joblessness, illiteracy, welfare dependency, or drug abuse problems that have come to define inner-city America.

Therein lies the moral dimension of the nation's urban crime dilemma. Unless citizens like me feel a sense of civic obligation to the country's Irma Thomases, unless we hold ourselves morally responsible for caring about their tragic life circumstances, there is no reason why we should demand that our government act to promote security in their communities.

PROMOTING SECURITY IN INNER-CITY COMMUNITIES

I would like to argue that the federal government can and should act to promote security in inner-city communities where crime and disorder are rampant, and to specify a few of the public policies that are most likely to be effective. I understand that, where public policies are concerned, most Americans are less at home with talk of "civic obligation" or "moral responsibility" than they are with talk of constitutional rights. So, without falling into "law reviewese," let me translate the issue into a single, overarching question about inner-city crime, community, and civil rights. The question is this: Are the civil rights of the nation's Irma Thomases being violated; and, if so, what, if any, federal government action can and should be taken to remedy the situation by promoting security in inner-city communities?

Let me be clear about what I mean by "promoting security in inner-city communities." I mean more than lowering crime rates. I mean providing the security to life, liberty, and property that is necessary for these neighborhoods to flourish as neighborhoods—enabling the citizens who live in these places to pursue their individual and collective lives as they see fit without undue fear of having their lives disrupted of destroyed. I mean securing inner-city communities against criminals who assault, rape, rob, burglarize, extort, deal drugs, and murder. But I also mean securing them against the community-sapping disorders that are commonly associated with serious crime and the fear of serious crime—public drunkenness, aggressive panhandling, gangs loitering in parks, prostitutes soliciting on street corners, abandoned cars, rowdy taverns, unregulated sex and drug-oriented paraphernalia shops, gambling dens, unmaintained or abandoned buildings, and so on.

As studies by Wesley G. Skogan, James Q. Wilson, and other scholars have suggested, such social and physical disorders give rise to serious crime, foster constant fear, and contribute ultimately to neighborhood instability and decay by enervating the capacity of people in these communities to exercise control over neighborhood events and conditions.

The question, then, is whether the persistent failure of state and local governments to promote security in disorder-ravaged, crime-torn inner-city neighborhoods is tantamount to a failure to protect and enforce the civil rights of the citizens who live in these places.

It is hard to see how the civil rights of these citizens are not being violated. I am not interested in performing the sort of intellectual gymnastics that might constitute a fully developed argument in favor of this proposition. Instead, I wish only to point to 1954, the year that the United States Supreme Court upheld the civil rights of Linda Brown and all persons similarly situated by declaring in *Brown v. Board of Education* that "segregation of children in public schools solely on the basis of race" deprives "the children of the minority group of equal educational opportunities."

The little Linda Browns who live in today's inner-city neighborhoods are being deprived of all manner of individual and collective life opportunities. It is, of course, possible to hold to a conception of civil rights that requires government action against segregated schools but does not require it against violence-ridden ones. It is likewise possible to maintain that there is a civil rights interest in enabling children to attend the local public school of their choice, but none in enabling them to walk to school without having to dodge stray bullets, run from drug dealers, or wear colors that do not offend street gangsters.

But I do not see how either the letter or the spirit of the *Brown* decision, or of numerous other court decisions and public laws, can be honored unless the federal government assumes a civil rights interest in promoting security in predominantly poor, minority inner-city neighborhoods where security has been absent, and communal existence has been disrupted or destroyed for over a quarter-century. If state and local authorities have proven unable or unwilling to promote security in these disadvantaged communities, then it is the federal government's constitutional duty to do so by whatever constitutionally acceptable means are necessary.

FEDERAL ACTION AGAINST INNER-CITY CRIME

Admittedly, this view of inner-city crime, community, and civil rights is a novel one. I would not, therefore, wish to hang on it the case for federal government action against inner-city crime. There are ample, if less principled, precedents for federal action. As I explained in a recently-published Brookings Institution volume on domestic policy priorities, between 1967 and 1992, the federal government fought two "wars on crime," each of them focused on urban areas. The first war (1967–80) was against poverty; the second one (1980–92) was against criminals. In the first war, the social and economic "root causes" of crime were attacked; in the second war, the likelihood that criminals would be detected, arrested, prosecuted, convicted, and incarcerated was increased. Initially, each war was supported by impressive research and enjoyed widespread public support. Ultimately, each war was judged a failure and generated widespread public disillusionment.

The point, however, is that for the last quarter-century the federal government has assumed some direct responsibility for meeting the problems of crime and disorder, especially within the nation's inner cities. Even so, according to BJS, in 1988, (the last year for which there are complete spending data) direct and indirect federal expenditures on all criminal justice activities amounted to just under $8 billion, or 13 percent of all governmental expenditures on crime prevention and control. This is a pittance for domestic defense.

There are at least two areas where the federal government can and should act to promote security in inner-city neighborhoods: (1) community-policing for inner-city residents, and (2) drug treatment for inner-city offenders.

COMMUNITY POLICING

The unflattering but accurate image of contemporary police work in most big cities is that of cops cruising in patrol cars, physically and psychologically distant from the people of the communities they serve and "never around" when needed. Indeed, in the understaffed Los Angeles Police Department, the image is of cops in helicopters who swoop down on violence-ridden, drug-infested communities, police skypeople whose faces they can hardly see, then vanish, leaving the communities and their troubles untouched.

In Los Angeles, as in other urban areas, policing has evolved into an increasingly high-tech, bureaucratic game of "cops and robbers." The goal of community policing is to stop the game-playing and instead transform the big-city police into a community-oriented group of "cops and citizens." The image of policing it promises is of cops on foot patrol, listening to community residents, working with community leaders and groups, coordinating problem-solving activities with other government agencies, and using their authority and resources in ways that the community understands and approves.

There is as yet no definitive social science research on the effects of community policing. But the National Institute of Justice has launched several systematic research efforts, and Mark H. Moore's book *Beyond*

911 and over a dozen other existing studies indicate that good things happen wherever police get out of their cars, onto the streets, and into regular contact with citizens in the community. Street crime decreases. The community's fear of crime abates. Officer morale strengthens. Police-community relations improve.

But community policing requires a full-scale commitment. In the 1980s, as the inner-city drug-and-crime epidemic worsened, many big-city police departments were reduced. Today, hardly a major police force in the country has as many officers as it arguably needs. Few departments have enough to send battalions of officers on foot patrol in the most hard-hit neighborhoods.

The federal government can and should supply the human and financial resources needed to bring community policing to all inner-city residents. Police crackdowns in troubled neighborhoods rarely reduce crime and disorder because criminals and other troublemakers quickly move elsewhere. But it is reasonable to suppose that by doubling or tripling the number of officers on regular duty in and around drug-infested, crime-torn neighborhoods, and by deploying them in accordance with the precepts of community policing, the streets and sidewalks of even the most blighted inner city could be made secure enough for children to play and adults to stroll.

The federal government can see to it that all inner-city neighborhoods are well policed. As Police Chief Reuben Greenberg wrote in a recent issue of *Policy Review,* where the community's security is concerned, it is possible to "treat people in public housing as if they lived in a country club or upscale apartment." It is possible, but it cannot be done without significant federal support. To get a rough idea of what it might cost, to sustain a 20 percent increase in the police forces of the 222 local police departments that in 1990 served populations of 100,000 or more would cost about $1 billion a year.

Were the federal government to provide such aid, it would need to be sure that the money goes to police departments, that it is spent on community policing efforts, and that the new manpower is trained and deployed in the neighborhoods that need it, not used simply to reduce the local contribution to spending on police. In this regard, the intergovernmental history of the first federal war on crime furnishes a cautionary tale. The federal government's Law Enforcement Assistance Administration (1968–1982) spent billions, but little of the money ever reached the inner-city neighborhoods that needed it most.

DRUG TREATMENT

Federal corrections officials have long believed, and numerous studies have confirmed, that drug addiction is a "multiplier" of crime. People who become addicts often commit crimes before they become addicted, but the onset of addiction dramatically worsens criminal behavior. Research has shown that successful drug treatment programs for offenders have several features in common. As common sense would suggest, one key to successful drug treatment is keeping addicts in the program. The longer an addict stays in a properly structured drug treatment program, the better the chances of reducing drug abuse and crime. For example, studies show that success is likely in compulsory prison-based drug treatment programs that provide strict supervision, are available nine months to a year before the participant's release, and offer meaningful, community-based after-care.

In 1990 federal prisons held some 59,000 prisoners, about 47 percent of whom were classified by the federal Bureau of Prisons (BOP) as having moderate to serious drug abuse problems. Between 1990 and 1992, the BOP began to shape drug treatment around four main programs: drug education, drug abuse counseling, comprehensive and pilot residential drug treatment, and transitional services. By the end of 1992, thousands of federal prisoners had benefitted from these treatment programs.

It is now in order for the federal government to make such drug treatment programs available to prisoners in every state correctional system in the country—and to pay for them with federal dollars. In 1990 only 11 percent of state prisoners were receiving drug or alcohol counseling. A recent BJS survey indicates that many state prison systems have more than enough drug treatment capacity. But no one doubts that the number of untreated or undertreated inmates in state prisons is quite high. It is difficult to know how many state prisoners have serious but unmet drug treatment needs, and even harder to assess the quality of prison-based programs from one jurisdiction to the next. But it is clear that they vary widely in methods and quality, and that correction officials in many states lack the funds to train staff, hire specialists, or administer programs on a routine basis.

When we talk about state prisons, we are talking about places that draw a disproportionate fraction of their residents from the streets of inner-city America. By 1980 one of every 100 residents of some inner-city census tracts was behind prison bars. According to the Correctional Association of New York, in 1990 in New York state and other jurisdictions nearly one-quarter of all teenage and young adult African-American males were under some form of correctional supervision (behind bars or in the community on probation or parole), and over ten percent of them were incarcerated. They were twenty times more likely to be imprisoned than teenage and young adult white males.

There is, to be sure, a strong case to be made that the federal government should provide drug treatment on demand in inner-city neighborhoods. Perhaps if such treatment were more widely available, fewer inner-city youth would become criminals in the first place. But, whatever the case for other ways of delivering drug treatment to citizens who need it, it is hard to imagine why we would not want to provide it to convicted criminals who, as a result of receiving it, might prove less likely to victimize their neighbors in the future, and more likely to get and keep jobs and lead productive lives.

To get a rough idea of what universal prison-based drug treatment might cost, annual drug treatment expenditures in the federal prison system average about $300 per prisoner. Thus, to serve 800,000 state prisoners similarly would cost about $250 million a year. This federal expenditure might be worth the cost in lowering recidivism alone. As a bonus, the program would also help to repair drug-ravaged lives, restore drug-ravaged communities, and make potentially productive taxpayers out of former inner-city criminals.

THE CLINTON-GORE PLAN ON CRIME AND DRUGS

In 1989, I argued in *The Public Interest* that inner-city crime bred urban poverty as much as urban poverty bred inner-city crime. That argument struck many readers, several of my liberal friends among them, as dangerous if not reactionary. During the presidential campaign, however, Clinton and Gore offered a crime and drugs plan that was predicated on that understanding. The plan emphasized both community policing and drug treatment. It also stressed the expansion of boot camp prisons. The details of the Clinton-Gore proposals, however, raised some important questions.

The Clinton-Gore community policing proposal was centered on the creation of a 100,000-person "National Police Corps" that would offer "veterans and active military personnel a chance to become law enforcement officers." Democrats in Congress have repeatedly pushed a similar idea: namely, a tuition-for-service police corps consisting of recent college graduates. For several reasons, the Clinton-Gore version is better. Good policing does not require officers to have advances degrees or college diplomas, and there is absolutely no evidence that college graduates make better police officers. To link community policing initiatives with efforts to pin badges on college kids (or "kiddie corps" as some veteran officers have called the proposal) might only raise the odds against successful implementation by stirring unnecessary resentment in the ranks of local police departments. Mooveover, it has been estimated that the tuition-for-service approach could range as high as $1.7 billion a year. It is unlikely that any approach centered on veterans, active military personnel, or simply walk-in recruits would cost that much.

The Clinton-Gore drug treatment proposals were quite sweeping. The plan called for treatment on demand. We know that some types of prison-based drug treatment programs work. But we have much less knowledge about the effects, if any, of treatment on demand. Even if treatment efforts were focused exclusively on adult and juvenile offenders, we would be talking about extending it to over four million people. The likely administrative quagmire of attempting to offer programs in thousands of local jails, probation, and parole systems should give anyone pause. Whether this could be done with predictable and desirable consequences, and a cost that is not prohibitive, remains in grave doubt.

Democrats in Congress have favored prison-based drug treatment, but linked the proposal to sentence reductions for prisoners who participate. But there is no evidence that such "good time" provisions either improve prisoners' institutional behavior or make any difference in their post-release behavior (going straight, getting jobs).

Finally, the Clinton-Gore plan favored the development of boot camp prisons in which youthful, nonviolent offenders would live in a paramilitary environment, undergo regular drug testing, be required to work, and receive education and drug treatment. In 1992, boot camps were up and running in over two dozen states, Arkansas among them. As a report of the National Conference of State Legislatures noted, there is "considerable variation in how states have designed and operated boot camp programs." So far, there is no systematic evidence that boot camps either save money or reduce recidivism, and the anecdotal evidence remains quite mixed.

CONCLUSION: A LIMITED FEDERAL WAR ON CRIME

But if the Clinton-Gore administration honors the spirit, if not each and every letter, of its campaign plan on crime and drugs, the nation's inner-city crime problem will almost certainly be assuaged. No federal measures can solve the crime and disorder problem for Irma Thomas and her neighbors. But the Clinton-Gore administration has pledged to place the federal government more squarely in the fight to reclaim inner-city communities for the good people who are trapped in them. A line of the Democratic campaign plan read: "We cannot and we must not permit another generation of Americans to grow up on streets too unsafe to walk." To honor its own campaign rhetoric, not to mention our civic and moral responsibility, the new administration can and should begin to engage in a limited federal war on inner-city crime that we are not bound to lose.

25

A Mandate For Liberty: Requiring Education-Based Community Service

Benjamin R. Barber

The extraordinary rise in American interest in community service has inspired widespread participation by the nation's young in service programs. It has also provoked a profound and telling debate about the relationship of service to voluntarism on the one hand, and to civic education and citizenship on the other. Two complementary approaches to service have emerged that are mutually supportive but also in a certain tension with one another. The first aims at attracting young volunteers, particularly students, out of the classroom and into service projects as part of a strategy designed to strengthen altruism, philanthropy, individualism, and self-reliance. The second is concerned with integrating service into the classroom and into academic curricula in hopes of making civic education and social responsibility core subjects of high school and university education.

Underlying these two complementary approaches are conflicting though not altogether incompatible views of the real aim of student community service programs. The differences are exemplified by the issue of whether education-based service programs should be voluntary or mandatory. If the aim of service is the encouragement of voluntarism and a spirit of altruism—if service is seen as a supererogatory trait of otherwise self-regarding individuals—then clearly it cannot be mandated or required. To speak of coercing voluntarism is to speak in oxymorons and hardly makes pedagogical sense. But if service is understood as a dimension of citizenship education and civic responsibility in which individuals learn the meaning of social interdependence and become empowered in the democratic arts, then to require service is to do no more in this domain than is done in curricula decisions generally.

As it turns out, the educational justification for requiring courses essential to the development of democratic citizens is a very old one. America's colleges were founded in part to assure the civic education of the young—to foster competent citizenship and to nourish the arts of democracy. Civic and moral responsibility were goals of both colleges organized around a religious mission and secular land-grant colleges. The premise was that democratic skills must be acquired. We think of ourselves as "born free," but we are, in truth, born weak and dependent and acquire equality as a concomitant of our citizenship. Liberty is learned: it is a product rather than the cause of our civic work as citizens.

When we coerce behavior we impose beliefs heteronomously. When we require a certain pedagogy we aim at empowering the person and thus at cultivating autonomy. Those most in need of training in the democratic arts of citizenship are, in fact, least likely to volunteer. Complacency, ignorance and interdependence, apathy, and an inability to see the relationship between self-interest and broader community interests are not only the targets of civic education: they are obstacles to it, attitudes that dispose individuals against it. The problem to be remedied is here the impediment to the remedy. Education is the exercise of authority—legitimate coercion—in the name of freedom: the empowerment and liberation of the pupil. To make people serve others may produce desirable behavior, but it does not create responsible and autonomous individuals. To make people participate in educational curricula that can empower them, however, does create such individuals.

In most volunteer service programs, those involved have already learned a good deal about the civic significance of service. Students who opt to take courses incorporating service have often done extensive volunteer service prior to enrollment. Such programs reach and help students who have already made the first and probably most significant step towards an understanding of the responsibilities of social membership. They provide useful outlets for the expression of a disposition that has already been formed. But that preponderant majority of young people who have no sense of the meaning of citizenship, no conception of civic responsibilities, is, by definition, going to remain entirely untouched by volunteer programs.

Thinking that the national problem of civic apathy can be cured by encouraging voluntarism is like thinking that illiteracy can be remedied by distributing books on the importance of reading. What young people require in order to volunteer their participation in education-based community service courses are the very skills and understandings that these courses are designed to provide.

There are, of course, problems with mandating education of any kind, but most educators agree that an effective education cannot be left entirely to the discretion of pupils, and schools and universities require a great many things of students—things less important than the skills necessary to preserve American freedoms. It is the nature of pedagogical authority that it exercises some coercion in the name of liberation. Civic empowerment and the exercise of liberty are simply too important to be treated as extracurricular electives.

This account of education-based service as integral to liberal education in a democracy and, thus, as an appropriate subject for mandatory educational curricula points to a larger issue: the uncoupling of rights and responsibilities in America. We live at a time when our government has to compete with industry and the private sector to attract servicemen and women to the military, when individuals regard themselves almost exclusively as private persons with responsibilities only to family and job, with endless rights against an alien government, of which they see themselves, at best, as no more than watchdogs and clients, and at worst, as adversaries or victims. The idea of service to country or an obligation to the institutions by which rights and liberty are maintained has fairly vanished. "We the People" have severed our connections with "It" the state or "They" the bureaucrats and politicians who run it. If we posit a problem of governance, it is always framed in the language of leadership—as if the preservation of democracy were merely a matter of assuring adequate leadership, surrogates who do our civic duties for us. Our solution to problems in democracy is to blame our representatives. Throw the rascals out—or place limits on the terms they can serve. Our own complicity in the health of our system is forgotten, and so we take the first fatal step in the undoing of the democratic state.

Civic education rooted in service learning can be a powerful response to civic scapegoat-ism and the bad habits of representative democracy (deference to authority, blaming deputies for the vices of their electors). When students use experience in the community as a basis for critical reflection in the classroom, and turn classroom reflection into a tool to examine the nature of democratic communities and the role of the citizen in them, there is an opportunity to teach liberty, to uncover the interdependence of self and other, to expose the intimate linkage between rights and responsibilities. Education-based community service programs empower students even as they teach them. They bring the lessons of service into the classroom even as they bring the lessons of the classroom out into the community. A number of institutions around the country have been experimenting with programs, a few have even envisioned mandatory curricula. Many others, including Stanford University, Spelman College, Baylor University, Notre Dame, the University of Minnesota, and Harvard University, are beginning to explore the educational possibilities of service learning as a significant element in liberal education.

Rutgers University has tried to offer pedagogical leadership to sister institutions. In the spring of 1988, the late Rutgers President Edward Bloustein gave a commencement address in which he called for a mandatory program of citizen education and community service as a graduation requirement for all students at the State University of New Jersey. In the academic year 1988–89, I chaired a Committee on Education for Civic Leadership charged with exploring the president's idea, and trying to develop a program through which it could be realized. We began with nine governing principles—the foundation of the practical program—which continue to govern the development of the Rutgers program following the tragic death of President Bloustein in 1989:

- That to teach the art of citizenship and responsibility is to practice it: so that teaching in this domain must be about acting and doing as well as about listening and learning, but must also afford an opportunity for reflecting on and discussing what is being done. In practical terms, this means that community service can only be an instrument of education when it is connected to an academic learning experience in a classroom setting. But the corollary is also true, that civic education can only be effective when it encompasses experiential learning of the kind offered by community service or other similar forms of group activity.

- That the crucial democratic relationship between rights and responsibilities, which have too often been divorced in our society, can only be made visible in a setting of experiential learning where academic discussion is linked to practical activity. In other words, learning about the relationship between civic responsibility and civic rights means exercising the rights and duties of membership in an actual community, whether that community is a classroom, a group project or community service team, or the university/college community at large.

- That antisocial, discriminatory, and other forms of selfish and abusive or addictive behavior are often a symptom of the breakdown of civic community—both local and societal. This suggests that to remedy many of the problems of alienation and disaffection of the young requires the reconstruction of the civic community, something that a program of civic education based on experiential learning and community service may therefore be better able to accomplish than problem-by-problem piecemeal solutions pursued in isolation from underlying causes.

- That respect for the full diversity and plurality of American life is possible only when students have an opportunity to interact outside of the classroom in ways that are, however, the subject of scrutiny and open discussion in the classroom. An experiential learning process that includes both classroom learning and group work outside the classroom has the greatest likelihood of impacting on student ignorance, intolerance, and prejudice.

- That membership in a community entails responsibilities and duties which are likely to be felt as binding only to the degree individuals feel empowered in the community. As a consequence, empowerment ought to be a significant dimension of education for civic responsibility—particularly in the planning process to establish civic education and community service programs.

- That civic education is experiential learning, and community service must not discriminate among economic or other classes of Americans. If equal respect and equal rights are two keys to citizenship in a democracy, then a civic education program must assure that no one is forced to participate merely because he or she is economically disadvantaged, and no one is exempted from service merely because that individual is economically privileged.

- That civic education should be communal as well as community-based. If citizen education and experiential learning of the kind offered by community service are to be a lesson in community, the ideal learning unit is not the individual but the small team, where people work together and learn together, experiencing what it means to become a small community together. Civic education programs thus should be built around teams (of say five or ten or twenty) rather than around individuals.

- The point of any community service element of civic education must be to teach citizenship, not charity. If education is aimed at creating citizens, then it will be important to let the young see that service is not just about altruism or charity, or a matter of those who are well-off helping those who are not. It is serving the public interest, which is the same thing as serving enlightened self-interest. Young people serve themselves as members of the community by serving a public good that is also their own. The responsible citizen finally serves liberty.

- Civic education needs to be regarded as an integral part of liberal education and thus should both be mandatory and receive academic credit. Because citizenship is an acquired art, and because those least likely to be spirited citizens or volunteers in their local or national community are most in need of civic training, an adequate program of citizen training with an opportunity for service needs to be mandatory. There are certain things a democracy simply must teach, employing its full authority to do so: citizenship is first among them.

The program we developed on the foundation of these principles has been endorsed by representatives of the student body and by the Board of Governors and is currently being reviewed by duly constituted faculty bodies and by Rutgers' new president, Francis L. Lawrence. It calls for:

A MANDATORY CIVIC EDUCATION COURSE

A mandatory civic education course organized around (though not limited to) a classroom course with an academic syllabus, but also including a strong and innovative experiential learning focus utilizing group projects. A primary vehicle for these projects will be community service, as one of a number of experiential learning options; while the course will be mandatory, students will be free to choose community service or non-service projects as their experiential learning group project. The required course will be buttressed by a program of incentives encouraging students to continue to participate in community service throughout their academic careers at Rutgers.

COURSE CONTENT

Course content will be broad and varied, but should guarantee some coverage of vital civic issues and questions, including the following:

1. The nature of the social or civic bond; social contract, legitimacy, authority, freedom, constitutionalism—the key concepts of political community;
2. The meaning of citizenship—representation versus participation, passive versus active forms of civic life; citizenship and service;
3. The university community; its structure and governance; the role of students, faculty, and administrators; questions of empowerment;
4. The place of ethnicity, religion, race, class, gender, and sexual orientation in a community; does equality mean abolishing differences? Or learning to respect and celebrate diversity and inclusiveness? How does a community deal with differences of the kind represented by the dis-equalizing effects of power and wealth?
5. The nature of service: differences between charity and social responsibility; between rights and needs or desires. What is the relationship between community service and citizenship? Can service be mandatory? Does a state have the right to mandate the training of citizens or does this violate freedom?
6. The nature of leadership in a democracy: are there special features

to democratic leadership? Do strong leaders create weak followers? What is the relationship between leadership and equality?

7. Cooperation and competition: models of community interaction; how do private and public interests relate in a community?

8. The character of civic communities, educational, local, regional, and national. What is the difference between society and the state? Is America a "community"? Is Rutgers a community? Do its several campuses (Camden, Newark, New Brunswick) constitute a community? What is the relationship between them and the communities in which they are located? What are the real issues of these communities—issues such as sexual harassment, suicide, date rape, homophobia, racism, and distrust of authority?

A SUPERVISORY BOARD

A supervisory board will oversee the entire program, including its design and development, its standards, and its operation. This Board will be composed of students, faculty, community, and administrators who will act as the sole authority for the civic education program and who will also supervise the planning and implementation process in the transitional period. The board will work with an academic oversight committee, a senior faculty committee responsible for academic design and for ongoing supervision over and review of course materials. This committee will work closely with community representatives and School of Social Work experts to assure quality control over community service and other group projects. Course sections will be taught by a combination of volunteers from faculty, graduate students, and more senior students who have graduated from the program and wish to make seminar leadership part of their continuing service.

VARIATIONS ON THE BASIC MODEL

Variations on the basic model will be encouraged within the basic course design, with ample room for significant variations. Individual colleges, schools, and departments will be encouraged to develop their own versions of the course to suit the particular needs of their students and the civic issues particular to their disciplines or areas. The Senior Academic Committee and the Supervisory Board will assure standards, by examining and approving proposed variations on the basic course. Thus, the Engineering School might wish to develop a program around "the responsibilities of scientists," the Mason Gross School for the Arts might wish to pioneer community service options focusing on students performing in and bringing arts education to schools and senior centers in the community, or Douglass College might want to capitalize on its long-standing commitment to encouraging women to become active leaders by developing its own appropriate course variation.

EXPERIENTIAL LEARNING

Experiential learning is crucial to the program, for the key difference between the program offered here and traditional civic education approaches is the focus on learning outside the classroom, integrated into the classroom. Students will utilize group projects in community service and in other extra-seminar group activities as the basis for reading and reflecting on course material. Experiential learning permits students to apply classroom learning to the real world, and to subject real world experience to classroom examination. To plan adequately for an experiential learning focus and to assure that projects are pedagogically sound and responsible to the communities they may engage, particular attention will be given to its design in the planning phase.

THE TEAM APPROACH

The team approach is a special feature of the Rutgers proposal. All experiential learning projects will be group projects in which individuals learn in concert with others and experience community in part by practicing community during the learning process. We urge special attention be given to the role of groups or teams in the design both of the classroom format and the experiential learning component of the basic course.

COMMUNITY SERVICE

Community service is only one among the several options for experiential learning, but it will clearly be the choice of a majority of students, and is, in fact, the centerpiece of the Rutgers program. For we believe that community service, when related to citizenship and social responsibility in a disciplined pedagogical setting, is the most powerful form of experiential learning. As such, it is central to our conception of the civic education process.

AN INCENTIVE PROGRAM FOR CONTINUING SERVICE

An incentive program for continuing service is built into the Rutgers project, because our objective is to instill in students a spirit of citizenship that is enduring. It is thus vital that the program, though it is centered on the freshman year course, not be limited to that initial experience, and that there be opportunities for ongoing service and participation throughout the four years of college.

OVERSIGHT AND REVIEW

Oversight and review are regarded as ongoing responsibilities of the program. In order to assure flexibility, adaptability to changing conditions, ongoing excellence, and the test of standards, every element in the program will be subjected to regular review and revision by the faculty and the student body, as represented on the Supervisory Board, the Academic Oversight Committee, and the Administration. This process of review will be mandated and scheduled on a regular basis, so that it will not come to depend on the vagaries of good will.

In a vigorous democracy capable of withstanding the challenges of a complex, often undemocratic, interdependent world, creating new generations of citizens is not a discretionary activity. Freedom is a hothouse plant that flourishes only when it is carefully tended. It is, as Rousseau once reminded us, a food easy to eat but hard to digest, and it has remained undigested or been regurgitated more often than it has been assimilated by our democratic body politic. Without active citizens who see in service not the altruism of charity but the necessity of taking responsibility for the authority on which liberty depends, no democracy can function properly or, in the long run, even survive.

National service is not merely a good idea, or, as William Buckley has suggested in his new book endorsing a service requirement, a way to repay the debt owed our "patrimony." It is an indispensable prerequisite of citizenship and thus a condition for democracy's preservation. Democracy does not just "deserve" our gratitude: it demands our participation as a price of survival.

The Rutgers program and others like it offer a model which integrates liberal teaching, experiential learning, community service, and citizen education. It also suggests a legislative strategy for establishing a national service requirement without raising up still one more elephantine national bureaucracy. Require service of all Americans through federal guidelines, but permit the requirement to be implemented through service learning programs housed in schools, universities, and, for those not in the school system, other local institutions. Using the nation's schools and colleges as laboratories of citizenship and service might at once offer an attractive way to develop civic service opportunities for all Americans and help educate Americans in the indispensable obligations of the democratic citizen. This would not only serve democracy, but could restore to our educational institutions a sense of mission they have long lacked.

26

Social Science Finds: "Marriage Matters"

Linda J. Waite

As we are all too aware, the last few decades have witnessed a decline in the popularity of marriage. This trend has not escaped the notice of politicians and pundits. But when critics point to the high social costs and taxpayer burden imposed by disintegrating "family values," they overlook the fact that individuals do not simply make the decisions that lead to unwed parenthood, marriage, or divorce on the basis of what is good for society. Individuals weigh the costs and benefits of each of these choices to themselves—and sometimes their children. But how much is truly known about these costs and benefits, either by the individuals making the choices or demographers like myself who study them. Put differently, what are the implications, for individuals, of the current increases in nonmarriage? If we think of marriage as an insurance policy—which it is, in some respects—does it matter if more people are uninsured, or are insured with a term rather than a whole-life policy? I shall argue that it does matter, because marriage typically provides important and substantial benefits, benefits not enjoyed by those who live alone or cohabit.

A quick look at marriage patterns today compared to, say, 1950 shows the extent of recent changes. Figures from the Census Bureau show that in 1950, at the height of the baby boom, about a third of white men and women were not married. Some were waiting to marry for the first time, some were divorced or widowed and not remarried. But virtually everyone married at least once at some point in their lives, generally in their early twenties.

In 1950 the proportion of black men and women not married was approximately equal to the proportion unmarried among whites, but since that time the marriage behavior of blacks and whites has diverged dramatically. By 1993, 61 percent of black women and 58 percent of black men were not married, compared to 38 percent of white men and 41 percent of white women. So, in contrast to 1950 when only a little over one black adult in three was not married, now a majority of black adults are unmarried. Insofar as marriage "matters," black men and women are much less likely than whites to share in the benefits, and much less likely today than they were a generation ago.

The decline in marriage is directly connected to the rise in cohabitation—living with someone in a sexual relationship without being married. Although Americans are less likely to be married today than they were several decades ago, if we count both marriage and cohabitation, they are about as likely to be "coupled." If cohabitation provides the same benefits to individuals as marriage does, then we do not need to be concerned about this shift. But we may be replacing a valuable social institution with one that demands and offers less.

Perhaps the most disturbing change in marriage appears in its relationship to parenthood. Today a third of all births occur to women who are not married, with huge but shrinking differences between blacks and whites in this behavior. One in five births to white mothers and two-thirds of births to black mothers currently take place outside marriage. Although about a quarter of the white unmarried mothers are living with someone when they give birth, so that their children are born into two-parent—if unmarried—families, very few black children born to unmarried mothers mothers live with fathers too.

I believe that these changes in marriage behavior are a cause for concern, because in a number of important ways married men and women do better than those who are unmarried. And I believe that the evidence suggests that they do better because they are married.

MARRIAGE AND HEALTH

The case for marriage is quite strong. Consider the issues of longevity and health. With economist Lee Lillard, I used a large national survey to follow men and women over a 20-year period. We watched them get married, get divorced, and remarry. We observed the death of spouses and of the individuals themselves. And we compared deaths of married men and women to those who were not married. We found that once we took other factors into account, married men and women faced lower risks of dying at any point than those who have never married or whose previous marriage has ended. Widowed women were much better off than divorced women or those who had never married, although they were still disadvantaged when compared with married women. But all men who were not currently married faced significantly higher risks of dying than married men, regardless of their marital history. Other scholars have found disadvantages in death rates for unmarried adults in a number of countries besides the United States.

How does marriage lengthen life? First, marriage appears to reduce risky and unhealthy behaviors. For example, according to University of Texas sociologist Debra Umberson, married men show much lower rates of problem drinking than unmarried men. Umberson also found that both married men and women are less likely to take risks that could lead to injury than are the unmarried. Second, as we will see below, marriage increases material well-being—income, assets, and wealth. These can be used to purchase better medical care, better diet, and safer surroundings, which lengthen life. This material improvement seems to be especially important for women.

Third, marriage provides individuals—especially men—with someone who monitors their health and health-related behaviors and who encourages them to drink and smoke less, to eat a healthier diet, to get enough sleep and to generally take care of their health. In addition, husbands and wives offer each other moral support that helps in dealing with stressful situations. Married men especially seem to be motivated to avoid risky behaviors and to take care of their health by the sense of meaning that marriage gives to their lives and the sense of obligation to others that it brings.

MORE WEALTH, BETTER WAGES—FOR MOST

Married individuals also seem to fare better when it comes to wealth. One comprehensive measure of financial well-being—household wealth—includes pension and Social Security wealth, real and financial assets, and the value of the primary residence. According to economist James Smith, in 1992 married men and women ages 51–60 had median wealth of about $66,000 per spouse, compared to $42,000 for the widowed, $35,000 for those who had never married, $34,000 among those who were divorced, and only $7,600 for those who were separated. Although married couples have higher incomes than others, this fact accounts for only about a quarter of their greater wealth.

How does marriage increase wealth? Married couples can share many household goods and services, such as a TV and heat, so the cost to each individual is lower than if each one purchased and used the same items individually. So the married spend less than the same individuals would for the same style of life if they lived separately. Second, married people produce more than the same individuals would if single. Each spouse can develop some skills and neglect others, because each can count on the other to take responsibility for some of the household work. The resulting specialization increases efficiency. We see below that this specialization leads to higher wages for men. Married couples also seem to save more at the same level of income than do single people.

The impact of marriage is again beneficial—although in this case not for all involved—when one looks at labor market outcomes. According to recent research by economist Kermit Daniel, both black and white men receive a wage premium if they are married: 4.5 percent for black men and 6.3 percent for white men. Black women receive a marriage premium of almost 3 percent. White women, however, pay a marriage *penalty,* in hourly wages, of over 4 percent. In addition, men appear to receive some of the benefit of marriage if they cohabit, but women do not.

Why should marriage increase men's wages? Some researchers think that marriage makes men more productive at work, leading to higher wages. Wives may assist husbands directly with their work, offer advice or support, or take over household tasks, freeing husbands' time and energy for work. Also, as I mentioned earlier, being married reduces drinking, substance abuse, and other unhealthy behaviors that may affect men's job performance. Finally, marriage increases men's incentives to perform well at work, in order to meet obligations to family members.

For women, Daniel finds that marriage and presence of children together seem to affect wages, and the effects depend on the woman's race. Childless black women earn substantially more money if they are married but the "marriage premium" drops with each child they have. Among white women only the childless receive a marriage premium. Once white women become mothers, marriage decreases their earnings compared to remaining single (with children), with very large negative effects of marriage on women's earnings for those with two children or more. White married women often choose to reduce hours of work when they have children. They also make less per hour than either unmarried mothers or childless wives.

Up to this point, all the consequences of marriage for the individuals involved have been unambiguously positive—better health, longer life, more wealth, and higher earnings. But the effects of marriage and children on white women's wages are mixed, at best. Marriage and cohabitation increase women's time spent on housework; married motherhood reduces their time in the labor force and lowers their wages. Although the family as a whole might be better off with this allocation of women's time, women generally share their husbands' market earnings only when they are married. Financial well-being declines dramatically for women and their children after divorce and widowhood; women whose marriages have ended are often quite disadvantaged financially by their investment in their husbands and children rather than in their own earning power. Recent changes in divorce law—the rise in no-fault divorce and the move away from alimony—seem to have exacerbated this situation, even while increases in women's education and work experience have moderated it.

IMPROVED INTIMACY

Another benefit of married life is an improved sex life. Married men and women report very active sex lives—as do those who are cohabiting. But the married appear to be more satisfied with sex than others. More married men say that they find sex with their wives to be extremely physically pleasurable than do cohabiting men or single men say the same about sex with their partners. The high levels of married men's physical satisfaction with their sex lives contradicts the popular view that sexual novelty or variety improves sex for men. Physical satisfaction with sex is about the same for married women, cohabiting women, and single women with sex partners.

In addition to reporting more active and more physically fulfilling sex lives than the unmarried, married men and women say that they are more emotionally satisfied with their sex lives than do those who are single or cohabiting. Although cohabitants report levels of sexual activity as high as the married, both cohabiting men and women report lower levels of emotional satisfaction with their sex lives. And those who are sexually active but single report the lowest emotional satisfaction with it.

How does marriage improve one's sex life? Marriage and cohabitation provide individuals with a readily available sexual partner with whom they have an established, ongoing sexual relationship. This reduces the costs—in some sense—of any particular sexual contact, and leads to higher levels of sexual activity. Since married couples expect to carry on their sex lives for many years, and since the vast majority of married couples are monogamous, husbands and wives have strong incentives to learn what pleases their partner in bed and to become good at it. But I would argue that more than "skills" are at issue here. The long-term contract implicit in marriage—which is not implicit in cohabitation—facilitates emotional investment in the relationship, which should affect both frequency of and satisfaction with sex. So the wife or husband who knows what the spouse wants is also highly motivated to provide it, both because sexual satisfaction in one's partner brings similar rewards to oneself and because the emotional commitment to the partner makes satisfying him or her important in itself.

THE IMPACT OF MARRIAGE ON CHILDREN

To this point we have focused on the consequences of marriage for adults—the men and women who choose to marry (and stay married) or not. But such choices have consequences for the children born to these adults. Sociologists Sara McLanahan and Gary Sandefur compare children raised in intact, two-parent families with those raised in one-parent families, which could result either from disruption of a marriage of from unmarried childbearing. They find that approximately twice as many children raised in one-parent families than children from two-parent families drop out of high school without finishing. Children raised in one-parent families are also more likely to have a birth themselves while teenagers, and to be "idle"—both out of school and out of the labor force—as young adults.

Not surprisingly, children living outside an intact marriage are also more likely to be poor. McLanahan and Sandefur calculated poverty rates for children in two-parent families—including stepfamilies—and for single-parent families. They found very high rates of poverty for single-parent families, especially among blacks. Donald Hernandez, chief of marriage and family statistics at the Census Bureau, claims that the rise in mother-only families since 1959 is an important cause of increases in poverty among children.

Clearly poverty, in and of itself, is a bad outcome for children. In addition, however, McLanahan and Sandefur estimate that the lower incomes of single-parent families account for only half of the negative impact for children in these families. The other half comes from children's access—or lack of access—to the time and attention of two adults in two-parent families. Children in one-parent families spend less time with their fathers (this is not surprising given that they do not live with them), but they also spend less time with their mothers than children in two-parent families. Single-parent families and stepfamilies also move much more frequently than two-parent families, disrupting children's social and academic environments. Finally, children who spend part of their childhood in a single-parent family report substantially lower quality relationships with their parents as adults and have less frequent contact with them, according to demographer Diane Lye.

CORRELATION VERSUS CAUSALITY

The obvious question, when one looks at all these "benefits" of marriage, is whether marriage is responsible for these differences. If all, or almost all, of the benefits of marriage arise because those who enjoy better health, live longer lives, or earn higher wages anyway are more likely to marry, then marriage is not "causing" any changes in these outcomes. In such a case, we as a society and we as individuals could remain neutral about each person's decision to marry or not, to divorce or remain married. But scholars from many fields who have examined the issues have come to the opposite conclusion. Daniel found that only half of the higher wages that married men enjoy could be explained by selectivity; he thus concluded that the other half is causal. In the area of mental health, social psychologist Catherine Ross—summarizing her own research and that of other social scientists—wrote, "The positive effect of marriage on well-being is strong and consistent, and the selection of the psychologically healthy into marriage or the psychologically unhealthy out of marriage cannot explain the effect." Thus marriage itself can be assumed to have independent positive effects on its participants.

So, we must ask, what is it about marriage that causes these benefits? I think that four factors are key. First, the institution of marriage involves a long-term contract—" 'til death do us part." This contract allows the partners to make choices that carry immediate costs but eventually bring benefits. The time horizon implied by marriage makes it sensible—a rational choice is at work here—for individuals to develop some skills and to neglect others because they count on their spouse to fill in where they are weak. The institution of marriage helps individuals honor this long-term contract by providing social support for the couple as a couple and by imposing social and economic costs on those who dissolve their union.

Second, marriage assumes a sharing of economic and social resources and what we can think of as co-insurance. Spouses act as a sort of small insurance pool against life's uncertainties, reducing their need to protect themselves—by themselves—from unexpected events.

Third, married couples benefit—as do cohabiting couples—from economies of scale.

Fourth, marriage connects people to other individuals, to their social groups (such as in-laws), and to other social institutions (such as churches and synagogues) which are themselves a source of benefits. These connections provide individuals with a sense of obligation to others, which gives life meaning beyond oneself.

Cohabitation has some but not all of the characteristics of marriage and so carries some but not all of the benefits. Cohabitation does not generally imply a lifetime commitment to stay together; a significant number of cohabiting couples disagree on the future of their relationship. Frances Goldscheider and Gail Kaufman believe that the shift to cohabitation from marriage signals "declining commitment within unions, of men and women to each other and to their relationship as an enduring unit, in exchange for more freedom, primarily for men." Perhaps as a result, many view cohabitation as an especially poor bargain for women.

The uncertainty that accompanies cohabitation makes both investment in the relationship and specialization with this partner much riskier than in marriage and so reduces them. Cohabitants are much less likely than married couples to pool financial resources and more likely to assume that each partner is responsible for supporting himself or herself financially. And whereas marriage connects individuals to other important social institutions, cohabitation seems to distance them from these institutions.

Of course, all these observations concern only the average benefits of marriage. Clearly, some marriages produce substantially higher benefits for those involved. Some marriages produce no benefits and even cause harm to the men, women, and children involved. That fact needs to be recognized.

REVERSING THE TREND

Having stated this qualification, we must still ask, if the average marriage produces all of these benefits for individuals, why has it declined? Although this issue remains a subject of much research and speculation, a number of factors have been mentioned as contributing. For one, because of increases in women's employment, there is less specialization by spouses now than in the past; this reduces the benefits of marriage. Clearly, employed wives have less time and energy to focus on their husbands, and are less financially and emotionally dependent on marriage than wives who work only in the home. In addition, high divorce rates decrease people's certainty about the long-run stability of their marriage, and this may reduce their willingness to invest in it, which in turn increases the chance they divorce—a sort of self-fulfilling prophecy. Also, changes in divorce laws have shifted much of the financial burden for the breakup of the marriage to women, making investment within the marriage (such as supporting a husband in medical school) a riskier proposition for them.

Men, in turn, may find marriage and parenthood a less attractive option when they know that divorce is common, because they may face the loss of contact with their children if their marriage dissolves. Further, women's increased earnings and young men's declining financial well-being may have made women less dependent on men's financial support and made young men less able to provide it. Finally, public policies that support single mothers and changing attitudes toward sex outside of marriage, toward unmarried childbearing, and toward divorce have all been implicated in the decline in marriage. This brief list does not exhaust the possibilities, but merely mentions some of them.

So how can this trend be reversed? First, as evidence accumulates and is communicated to individuals, some people will change their behavior as a result. Some will do so simply because of their new understanding of the costs and benefits, to them, of the choices involved. In addition, we have seen that attitudes frequently change toward behaviors that have been shown to have negative consequences. The attitude change then raises the social cost of the newly stigmatized behavior.

In addition, though, we as a society can pull some policy levers to encourage or discourage behaviors. Public policies that include asset tests (Medicaid is a good example) act to exclude the married, as do AFDC programs and most states. The "marriage penalty" in the tax code is another example. These and other policies reinforce or undermine the institution of marriage. If, as I have argued, marriage produces individuals who drink less, smoke less, abuse substances less, live longer, earn more, are wealthier, and have children who do better, we need to give more thought and effort to supporting this valuable social institution.

IV

THE COMMUNITY OF COMMUNITIES

27

Democracy and the Politics of Difference

Jean Bethke Elshtain

The American Founders were well aware of the vexations attendant upon the creation of a new political body. As men of the Enlightenment, they rejected the images of the body politic that dominated medieval and early modern political thinking. For Jefferson and Madison, John of Salisbury's twelfth-century visualization of a body politic with a prince as the head and animator of the other members was too literalist, too strongly corporatist, and too specifically Christian to serve the new secular order. But they were nevertheless haunted by Hebrew and Christian metaphors of a covenanted polity: The body is one but has many members. There can be unity with diversity.

Indeed, it is this incorporation, this enfolding of individuals within a single body that makes meaningful diversity possible. As political philosopher Charles Taylor writes, ". . . my discovering my own identity doesn't mean that I work it out in isolation, but that I negotiate it through dialogue, partly overt, partly integral, with others. . . . My own identity crucially depends on my dialogical relations with others." We cannot be different all by ourselves. The great challenge was to create a political body that brought people together and created a "we" but still enabled people to separate themselves and recognize and respect one another's individualities. This remains the great challenge for all modern democrats.

Practitioners of a phenomenon I tag the "politics of displacement" try to solve this problem by smashing it to bits. Rather than negotiating the complexity of public and private identities, they disdain all distinctions between citizenship and any other identity and seek full public recognition, not as a citizen but as a person with a handicap, as having a particular sexual orientation, as a member of ethnic or racial groups, or as a man or woman. When such marks of difference triumph, once they gain public recognition, acceptance, legitimation, and even preferred status and treatment, what we hold in common loses ground. The result is a public world with many "I's" who form a "we" only with people exactly like themselves.

Persons of democratic disposition are troubled by such developments. The rush for recognition of difference represents a legitimate, modern concern, and some form of equal recognition must form the very lifeblood of a democracy. But what sort of recognition? Claiming, "I am different, you must recognize me and honor my difference" says nothing at all. Should I honor someone or recognize her simply because she is female or proclaims a particular sexual identity? I may disagree profoundly with her about everything I find important—from what American policy ought to be in the Balkans, to how to stem the tide of deterioration of America's inner cities, to whether violence on television is a serious concern or just an easy target for riled parents. My recognition of her difference—by which I mean my preparedness to engage her as an interlocutor *given* our differences on equality, justice, freedom, fairness, authority, and power—turns on the fact that I share something with her. She, too, is a citizen. We both, I hope, operate from a stance of goodwill and an acceptance of the backdrop of democratic, constitutional guarantees. We both share democratic habits and dispositions, an energetic desire to forge at least provisional agreements on highly controversial issues and, failing that, to remain committed nonetheless to the centrality of dialogue to our shared way of life. If I am her enemy—because I am white, or heterosexual, or a mother, or an academic—her only desire can be to wipe me out. One makes war with enemies; one does democratic politics with opponents.

INTELLECTUAL ABOUT-FACE

Not all that long ago it was the liberal position that emphasizing human differences sanctions inequality. Our sameness alone, argued liberal thinkers, secures an egalitarian, democratic regime. American society is unique among nations in its strong presumption of equality as one of the touchstones of our national identity: all men are created equal (to be sure, slaves and women were omitted from the original intent of the phrase, but the formulation named the continuing aspiration as well as the imperfect reality). Many conservatives, by contrast, claimed that manifest natural differences between people amount to natural human inequality. Equating equality with sameness and inequality with difference, such thinkers insisted that society must reflect this human inequality and that widespread social inequality is therefore inevitable. Moreover, they argued, attempts to alter institutions to eliminate or reduce inequality are a nasty form of social surgery designed to eliminate human differences themselves. Liberals insisted that such Social Darwinism strained credulity: could all those who were well placed have fully earned it? Could their power and privilege simply have flowed from their being different—unequal—from the rest of us?

Alas, the radical egalitarian response became as tendentious as its ideological opposite. Rather than challenging the view of equality that equated it with sameness, many critics implicitly embraced it, envisioning a fuzzy, utopian world in which people were as indistinguishable from one another as happy peas in an egalitarian pod. Arguments for the continuing need to assess the disparate merits of diverse human capacities, abilities, and achievements melted away. Over the past 30 years, the argument has been vehemently pressed that standards themselves are inherently anti-democratic. A therapeutic mentality, holding that we should all "feel comfortable" and that the faculty of judgement is suspect, has gained credence.

Kurt Vonnegut, in his short story "Harrison Bergeron," satirizes this ideology of bland equality of sameness, promoted by many calling themselves egalitarians. Vonnegut writes: "The year was 2081 and everybody was finally equal. They weren't only equal before God and the law. They were equal every which way. Nobody was smarter than anybody else. Nobody was better looking than anybody else. Nobody was younger or quicker than anybody else. All this equality was due to the 211th, 212th, and 213th Amendments to the Constitution, and to the unceasing vigilance of agents of the United States Handicapper General." Vonnegut portrays a future society in which all differences, all particular and unique human talents and gifts, have been counterbalanced in order to achieve the "equal society." Thus, ballet dancers, naturally gifted and trained to be lithe and limber, must dance with huge weights and irons on their legs. This guarantees that those who haven't the grace to be ballet dancers won't have to watch others leap any higher or move any more gracefully than they can.

THE HARM WROUGHT

In the academy, the equation of equality and sameness led to a muddle-headed assault on any notion of distinctiveness or value. Core curricula, for example, were jettisoned on the presumption that a core hampers individual liberty and is suited only for elitists. Some institutions of higher learning gave up grading students altogether. Others moved to a "Pass/ Fail" system which amounts to the same thing. Textbook publishers knowingly began to "dumb down" texts in history, science, and literature. In an understandable and justifiable urge to improve the lot of the many, the distinctiveness of the one was forgotten or even disdained.

Writer Richard Rodriguez, in his poignant autobiography about growing up the son of Mexican immigrant parents in California and becoming a "scholarship kid," writes of the condescending paternalism he encountered at the hands of interventionist egalitarians. Rodriguez's particular target is affirmative action and his own legal categorization as a "minority" by policymakers allegedly working on his behalf. Rodriguez notices that, although he received an excellent parochial education, he was treated as a victim of cultural deprivation; the working assumption, of course, was that he was both ignorant and incapable of defending himself. He notices that educators make all sorts of "allowances" for poorly educated Mexican-American students and push them through the system ill prepared, assuming that standards of merit and achievement are themselves impositions by an Anglo majority on minorities.

Rodriguez writes: "The conspiracy of kindness became a conspiracy of uncaring. Cruelly, callously, admissions committees agreed to overlook serious academic deficiency. I knew students in college then barely able to read, students unable to grasp the function of a sentence. I knew nonwhite graduate students who were bewildered by the requirement to compose a term paper and who each day were humiliated when they couldn't compete with other students in seminars. . . . Not surprisingly, among those students with very poor academic preparation, few completed their courses of study. Many dropped out, blaming themselves for their failure. One fall, six nonwhite students I knew suffered severe mental collapse. None of the professors who had welcomed them to graduate school were around when it came time to take them to the infirmary or the airport. And the university officials who so diligently took note of those students in their self-serving totals of entering minority students finally took no note of them when they left."

Unsurprisingly, when Rodriguez published his book, many attempted to discredit him as a spokesman for right-wing reaction; by doing so, they could ignore his arguments. Rodriguez's critics made evident the Left's general inability to tolerate diversity in the ranks of minority groups— presumably they should all think alike and have identical needs that whites can minister to. Ironically, under the rubric of difference, this intolerance has grown more, not less, pronounced in the past decade.

Consider how quickly the rhetoric of difference has supplanted the rhetoric of equality. At a conference on women and feminism in 1989, I was perplexed to hear two and one-half days of assaults on the very idea of equality. Equality meant "the same." It was the mark of masculinism. It was the stigma of heterosexism. It was every nasty thing you could come up with a name for. Even the Nazis became perverse egalitarians in their rush to exterminate the different. Equality, I learned, meant "homologization with the male subject."

The rush to eliminate equality from our political idiom and our political aspiration strikes me as daft, for democracy without equality is an impossible proposition. But at least some of those immersed in what they call the "discourse of difference" are not so keen on constitutional democracy. One participant in the conference was quite candid about this. The task of feminism, she claimed, was celebrating female "will-to-power." She either didn't know or didn't care how disastrously that particular slogan had been deployed in the not-too-distant past.

Repudiating the sameness of equality for its supposed (and supposedly intentional) homogenizing effect, difference ideologues embrace their own version of sameness—an exclusionist sameness along lines of gender, race, ethnicity, and sexual preference. There is no apparent end to this process, as identities get shaved off into thinner and thinner slivers: lesbian women of color or white heterosexual men who were abused by their fathers. Ironically, writes political theorist Sheldon Wolin, it has traditionally been the "non-democratic rulers, the men who justify their rule by appealing to differences—hereditary, divinity, merit, knowledge— who reduce populations to a common condition." We now impose a common condition on ourselves in the name of diversity.

Political philosopher George Kateb notes: "To want to believe that there is either a fixed majority interest or a homogenous group identity is not compatible with the premises of rights-based individualism." Although I prefer to speak of democratic "individuality" rather than "individualism," Kateb's point is perceptive. To the extent that citizens begin to retribalize into ethnic or other "fixed-identity groups," democracy falters. Any possibility for human dialogue or democratic commonality vanishes as so much froth on the polluted sea of phony equality, and difference becomes more and more exclusivist. If you are black and I am white, by definition I do not "get it." There is no way to negotiate the space between our pregiven differences. We're just stuck with them and mired in the cement of our own identities; we need never deal with one another. One of us will win and one of us will lose, and that's what it's all about: nothing but power of the most imposing sort.

If someone has consigned equality to the discursive trash heap and proclaims that she'll have none of it; if, instead, she insists that politics must consist of my acknowledging and recognizing her differences but, at the same time, I am not allowed to engage her about these differences because we have nothing to say to one another, then I can only respond that she is not thinking and acting like a democratic citizen. She is thinking and acting like a royal pain in the neck, and the sooner I can get her out of sight and mind, the better, not because I am a racist or a sexist or a homophobe or any of the other handy labels we toss around all too easily these days, but because I am weary of being accused of bad faith no matter what I do or say, or refrain from doing or saying.

EDUCATION AND CIVIC SENTIMENT

It was taken for granted from the start of the American democratic experiment that the survival of the republic for any length of time would depend heavily on cultivating civic sentiments among the young. The Founders' optimistic hope was that national character itself could be formed by carefully molding the children of each new generation. The American Founders debated education, rejecting explicitly the classically harsh and martial Spartan example, because it demanded and likely yielded homogeneity and sameness. Their version of difference involved awareness of different opinions: we don't all think alike. The claims to difference were couched in epistemological rather than in ontological terms, in sharp contrast to much contemporary multiculturalism, according to which there is such a thing as "thinking black" or "thinking white" which is innate and inevitable to blacks and whites. To the extent that schools put themselves at the service of this latter version of multiculturalism, they disastrously abandon the turf they were deeded.

Imposed uniformity—whether of sameness or difference—cannot prepare citizens of a democracy to exercise civic and social responsibilities. So-called "multicultural" curricula are designed explicitly to entrench differences. As a form of ideological teaching, multicultural absolutism isolates us in our own skins and equates culture with racial or ethnic identity. "Resegregation," some call it. How long will it take before we move from separate approaches for black children in the name of Afrocentrism, to a quest for entirely separate schools? The glory of American public education has been its mingling of classes, genders, ethnicities, and races.

Richard Rodriguez, in *Days of Obligation*, notes that "American educators have lost the confidence of their public institution. . . . There are influential educators today, and I have met them, who believe that the purpose of American education is to instill in children a pride in their ancestral pasts. Such a curtailing of education seems to me condescending; seems to me the worst sort of missionary spirit. Did anyone attempt to protect the white middle-class student of yore from the ironies of history? Thomas Jefferson—that great democrat—was also a slaveowner.

Need we protect black students from complexity? Thomas Jefferson—that slaveowner—was also a democrat. American history has become a pageant of exemplary slaves and black educators. Gay studies, women's studies, ethnic studies—the new curriculum ensures that education will be flattering. But I submit that America is not a tale for sentimentalists."

If we are flattered and cajoled into thinking ours is a tale of victimization and thus one also of purity, we become sentimentalists. As Rodriquez insists, newcomers to this country need to know about seventeenth-century Puritans and, yes, about cowboys and Indians, for these are the building-block dramas of American society. Teaching exotic, mythic, and altogether "foreign" pasts doesn't prepare students for a culture that is both "in common" and forever changing. If we act too quickly on the notion of educational relevance—teaching minority students practical subjects so they can get jobs when they leave school—we stress watery adaptation above authentic excellence. If we concentrate exclusively on the few, assuming the many to be less vital, democratic culture withers on the vine. If we say education must be for the many, yet we have no faith in the many's potential, we abandon excellence for a lowest common denominator and throw out Jefferson's aristocracy of virtue and talent.

POLITICIZATION OF SCHOOLS

A thin line separates an awareness that education is never without political context (and therefore content) from a willingness to politize education actively. Education is always cast as the means whereby citizens of a society learn to live with one another. It always reflects a society's views of what is excellent, worthy, and necessary. These reflections are continually refracted and reshaped as social definitions and objectives shift as a result of democratic contestation. In this sense, education is necessarily political. But this is different from being directly and blatantly politicized, that is, from serving interests and ends imposed by militant groups committed to true Biblical morality, heightened racial awareness, androgyny, therapeutic self-esteem, or any of the other enthusiasms in which we are currently awash.

Consider the following example: A class takes up the Declaration of Independence and the grand pronouncement that "All men are created equal." But women (and many men) were disenfranchised. Slaves were not counted as full persons. How could this be? What meaning of equality did the Founders embrace? Were any of them uneasy about this? How did they square this shared meaning with what we perceive to be manifest inequalities? What political and moral exigencies of that historic moment compelled what sorts of compromises? Might things have gone differently? By raising such questions, teachers and students take part in a reflective and uniquely democratic political education, confronting our perennial dilemma of the one and the many.

But let me offer two other examples, exaggerated in order to mark the differences between these and my first example as clearly as I can. A teacher declares that the Founders were correct in every respect. To be sure, slavery is an unfortunate blemish, but that got corrected. Our purpose as democratic educators at the end of the twentieth century is to reaffirm our devotion to the Founders and their Republic. After all, did they not distill the essence of the wisdom of the ages in their handiwork? Here uncritical adulation triumphs.

The hagiographer's mirror image is offered by the teacher who declares that nothing good ever came from the hand of that abstract, all-purpose villain, the "dead, white, European male." The words and deeds of such men, including the Founders, are nefarious. They were nothing but racists and patriarchalists, blatant oppressors who hid behind fine-sounding words. All they created is tainted and hypocritical. All, presumably, has been exposed. To express a different point of view is to betray one's own venality, false consciousness, or white, patriarchal privilege. Here demonology triumphs.

These latter two examples of teacherly malfeasance I take to be instances of unreflective, dogmatic politicization. Each evades the dilemmas of democratic equality rather than offering us points of critical reflection on those dilemmas. This sort of education fails in its very particular and important task of preparing students for a world of ambiguity and variety. It equips them only for resentment or malicious naïveté. Let me be clear: I am not indicting education, whether public or private, elementary, secondary, or college level, for our growing balkanization. But I am suggesting that the schools, which once took as their mission instilling some measure of commonality across differences, now suffer under the claim that that effort itself was but another name for "normalization" and cultural imperialism. All those dedicated teachers in all those public schools (the vast majority of them women), working long hours for not-very-good pay, are now relegated to the status of agents of domination.

GETTING PERSONAL

I think of my own education, and my democratic dreams, as they were nurtured in the rural Colorado village in which I grew up. The Timnath Public School, District Number 62, incorporated grades 1–12 in a single building: there weren't that many of us. I remember that we memorized the Declaration of Independence and the Gettysburg Address. The Gettysburg Address recitation, when my classmates and I were in the single seventh and eighth grade classroom under the firm if somewhat eccentric tutelage of Miss McCarthy, was always quite an event. We would line up in a single row around the classroom. On Miss McCarthy's signal, we would begin to hum the stirring song of the American Civil War, "The Battle Hymn of the Republic," as Miss McCarthy recited the Gettysburg Address with flourish and fervor. She had a way of trailing off each sentence in a trembly, melodramatic whisper that sometimes left the hummers in stitches. But I never forgot the Gettysburg Address and its promise of democratic equality.

By the time we reached high school in that isolated little place, our text for English class was called *Adventures in Reading.* I still have my copy, having purchased it from the school because I loved so many of the stories and poems it contained. The table of contents was divided into "Good Stories Old and New" with such bracing subsections as "Winning Against the Odds," "Meeting the Unusual," and "Facing Problems." We read "Lyrics from Many Lands" and "American Songs and Sketches." I looked at this text recently as I thought about democracy and education. By no means was this a book dominated by the single point of view of the dread, dead, white, European male. We read Mary O'Hara, Dorothy Canfield, Margaret Weymouth Jackson, Elsie Singmaster, Selma Lagerlöf, Rosemary Vincent Benet, Kathryn Forbes, Sarojini Naidu, Willa Cather, and Emily Dickinson. We read the great abolitionist, Frederick Douglass and the black reformer, Booker T. Washington. We read Leo Tolstoy and Pedro de Alarcón. We read translations of Native American Warrior Songs.

This reading wasn't done under the specific rubric of multiculturalism. But it was undertaken with the assumption that life is diverse and filled with many wonders. Through *Adventures in Reading,* we could make the lives and thoughts of others somehow our own. In my imaginings and yearnings, I didn't feel constrained because some of those I most admired were men. I was taught, "Reading is your passport to adventure in faraway places. In books the world lies before you, its paths radiating from great cities to distant lands, to scenes forever new, forever changing. . . . Reading knows no barrier, neither time nor space nor bounds of prejudice—it admits us all to the community of human experience." Clearly, I was a lucky child, a lucky democratic child, for I learned that, in political philosopher Michael Oakeshott's words, "Learning is not merely acquiring information . . . nor is it merely 'improving one's mind'; it is learning to recognize some specific invitations to encounter particular adventures in human self-understanding."

This work of human self-understanding can be neither the exclusive purview of the family nor of some overweening state bureaucracy, whether it is pushing homogeneity or multiculturalism. It is primarily a task of civil society, of which schools are a part. Of course, education in a democratic culture is a porous affair, open to the wide world outside the door and beyond the playground, but that does not mean it must become the purveyor of passing enthusiasms, whether political or pedagogical. The danger in continuing down our present path is that our understanding of education itself is increasingly imperiled. We have done too little to protect education from heavy-handed intrusion by those who would have both education and children serve political masters or ideological purposes, whether in the name of change or in defense of some status quo. Thus, we increasingly give over to education all sorts of tasks it is ill equipped to handle. At the same time, we seem intent on stripping it of what it actually ought to be: an invitation to particular "adventures in human self-understanding," in Oakeshott's terms.

CONCLUSION

The danger in any ideological definition of education is that it undermines an essential element of democracy, that of self-limiting freedom. If democracy is the political form that permits and requires human freedom as responsibility, any definition or system that sanctions evasion of responsibility imperils democracy. Once a world of personal responsibility with its characteristic virtues and marks of decency (honor, friendship, fidelity, fairness) is ruptured or emptied, what rushes in to take its place is politics as a "technology of power," in Václav Havel's words. Responsibility, according to Havel, flows from the aims of life "in its essence," these being plurality and independent self-constitution, as opposed to the conformity, uniformity, and stultifying dogmas of left- and right-wing ideologues, who abandon reality and assault life with their rigid, abstract chimeras. To live "within the truth," as Havel calls it, is to give voice to a self, and a citizen, that has embraced responsibility for the here and now. As he writes, "That means that responsibility is ours, that we must accept it and grasp it here, now, in this place where the Lord has set us down, and that we cannot lie our way out of it by moving somewhere else, whether it be to an Indian ashram or to a parallel polis." This is tough stuff. But, then, democracy is for the stout of heart who know there are things worth fighting for in a world of paradox, ambiguity, and irony. This democratic way—moderation with courage, openness to compromise without sacrificing principle—is the rare but now and then attainable fruit of the democratic imagination and the democratic citizen.

28

Pluralism vs. Particularism in American Education

Diane Ravitch

The history of American public education contains numerous examples of racial, religious, and ethnic conflict. This is not surprising since the schools tend to be the most sensitive cultural barometers in society. The curriculum of the schools is often seen by parents, policymakers, and interest groups as a means to shape the minds and values of the next generation. As long as there has been public education in this country, the schools have provided an arena for social conflict in which groups clash over whose values are taught in the schools.

During the nineteenth century, Catholics fought to remove the Protestant influence on textbooks and curricula. Battles over school prayer and over the presence of religious activities in school still divide communities nearly thirty years after the Supreme Court forbade prayer in the schools. The advance of secularism has prompted fundamentalist Christians to campaign against textbooks and library books that offend their religious views and for science courses that teach creationism on an equal footing with evolution. For the past four decades, the movement to eliminate racial segregation and its lingering effects from the schools has changed the nature of American schools and American society.

Although educators and policymakers must strive to keep the schools free from partisan struggles, the schools inevitably are drawn into controversies that reflect the differences among values among people in a diverse society. Sometimes these controversies have been ultimately beneficial to the schools, for example, by removing biased materials from textbooks, or by creating programs to encourage more girls to study mathematics and science.

But not all controversies have happy outcomes, not all stories have happy endings. Textbooks suffer, as does instruction, when publishers remove literary selections with myths or fables or themes that offend someone, somewhere. Science programs are weakened when teachers are afraid to teach about AIDS or sex education or evolution because some parents object. History instruction is distorted when interest groups exert political pressures on teachers, textbook publishers, and school board members to have the past taught their way. Such political pressures on the schools threaten public education itself, making it difficult to teach history and controversial issues honestly and making other subjects in the curriculum vulnerable to political campaigns.

The decade's coming battle over values will determine how *we provide our students with a multicultural education. Such an education is a necessity.* The children in our schools come from many different racial and ethnic backgrounds, and some are recent immigrants from Latin America, Africa, Asia, or Europe. This cultural diversity in the classrooms of our nation has created a growing demand for school programs that reduce prejudice and teach children to appreciate others whose race and ethnicity are different from their own. For these reasons many states, school districts, and even individual schools and classrooms have established various sorts of multicultural programs. Properly conceived, these programs enrich students' understanding of history and contribute to their appreciation of American diversity.

But almost any idea carried to its extreme can become ridiculous or destructive. Such is the turn being taken by certain advocates of multicultural education. Pluralistic multiculturism is now contending with particularistic multiculturalism. *The pluralists,* like New York City's Mayor David Dinkins, say that we are all parts of this nation's "gorgeous mosaic" of racial and ethnic groups; as citizens of the same society, we are all responsible for one another. By contrast, *the particularists* neglect the bonds of mutuality that exist among people of different groups and encourage children to seek their primary identity in the cultures and homelands of their ancestors.

For many years the public schools attempted to neutralize controversies over race, religion, gender, and ethnicity by ignoring them. The textbooks minimized inter-group problems and social injustices and taught a sanitized version of history. Race and ethnicity were presented as minor elements in the American pageant; slavery was treated as an episode, as was immigration, and women were largely absent. The textbooks concentrated on presidents, wars, and national politics. An occasional "great black" or "great woman" received mention, but the main narrative paid little attention to minority groups and women.

Since the 1960s, there has been a great deal of new scholarship about the history of women, blacks, and various ethnic minorities. Much of this has found its way into university-level textbooks. At first, the multicultural content was awkwardly incorporated as little boxes on the side of the main narrative. Then some of the new social historians (like Stephan Thernstrom, Mary Beth Norton, Gary Nash, Winthrop Jordan, and Leon Litwack) themselves wrote textbooks, and the main narrative itself began to reflect a broadened historical understanding of race, ethnicity, gender, and class, in the American past.

In recent years, history and literature textbooks for elementary and secondary students have been revised to incorporate this broader perspective of the American past, but in all too many cases, the additions remain merely add-ons, sidebars to the main story. In elementary and in secondary texts, as in college texts, the story itself must be told as the forging of a new people who are learning to live amicably with others who are different. It is a story in which people of many different backgrounds have joined together to become one nation, all Americans.

Wisely and intelligently designed, what has come to be known as the multicultural curriculum is a tool with which to broaden and transmit the common culture that we all share. Indeed, the unique feature of the United States is that its common culture has been formed by the interaction of its subsidiary cultures. It is a culture that has been influenced over time by immigrants, American Indians, and African slaves and their descendants. American music, art, literature, language, food, and customs all show the effects of the commingling of diverse cultures in one nation. Paradoxical though it may seem, the United States has a common culture that is multicultural.

This understanding of the pluralistic nature of American culture has taken a long time to forge. It is based on sound scholarship and had led—and is still leading—to major revisions in what children are taught and what they read in school. Making these changes is difficult, raises tempers and controversies, but gives a more interesting and more accurate account of American history. Accomplishing these changes is valuable, too, because there is a useful lesson for the rest of the world in America's relatively successful experience as a pluralistic society. Throughout history, the clash of different cultures, races, ethnic groups, and religions has usually been and is still today the cause of bitter hatred, civil war, and international war. Thus, it is a matter of more than parochial importance that we closely examine and try to understand that part of our national history in which different groups competed, fought, suffered, but ultimately learned to live together in pease and even achieved a sense of common nationhood.

PLURALISM WITHIN UNITY

We are a multicultural people, but also a single nation knitted together by a common set of political and moral values. In the education that we provide to our students, how do we reconcile our *pluribus* and our *unum?* How do we ensure that education promotes pluralism, nor particularism?

The movie *Glory* is a fine example of plural education at its best. This depiction of the most famous black Civil War regiment demonstrates the courage and determination of the black soldiers; it shows whites who were vicious racists, and whites who gave their lives to the cause of black freedom. Everyone who sees the movie leaves with a greater understanding of the black contribution to the building of America and can identify with the heroism of the Massachusetts 54th.

The California History-Social Science Framework, which I helped to draft, is an example of an excellent full-length multicultural curriculum. The California History-Social Science curriculum was developed over a two-year period by a framework committee made up of teachers and historians. The framework committee agreed that the new curriculum should center on the study of history, that it must be multicultural, and that it must place a premium on civic education.

With these goals in mind, the framework committee decided that world history must be increased to three required years, providing enough time to examine the civilizations that developed in Africa, the Near East, China, India, and elsewhere; the civilizations of the Mayas, Incas, and Aztecs; the growth of western civilization in Europe; and the problems of the twentieth-century world. Teachers of these courses are encouraged to use the literature and art of diverse cultures, their myths, legends, religious literature, poems, novels, biographies, and so on.

In the teaching of American history, racial and ethnic minorities are woven into the central story, not represented as mere footnotes. For example, major attention is paid to slavery in American history; to the abolition movement; to the rise of Jim Crow laws and segregation after the Civil War; and a full unit is devoted to the civil rights movement of the twentieth century. Wherever historically appropriate, the curriculum recognizes the importance of ethnic groups in the building of the nation. Students learn about the Hispanic roots of the Southwest, the cultures of Native American tribes, and Asian and Chicano immigration to California. And, the internment of Japanese-Americans during World War II is confronted and honestly treated as a violation of basic human rights.

Multiculturalism is treated as a dynamic aspect of American culture, not as an alternative to it. A major strand of the curriculum is called "National Identity." This is described as follows: "Students must: *Recognize that American society is now and always has been pluralistic and multicul-*

tural. From the first encounter between indigenous peoples and exploring Europeans, the inhabitants of the North American continent have represented a variety of races, religions, languages, and ethnic and cultural groups. With the passage of time, the United States has grown increasingly diverse in its social and cultural composition. Yet, even as our people have become increasingly diverse, there is broad recognition that we are one people. Whatever our origins, we are all Americans." This strand concludes with the admonition that students should: *"Realize that true patriotism celebrates the moral force of the American idea as a nation that unites as one people the descendants of many cultures, races, religions, and ethnic groups."*

The California history framework explicitly recognizes the positive value of pluralism in American society. Pluralism is presented as a key to understanding and defining the American community—a society and a culture to which we all belong. If there is no overall community, if all we have is a motley collection of racial and ethnic cultures, there will be no sense of the common good. Each group will fight for its own particular interests, and we could easily disintegrate as a nation, becoming instead embroiled in the kinds of ethnic conflicts that often dominate the foreign news each night. Without a sense of community that embraces all of us, we have no means to mobilize on behalf of the social good. There will be, for example, no reason to support public education. Public education is paid for by tax dollars to educate all children for their own good and for the good of the larger community. If there is no larger community, then each group will want to teach its own children in its own way, and public education will cease to exist.

PARTICULARISM

Contrast California's pluralistic approach with the particularism that gained a major forum when, last fall, New York State Commissioner of Education Thomas Sobol released a report called "A Curriculum of Inclusion." The report, the product of a Task Force on Minorities created by Sobol to review the state's curriculum guides for any instance of bias, disparages any common elements in our history, society, and culture.

The task force report denounces New York state's existing curriculum guides for "projecting dominant European-American values" that belittle the contributions of American minorities and non-western civilizations and for its "hidden assumptions of white supremacy" and "white nationalism." It claims that "negative characterizations or the absence of positive references have a terribly damaging effect on the psyche of the young people of African, Asian, Latin, and Native American descent" and, moveover, that the failure of the curriculum to portray positively non-European cultures has led to the low self-esteem and, therefore, the poor school performance of minority children.

If these charges about New York state's curriculum were true, it would, indeed, be urgent to revamp the curriculum, as the task force demands. But the charges have little merit. "A Curriculum of Inclusion" is remarkable in that it manages to denounce bias without being able to identify a single instance of it in the curricula guides under review. Instead, the consultants to the task force treat every disagreement they have with the curriculum as if it were proof of racial bias. For example, the African-American consultant excoriates the curriculum for its "White Anglo-Saxon [WASP] value system and norms," its "deep seated pathologies of racial hatred," and its "white nationalism," yet the only example of "bias" he found was that Egypt is studied as part of the Middle East instead of as part of African civilization. As it happens, scholars disagree about whether Egypt should be considered part of Africa or part of the Middle East; choosing one alternative rather than the other is not evidence of bias. The "Latino" consultant criticizes the use of the term "Spanish-American War" instead of "Spanish-Cuban-American War."

A full reading of the report suggests that the task force wants the curriculum to accept and teach its claim that European values are themselves "racist" and "oppressive" and responsible for producing "aggressive individuals and nations that were ready to discover, invade, and conquer foreign lands because of greed, racism, and national egoism."

The report is Europhobic. It repeatedly reproaches the state's curriculum for being "Eurocentric," as though this were a matter of racism, rather than the matter-of-fact consequences of European influence and European immigration. Nearly eighty percent of the population of the United States today is of European descent; the political and economic institutions of the United States were deeply influenced by European ideas. Europe's legacy to us is the set of moral and political values that we Americans subsequently refined and reshaped to enable us, in all our diversity, to live together in freedom and peace.

But in the particularist view, such commonly held values are of little concern. What is highlighted are our differences. Particularistic education teaches children to see history as a story of victims and oppressors, and it endorses the principle of collective guilt. In other words, "Your ancestor oppressed my ancestor." This approach encourages a sense of rage and victimization in those who are the presumed descendants of victims and a sense of resentment in those who are presumed descendants of oppressors. Instead of promoting reconciliation and a sense of shared community, particularism rekindles ancient hatreds in the present; its precepts set group against group. Instead of learning from history about the dangers of prejudging individuals by their color or religion, students learn that it is appropriate to think of others primarily in terms of their group identity.

The New York report divides the American people into five groups: African-Americans, Asian-Americans, Native Americans, Latinos/Puerto Ricans, and European Americans. In the eyes of the task force, each of these labels represents a group with a specific culture and history. In reality, none of the five labels used by the task force represents a single culture. If multiculturalism is to have real meaning and value, teachers and students must understand that children who speak the same language or have the same skin color may come from very different cultural backgrounds. The child from Cambodia has a cultural background different from the Japanese or Korean child. So, too, do cultural differences exist between children from Puerto Rico and those from Mexico and among black children from different parts of America or the world. But these differences are largely obscured by the five blanket labels that the New York task force adopts.

In the same stereotypical way, the report describes "European-Americans" in ways that are culturally inappropriate, indeed, in ways that are offensive, insensitive, and biased. All people with a white skin color are referred to as Europeans or "Anglo-Saxons." In the view of the task force, Jews and Germans, Irish and Russians, French and Italians, Bulgarians and Spanish are all members of the same group, all "Anglo-Saxons."

SELF-ESTEEM

Behind the "Curriculum of Inclusion" lies a pedagogical theory, a conviction that changes in the curriculum will raise the self-esteem of children from racial and ethnic minorities and will lead to improved academic performance. According to the theory, minority children who presently perform poorly will have higher self-esteem and higher performance if their teachers featured the achievements of minority cultures instead of the achievements of Europeans and white Americans.

The problem with this theory is that it confuses the obvious and the dubious. By now, it should be obvious to American teachers that they must make a special effort to promote respect among children of different racial and ethnic backgrounds and to instill self-respect in all children. But it is dubious to assert that programs to bolster racial pride will raise children's self-esteem or their academic performance. For one thing, there is no evidence to support this claim; for another, international assessments have shown that American students have *higher* self-esteem than their counterparts in other countries but do *worse* on academic tests. Genuine self-esteem means self-respect and confidence in one's ability; self-confidence is the product of experience, the reward that comes as a result of working hard to achieve one's goals.

Perhaps the sharpest commentary on the task force's notion that curricular change can build self-esteem has come from Dr. James Comer, who has worked closely with the schools in New Haven, Connecticut. He said that if you want to build self-esteem "you get parents involved in the school so that students see mutual respect between members of their own group and the mainstream. You arrange exposure to living role models and make sure that students understand why their groups have not been well represented. Rewriting the curriculum in isolation from their own experience is well down the list."

It is also questionable whether teachers of history should be directed to use history as a mechanism for instilling self-esteem and excessive reverence for one's ancestors. If teachers are expected to use history to build self-esteem by showing children that their ancestors were great and glorious, will they also be expected to hide that part of each group's history that is not heroic and admirable? Will they hesitate to introduce anything critical of any culture for fear of damaging the self-esteem of children in the classroom? What will these constraints do to the teacher's ability to teach critical thinking and to deal honestly with controversial issues?

New York may be the most famous proponent of particularist multiculturalism, but it is not alone. One can scarcely pick up an educational journal without reading about a school district that is converting to an ethnocentric curriculum in an attempt to promote "self-esteem." A state-funded project in a Sacramento high school is teaching young black males to think like Africans and to develop the "African Mind Model Technique," in order to free themselves of the racism of their own culture.

In one current proposal, a largely Hispanic student population is to learn botany through the study of the agricultural techniques of the Aztecs. Furthermore, "ethnobotanical" classifications of plants are to be substituted for the Eurocentric Linnaean system. (It may seem curious that Hispanic children are deemed to have no cultural affinity with Spain; but to acknowledge the cultural tie would be to confuse the ideological assault on Eurocentrism.)

The new particularism is unabashedly filiopietistic. It teaches children that they must immerse themselves in their "native" culture in order to understand subject matter that is taught in school. That the culture they live in is not their native culture. That American culture is "Eurocentric," and therefore hostile to anyone whose ancestors are not European. Whether they intend it or not, the message of the particularists implies that children who are members of racial and ethnic minorities are not part of American culture; that they must look elsewhere for their heritage; and that American culture belongs to white Europeans. Since these children live in American society and must find their place in this society, the particularist message may actually damage the self-esteem of minority children by implying that they are not part of the mainstream culture and that their ancestors had little or no part in shaping the common culture. If children are taught that their real identity must be found on another continent or in a vanished civilization, they may suffer an intense sense of marginalization in relation to the culture in which they now live.

Another current proposal suggests that Mexican-American and Puerto Rican children should not only learn about the mathematical accomplishments of the Mayas, but should be taught the Mayan mathematical system. Perhaps what this demonstrates best is how a sensible idea—teaching children that the Mayas developed a fascinating and sophisticated civilization—becomes ludicrous when it is carried to the extreme of believing that any children whose families emigrated from Latin America or Puerto Rico must be taught Mayan mathematics if they are to succeed. For one thing, neither Puerto Ricans nor most Mexicans are descendants of the Mayas. Yet the idea of teaching Mayan mathematics is supposed to motivate them.

A very different approach to teaching Mexican-American children is depicted in the popular movie *Stand and Deliver,* in which the teacher, himself an immigrant from Bolivia, inspires a class of Mexican-American children to learn advanced mathematics. He mentions that the Mayans discovered the concept of zero, but he also demands that they do homework and attend school on Saturdays and during Christmas vacation so that they might pass the advanced-placement test. He teaches his students to work hard and to master the kind of mathematics they need to succeed in the world as it is today; he does not teach them "Mayan mathematics."

These proposals to teach them "ethnomathematics" come at a time when American mathematics educators are trying to overhaul the present curriculum and practices because of the poor performance of American children on national and international assessments. Mathematics educators are attempting to change the teaching of their subject so that children can see its uses in everyday life. There would seem to be an incipient conflict between those who want to introduce real-life applications of mathematics and those who want to teach the mathematical systems used by ancient cultures. I suspect that most mathematics teachers would enjoy doing a bit of both if there were time or student interest. But any widespread movement to replace modern mathematics with ancient mathematics runs the risk of disaster in a field that is struggling to update existing curricula. If, as seems likely, ancient mathematics is taught mainly to minority children, the gap between their achievement levels and those of middle-class white children seems likely to grow.

Particularism is premised on the spurious notion that cultural traits may be inherited. It implies a dubious, perhaps dangerous, form of cultural predestination. Children are taught that if their ancestors could do it, so can they. But what happens if a child is from a cultural group that made no significant contribution to science or mathematics: Does this mean that children from that background must find a culturally appropriate field in which to strive? How does a teacher find the right cultural buttons for children of mixed cultural heritage? And how in the world will teachers use this technique when the children in their classes, as is usually the case, are drawn from many different cultures? By the time that every culture gets its due, there may be no time left to teach the subject itself.

CENTRAL ISSUES

Two issues are central to this controversy: First, is American education Eurocentric? And, second, do children need to be immersed in their own particular cultural heritage in order to succeed academically?

As I mentioned earlier, there is good reason for American education to reflect the substantial influence of Europe on the formation of the United States. That influence is a historical fact, reflected in our Constitution as well as our cultural and economic institutions. But this does not mean that the curriculum in American schools is Eurocentric. If anything, American education is centered on American life; it is "Americentric." Most American students know little about Europe, and even less about the rest of the world. Their minds are rooted solidly in the here and now. Most seem to think that the United States is the world. One of the most difficult and demanding tasks of teachers today is to break through this parochialism and to introduce students to the world beyond our borders. Eurocentrics is not the problem; ignorance is.

Second, the claim that children will do better if they study their ancestor's achievements sounds dangerously like a panacea that may detract from the real needs of students today. Many children from racial and ethnic minorities leave school without graduating and perform poorly in academic classes. Probably they would fare better in school if they had well-educated and well-paid teachers, small classes, good materials, encouragement at home and school, summer academic programs, a quiet study place, and protection from the drugs and crime that ravage their neighborhoods. These are expensive and time-consuming remedies. The lure of particularism is that it offers a less complicated anodyne, one in which the children's academic needs may be addressed (or ignored) by inflating their racial and cultural pride.

Moreover, the rising tide of particularism encourages the politicization of all curricula in the schools. If educational bureaucrats bend to the political and ideological winds, as is their wont, we can anticipate a generation of struggle over the content of curriculum. There is already too much receptivity by state and local school-board members to fundamentalists, anti-evolutionists, and interest groups who want to censor textbooks, remove library books, and determine what may be taught in history, literature, and science.

Any reconstruction of the curriculum, whatever the subject, must proceed on the best knowledge available to experienced teachers and scholars. At the same time, it is important to teach students about conflicting interpretations and about debates among experts. Every subject field has disagreements among the experts, and the study itself becomes more interesting if students are let in on these disagreements. History is not just a bunch of facts and dates and names that must be regurgitated for tests; it is a field that is alive with controversy.

Students should learn, for example, that scholars disagree about whether Egypt was a black African civilization or a multiracial civilization. Some scholars believe that what is now called "western civilization" can be traced to African origins, via Egypt and Greece. Others believe that contemporary interest in the color of ancient Egyptians reflects our obsession with race. Let students investigate the question; such an inquiry would send many students to books about ancient Egypt as well as to museums with Egyptian collections.

One thing that these investigations will produce is an awareness of the way that cultures influence each other, exchanging ideas, customs, art, and technology. From this they will learn that great civilizations do not exist in isolation; they grow by learning from others. Such an insight might help students understand how American culture has been transformed by the contributions of its many different minorities.

To the extent that children come to understand that history is a study that is constantly revised and interpreted, they will realize that historical study has political implications, that it is written by fallible humans like themselves who make conscious choices among facts, that some historical theories are wrong, that what they learn in the textbooks is conditional, and that the historian often works like a detective.

In studying history, students must come to understand that the historical record is not fixed and that it changes as a result of new scholarship and debates among historians. In no event should the history taught in school be determined by political pressures brought to bear on legislators, school boards, textbook publishers, and state education departments. Whatever the subject field, teachers must be free to teach honestly and critically. They must feel free to show different sides of the issues. They must not be turned into ethnic cheerleaders who, for the supposed sake of their students' self-esteem, are pressed to teach spurious history in order to make sure that everyone's ancestors are presented as accomplished and glorious.

Sooner or later, educators must directly refute the widespread filiopietistic belief that children will succeed in school only if they have learned a glorified history of their own race and ethnic group. If history is taught honestly, it gives no grounds for excessive racial pride. People of every race, at some point in its history, have committed terrible crimes, often against people of the same group. Some whites practiced or condoned slavery; certain whites were responsible for the Holocaust. People of other racial groups have also committed comparable crimes. Remember that white slave traders bought African slaves from Arab slave traders, who bought them from African tribes who had enslaved their captives during the war. Mayan and Aztec peoples practiced human sacrifice and slavery. Before World War I, the Turkish government massacred hundreds of thousands of Armenians. In Africa in the late 1960s, a million or more Ibo people were starved to death by the Nigerian government when they tried to create a secessionist Biafran state. In China, the Maoist government killed millions of Chinese people. Japan slaughtered tens of thousands of Chinese during the infamous "Rape of Nanking" in the 1930s. The Khmer Rouge government of Cambodia slaughtered more than a million of its own people in the 1970s.

IN CONCLUSION

No race has a corner on virtue or vice. Each child should learn to value himself or herself as a member of the human race. Self-esteem ultimately must derive from one's own hard work and accomplishments, not from pride in one's skin color, which is an inherited attribute rather than an accomplishment.

Ultimately, the best guarantee of a fair and just society, where people of different cultural backgrounds can live in peace and mutual respect, is the democratic political tradition. It is found in many societies—east and west, north and south—wherever the central values are liberty, equality, and justice. It is the democratic tradition that requires us to respect basic human rights, to listen to dissenters instead of jailing them, to have a multiparty system, a free press, free speech, freedom of religion, freedom of assembly, and free trade unions. In our society, the democratic tradition was shaped by the Enlightenment, Thomas Jefferson, Horace Mann, Abraham Lincoln, Frederick Douglass, Elizabeth Cady Stanton, Susan B. Anthony, Samuel Gompers, John Dewey, Jane Addams, A. Philip Randolph, Franklin Delano Roosevelt, Martin Luther King, Jr., Bayard Rustin, and millions of other people from different backgrounds.

We teach our children about their society for many reasons. We want them to see how it evolved and what it is becoming so that they will be able to understand it, make their way in it, learn its symbols and language, and participate as knowledgeable citizens in the present and the future. All of them will be eligible to vote; all are likely to live and work in a variety of contexts, sometimes with people of their own group, but more often with people from other backgrounds.

What we should be teaching our children is that race hatred is wrong, racial chauvinism is wrong, and racism is wrong. People are people. Cut us and we bleed. If we lose a child, we cry. The human heart is the same in all of us, regardless of skin color or language. It is the job of public education to teach everyone, whatever their ancestry, that we are all Americans and we all reside in the same world. We must all discover what W.H. Auden wrote fifty years ago, as a new world war began: "We must love one another or die."

29

Immigration and Political Community in the United States

Daniel J. Tichenor

Illegal immigration and the arrival of unprecedented numbers of asylum-seekers both haunted American policymakers in the 1980s. Our nation's borders had become porous and inadequately regulated, and as always, racial issues loomed large in American immigration politics. By 1980 non-white newcomers from Asia, Latin America, and the Caribbean dominated all forms of migration to the U.S. Europe, once the origin of nearly all immigration to America, has accounted for only ten percent of total immigration since the 1970s. The uninvited influx of asylum-seekers and illegal immigrants prompted a decade of polarizing debate among policymakers over the entire structure of American immigration and refugee policy. Two major laws, the Immigration Reform and Control Act of 1986 (IRCA) and the Immigration Act of 1990, and their subsequent judicial and administrative interpretation, represent the culmination of this period of policy change. The treatment of aliens in this burst of policymaking reveals both a promising inclusiveness and a disquieting enervation of the responsibilities and perceived worth of citizenship.

A BREAK WITH THE PAST

The widespread support during the 1970s and 1980s for curtailing immigration was nothing new in American politics. Policymakers have long sought to restrict or bar outsiders of non-European races or ethnicities from entering the country. For example, the exclusion of Chinese in the 1880s and the National Origins Quota system of the 1920s were both efforts to block entrance to all but Northern and Western European newcomers. Policymakers also historically have responded to worrisome illegal immigration by launching campaigns to seize and deport undocumented aliens (particularly Mexicans) en masse. Operation Wetback in 1954 led to the expulsion of over one million Mexican aliens, many of whom were legal residents. The Hart-Celler Act of 1965 stripped away racist national origins quotas, but most reformers intended a new emphasis on family reunification to limit drastically the number of visas available to Third World immigrants.

Recent immigration reform represents a decisive break with this nativist tradition. The 1986 and 1990 laws made no effort to stop non-white, non-European migrants from dominating immigration into the U.S. Not only did these laws not restrict "new immigration," they also allowed significant increases in migration from these regions. The IRCA dealt with the illegal population residing in the country by granting legal status to over 3 million illegal aliens. The Immigration Act of 1990 granted stays of deportation to family members of aliens legalized under the IRCA. The 1990 law also raised the cap on legal immigration and allowed even that ceiling to be exceeded by relatives of citizens. In short, immigration reforms expanded alien rights and increased migration to the U.S., even though the original impetus for the law had been restrictionist.

Immigration reform also produced an ideological convergence in favor of sustained immigration. This development was undergirded by two important forces in American politics: the legacy of the Civil Rights movement and the resurgence in the 1980s of free-market economics. The first extensive federal regulations on immigration were enacted amidst the drastic economic and social dislocations of the late nineteenth and early twentieth centuries. As ties between members of the national community assumed greater importance, an agitated society directed its venom against emancipated blacks and new immigrants from both Asia and from Southern and Eastern Europe. These were people whom white America largely saw as imperiling the American way of life. Although the Jim Crow laws produced by this racially exclusive nationalism were undoubtedly more pernicious than immigration restrictions, immigration policy was linked thereafter in the minds of progressive politicians and activists with the black struggle for full citizenship.

As 1980s immigration advocates on the Left sought to grant entry and protection to powerless alien groups (particularly non-white illegal aliens and refugees), free-market immigration advocates sought to unfetter the labor market and allow the labor supply to accommodate the demands of employers. Conservative think tanks and editorial pages encouraged not simply the free movement of goods, technology, and capital, but the free movement of people across borders. Hudson Institute scholar Stephen Moore praised immigrants for "their propensity to start new businesses" and "their contribution in keeping U.S. businesses internationally competitive." The key goal of the expansionist Right was to provide American businesses greater access to the immigrant labor market and relief from new regulations such as employer sanctions and job and discrimination protection for aliens.

Significantly, the ideological convergence in favor of sustaining robust immigration generated not consensual politics, but a new divide between market-oriented and rights-oriented expansionists. The locus of conflict seemed to shift from a question of *whether* there should be expansive immigration, to a struggle over *who* should benefit from an opening of the gates. In the legislative arena, free market expansionists secured sharp increases in employer-sponsored and skilled-worker visas, as well as cheap alien labor for the agricultural, garment, and hotel sectors. Rights-oriented expansionists secured a generous amnesty program for illegal aliens, a new civil rights agency charged with combating job discrimination against aliens, new protections for temporary farmworkers, legal status for previously excluded refugee groups, generous allocations of family reunification visas, and the removal of many ideological and sexual orientation restrictions.

Obscured among these initiatives was the original purpose of reform: to curb illegal immigration and regain control of porous borders. Instead of representing the centerpiece of immigration reform, the enactment of an immigration control mechanism in 1986—employer sanctions—was clearly subordinate to the decade's expansionist reforms. Civil rights activists and market libertarians successfully opposed the creation of a new counterfeit- and tamper-resistant employee identification system. When a pilot program was proposed by Senator Alan Simpson (R-WY) in 1990 to use driver's licenses in conjunction with employer sanctions, it was defeated on the House floor by members of the Hispanic Caucus who likened it to South Africa's apartheid system of passbooks for blacks. Free-market expansionists exempted small businesses from employer sanctions, which the Reagan and Bush administrations viewed as another regulatory burden on U.S. businesses and never enforced strictly. Dampened briefly after the IRCA was enacted, illegal immigration soon returned to peak levels of the pre-reform era.

NOTHING NEW

These distinct rationales for expansive immigration are hardly novel. In his *Report on Manufactures*, Alexander Hamilton noted that it was in the national interest "to open every possible avenue to emigration from abroad." Consistent with his vision of commercial empire, Hamilton perceived aliens as "an important resource, not only for extending the population, and with it the useful and productive labor of the country, but likewise for the prosecution of manufactures." Almost a century later, Andrew Carnegie praised open immigration as "a golden stream which flows into the country each year." He added crassly: "these adults are surely worth $1500 each—for in former days an efficient slave sold for that sum."

Whereas Hamilton emphasized the financial empire to be reaped from open immigration, Thomas Jefferson's enlightened idealism expressed a special obligation to newcomers. Although he had opposed immigration as a young man, Jefferson wrote in 1817 that the U.S. should be a new Canaan where outsiders would be "received as brothers and secured against . . . oppression by participation in . . . self-government." In contrast to Carnegie's economic pragmatism, Ralph Waldo Emerson exalted in 1878 that "our whole history appears like a last effort of the Divine Providence in behalf of the human race." He extolled American opportunity—"opportunity to civil rights, of education, of personal power"—which he saw as an "invitation to every nation, to every race and skin."

The American political community is often characterized as lagging well behind the industrial democracies of Europe in terms of welfare rights. Sociologist Ann Shola Orloff, for instance, emphasizes that the American framers' penchant for dividing political authority has produced an attenuated, even anemic, system of social welfare that pales in comparison to its European counterparts. "Against the backdrop of European welfare states," Orloff writes, "the American system of public social provision seems incomplete and belated." But the issue of how a nation treats those from outside its boundaries reminds us that inclusivity and benevolence encompass more than welfare provision. At the same time, the potential for immigration to erode feelings of mutual economic obligation in a political community and to hurt the nation's poorest citizens most, underscores the limits of viewing immigration policy as a measure of a polity's benevolence.

THE EUROPEAN COMPARISON

The fact that the U.S. permitted increases in alien admissions and extended new rights to non-citizens is striking compared to the political response of many west European nations. European politicians struggled between "national identity" and obligations owed to foreigners residing and working within their borders. In the midst of stunning postwar economic growth, Britain, France, Switzerland, West Germany, and other nations recruited millions of foreign guestworkers (from the Middle East and Northern Africa) to prevent labor shortages and to keep wages in check. In the 1970s, a time of employment scarcity among citizens, anti-immigrant voices began challenging the presence of guestworkers. The politicization of immigration was fueled further by waves of asylum seekers and illegal aliens seeking entry into these culturally homogenous societies. Many people began to wonder whether European civic cultures were capable of assimilating new ethnic and racial groups. New restrictionists in Europe warned that aliens undermined the solidarity and loyalty that common ethnicity and historical experience engenders. As German scholar Kay Hailbronner notes, Germans "think of their nation not as a political unit but as a cultural, linguistic, and ethnic unit."

Several political parties (most notably the National Front parties of France and Great Britain and the *Republikaner* party in Germany) emerged as standard-bearers of this new breed of nationalist politics. "These movements were built, not surprisingly, on the edifice of anti-immigrant, racist and xenophobic appeals," writes political scientist James Hollifield. Jean-Marie Le Pen, leader of the French National Front, garnered at least ten percent of the vote in elections throughout the 1980s, sounding the battlecry "La France aux Français" (France for the French).

As a result, the European mainstream was forced to accommodate the Right's attitude toward immigration. Le Pen's consistent appeal, drawing on nationalist subcultures of Jacobinism on the Left and Gaullism on the Right, prompted other parties in France to shift their immigration position. The National Front in Britain was weakened not only by a strong two-party system and stout resistance from Prime Minister Margaret Thatcher, but by the co-opting by the Conservative Party of the National Front's anti-immigrant stance. Britain's 1981 Nationality Act established gradations of citizenship for immigrants from former colonies. It also instituted conditional birthright citizenship; children born in Britain to parents without permanent residency status are no longer guaranteed full membership. Even Sweden and Denmark, known for their generosity to refugees, imposed strict denial rates of asylees. As immigration scholar Lawrence Fuchs notes, "Europeans generally [have] asked about foreigners, How can we get these outsiders to go home? or, failing that, How can we keep them outside the polity a while longer even as they work among us?" Significantly, the resurgence of restrictive nationalism occurred when most of the migrants seeking membership were non-whites.

Though the U.S. is currently absorbing a similar influx of non-white, Third World nationals, nativist voices reminiscent of the Know-Nothings, American Protective Association, and the Immigration Restriction League were largely muted in the 1980s. Whereas European policymakers restricted the flow of immigrants and refugees to their countries, summarily deported illegal aliens and asylees, and denied full membership to foreign guestworkers (regardless of how long these "guests" lived and labored in their societies), their American counterparts increased alien admissions, made citizenship easier to gain, and expanded the opportunities and protection of illegal aliens and temporary workers.

One can overstate the generosity of pro-immigration reforms. After all, the new employer-sponsored and skills-based visas reflect more strongly a concern for labor-market demands than one for the well-being of newcomers. But pro-immigration reforms certainly reflect an inclusive vision of membership as well as self-interested economic calculations.

THE DOWNSIDE

If the recent expansion of alien admissions and rights demonstrates a promising inclusiveness of outsiders, it also describes an enervation of the bonds between Americans. During the Great Depression, John Dewey argued that freedom in the 20th century required government to secure not only the natural rights of individuals, but also their economic well-being. This new social contract, the heart of the New Deal, raises the question of whether certain obligations owed to disadvantaged members of a political community must be met before newcomers are granted admission and membership goods.

The agenda of rights-oriented expansionists focused resolutely on the compelling needs of individual aliens, yet ignored how increases in alien admission might affect disadvantaged citizens. At its most absurd extreme, political champions of the special lotteries and "diversity" visas, which had been designed principally to benefit Irish aliens, defended those programs using civil rights language and described European immigrants as "disadvantaged" persons.

Absent from this calculus is any serious consideration of policy costs or trade-offs. The absoluteness of rights-based arguments often derails meaningful deliberation of contending claims: whether the presence of numerous unskilled and vulnerable foreign workers perpetuates a segmented labor force, for example, or whether it forces unskilled domestic workers to choose between low-wage jobs with poor working conditions or unemployment. These are questions that never figured prominently in policy debate. Nor were the civic merits of asking U.S. companies (or the state) to retrain citizens to fill skilled positions fully weighed by most policymakers.

The responsiveness of immigration policy reform to the rights claims of aliens and American employers also caused it to ignore how reforms affected the nation's poorest citizens, of whom a disproportionate number are African-Americans. While economists for several decades had shown that immigrants contribute to the overall economic well-being of American society, less attention has been devoted to their impact on the economic underclass. Significantly, several observers suggest that many Americans are more partial to Asian, Central American, European, and Mexican newcomers than to urban blacks. For example, sociologist William Julius Wilson found in 1992 that the loss of manufacturing jobs in Chicago affected blacks and new immigrant groups very differently. Though less formally educated than black workers, Mexican and other immigrants still lost fewer jobs. When displaced from blue-collar jobs, immigrant workers found new employment faster. Wilson discovered in interviews with Chicago-area employers that employers viewed these groups very differently one from another. Inner-city blacks (especially young black males) were seen as "uneducated, unstable, uncooperative, and dishonest." Mexicans and other Third World immigrants, by contrast, were "perceived to exhibit better 'work ethics' than native workers" largely because they endured poor working conditions, meager pay, and few opportunities to advance. Wilson suggests that the unwillingness of many native blacks to tolerate these wages and conditions has shaped employer attitudes. His findings are supported by a General Accounting Office report claiming that janitorial firms in Los Angeles replaced unionized black workers with non-unionized immigrants.

The preference for immigrant labor is not a new development. More than a century ago, Frederick Douglass lamented that "every hour sees the black man elbowed out of employment by some newly arrived immigrant." Stanley Lieberson's study of job competition in the expanding urban labor markets of the late nineteenth century suggests that new immigrants were preferred over southern blacks who had migrated north.

Competition for employment is compounded by the fact that immigrants place special strains on government services in major cities and metropolitan areas. Six cities and metropolitan areas—New York, Los Angeles, San Francisco, Chicago, Miami, and Houston—account for the settlement of three-quarters of current immigration. For much of this century, the problems of urban America—school decline, limited tax revenues, crumbling infrastructure, an economic underclass—have been largely the problems of black America. While studies indicate that immigrants pay more in taxes than they cost in government services, newcomers do place great burdens on city and state services such as education and emergency health care. The Los Angeles County Board of Commissioners found that providing services to legal immigrants, amnesty aliens, and illegal aliens represented an estimated 31 percent of the county's costs in 1991–92. And San Diego County officials discovered that two-thirds of emergency medical funds for the poor were spent on aliens.

Ironically, even as immigration reform drew residual energy from the civil rights movement, policymakers showed a profound inattention to the most intractable problems of African-Americans. This quality of immigration policymaking seems to exemplify a political community of citizen-strangers, in which many white members express a greater affinity for and identification with newcomers than with fellow black members. Moreover, the estrangement of citizens is reinforced by the flight of white citizens from cities to fortress communities offering safe havens from urban problems. It is worth adding that those aliens whom black citizens most hoped to see admitted—Haitian refugees and African immigrants—benefitted least from immigration reform.

All this is not to say that new immigration has to represent a zero-sum game, in which the economic and political ends of newcomers are at odds with native blacks. Alliances between black and Hispanic leaders may produce important economic and political cooperation. But it is profoundly disturbing that policymakers never thoroughly examined so many fundamental questions about how immigration reform might affect the nation's urban poor.

ALIENS AS SCAPEGOATS

The economic burdens posed by new immigrants and refugees on a few key cities and states have contributed significantly to new restrictionism in American public opinion and politics. Immigration policymaking of the 1980s was an insulated process, dominated by organized groups, professional lobbyists, and policymakers in Washington. Recently, however, policymakers have played to public fears about crime, welfare dependency, and unemployment by using aliens as convenient scapegoats. Indeed, it has become a popular sport in Congress to propose amendments denying aliens (even legal, taxpaying aliens) income support, health care, educational benefits, disaster relief, and other forms of public support. Many legislators have also called for sweeping reductions in immigration. Despite having championed a foreign guestworker program when he was a senator in the 1980s, California's governor Pete Wilson has blamed immigrants for unemployment and budgetary woes in his state. Some California and Texas politicians have called for a wall of troops to guard the U.S.-Mexican border, while others advocate a constitutional amendment denying the children of undocumented aliens birthright citizenship.

Tellingly, this new burst of restrictionist populism has shown as much disdain for informed public deliberation as did the last decade of immigration politics. Recent political efforts to scale back total immigration and alien rights have discouraged discussion of several important questions concerning the nation's social and humanitarian goals. Given that most immigrant visas are distributed to relatives of American citizens and permanent residents, are we willing to sacrifice the social goal of family unity for that of having fewer immigrants? Are we willing to apply strict numerical ceilings on refugee admissions, regardless of the persecution asylees may be fleeing? The last time our nation stridently rejected humanitarian obligations to refugees, millions died at the hands of Germany's Nazi regime. Likewise, is it just to deny public benefits to *all* aliens, including those who are legally admitted and pay taxes? Do we owe special obligations to the children of illegal aliens, whom the Supreme Court has recognized as "innocents" and many of whom are U.S. citizens? And how far are we willing to go in denying health care to undocumented aliens? Would that include such necessities as prenatal or emergency care?

Recent immigration politics also have obscured important information that might elevate the debate. In their haste to reap political gain at the expense of newcomers, "born-again" restrictionist politicians conveniently fail to make critical distinctions between the economic and social characteristics of legal and illegal migratory streams. For example, several economic studies show that legal immigrants are far less likely than illegal aliens *or citizens* to become welfare dependent. Nevertheless, legal immigrants and refugees have been held political hostage largely because of a continued failure to curb illegal immigration.

CONCLUSION

Several observers see the latest wave of Third World newcomers as a formidable threat to American culture. These observers often focus their concerns on Latin Americans, drawing attention to linguistic separatism and dramatically low levels of naturalization. This is nothing new. Throughout American history, natural-born citizens blamed new immigrant groups for failing to become fully integrated members of society. Political scientist Rodolfo de la Garza offers an alternative explanation for why Mexican-Americans and other Hispanics have been slow to embrace American culture: "Mexican-Americans have retained a 'Mexicanness' only because they were so long denied access to American institutions." For most of the nineteenth century, new immigrants were incorporated into the political community by Martin Van Buren's compromise between republican virtue and modern democracy—decentralized political parties. These imperfect "civic associations," to borrow a phrase from political philosopher Wilson Carey McWilliams, linked the interests of immigrants to something larger than themselves. The civic educator of today's immigrants, by contrast, has been a centralized, rights-based regime that teaches little about obligations and the value of participation.

Scholarly debates concerning alien admissions and rights have generally oscillated between national and global perspectives, either challenging or vindicating the sovereign right of nation-states to control their borders. On the one hand, political theorists Joseph Carens and Judith Lichtenberg and other proponents of an internationalist view have stressed that the equal moral worth of individuals discards distinctions between aliens and citizens. This perspective reminds us that new migratory pressures are produced by a vast disparity in wealth between First and Third World peoples. On the other hand, political philosophers Michael Walzer, Bruce Ackerman, and Mark Gibney argue that open borders would render communal life meaningless and sacrifice essential bonds and duties between national citizens. In both arguments the voices of local communities expressing their distinct needs and concerns are often neglected.

Recent immigration reform reflects this neglect and thus exposes an American political community with remarkably weak ties and obligations among citizens. Fragmentation of national institutions accentuated divisions between policymakers, producing contradictions and cross-purposes in the legislation. The failure to engage citizens and localities in policymaking may result in a strong political backlash against recent expansions in alien admissions and rights. By insulating meaningful policymaking from local communities and public deliberation, national decisionmakers have unintentionally provided a window of opportunity for irresponsible politicians to translate xenophobic appeals to votes. The new volatility of American immigration politics has increased the likelihood of dramatic policy changes as political pressure for new restrictions builds in the next few years.

Engaging citizens and local communities in deliberation over immigration policy involves considerable risk for expansionists. Public opinion polls have usually found Americans generally opposed to large-scale immigration and refugee admissions. Yet the alternatives to public education and informed dialogue on this issue are hardly appealing. Centralized and insulated policymaking in the 1980s often ignored important trade-offs as well as the reasonable concerns of local communities. One residual effect of this process is that certain cities and states have unfairly been asked to absorb a disproportionate share of the initial costs of new immigration. In turn, the populist restrictionism of recent immigration politics has invited irresponsible politicians to perpetuate anti-immigrant stereotypes even as they pay no attention to the potential economic, social, and moral costs of their knee-jerk policies.

Requiring immigration policymakers to be attentive to the concerns of citizens and local communities might bring important costs and trade-offs to the surface, providing an opportunity for public officials and citizens to educate one another. It may also give aliens greater incentive to pursue cultural and political membership so that they may participate in a meaningful deliberative process. Finally, it may enable American political communities to respond to the needs of citizens and newcomers of diverse ethnic and racial groups without diffusing the special commitments and obligations that foster attachments among members.

30

Who Killed Modern Manners?

Judith Martin

It was idealism that murdered modern manners.

Those whose daily lives include being cut off on the highway and shoved on the sidewalk, ignored by service people or insulted by customers, addressed as equals or inferiors by juniors and intimates by strangers, and cursed if not shot by anyone who is simply feeling surly and finds them a convenient target, tend to blame people of ill will. Surely no one would be so villainous as to attack the premise that is the philosophical basis of etiquette: that people must agree to restrain their impulses and follow a common language of behavior in order to avoid making communal life abrasive, unpleasant, and explosive.

But attack this premise is exactly what some did. During the idealism of the 1960s, people who were willing to put more thought and energy into getting out of the social tasks they had been taught than in simply performing them, came up with the following astounding revelations:

1. Good surface behavior is not a truth-in-packaging guarantee of a virtuous heart inside.
2. Teaching children manners inhibits them from behaving as their natural impulses may prompt them.
3. Many conventions of etiquette are arbitrary, and cannot be functionally justified—for example, the necktie does not do the sort of valiant and obviously useful job a belt does.
4. Among our inherited etiquette traditions are patterns of behavior apparently based on ideas that we now find repugnant, such as that ladies are weaker than gentlemen and must therefore be given protective treatment.
5. Specialized forms of etiquette practiced by a particular social subgroup—the prime example being rich people who use peculiar sil-

verware to baffle and embarrass the uninitiated—serve to distinguish those people from outsiders, and may encourage them to feel superior.

All of these points are true to the point of having been taken for granted by those who gave civilized human behavior any real thought. One must then go beyond them to realize that:

1. It is not therefore true that a virtuous heart excuses surface behavior if it inadvertently inconveniences, antagonizes, or disgusts others. And an evil heart that is constrained by the demands of politeness is less of a public menace than one freer to follow its evil impulses.
2. The children who are most paralyzed by inhibitions turn out to be the ones who are thrown into the complications of life without being told what behavior is expected of them, or warned how their actions will be interpreted.
3. Etiquette sometimes employs symbolism, and symbolism is, by definition, arbitrary, although this does not prevent it from being useful. A tie symbolizes respect and seriousness, as T-shirts or bare chests with gold chains, no matter how much more comfortable, washable, and alluring, do not.
4. Because etiquette is based on tradition, and people often have affection for the traditions of their youth, its customs tend to lag behind developing sociological thought. Yet etiquette can, and does, change over time to accommodate new ways of living. "Ladies first" was never a permanent rule of etiquette, having replaced the fifth century Greek rule, "ladies never." It is now gradually changing to a precedence system based on age (and, in any case, was never proper in the work place, where rank, not gender, is what counts).
5. The rich are not the only group to have specialized manners: The attention to clothing, forms of greeting, and the social hierarchy practiced by any teenaged street gang are, for example, far more complicated. But when knowledge of special forms moves from cultural identification to snobbery, the practice is classified as bad manners. Through the principle of noblesse oblige, etiquette requires the powerful to be especially polite to those less powerful, rather than to follow the more rational rule of "might makes right" and then buy their way out of any trouble they may cause.

THE TRIUMPH OF "HONESTY"

The idealists who thought that the world would be a better place if good manners were quashed also held charming beliefs about human nature that unfortunately do not correspond to human experience. They felt that children are born not only good but creative, and that civilizing them only destroys virtue and artistry that would otherwise blossom. And they believed that we would all love one another if only we could really open up our hearts and minds, without the artificial barriers of learned behavior.

But children seem rather to be born thinking that they are the center of a universe that must cater to their needs: Where is the infant who decides that he or she is not really all that hungry, and could let those exhausted people get a bit more sleep before demanding breakfast? And if they are such great artists, why is it that the children's drawings that we so proudly display on our refrigerators all look alike?

The idea that we would all love one another, if only we communicated everything we thought and felt, trivializes real differences—emotional, intellectual, philosophical—that well-meaning people may sincerely hold. Manners that disguise fundamentally opposing and hotly held differences are, rather, what enable us to live on peaceful terms with our opponents.

Paradoxically coexisting with this sweet delusion was the self-assertiveness movement, which encouraged looking after oneself, often suggesting highly provocative techniques for taking advantage of others. The idea behind this was that the only way to avoid being treated unfairly was to fight for oneself and against others, which necessitated abandoning the mannerly goal of communal good.

When all these ill-thought-out concepts were raised, the habit of following good manners easily collapsed. It apparently does not take much to persuade people to stop bothering to write thank you letters, train their children not to destroy other people's property, pretend that they appreciate disappointing presents, or extend hospitality without any anticipation of a career advantage.

"Honesty"—which came to mean the undisguised communication of unattractive, often insulting, opinions—came to be considered the first among virtues, against which such a gentle virtue as human kindness did not have a chance.

But civilization cannot really exist without etiquette, as is acknowledged in both Western philosophy (from Socrates with his question of how one should live, to Erasmus, who wrote a renaissance etiquette book, to Emerson, who anticipated me in the 19th century by calling his work "On Manners") and Far Eastern philosophy (including Confucianism, Taoism, and Buddhism). Evidence of etiquette dates from our earliest definitions of civilization, which are associated with the ceremonial burial of the dead. Even those who now argue that etiquette must justify itself by being of immediate functional value do not maintain that it would be more practical to put corpses down a garbage disposal, rather than to go through some form of funerary ritual.

THE ROLE OF MANNERS

Ritual serves one of three major functions of manners. Oddly enough, the greatest scoffers at the traditions of American etiquette, who scorn the rituals of their own society as stupid and stultifying, voice respect for the custom and folklore of Native Americans, less industrialized peoples, and other societies they find more "authentic" than their own.

Americans who disdain etiquette in everyday life often go into an etiquette tailspin in connection with marriage. Although the premise on which the 20th-century American wedding forms were based—that a young girl is given by the father whose protection she leaves to a husband who will perform the same function—has changed, the forms retain their emotional value. If it happens that the bride has been supporting the bridegroom for years in their own household, she may well ask their own toddler age son to "give her away" just to preserve the ritual.

Ritual provides a reassuring sense of social belonging far more satisfying than behavior improvised under emotionally complicated circumstances. Rituals of mourning other than funerals have been nearly abandoned, but at a great emotional cost. Not only are the bereaved unprotected from normal social demands by customs of seclusion and symbols of vulnerability, but they are encouraged to act as if nothing had happened—only to be deemed heartless if they actually succeed.

A second function of manners is the symbolic one. It is the symbolic function that confuses and upsets people who claim that etiquette is "simply a matter of common sense" when actually, the symbols cannot be deduced from first principles, but must be learned in each society, and, within that society, for different times, places, ages, and social classes.

Because symbols are arbitrary, it can happen that opposite forms of behavior may symbolize the same idea, as when a man takes off his hat to show respect in a church, but puts on his hat to show respect in a synagogue. But once these rules are learned, they provide people with a tremendous fund of nonverbal knowledge about one another, helping them to deal appropriately with a wide range of social situations and relationships. Forms of greeting, dressing, eating, and restraining bodily functions can all be read as symbols of degrees of friendliness or hostility, respect or contempt, solidarity with the community or alienation from it. It is safe to assume that a person who advances on you with an outstretched hand is symbolizing an intent to treat you better than one who spits on the ground at the sight of you.

The law, the military, diplomacy, the church, and athletics have particularly strict codes of etiquette, compliance with which is taken to symbolize adherence to the particular values that these professions require: fairness, obedience, respect, piety, or valor. And following the conventions of the society is taken as a measure of respect for it—which is why people who are facing juries are advised by their own lawyers to dress and behave with the utmost convention.

It does not matter how arbitrary any of the violated rules may be—ignoring them is interpreted as defiance of, or indifference to, or antagonism toward, the interests of the person or community whose standard is being ignored. The person who wears blue jeans to a formal wedding, or a three-piece suit at a beach party, may protest all he likes that his choice had only to do with a clothing preference, but it is hard to imagine anyone so naive as to believe that the people whose standards he is violating will not interpret the choice as disdain. In New York, a 15-year-old was shot on the street in a gang fight started over his refusal to return another teenager's high five sign of greeting. "Dissin'," the current term for showing disrespect, is cited as a leading provocation for modern murder.

The third function of etiquette is the regulative function, which is less troublesome to the literal-minded, because those rules can be understood functionally. Between them, etiquette and law divide the task of regulating social conduct in the interest of community harmony, with the law addressing grave conflicts, such as those threatening life or property, and administering serious punishments, while etiquette seeks to forestall such conflicts, relying on voluntary compliance with its restraints.

This is why etiquette restricts freedom of self-expression more than the law does (and why etiquette rejects encounter group theories of achieving harmony through total communication). It is within my legal right to tell you that you are ugly, or that your baby is, but this is likely to lead to ugly—which is to say dangerous—behavior, which it will require the law to address, no longer as a mere insult, but as a more serious charge of slander, libel, or mental cruelty.

But the danger of attempting to expand the dominion of the law to take over the function of etiquette—to deal with such violations as students calling one another nasty names, or protesters doing provocative things with flags—is that it may compromise our constitutional rights. For all its strictness, a generally understood community standard of etiquette is more flexible than the law and, because it depends on voluntary compliance, less threatening.

Jurisprudence itself cannot function without etiquette. In enforcing standards of dress, rules about when to sit and when to stand, restricting offensive language and requiring people to speak only in proper turn, courtroom etiquette overrides many of the very rights it may protect. So does the etiquette of legislatures, such as that specified in *Robert's Rules of Order*. This is necessary because the more orderly is the form of a social structure, the more conflict it can support. Etiquette requires participants in adversarial proceedings to present their opposing views in a restrained manner, to provide a disciplined and respectful ambience in which to settle conflicts peacefully.

RESPONDING TO CHANGING TIMES

That we cannot live peacefully in communities without etiquette, using only the law to prevent or resolve conflicts in everyday life, has become increasingly obvious to the public. And so there has been, in the last few years, a "return to etiquette," a movement for which I am not totally blameless. It has been hampered by the idea that etiquette need not involve self-restriction. Those who must decry rudeness in others are full of schemes to punish those transgressors by treating them even more rudely in return. But the well-meaning are also sometimes stymied, because they understand "etiquette" to consist of the social rules that were in effect approximately a generation ago, when women rarely held significant jobs, and answering machines and Call Waiting had not yet been invented. As the same social conditions do not apply, they assume that there can be no etiquette system, or that each individual may make up his or her own rules.

One often hears that etiquette is "only a matter of being considerate of others," and that is certainly a good basis for good behavior. Obviously, however, it does not guide one in the realms of symbolic or ritual etiquette. And if each individual improvises, the variety of resulting actions would be open to misinterpretations and conflicts, which a mutually intelligible code of behavior seeks to prevent.

Yet many of the surface etiquette issues of today were addressed under the codes of earlier times, which need only be adapted for the present. As previously noted, a system of precedence must exist, although it need not be "ladies first." One must regulate the access of others to one's attention—if not with a butler announcing the conventional fiction that "Madam is not at home," then by a machine that says, "If you leave a message after the beep. . . ." But dropping one unfinished conversation to begin another has always been rude, and that applies to Call Waiting. Usually, changes happen gradually, as, for example, most people have come to accept the unmarried couple socially, or to issue their wedding invitations in time for guests to take advantage of bargain travel prices.

There is, of course, ideologically motivated civil disobedience of etiquette, just as there is of law. But people who mean to change the behavior of the community for its own supposed benefit by such acts must be prepared to accept the punitive consequences of their defiance. They would be well advised to disobey only the rule that offends them, carefully adhering to other conventions, if they do not wish to have their protests perceived as a general contempt for other people. Thanks to her symbolic meaning, the well-dressed, soft-spoken grandmother is a more effective agitator than the unkempt, obscenity-spouting youth.

Ignorance of etiquette rules is not an easily accepted excuse, except on behalf of small children or strangers to the community. An incapacity to comply is acceptable, but only if convincingly explained. To refuse to shake someone's hand will be interpreted as an insult, unless an explanation, such as that one has crippling arthritis, is provided.

Such excuses as "Oh, I never write letters" or "I just wasn't in the mood" or "I'm not comfortable with that" are classified as insolence, and disallowed. Etiquette cannot be universally abandoned in the name of individual freedom, honesty, creativity, or comfort, without social consequences.

In 1978, when I began chronicling and guiding the legitimate changes in etiquette, and applying the rules in specific cases, where there may be extenuating circumstances or conflicting rules—as a judge does in considering a case—it was difficult to get people to agree that etiquette was needed. Now it is only difficult to get people to comply with its rules.

Index

ABA. *See* American Bar Association
abnormals, 191
abortion, 51, 52, 53
Abortion and Divorce in Western Law
(Glendon), on children/divorce,
153–54
absoluteness, illusion of, 111, 112, 113
absolutism, 7, 13, 26, 264
Academic Oversight Committee, for
civic education, 245
Accel Transportation project, 206
Ackerman, Bruce: on open borders,
292
ACLU. *See* American Civil Liberties
Union
acquired immunodeficiency syndrome
(AIDS), 135; curbing spread of,
xxxiv, xxxv; heterosexual transmission of, 136
acquired immunodeficiency syndrome
(AIDS) prevention programs; culturally sensitive, 131–34; public
health and, 136–37
ACT-UP. *See* AIDS Coalition to Unleash Power
Addams, Jane, 280
Adoption Assistance Act, The, 181
advertising, 119, 122; subliminal suggestion and, 121
advocacy politics, judicial review and,
52
AFDC programs, marriage and, 255

affirmative action, 64, 207, 209; attack
on, 208, 212, 262
African Americans: AIDS prevention
and, 135–36; crime and, 228; immigrants and, 289; net worth of, 204;
teaching about, 271; unmarried,
247–48
African Mind Model Technique, 276
Agnos, Art, 188
AIDS. *See* acquired immunodeficiency
syndrome
AIDS Coalition to Unleash Power
(ACT-UP), 135, 136
Airhihenbuwa, Collins: on HIV/AIDS
education, 131
Alarcón, Pedro de, 267
Albert, Michel, 79
alcohol: damage from, 220, 250; policies toward, 222. *See also* drinking
aliens: admission of, 286, 288, 292–93;
treatment of, 283, 285, 288, 287,
290–91
altruism, 61, 241, 245
"America on the Line," 56, 57–58, 59
American Association of Marriage
Counselors, 160
American Association for Marriage
and Family Therapy, 160
American Bar Association (ABA), Section of Individual Rights and, 99,
101
American Civil Liberties Union

(ACLU), xi, 21, 38, 39, 139; *Acuna* case and, 141; Billy Boggs and, 193; criticism of, xxxiv–xxxv

American Enterprise, 147

American Medical Association, 23

American Protective Association, 287

American Scholar, 189

Americans with Disabilities Act, 215

Amos, Kent, 200

Anarchy, State, and Utopia (Nozick), 22

Anderson, Thomas, 128

anomie, spread of, 85, 86

Anthony, Susan B., 280

anti-begging ordinances, 195

Aristotle, ix

Arnold, Thurman: on property, 111

Asia That Can Say No, The (Mohammed), 86

Assets for Independence Act, 205

association rights, violation of, 141

associations, 18, 141; civic, 291; community, 169–70; participating in, 168; social isolation and, 167

asylum-seekers, 76, 283, 287

Atlantic Council, civic values and, 101

Auden, W. H., 281

authoritarian conservatives, drug policy and, 216, 219, 220–21, 224

authoritarianism, temptations of, 85–86, 87, 88–89, 90

autonomy, 35, 36; moral, 5; respecting, 119

Bailey v. City of National City, 141

Baker, James, III, xx

Baker, Karl: street preachers and, 126–27, 130

Barber, Benjamin: strong democracy and, xix

Barmby, Universal Communitarian Association and, ix

Bates, Steven: street preachers and, 127

Begun, Martin: on mental health system, 194

behavior, 296, 297; antisocial, xii, xiii, 45, 240; problems with, 295

Bell, Daniel A., x, 30

Bellah, Robert, x

Benedict, Ruth, 191

Benet, Rosemary Vincent, 267

Bennett, Bill, 179

Bennett, William, 220

Bentham, Jeremy: victimless crimes and, 190

Berlusconi, Silvio, 87

Beyond 911 (Moore), 231–32

bias, 274

BIDs. *See* Business Improvement Districts

Bill of Rights, xv, 6, 98; absolute rights and, 112

"Billy Boggs" affair, 193

BJS. *See* Bureau of Justice Statistics

Blacks. *See* African Americans

Blackstone, William, 109, 112

Blair, Tony, x, xx

Bloustein, Edward: on education/community service, 240

body politic, creation of, 259

Boggs, Billy, 193

Bone, Janice, 44

boot camp prisons, 234, 235

BOP. *See* Bureau of Prisons

Bork, Robert, 214

Boswell, Jonathan, 18

"Bowling Alone" (Putnam), 172

Boys and Girls Club, safe haven by, 200

Boyz 'N the Hood (movie), 205

Bradburn, Norman: SLOPs and, 57

Bradley, Bill, xx; on civil society, 167–68

Bratton, William, 192

Briggs, Orin: street preachers and, 127

Bronx Parent Association, 203

Brookings Institution, 230

Brown, Joyce, 193

Brown, Linda, 230

Brown v. Board of Education, 51, 209–10, 230; separate but equal and, 208

Bryant Park, 183, 186, 195

Buber, Martin, ix

Buchanan, Patrick: subsidiarity and, 19
Buckley, William: service requirement and, 245
Buddhism, etiquette and, 297
Buffalo Law Review, 98
Bureau of Justice Statistics (BJS), 228, 231, 233
Bureau of Prisons (BOP), drug treatment and, 233
Burger, Warren, 103, 208
Burke, Edmund, 9, 32
Bush, George, 57
Business Improvement Districts (BIDs), 195
Business Week, xix

California History-Social Science Framework, multicultural curriculum and, 272
California Law Review, The, 102
California Penal Code, on public nuisance, 140–41
California Supreme Court, gangsters and, 140
Call Waiting, etiquette and, 300
campaign contributions, xxxii–xxxiii
Canfield, Dorothy, 267
capitalism, changes in, 87
Capitalism against Capitalism (Albert), 79
Capitello, Grace, 204, 205
"captive audience" doctrine, 128
Carens, Joseph, 292
Carlyle, Thomas, 39
Carnegie, Andrew, 286
Carter, Jimmy: straw polls and, 59
castes, 64, 67
Cather, Willa, 267
CBS Evening News, sound bites from, 57
CC&Rs. *See* covenants, conditions, and restrictions
Centers for Disease Control and Prevention, AIDS prevention programs and, 133
centralization, 47–48, 49, 92
Central Ward (Newark), loans for, 202

"Challenge of Secularism to Christian Education, The" (Fisher), 104
change, responding to, 300–301
Change (journal), 100
Character Development Act, The, 180
charity, 241, 245
Chase-Lansdale, Lindsay: on children/divorce, 149
Cherlin, Andrew: on children/divorce, 149
Chicago School of Economics, theories of, 212
childbearing, unmarried, 153, 254
children, 203; divorce and, 147, 148–49, 152–54, 160, 164; focus on, 145–46, 154; marriage and, 252; one-parent families and, 147, 149, 150, 252; poverty and, 252; rights of, 115; smoking and, 119; teaching manners to, 295; two-parent families and, 252
Childress, James: on expressing/imposing community, 146
choices, 35, 217; protecting, 116, 121
choice theory, interest theory and, 115
Chung, Connie, 57
Cipollone, Rose, 117–22
citizenship, 24, 82, 92, 240; civil society and, 76; community service and, 245; inequality and, 76–77; meaning of, 238, 242; teaching, 237, 238, 241
City Lands Corporation, 201
City of Dallas v. Stanglin, The, 141
City of Ladue v. Gilleo, 171
civic bonds, 35, 242
civility: piety and, 65; public realm and, 37–39
civil liberties, 26, 196; restrictions on, 73
civil rights, 89, 97; violation of, 128, 229, 230
Civil Rights Act (1964), 154, 209, 210, 213, 214; affirmative action and, 208, 212; policy following, 215
Civil Rights movement, 75, 284
civil society, xxxi, 74, 75, 79, 89, 146; associations and, 167–68; citizen-

ship and, 76; community and, 93; economic development and, 87; globalization and, 81–85, 92; justice and, 24; pressures on, 73, 81–85, 91

Clinton, Bill, 58; on social reform, 177–78; straw polls and, 59

Coates v. Cincinnati, loitering statute and, 190

Coats, Dan: bills introduced by, 180–81

cocaine, import of, 221

cohabitation, 247, 248; financial benefits of, 250; marriage and, 253–54; women and, 254

Coke, Sir Edward, 107

Coleman, James, 149

collective will, 11, 12

Color-Blind Constitution, The (Kull), 213

color-blindness, 212–13

Comer, James: on self-esteem, 276

commitment: depth of, 162–64, 253; marriage and, 158, 165, 166; moral, 162, 164

Committee on Education for Civic Leadership, 240

common good, 10–13, 297

communitarianism, ix, xii, xiii, xxv–xxvi, 62, 63, 84; criticism of, xix; democratic, 17–19; liberal theory and, 39; neo-progressive, xxxiii

community, xii, xxxv–xxxvi, 66, 70, 92; bonds of, 65, 243; CC&Rs and, 172–75; communitarian response and, 13; conflict in, 16, 214–15, 240; cultural, 49; defining, xiii–xvi, 15–16; democratic, 19; education and, 273; expressing/imposing, 146, 199; morality and, xxxvi; political, 12, 19, 56, 293; pluralism and, 273

community capital partnerships, 201–2

community development loan funds, 203

Community and the Economy: The Theory of Public Co-operation (Boswell), 18

community interests, 11, 126–27; self-interest and, 238

community policing, 195–96, 231–32, 234

Community Reinvestment Acts, 203

Community Schools, 200

community service: citizenship and, 245; education and, 239, 240, 241, 244; encouraging, 237, 242; incentive program for, 244–45

Compassion Credit Act, The, 181

compassion fatigue, 179

competitiveness, 80, 84, 89, 93, 243

compromise, forging, 52–53

Condorcet, 27

Confucianism, 87; etiquette and, 297; social cohesion and, 86

consensus, 16, 52–53

Conservative Party, immigration and, 287

Consideration of Representative Government (Mill), 24, 29

Constitution: majority rule and, xv; property rights and, 112

Constructing Community: Moral Pluralism and Tragic Conflicts (Moon), 11

cooperation, 66, 243

corporations: moral order and, 43–44; private behavior and, 44

Correctional Association of New York, imprisonment by, 233

Coughlin, Richard M.: communitarianism and, xxiin18

counselors. *See* therapists

counterspeech, freedom from, 43

couples therapy/counseling, 161

covenants, conditions, and restrictions (CC&Rs), 169; control and, 172; terminating/modifying, 170, 171

Cramton, Roger C., 100

credit unions, community loans from, 203

crime, 141, 177; African Americans and, 228; broken families and, 148; drug abuse and, 225, 234; low-level

disorders and, 192; root causes of, 231; underclass and, 228; urban, 229, 232; victimizing, 192; victimless, 190–92, 196; violent, 228; war on, 230, 231, 234–36
critical thinking, 276
cultural diversity, 270; inclusion and, 69–70
cultural heritage, 151, 275
cultural sensitivity, 131–33; pluralism and, 132; principles of, 134–36; public health and, 133–34
culture: conservative critique of, 61–62; loss of, 10; pluralistic nature of, 271
Cuomo, Mario: on violent mental patients, 192
Current Law Index, xviii, 100
"Curriculum of Inclusion, A" (Sobol), 273, 274, 275

Dalton, Harlon, 132, 135
Danforth, John: Community Schools and, 200
Daniel, Kermit: on marriage/economics, 250, 253
Dasgupta, Partha: social well-being and, 90
Days of Obligation (Rodriguez), 264
Death and Life of Great American Cities, The (Jacobs), 190
death rates, nonmarriage and, 249
decentralization, 24, 48, 53
Declaration of Independence, 266; disenfranchisement and, 265; moral equality and, 4
"Defining Defiance Down" (Moynihan), 189
deinstitutionalization, 190, 192–94
de la Garza, Rodolfo: Mexicanness and, 291
deliberation, 8, 58–59; face-to-face, 56, 60; free speech and, 8
democracy, 52, 53, 71, 75, 168; alternative forms of, 56; direct, 55, 56; education and, 268; equality and, 263; failure of, 47; freedom and, 39–40;

leadership in, 242–43; public realm and, 184; unemployment and, 78
depression, marital problems and, 159, 162
Derber, Charles: on consensual values, xiv
deregulation, 80
Desai, Meghnad: social well-being and, 90
development, individual, 204–5
Dewey, John, 3, 7, 67–68, 280, 288
Dicey, A. V., 22
Dickinson, Emily, 267
DiClemente, Ralph, 133
difference, 262; cultural background and, 275; emphasizing, 260–61
differentiation, xv
Dilger, Robert Jay, 175; on CC&Rs, 170; on civic virtue, 173; NIMBY and, 174
Dinkins, David, 270
disadvantaged, singling out, 222–23
discrimination, xxxv, 102; abolishing, 209, 211, 214, 216; drug abuse and, 222; hiring, 208; invidious, 63–64; market, 210–12; protection vs., 5, 63, 99; self-interest and, 211
displacement, politics of, 259–60
distributive policies, 31–33
Disuniting of America, The (Tocqueville), 81
diversity, 12; appreciation of, 240–41, 270; moral equality and, 5–6; mutuality and, 65
divided public, 49
divorce, 247, 248, 249, 254; children and, xxix, 147, 148–49, 152–54, 160, 164; communitarian perspective on, 164; covenant marriage and, xxiiin31; expressive, 161; financial well-being and, 153, 250–51; impact of, 147, 148, 149; no-fault, 153, 251; rates of, 147, 151
"Divorce Busting" workshops, 161
Divorce Culture, The (Whitehead), 161
divorce law, 45, 180; reform of, xxix, 152–54, 251

domestic disarmament, xxxv
domination, restraining, 66–67
Douglass, Frederick, 267, 280; on blacks/immigrants, 289
drinking, 229; decriminalization of, 190; licensing, 224. *See also* alcohol
drug abuse, 229; Clinton-Gore plan on, 234–35; crime and, 225, 234; damage from, 220; government intervention in, 218–19; hostility toward, 221; inner-city, 232; libertarians and, 216–17, 219; marriage and, 250; poor/affluent and, 223; punishment for, 222; as rational act, 218; reducing, 225; values and, 220
drug dealers, 223, 230
drug policy, 190; communitarian approach to, 224–25; unintended consequences of, 221
drug testing, xi, 279
drug treatment programs, 231, 232–34; compulsory, 233, 234, 235; education and, 235
drunk driving, xxxv, 218, 224
Durkheim, Emile, ix
Dworkin, Ronald: on free speech, 7, 8

economic growth, 74, 79, 86, 90; autonomy and, 36; limits of, 177, 210; social stability and, 87
economism, 77, 90
education, 146, 245, 273; changes for, 266; citizen, 245; civic, 237, 238, 239, 240, 241, 242, 243–44, 264–65; community service and, 240; democracy and, 268; drug treatment and, 235; employment and, 91–92; Eurocentric, 278; freedom and, 238; mandating, 238–39; mathematics, 277; moral, xix, xxviii, xxix–xxx, 103; multicultural, 270; particularistic, 273–75; pluralism and, 272; political pressures on, 269, 270; protecting, 268; purpose of, 264–65, 281; segregation and, 269; women's, 251; work and, xxx, 91–92. *See also* schools

"Education and Freedom" (Howard), 99
Ellwood, David, 147
Emerson, Ralph Waldo, 286, 297
eminent domain, 110
employment: education and, 91–92; parenting and, xxviii–xxix
empowerment, 53, 54
Ennis, Bruce: on institutionalization, 193
Enterprise Foundation, 199
entitlements, 33, 91
entrepreneurship, encouraging, 23, 202–3
Entrepreneurship Training Program, 203
environmentalists, 68, 89
Epstein, Richard, 212, 216; civil rights laws and, 207, 213, 214; discrimination and, 209, 211; symbols and, 213–14, 215
equality, xxxi, 3, 70, 261–64, 266, 280; democracy and, 263; Founders and, 265; freedom and, 22; liberal, 23–24; moral, 4–6, 63, 64, 65, 67; mutuality and, 66; social, 4; social justice and, 62–64
Erasmus, 297
ethnic studies, 265, 270
ethnocentrism, 6, 35
ethnomathematics, 277
etiquette: civil disobedience of, 300–301; civilization and, 297; law and, 299–300; marriage and, 298, 299; self-expression and, 299; symbolism and, 295, 296; teaching, 295–96; tradition and, 296
Etzioni, Amitai: on community, 62
Eurocentrism, 274, 276, 278
Europe of Regions, 92
exclusion, politics of, 50
Exit, Voice and Loyalty (Hirschman), 84
experiential learning, 244, 245
externalities, controlling, 67–68

Fable of the Bees (Mandeville), 21
family, 83, 145–46; children and, 147,

152; debate about, xiii, 150–51; decline of, 103, 146–52, 177, 189, 247; moral understanding of, xxviii, 103, 145, 151; respect for, 45, 180; responsibilities and, 151; role models and, 179–81; role of, 103
Family Housing Act, The, 180–81
family policy, 35–36, 150
family therapy, 160; mainstreaming of, 161–62
"Fathering, Mentoring, and Family," 179
Federal Bureau of Investigation (FBI) Uniform Crime Report, on Philadelphia crime rate, 228
Federal Housing Administration, RCAs and, 176
Federalist Papers, The, 24, 28, 81
feminism, 48, 263
Field, Frank, 91
Fifteen-Month Houses, 203–4
Fifth Amendment, property rights and, 110, 112
Filmer, Sir Robert: freedom and, 26
First Amendment, xv, xvii, xxxiii, 125; balancing, 141–42; privacy issue and, 128, 129, 130; public forums and, 128
Fisher, Ben C.: on brotherhood of man, 104
Fishkin, James, xvii
Fitzpatrick, Daniel: Sokolow/Levin and, 107
fixed-identity groups, 263
flexibility, 80, 81, 83–85
Florida Democratic Party Straw Poll, 59
Flynn, Patrick: street preachers and, 127
Foley, Robert: gangster case and, 139
Forbes, Kathryn, 267
Forbidden Grounds (Epstein), 208, 212, 216
Fordham, Jefferson B., 99, 100
Foundation for Teaching Entrepreneurship, 203

fragmentation, 49–51, 292; fighting, 53
France, Anatole, 4
freedom, 245, 280; civic, 86; decontextualization of, 23–25; democracy and, 39–40; education and, 238; equality and, 22; individual, 102, 146; liberal, 27, 146; maximization of, 22; obligation and, 24; oversimplifying, 25–27; political, 73, 85, 86, 90; property policy and, 37; restrictions on, 172; undermining cultural basis of, 27–30
Freedom and Rights (Milne), 98
free speech, xv–xvi, xvii, xxxiii; controversies over, 7–8; governing, 8–9; privacy rights and, 130; protecting, 38, 43, 125; street preachers and, 128–29
Friedan, Betty, xx
Friedman, Milton, 25, 35, 38; individual rights and, 21
Friedman, Paul: on institutionalization, 193
fundamentalism, xi, 11, 81

Galileo, 27
Gallo, Joan: gang problems and, 139
Galston, William A., xvii, 43
gangsters, 141, 187, 229, 230; rights of, 139–40, 142
Garcetti, Gil, 139
Gauthier, David: on justice/self-interest, 66
gay community, public health and, 134–35
gay studies, 265
Geis, Gilbert: on victimless crime, 192
Gemeinschaft, x, 15, 16
General Accounting Office, on immigrants, 289
Gesellschaft, x
Gibney, Mark: on open borders, 292
Gillette, Clayton: on protection of groups, 172
Glasser, Ira: on communitarians, xiv
Glazer, Nathan, 101–2

Glendon, Mary Ann, xvii; on divorce/
children, 153–54
globalization; centralization and, 92;
challenges of, 85, 89–90, 93; choices
of, 77–81; civil society and, 81–85;
constraints of, 77–81
Glory (movie), pluralism and, 272
goals, defining, 16
Goffman, Erving: on deinstitutionalization, 192–93
Goldscheider, Frances: on cohabitation, 253
Gompers, Samuel, 280
Gospel Mission, The, 179
government: curbing, 180; excessive,
210
graffiti, 188, 189
Gray, John, x
Greenberg, Reuben, 232
guestworkers, 76, 287
Guidubaldi, John: on children/divorce,
148

Habermas, Jurgen, 17
Habits of the Heart (Bellah), 15
Hafen, Bruce, 99, 103
Hailbronner, Kay, 287
Hamilton, Alexander, 285, 286
harm principle, 10
"Harrison Bergeron" (Vonnegut), 261
Hart, Gary, 58
Hart-Celler Act (1965), quotas and,
284
hate codes, xvi
Havel, Václav, 268
Hayek, Friedrich, 21, 29
health: behaviors affecting, 44; mar-
riage and, 248–49
Hentoff, Nat, xv
Herakleitos, 77
Hernandez, Donald, 252
heroin, 221, 223
Hirschman, Albert, 84
Hispanic Caucus, employee identifi-
cation system and, 285
history, studying, 270, 279–80
Hobbes, Thomas, 26, 28, 29

Hogue, Larry, 194
Hollifield, James, 287
Holmes, Steven, xiv
homeowner associations, 169–70, 188
honesty, triumph of, 296–98
Howard, John A., 99, 104
human dignity, xxv, 178
human rights, 6, 70–71, 90, 97

Icard, Larry: on cultural sensitivity,
133
IDA. *See* Individual Development Account
identity, 6, 65, 70, 286
illiteracy, 229, 238
immigrants: blacks and, 289; as scapegoats, 290–91; work ethics of, 289
immigration, 274, 292–93; curtailing,
283–84, 285, 292; illegal, 283, 284,
291; politicization of, 283, 287,
290–91; reform of, 284, 288, 289–
90, 292; social well-being and, 74;
sustaining, 285
Immigration Act (1990), 283, 284
Immigration Reform and Control Act
(IRCA) (1986), 283, 284, 285
Immigration Restriction League, 287
impediment, absence of, 26, 27
*Imperial Germany and the Industrial
Revolution* (Veblen), 75
inclusion, 62; social justice and, 69–71
Index to Legal Periodicals, 100
individual, 16–17; development of,
204–5; sacredness of, 18
Individual Development Account
(IDA), 205
individualism, 11, 74, 84, 92, 99; abstract, 34; ascendancy of, 158; liberal
democracy and, 146; ontological,
17; rights-based, 263
Individual Retirement Accounts
(IRAs), 204, 205
individual rights, xvi, 100; exaggeration
of, 112–13
inequality, 82–83, 260; citizenship and,
76–77; reducing, 261
inhibitions, paralysis from, 296

innovation, flaws in, 57
institutionalization, limited, 194–95
institutions: culture and, 28, 29; decay of, 177, 292; strengthening, 180
integrity, principled conduct and, 7
interest theory, 116; choice theory and, 115
intimacy, improved, 251
intolerance, 41, 262
invisible hand, 25
IRAs. *See* Individual Retirement Accounts
IRCA. *See* Immigration Reform and Control Act
Ishihara, Shintaro, 86

Jackson, Kenneth, 176
Jackson, Margaret Weymouth, 267
Jacobs, Jane: on public space, 190
Janowitz, Morris, 101
Japan That Can Say No, The (Ishihara), 86
Jefferson, Thomas, 280; body politic and, 259; collective will and, 12; immigration and, 286; moral equality and, 4; slavery and, 264–65
Jim Crow laws, 209, 210, 211, 272, 284
Joas, Hans, x
John of Salisbury, body politic and, 259
Jordan, Frank, 188
Jordan, Winthrop, 271
judicial review, advocacy politics and, 52
justice, xxvii, 66, 71, 280; civil society and, 24; distributive, 32

Kamarck, Elaine Ciulla, 146
Kant, Immanuel: on critical morality/ received morality, 9
Kateb, George, 263
Kennedy, John F., 25, 74, 104
Kiernan, Kathleen: on children/divorce, 149
King, Martin Luther, Jr., 281
Know-Nothings, 287
Kornhauser, William, ix

Kramer, Larry: on gay community/ AIDS prevention, 134
Kristol, Irving: on underclass, 177
Kristol, William: on curbing government, 180
Ku Klux Klan, xiv
Kull, Andrew: on race-conscious policies, 213

Labor movement, 85, 89
Lagerlöf, Selma, 267
Landon, Alf, 57
language: awareness of, 132–33; family, 150–51; moral, 164; official, 150–51, 152
Lasch, Christopher: on nostalgia, 15
Latham & Watkins (law firm), gangster case and, 139
law: anti-discrimination, 208–10; civil, 217; criminal, 217; divorce, xxix, 45, 152–54, 180, 251; drunk driving and, 218; etiquette and, 299–300; family, 155; force of, 44–45; Jim Crow, 209, 210, 211, 272, 284; moral order and, 45; rights/ responsibilities and, 97, 100; rule of, 51, 70, 77; social/moral values and, 45
Law Enforcement Assistance Administration, 232
Lawrence, Francis L., 242
Learnfare, 45
Le Clair Court housing project, transportation barrier for, 205–6
Legal Resource Index, 100
Lehr v. Robertson, 104
Le Pen, Jean-Marie, 287
liberalism: classical vs. welfare, 3, 4; communitarian, 3, 6; contemporary, 4; equality/community and, 23; moral equality and, 5; popular vs. theoretical, 3
libertarianism: critiquing, 22–23, 30, 31; development of, 21–22
libertarians: drug abuse and, 216–17, 219, 223–24; Hobbesian concept and, 26–27; leftist/rightist, 21–22, 37; responsibility and, xxxvi

liberty, xxv, 3, 23, 90, 280; learning, 238; libertarians and, 6–9, 25, 26; as license, 88; maximizing, 35, 36; political, 74, 79; positive, 25–26; property and, 110–11; serving, 241
Lichtenberg, Judith, 292
Lieberson, Stanley: on blacks/immigrants, 289
Lillard, Lee, 248
Lincoln, Abraham, xxvi, 4, 280
Linder, William: New Community and, 201–2
Literary Digest, straw polls by, 57
Litwack, Leon, 271
"Living Civilly in an Urban Hell" (Purdy), 227
Lochner v. New York, 210
Locke, John, 24, 26, 27, 39, 109
London *Economist:* on neopuritanism, 41; on new morality, 44–45; on Punitive Society, 42
Los Angeles County Board of Commissioners, immigrant/alien services and, 289
Los Angeles Police Department, 231
Los Angeles Times, gangsters and, 140
Luther, Martin, 27
Lye, Diane, 252
Lynch, Michael: on gay community/AIDS prevention, 134

MacDonald, Heather: Hogue and, 194
McGrath, Janet, 133
MacIntyre, Alasdair, xxiin9
McKenzie, Evan, 171; on civic virtue, 173; on community associations, 169–70; on double taxation, 175; RCAs and, 174
McLanahan, Sara: on children/two-parent families, 252
MacLaury, Bruce, xx
McWilliams, Wilson Carey: civic associations and, 291
Machan, Tibor: criticism by, xix
Madison, James, 24, 29, 39; body politic and, 259; on community interest,

11; on Hobbes/human nature and, 28
Mandeville, Bernard: self-interest and, 21
Manhattan State Hospital, Hogue and, 194
Mann, Horace, 280
manners, 298–300; idealism and, 295; learning, 295, 296–97
Manoff, Robert, 134
Marcuse, Herbert: radical desublimation and, 189
marijuana, decriminalization of, 220
Mariotti, Steve, 202
marital suicide, therapist-assisted, 159, 165–66
marital therapy: communitarian approach to, 164–66; development of, 159–60, 166; mainstreaming of, 161–62; problems with, 157–58, 163–64; seeking, 164–65
markets, discrimination in, 210–12
marriage, xviii; benefits of, 180, 252–53, 254; changes in, 248; children and, 248, 252; cohabitation and, 253–54; commitment and, 165, 166; consequences of, 250–51, 252; covenant, xviii, xxiiin31; decline in, 247, 248; education for, 165; etiquette and, 298, 299; health/well-being and, 164, 248–51, 254; saving, 159, 160, 161
marriage penalty, 250, 255
marriage premium, 250
Marx, Karl, 39
Mason Gross School for the Arts, 243
Maternity Shelter Act, The, 181
Mays, Vickie: on gay community/language, 132–33
MCA. *See* Motion Picture Corporation of America
meaning, 178–79
Medicaid, marriage and, 255
mentors, role of, 179–80
Michigan Law Review, 99
Miegel, Meinhard, x

Mill, John Stuart, 24, 39, 217; on governmental forms, 29; harm principle and, 10
Milne, A.J.M.: on responsibilities, 98
minority groups, teaching about, 270, 271
mobility: increasing, 205–6; social, 39
"Mobility for Work" initiative, 206
Mohammed, Mahathir, 86
Mondale, Walter, xvii, 58
Moon, J. Donald, 11
Moore, Mark H., 231
Moore, Stephen: on immigrants, 284
moral agency, 8–9
moral decay, 10, 146–47, 190
moral equality, 4–6, 64; commitment to, 67; demands for, 65; social subordination and, 63
morality, xix, xxi, xxviii, xxxiv, 23, 28, 41, 63, 64, 66, 151, 197; civil, 29; communitarian, 13; community and, xxvii, xxxvi; critical, 9, 71; family, 103–4; institutional, 7; personal, 61; politics and, 19; promoting, 103; puritanism and, 42; social, 98
Moral Majority, 41
moral order, 70; corporations and, 43–44; law and, 45
moral reawakening, 41, 45
moral relativism, 28, 152
moral voice, xxvi, 41, 42–43, 146; divorce and, 154–55; restoring, xxvii–xxx
Morgan, Charles: on ACLU, 193
Motion Picture Corporation of America (MCA), City Walk and, 188
motorcycle-helmet laws, 113
Moynihan, Daniel: on New York/poverty, 189
multiculturalism, 6, 35, 49, 70, 264, 267, 268, 275; particularistic, 270, 276; pluralistic, 270; recognizing, 271, 272–73
Murphy, Cullen, 100
Murray, Charles, 173

mutuality, 62; equality and, 66; social justice and, 64–68

Naidu, Sarojini, 267
Nash, Gary, 271
National Commission on the Causes and Prevention of Violence, on violent crime, 228
National Conference of State Legislatures, on boot camps, 235
National Foundation for Teaching Entrepreneurship, 202
National Front parties, immigration and, 287
National Institute of Justice, 231
nationalism, restrictive, 287
Nationality Act (1981), 287
National Origins Quota system, 283
National Police Corps, 234
National Rifle Association (NRA), xxxv
national service, xxxi, 34, 245
Nedelsky, Jennifer: on property rights, 109
needle exchange programs, risks/benefits of, 136
Neighborhood Politics: Residential Community Associations in American Governance (Dilger), 170
Neighborhood Reconstruction Corps, 199–200
Nelson, Lars-Erik, 187, 192
neopuritanism, 41, 44
New Community Corporation, 201–2
New Economics for Women, 203
Newman, Oscar: on defensible space principles, 188
New York Civil Liberties Union (NYCLU), Boggs and, 193
New York Times, on neopuritanism, 41
Niebuhr, Rienhold: on democracy/freedom, 39–40
NIMBY. *See* Not In My Back Yard
Nisbet, Robert, ix, x
noise, banning, 125
nonmarriage: death rates and, 249; increase in, 247

Norton, Mary Beth, 271
Not In My Back Yard (NIMBY), 174
Nozick, Robert, 21, 22; libertarianism of, 218; on redistributive principles/justice, 32–33
NRA. *See* National Rifle Association
nuisance, 125; defining, 140–41
NYCLU. *See* New York Civil Liberties Union

Oakeshott, Michael: on learning, 267, 268
Oaks, Dallin H., xx
obligation, 62, 66, 98, 101, 215; civic, 33–35, 229; freedom and, 24; moral, 33; mutual, 65. *See also* responsibilities
OECD. *See* Organization for Economic Co-operation and Development
Official Rules, The (Dickson), 102
O'Hara, Mary, 267
Olasky, Marvin: on compassion, 178
one-parent families, children and, 147, 149, 150, 252
"1,112 and Counting" (Kramer), 134
"On Manners" (Emerson), 297
Operation Wetback, 284
opportunity, equality of, 67
Ordinary Religion of the Law School Classroom, The (Cramton), 100
Organization for Economic Co-operation and Development (OECD), 74
Organization for European Economic Cooperation, 74
Orloff, Ann Shola, 286
Orwell, George, xi

Pagan, Antonio, 196
panhandling, 187, 188, 194, 195, 229
parenting: bolstering, 151; marriage and, 248; employment and, xxviii–xxix; responsibilities of, 99; role of, 179–80; unwed, 151, 247, 248, 254. *See also* one-parent families; two-parent families
Park, Robert E., ix

parks, building/maintaining, 183, 185–86
Parsons, Talcott, ix
participation, xxxii, 10, 52, 68, 93; civic, 66; political, 73–76, 175; rationality and, 65; social, 76
particularism, xxxv, 70, 270, 273–75; ethnic/national, xxxvi; rise of, 276, 278, 279
paternalism, 44, 262; case against, 118–19; decline of, 115; permissible, 119–20; rights theory and, 116; scope of, 116–17; smoking and, 122–23
Paths to Utopia (Buber), ix
Pawel, Michael: Hogue and, 194
Perot, H. Ross, 56, 57
Philadelphia House Authority, 227
Philadelphia Inquirer, The, 227
physiocrats, 27
Pierce v. Society of Sisters, 104
piety, civility and, 65
Plessy v. Ferguson, 209, 210
pluralism, 270; cultural sensitivity and, 132; community and, 273; education and, 272; recognizing, 272–73; respect for, 240–41; unity and, 271–72
police: community, 195–96, 231–32, 234; private, 188; spending on, 232
Policy Review, 232
Political Liberalism (Rawls), 12
political liberty, 74, 79; economic development and, 87
political system: equilibrium in, 54; public sphere and, 49
politics, xxxii; inclusion and, 69; as judicial review, 52; morality and, 19; special-interest, 50–52, 53, 89
polity, 30, 259; cleaning up, xxxii–xxxiii
polls, 55, 57, 58, 59
Popper, Karl, 77
poverty, 189, 205; children and, 252; civil society and, 83; debt and, 204; drug abuse and, 222, 223; war on, 231
power: centralization of, 47–48; decentralization of, 53, 66

preachers. *See* street preachers
preferences: authentic, 121; evaluating, 117–18; implanted, 121; personal, 121; preferred, 117, 120; relevant, 117, 118–19; settled, 117, 119–20
prejudice, 64, 67, 267
premarital counseling, xviii
President's Commission on Law Enforcement and Administration of Justice, Task Force Report of, 191
Prim, Theresa, 206
primaries, 55, 58, 59
privacy rights, 171; First Amendment and, 128, 129; free speech and, 130
private governments, xxvii, 188
private groups, 178; public groups and, xxxi
"private vice, public virtue" doctrine, 28
Privatopia: Homeowner Associations and the Rise of Residential Private Governments (McKenzie), 169
productivity, 83, 84
profitability, 69, 84
Progressive Policy Institute, 146
Project for American Renewal, The, 179, 180
Project for Public Space, The, 195
property: freedom and, 37, 110–11; reasonable regulation of, 108
property paradigm, 110, 111
property rights, 188; absoluteness of, 109–10; Constitution and, 112; good society and, 36–37; invoking, 108; legal limitations on, 110; libertarian theory on, 36; subordination of, 110
prostitution, 192, 196, 229
protection, 77; discrimination vs., 5
public agenda, determining, 48
public health, xxxiv–xxxv; African Americans and, 135–36; AIDS prevention and, 136–37; cultural sensitivity and, 133–34; gay community and, 134–35
public housing, 180, 196

public interest, xxxiii, 11
Public Interest, The (Glazer), 101–2, 234
public realm: civility and, 37–39; democracy and, 184
public safety, concerns about, xxxiv–xxxv
public space, 184, 195; developing, 185–86, 194; libertarianism and, 37–38; loss of, 187
public sphere, enlargement of, 48–49
punitiveness, 88; equity and, 42
Purdy, Matthew, 227
puritanism, morality and, 42
Putnam, Robert D., x, 167, 172
"Putting Children First" (Progressive Policy Institute, Kamarck), 146

quotas, 207, 283, 284

race, teaching about, 270
racism, 213, 216, 274; elimination of, xvii, 210, 211, 276; teaching, 281
Randolph, A. Philip, 280–81
rationality, 3; participation and, 65; speculative reason and, 9–10
Ravitch, Diane, 175
Rawls, John, 12, 63; moral principles and, 5; redistributive principles and, 32–33
RCAs. *See* Residential Community Associations
recidivism, 234, 235
reciprocity, 65, 66
reconciliation, fostering, xxxi
Reconstruction of Patriotism—Education for Civil Consciousness, The (Janowitz), 101
Red Hook Houses, problems at, 196
redistributive policies, 32, 33
referendums, 55, 58, 59
reform, 178–79
regionalism, 80–81
Rehnquist, William, 208
Reich, Charles: on property, 111
Reich, Robert: inequalization and, 82
relevant preferences, 117, 118–19

religious charities, 178
Report on Manufactures (Hamilton), 285
Republikaner party, immigration and, 287
Residential Community Associations (RCAs), 168–69, 170; control and, 171, 172; formation/expansion of, 175, 176; politics and, 173, 174–75; property values and, 174; urban planning and, 176
respect, xxxi, 70
responsibilities, xxxiv, 105, 129–30, 240; civic, 62, 101, 238, 241; divorce law and, 152–54; explanation of, 100; family and, 145–46, 151; fiduciary, 69; fulfillment of, 102, 104; human dignity and, 178; law and, 97; moral, 8, 9, 61, 165, 229, 238; parental, 99; personal, xxvi, 61, 62, 103; public coercion for, 154, 155; question of, xxxvi–xxxvii; rights and, xvi, xxv–xxxvii, 97–98, 100, 101, 239, 240; social, xxvi, 103, 237; superior rationality of, 98–99. *See also* Obligation
Responsive Communitarian Platform, xi, xiii; signatories for, xxxvii–xxxviii; text of, xxv–xxxvii
Responsive Community, The, xii, xiii, 167; communitarian thinking and, xi; development of, x, xvi; editorial board for, xx–xxi; electronic addresses/telephone numbers for, xx; themes/issues of, xix
rhetoric, 7, 11, 58, 110, 113, 114
Rhett, Billy: street preachers and, 126
Richardson, Elliot L.: on obligations, 98
rights, 99; absoluteness of, 112; enforcement of, 51, 101; fundamental, 139; judicial enforcement of, 102; law and, 97; relinquishing, 171–72; responsibilities and, xvi, xxv–xxxvii, 97–98, 100, 101, 239, 240; rightness vs., xxxiii–xxxiv

Rights and Responsibilities, xi
rights-and-welfare liberalism, drug abuse and, 216, 221–22
rights theorists, 115, 288; paternalists and, 116
Riordan, Richard, 188, 189
rituals, 298
Robb, Senator and Mrs. Charles, xx
Robert's Rules of Order, etiquette and, 300
Robert Wood Johnson Foundation, 204
Rodriguez, Richard, 262, 264, 265
Roe vs. Wade, 51
role models, 148, 179–81
Roosevelt, Franklin D., 4–5, 57, 74, 281
Ross, Catherine: on marriage, 253
Rouse, James: Enterprise Foundation and, 199
Rousseau, Jean-Jacques, 24, 245
rule of law, 51, 70, 77
Rustin, Bayard, 281

Sandefur, Gary: on children/two-parent families, 252
Sandel, Michael J., ix, x, xiv, xxiin9
Schlesinger, Arthur, Jr., 215
schools: community, 200; moral education and, xxix–xxx; partisan struggles within, 269; politicalization of, 265–66. *See also* education
Schur, Edwin: on victimless crime, 191
Schwartz, Amitai, 140
seat-belt laws, 113
Second Amendment, NRA and, xxxv
Second Chances: Men, Women, and Children a Decade After Divorce (Wallerstein), 148
Second Treatise (Locke), 26
Section of Individual Rights (ABA), 99, 101
secularism, xiii, 269
security, inner-city, 229–30, 231
segregation, 5, 264, 272; economic power and, 210; education and, 230, 269
self-esteem, 67, 280; damage to, 276, 277; raising, 275–78

self-governance, 27, 29
self-interest, 21, 66, 68, 207; community interests and, 238; discrimination and, 211; enlightened, 241; maximization of, 211; pursuing, 35, 214
self-preservation, 66, 180
self-selected listener opinion polls (SLOPs), 57
Selznick, Philip, x
Sen, Amartya: social well-being and, 90
separate but equal doctrine, 208, 209
separatism, linguistic, 291
service, national/local, xxxi
settlements, fair/conciliatory, xxxi
sex life, improved, 251
Shaffer, Thomas L., 102
Sharoing, Rudolf, xix–xx
Shorebank, 201, 202
simplism, conceptual/moral, 25
Simpson, Alan, 285
Singer, Merrill, 133
Singmaster, Elsie, 267
Sinnot, Timothy: criticism by, xix
situationists, 191
Skogan, Wesley G., 229
slavery, accounting for, 264–65
SLOPs. *See* self-selected listener opinion polls
Smith, Adam, 21, 25, 39, 103
Smith, James, 249
smoking: children and, 119; damage from, 119, 220; liberal perspective on, 222; paternalism and, 122–23; policies on, 117–18, 122. *See also* tobacco
Sobol, Thomas, 273
sobriety checkpoints, xxxiv, xxxv
social cohesion, 73, 86, 88, 90, 242
social conditions, changing, 222
Social Darwinism, 84, 261
social environments, xxv, xxxvi
social justice, xxvii, 62, 168; communitarian understanding of, xxxiv, 61; as moral imperative, 61; mutuality and, 66

social policy, 63, 178
social problems, 178, 191
Social Security, 111, 153, 249
Social Statics (Spencer), 21
social theory, weakness of, 37
society: guaranteeing, 280; regulating, xxxvi
soft despotism, 50
Soifer, Aviam: on property rhetoric, 110
Sokolow, Marvin, 107–8, 111, 112
solidarity, value of, 18
Sonnabend, Joseph: on gay community/AIDS prevention, 134
Sorrentino, Constance: on divorce rates, 147
Soul Searching: Why Psychotherapy Must Promote Moral Responsibility (Doherty), 158
sound bites, problems with, 57, 58
South Carolina Supreme Court, street preachers and, 127
speculative reason, limits of, 9–10
speech, loud, 128–29
Spencer, Herbert, 21
stakeholders, 92–93, 159
Stand and Deliver (movie), message from, 277
Stanton, Elizabeth Cady, 280
state, positive role for, 93–94
State of California v. Carlos Acuna, et al., The, 139, 141, 142
stepfamilies, children and, 252
stewardship, 62; social justice and, 68–69
Stolzer, Bea: New Economics for Women and, 203
Stoneman, Dorothy: Youth Build and, 199
straw polls. *See* polls
street preachers, 126, 127; free speech and, 128–29; tolerance for, 130
strong democracy, xix, xxvii
subsidiarity, 19, 54
Supervisory Board, for civic education, 243, 245

symbols, 213–14, 215; arbitrariness of, 298; etiquette and, 296

"takings" power, 110
Tamir, Yael: on group life, 168
Taoism, etiquette and, 297
Task Force on Minorities, 273
Task Force Report (President's Commission on Law Enforcement and Administration of Justice), 191
taxation, xxxii, 180; double, 175; progressive, 68
Taylor, Charles, ix, xxiin9; on discovering identity, 259; on politics of recognition, 132
technology, impact of, 79, 80
Teir, Robert, 195, 196
teledemocracy, problems with, 56–57
Thatcher, Margaret, 87, 287
therapists: associations of, 160; marriage and, 157–59, 160
therapy: couples, 161; mainstreaming of, 161–62
There's No Such Thing as Free Speech (Fish), 9
Thernstrom, Stephan, 271
Thomas, Irma, 227, 228, 229, 235
Tiananmen Square, demonstrations in, 184
Time, x, 41, 43
tobacco: advertising for, 122; case against, 117–18, 121. *See also* smoking
Tocqueville, Alexis de, 81, 112; associations and, 167; on citizen apathy, 50; on citizen mobilization, 47; decentralization of power and, 53; local politics and, 174
tolerance, 41, 129, 130, 262; fostering, xxxiii, 125; political, 28; racial, xviii
Tolstoy, Leo, 267
Tönnies, Ferdinand, ix, x
Torrey, E. Fuller: on psychotic rights, 195
totalitarianism, xi, 86
Tsongas, Paul, 58

two-parent families, 149–50; children and, 252

Umberson, Debra, 249
underclass, 91, 177, 228
unemployment, 78, 83
U.S. Supreme Court: RCAs and, 171; school prayer and, 269; street preachers and, 127
U.S. Surgeon General, recidivism and, 120
Universal Communitarian Association, ix
Urban Land Institute, on home associations, 172
urban planning, RCAs and, 176

values: civic, 101; community-shared, 16; drug abuse and, 220; moral, xxvii, 103–4; violation of, 43
Van Buren, Martin: immigrants/political community and, 291
Veblen, Thorstein, 75
Velvet Revolution, 184
victimless crime, 190–92, 196
violence, urban, 227, 228
virtues, 53–54; civic, xxvi, xxxvii; moral, xxvi; personal, 61
vocational training, 91, 92
voice, moral, xxvi, xxvii–xxx, 41, 42–43, 146, 154–55
voluntarism, xxxi, 237, 238
von Mises, Ludwig: individual rights and, 21
Vonnegut, Kurt: on equality, 261
voting, participating in, xxxii, 52
Voting Rights Act, 154

Wallerstein, Judith: on children/divorce, 148–49
Walzer, Michael, ix, xxiin9; on open borders, 292
Washington, Booker T., 267
wealth creation, 73, 90
Wealth of Nations (Smith), 25
Weber, Max: on Calvinism, 87
weddings. *See* marriage

Weiner-Davis, Michele: on solution-oriented therapy, 161
Wenceslas Square, 184
Western civilization, roots of, 279
White, Michael, 187
Whitehead, Barbara Dafoe, 150, 152, 161
Whyte, William H., 188
widowhood, 248; financial well-being and, 250–51
Will, George, xv
Willetts, David, x
Williams, Roger, 128
Wilson, James Q., 229
Wilson, Pete: on immigrants/unemployment, 290
Wilson, William Julius, 82, 289
Wingood, Gina, 133

Wolin, Sheldon, 263
women, teaching about, 270, 271
women's studies, 265
Woo, Michael, 188–89
Woods, John, 179
Woodson, Robert, Sr., 178
work: inclusion and, 69; school and, 91–92
World Health Organization, recidivism and, 120
Wright, Robert, x
Wurtzel, Alan and Irene, xx

Yew, Lee Kwan, 86
YMCA, safe haven by, 200
Youth Build, 199

Zinsmeister, Karl, 147
zoning, 176, 188

About the Contributors

Robert N. Bellah is professor of sociology at the University of California, Berkeley, and coauthor of *Habits of the Heart*.

Amitai Etzioni is university professor at the George Washington University. He is author of *The New Golden Rule*.

Thomas A. Spragens, Jr., is professor of political science at Duke University. He is author of *Reason and Democracy* and *Irony of Liberal Reason*.

James Fishkin is professor of ethics and American society at the University of Texas, where he is also the chair of the department of government. He is author of *Democracy and Deliberation: New Directions for Democratic Reform*.

Charles Taylor is professor of philosophy at McGill University and author of *Multiculturalism and the Politics of Recognition*.

Philip Selznick is professor emeritus at the School of Law at the University of California, Berkeley. He is author of *The Moral Commonwealth: Social Theory and the Promise of Community*.

Ralf Dahrendorf is a member of the House of Lords. He is the author of *After 1989—Morals, Revolution and Civil Society*.

Dallin H. Oaks is a member of the Quorum of the Twelve Apostles, serving a life-time position in answer to the call of the Mormon Church.

Robert E. Goodin is professional fellow in philosophy at the Australian National University.

Mary Ann Glendon is professor of law at Harvard University.

Roger L. Conner is executive director of the Center for the Community Interest. He is also coauthor of *The Winnable War: A Community Guide to Eradicating Street Drug Markets* and also *Citizens Action for Neighborhood Safety.*

Ronald Bayer is professor at the Columbia University School of Public Health.

Benjamin R. Barber is professor of political science and director of the Whitman Center at Rutgers University. He is author of *Strong Democracy.*

John J. DiIulio, Jr., is professor of politics and public affairs at Princeton University and Nonresident Senior Fellow in Governmental Studies at the Brookings Institution.

Mark Kleiman is professor of policy studies at the University of California School of Public Policy and Social Research. He is the author of *Against Excess: Drug Policy for Results and Marijuana: Costs of Abuse, Costs of Control.*

Alan Wolfe is professor of sociology and political science at Boston University. He is the author of *One Nation, After All* due out in winter, 1997.

Bill Bradley is a former Democratic senator from New Jersey and chair of the National Civic League. He is the author of *Time Present, Time Past.*

Fred Siegel is professor of history at the Cooper Union and Senior Fellow at the Progressive Policy Institute. He is the author of *The Future Once Happened Here: New York, D.C., L.A.* and *The Fate of America's Big Cities.*

Peter Katz is a San-Francisco-based consultant. He is author of *The New Urbanism: Toward an Architecture of Community.*

Daniel A. Bell is professor of philosophy at the University of Hong Kong. He is the author of *Communitarianism and Its Critics* and coauthor of *Towards Illiberal Democracy in Pacific Asia.*

Dan Coats is a Republican senator from Indiana.

Linda J. Waite is professor of sociology at the University of Chicago, where she directs the Center on Aging. She is the author of *Does Marriage Matter.*

William Galston is professor in the School of Public Affairs at the University of Maryland at College Park and director of the university's Institute for Philosophy and Public Policy. He is author of *Social Mores Are Not Enough.*

William J. Doherty is professor of family social science and director of the Marriage and Family Therapy Program at the University of Minnesota. His most recent book is *The International Family.*

Diane Ravitch is senior research fellow at Brookings Institution and senior research scholar at the New York University.

Jean Bethke Elshtain is professor of social and political ethics at the University of Chicago.

Daniel J. Tichenor is professor of political science at Rutgers University and Visiting Fellow at the Eagleton Institute.

Judith Martin is syndicated columnist Miss Manners. She is author of *Miss Manners Rescues Civilization from Sexual Harassment, Frivolous Lawsuits, Dissing, and Other Lapses in Civility.*